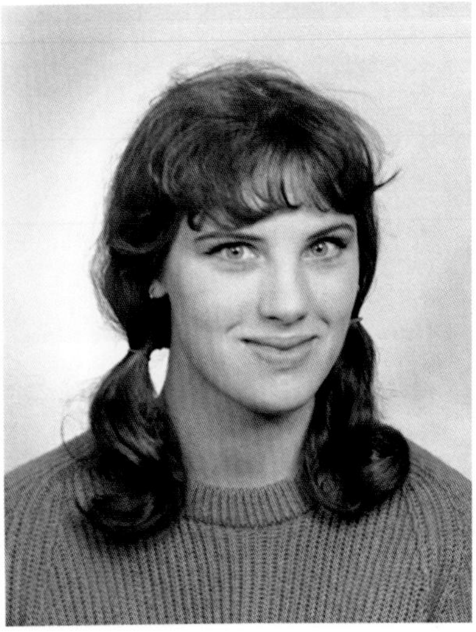 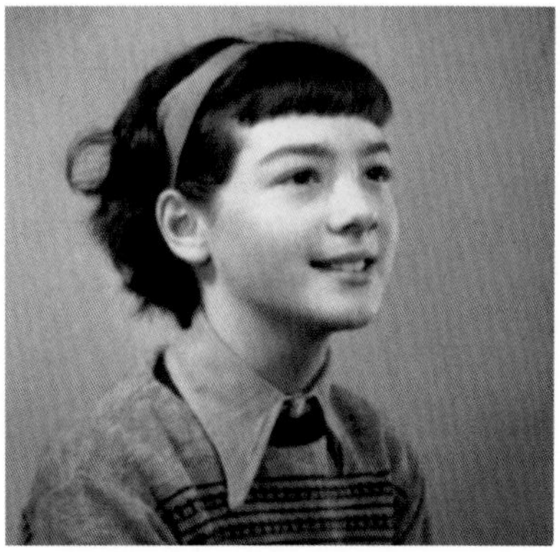

Dedicated to Andrew, Freddie and William, Mick Rooney, my mother, Diane, my mother-in-law, Geraldine, and to mothers everywhere.

Huge gratitude to everyone who helped with the book including:

Angela and Margherita Missoni, Sofia Del Bene, Andrea Vásquez Medina and Sara Crosta
Lali Dzhinikashvili and David Koma, Maria Tkachenko
Serena Rees, Bridget Rees, Cora Corre
Courtney Love and Tiina Lee
Sadie Frost, Iris Law and Mary Davidson, Rankin and Ellen Wallage
Lulu Guinness, Madeleine Guinness and Tara Kelway-Bamber
Herbie Mensah and Sarah McHale
Penelope Tree
Edina Ronay and Max Ronay
Kristen Gabrielle and Kathy Sledge
Pauline Black and Daniel Rachel
Lydia Corbett aka Sylvette, Alice Corbett and Isabel Coulton
Suzanne Kay
Quinn Tivey, Naomi deLuce Wilding, Tim Mendelson
Pippa Healy
Gina Gibbons
Alex Garman
Paul Simonon
Lillian Bucke
Francine Bosco
Michael Costiff
Winn Austin

Very special thanks to: Carrie Kania, James Smith, Alice Bowden, Mariona Vilarós, and Andrew Whittaker.

Terry Newman

Cool Mothers

AN APPRECIATION OF STYLE

★

ACC ART BOOKS

"Did mothers always try to press unto their daughters the itineraries of which they themselves had dreamed. Did I?"

Joan Didion,
2005

Introduction

★

Fashion for women, mothers, daughters and grandmothers is a special multi-layered dialogue: it fuses heritage, practicality, personal identity, rebellion and mentorship. Clothing is not just decoration – it is a lived, generational and socially navigated experience that can challenge norms, assert autonomy or maintain continuity. Clothes are an extension of self-expression and cultural critique, not just fashion. What our mothers wear is key to understanding who they are. It helps fashion their uniqueness as women of their time and tells us how they wanted to be seen. It explains and informs their life-long stories. Their wardrobe is not merely about mum-jeans, wedding hats and graduation dresses. The most famous 'waiting-list' bag in the world – the Birkin by Hermès – was created because Jane Birkin needed something to carry her baby things in. What mothers wear is a clue to class, personality, times, tastes and politics, and combining personal interviews with revealing research, *Cool Mothers: An Appreciation of Style* brings these stories to life.

Navigating motherhood with effortless grace is tricky. Even megastar Rihanna, who has so publicly redefined what it means to balance fame, style and family in the 21st century, admits it's hard work. It's far from easy to show up and sparkle as a fashion icon while pregnant or with two children under five in tow, but she succeeded in a Dior baby-doll dress on the red carpet during Paris Fashion Week while pregnant with her first baby. And, again, when she dressed her two eldest children in Dior menswear straight off Jonathan Anderson's debut Spring 2026 runway on a family visit to the premiere of the *Smurfs* (2025) movie. In a February 2025 *Harper's Bazaar* interview, RiRi admitted that looking after RZA and Riot is tough: "Every decision I make revolves around them, but everything that I do that I love robs me from them... I have to keep reminding myself that I asked for this, I love this. I try to figure out a balance so that I can feel fulfilled" (Sanchez, 2025). It may have felt revolutionary for Rihanna to wear a see-through négligée while heavily pregnant, but musician and actress Courtney Love styled the same look in a 1992 issue of *Vanity Fair* while she was expecting her daughter Frances, though to less gracious applause.

The role of being a mother is heavy with connotation and has been decoded very differently over the decades. Chic motherhood is something specially fascinating. Elizabeth Taylor visited Bertram Mills Circus in London back in 1961 with her daughter Liza Todd, both of them wearing matching tweed Dior suits to enjoy the rough and tumble of the fair. It was the same year Taylor won her first Best Actress Oscar for her role in *BUtterfield 8* (1960) when she chose to wear the tiny-waisted 'Soirée à Rio' corseted gown, designed by Marc Bohan for Dior and decorated with flowers and insects, to accept the award. Tim Mendelson, her close assistant for 20 years, revealed that she confided "it wasn't designed for her but instead (she) went to her local Dior and bought it off the rack". At the time, she was a mother of three children. Along with Liza, she had two sons, Michael Wilding Jr and Christopher Wilding, and would go on to adopt a fourth, Maria. Amazingly, Taylor always looked immaculate and glamorous; a hard task for anyone, let alone a hands-on mother and movie star. But the bewildering traditional rules of 'good mothering' – the historical expectations and subtle or not-so-subtle pressures of what a mother can and cannot be – is a weight to bear, and those who choose to wear clothes that empower them, or that express their true identity, take on a challenge.

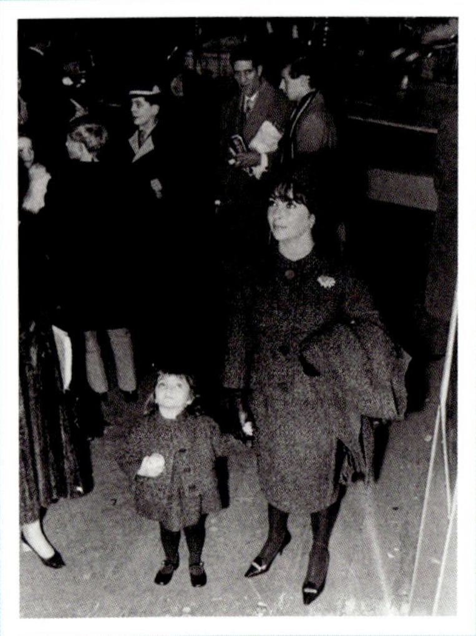

"Whether that's denim cut offs and a customised T-shirt or an evening gown, my mom says you have to be able to serve it and one thing I can say that my mom has always been good at is serving what she's wearing."

Kristen Gabrielle Lightfoot,
2025

Bianca Jagger's daughter, Jade, was just five years old when her mother turned heads wearing an off-the-shoulder disco dress, sitting on a horse at New York City's legendary nightclub Studio 54 in 1977. With the same poise and style that had inspired Yves Saint Laurent and Andy Warhol, the human-rights activist changed nappies and continued to wear her swish wardrobe without missing a beat when she had her child. Mother muses are valuable. Jagger's mother, Dora Macias Somarriba, managed as a young woman alone in Nicaragua, raising three children without any support. But she wasn't just surviving; she was an icon in her own right, and is Bianca's enduring authority to this day.

When London-based fashion designer David Koma became creative director of the House of Mugler, one of his first collections there was inspired by a Thierry Mugler suit that his mother had bought in the 2000s when he was a child, prompting him to reimagine it with a contemporary twist. Simon Porte Jacquemus, too, honours his late mother, Valérie Jacquemus, with his work. In an interview, he described her as "very warm, and also a bit childish in the way she would wear big pantaloon trousers or granny dresses. Without any money, she could look very special and artistic. She wasn't 'French chic'. She was too smiley for that, with her shiny eyes and shiny persona". Following his mother's untimely death, Jacquemus set up his own fashion brand, naming it after his mother's maiden name and creating a collection that was "designed for the girl my mother was" (Lau, 2016).

The emotional ties of families can encourage design creativity; most famously, after her daughter Marguerite was born in 1897, couturière Jeanne Lanvin began making the most exquisite clothes for her. The label's childrenswear became an enduring feature of the fashion house, sparking a trend for 'mummy and me' twinning outfits. It's a design principle they use to this day: Lanvin's 2015 campaign shot mother–daughter imagery, including models Pat and Anna Cleveland wearing identical outfits. A mother's identity is a catalyst for the way she dresses her children. The clothes a mother crafts for her child needn't be couture to resonate – many children's favourite fashion memories are of the outfits their mother made for them. Singer Janis Joplin's mother, Dorothy, used to make homespun frocks for her and her sister (Runtagh, 2021), while the American artist Betye Saar would buy a roll of fabric and use it to make outfits for all her children. Daughter Tracye reminisced in a *Harper's Bazaar* interview that she and her sisters were "like the von Trapps! We were all dressed in the same fabric. I had the jumper, and you had the romper, and she had the A-line" (Isaiah, 2021).

Princess Diana's style evolution, from aristocrat in pie-crust-collared blouses to single parent in slinky John Galliano slip-dresses, ran in parallel to the pieces in which she dressed her sons, princes William and Harry. As she became more fashion-confident, she quietly defied royal protocol and allowed them to wear jeans and baseball caps instead of the formal wear expected. Becoming a mother brings poignant physical and real-world change as well as a transformed sense of self. Expectations of how to behave, along with fear of failure and the backbeat of gender politics, intensify a moment in time when who you are as a mother needs to be figured out. Examining clothing is a way of telling those stories, and looking at the clothes mothers wear offers a lens through which to examine the intersections of fashion, identity and the experience of motherhood. Garments worn as a mother often become markers of emotional states during what can be a time of profound transformation. What you wear can reveal resilience, creativity, constraint and freedom, and exploring the clothes worn by all different kinds of mothers – from Yoko Ono and Judy Garland to Josephine Baker and Anna Wintour – adds another page to who they are and the worlds they lived in.

This is a book about fashion, and also about the way clothes can reveal the private and public dimensions of women's lives. Garments tell social stories and can be full of meaning, memory and sometimes resistance. Looking at the clothes mothers wear can contribute to a deeper understanding of women's lives through the language of dress. Reflections on not only what women wore as mothers, but also on how they remember their own mother and grandmother's clothes, opens up a conversation about character, generational influence and the evolving place of women in society. Reviewing their wardrobes helps to uncover how sartorial choices shape – and are shaped by – cultural narratives around femininity, care and domesticity. The House of Missoni, from its launch in 1953 to today, charts a lineage of powerful women: Rosita, Angela and Margherita all pioneered an artistic approach to business and fashion. The Missoni ladies and their clothes tell both a personal and collective story, and their unique wardrobes tell similar but different style stories.

Motherhood can also complicate lives and frustrate creativity; figuring out what to wear is often the last thing on the to-do list when up against a full day. Feminist poet Adrienne Rich's work *Of Woman Born: Motherhood as Experience and Institution* (1976) reflects on it as a means of oppression and subordination – as more to do with losing identity than asserting one. She presents the stereotypical stay-at-home mother as relegated and trapped. Women who have defied being pigeon-holed in this way have often been criticised. Julie Phillips's *The Baby on* *the Fire Escape* (2022) explores the difficult balance between making art and raising children. In a chapter called 'Outlaw Mothering', she focuses on the American painter Alice Neel, whose life inspired the book's title. Neel was far from a sentimental ideal of motherhood. She lost her first baby to diphtheria, became estranged from the daughter born after, and later had two sons when she was aged 39 and 41, raising them largely alone and supporting them through her art. Her life was complicated, unconventional and entirely self-directed. Phillips quotes Sally Eckhoff's *F*ck Art (Let's Dance)* (2013), describing a moment when Neel was nearly 80. A younger artist saw her in a "polka-dot dress, her hair pinned in a soft, grandmotherly twist" and wondered how "a bosom in patterned rayon" could contain "the heart of a soldier at arms". Clearly, even at that grand age, Neel was expected to dress in an outfit more befitting the iconography of a great artist or perfect textbook mother instead of just being herself, and here is reduced to a 'bosom in rayon'. Neel never seemed concerned. Photographs of her in 1930s Greenwich Village show a captivating bohemian in a beret, entirely sure of herself. Motherhood, especially the kind you invent as you go along, takes courage. No woman escapes judgement, whatever she wears. Neel simply refused to let it define her.

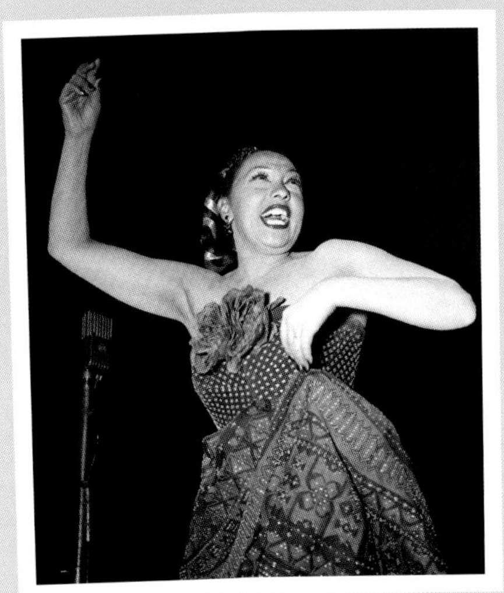

This book includes stories that engage the emotional territory of disappointment and regret alongside strength and purpose through the memory of clothes a mother has worn. For example, although Swinging Sixties fashion model Penelope Tree was enthralled by her mother Marietta's couture wardrobe stuffed with labels from Paris, she received limited maternal affection, which affected her profoundly. In Maya Angelou's 2013 memoir, *Mom & Me & Mom*, she recounts a pivotal interaction with her mother Vivian Baxter, whom she didn't want to claim as a mother but whose clothes fascinated her, nonetheless.

Public displays of affection between a mother and her children are not hard to find, however, and clothing can be a charming way for mothers, sons and daughters to connect and display their team spirit, especially on the red carpet. Take Timothée Chalamet and his mother, Nicole Flender. They both wore pieces from Virgil Abloh's 2019 'Off White' collection to celebrate the Golden Globes in 2019, when Chalamet was nominated for the Best Actor Award. Serena Williams and her daughter Olympia, meanwhile, sported matching catsuits by David Koma to the *King Richard* premiere in 2021. Equally, iconic archive pieces like the Alexander McQueen dress worn by Gwyneth Paltrow to the Oscars in 2002 are handed down and renewed. To the delight of her followers on Instagram, the actress posted an image of her daughter Apple wearing the iconic frock.

Salma Hayek's daughter, Valentina Pinault, wore Hayek's 1997 Isaac Mizrahi dress over a quarter of a century later to the 2023 Oscars. The familial fashion line is something Cora Corré, daughter of Serena Rees and Joseph Corré, and granddaughter of Vivienne Westwood, has been keenly immersed in since a very young age. She first walked Westwood's catwalk aged just four, alongside supermodel Veruschka, both wearing tiger-print dresses. Today, she heads The Vivienne Foundation, carrying forward the designer's philosophy to make the world a better place. When a mother or grandmother passes away, the clothes they wear become enshrined in memory and become touchstones to keep and treasure, as do their values. Sometimes, they live on as a celebration of who she was. Following the death of her mother Linda from breast cancer in 1998, Stella McCartney looked back on her mother's influence, telling *Vogue* back in 2000: "She wore the coolest clothes man – these beautiful Forties print skirts with a pop T-shirt, which is what I do. She was such a ballsy person" (Meter, 2000).

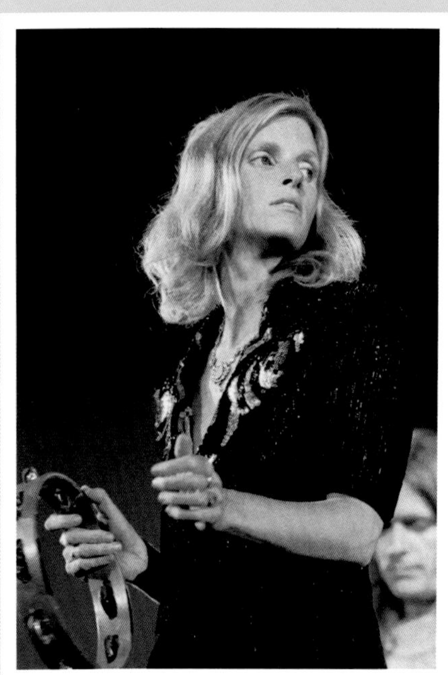

Equally, it's a mother's privilege to watch her offspring change and grow up and, perhaps, absorb their mother's style and attitude. Actress and director Sadie Frost reflected on her experience of seeing Iris, her daughter with actor Jude Law, mature:

> "It's so interesting when you see your daughters and their friends grow up; at first, they are just these things, and then they become fully fledged autonomous beings, and you can tell they've obviously been

watching and lapping things up and emerge like beautiful butterflies. This generation are very different; beautiful sassy girls like Iris and her friend Lila Moss [Kate Moss's daughter], who have had a great education and have this strength from being around such amazing creative people all their lives and have now emerged with such confidence to hold their own, much more than I was able to do when I was in my 20s. It's very different from my generation when we were just test-running everything and just hoping for the best. This generation can learn from our mistakes."

Remembering the stories of our mothers and the outfits they wore is an exercise in understanding their mistakes and triumphs, as well as appreciating the meaning of clothes as a record of women's lives. Whether your mum was a punk, a hippy or a Spice Girls fan, a power-suited career woman or a bohemian artist, the outfits she chose to wear can explain who she was and why, and that is why this is both a book of memory and empowerment, as well as a testimony and celebration of what clothes can tell us about our cool mothers.

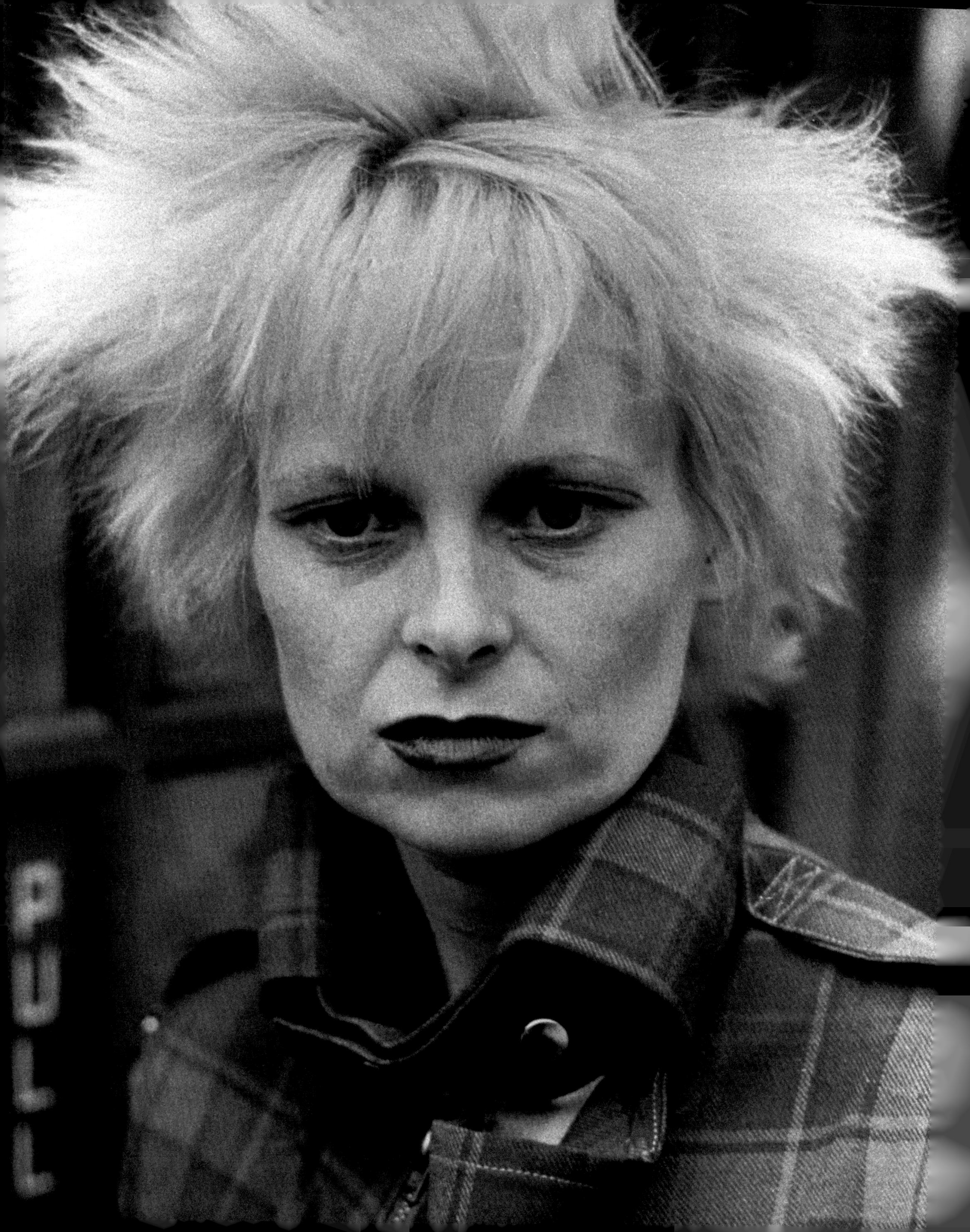
PULL

Vivienne Westwood, Bridget and Serena Rees, **and** Cora Corré

★

Cora Corré's mum and dad, Serena Rees and Joseph Corré, created Agent Provocateur, the playfully racy '90s lingerie brand, which conquered the world with its satin, lace frills and ruffles, and gave people an opportunity to have fun with their underwear. Her paternal grandmother, Vivienne Westwood, was an iconoclast and agitator. She didn't just reflect her time; she created it – with slogans, safety pins and a DIY attitude that, to this day, feels empowering.

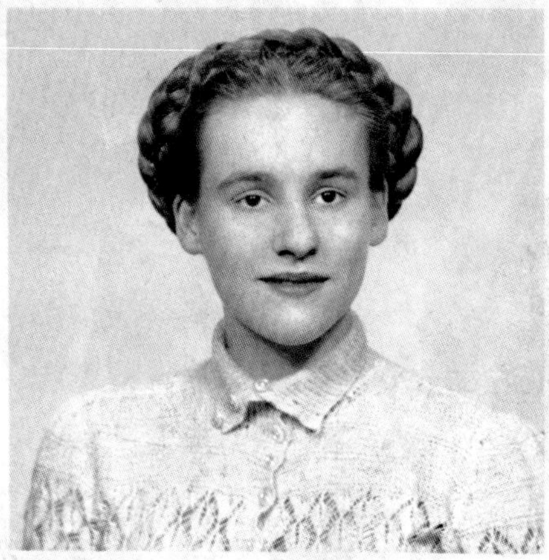

Bridget Rees, 18 years old, early 1950s.

Maternal grandmother Bridget Rees was a bohemian academic. She defied class and gender norms by studying at the University of Cambridge in the 1950s, wearing chic below-the-knee pencil-skirt suits. Her daughter, Serena, described her as "beautiful and quite McQueenish", though took a different path by creating Les Girls Les Boys, an androgynous selection of outfits that can be worn 'from bed to street', which turned the success of Agent Provocateur on its head. Despite her mother's subsequent leisurewear clothing brand, Serena's daughter Cora admits her nearest and dearest relations can't always comprehend the value of dressing down:

> "Tracksuits aren't something my family understands, but they are quite a big part of my life... I love an Adidas trackie top with a jean. But the idea of tracksuits has always been something my family has found hard to grasp outside of where they are necessary; the idea that someone would wear a slouchy tracksuit bottom for work is something that puzzled my grandmother Vivienne and still puzzles my dad."

Dressing to impress was far more commonplace than athleisure when Cora was growing up, and she goes on to reveal: "One of my earliest memories is coming home from primary school when we used to live in a flat above the Agent Provocateur office. I'd walk through the door and, in the hall, there was a glass desk with a lady behind it, wearing a pink Agent P dress and a heel, and I very much wanted that to be me." Now in her mid-20s, Corré has friends who are becoming mothers themselves. Reflecting on how personalities can change with responsibilities, she admits that it's not something that happened in her family.

> "I look back on both of my grandmothers, Bridget and Vivienne, and my mum Serena, and their maternal sides were always very much part of them, but they didn't let it become their identity and that is seen in their style. Serena didn't buy

into maternity wear, Vivienne definitely wouldn't have, and... I'm grateful for the way my mum brought me up. Motherhood didn't define her it just added to her."

It's a path Serena forged back in the '90s when she was expecting Cora.

"I loved being pregnant and the challenge of finding something to wear. I wore Westwood all the time. I found a stretchy dress and customised it to fit, and people thought I was crazy wearing heels all the time. When Cora arrived, I made her a part of our lives instead of making changes because of her. When she started school, I'd drop her off and all the other mothers would look down their noses at my outfit. I'd be fully Agent Provocateur-ed up."

It's something Cora remembers to this day:

"My mother used to pick me up from school in her everyday clothes and her everyday clothes very much differentiated her from the other mums. I used to tell Serena to stand away from the school gates. I have a very vivid memory – my mum has this long-sleeved Westwood top with a circle around each breast and a tube running from one to another, and she used to do the school run sometimes in it and that really got me. I just couldn't deal with it. I recently tried it on, it was an Anglomania remake and actually, although there are a lot of things of Serena's that I would absolutely love to wear, that still didn't work for me."

Cora's first day at school was equally noteworthy. Serena reveals:

"We did all these great bikinis at AP. There was a biker one with chains, badges and biker stuff and they were really cool. The team made a mini version for Cora. A little turquoise triangle bikini – it didn't have chains on it though if I remember. On her first day of school, we laid out her clothes the night before and in the morning I went into her room and she was putting on the bra top and knickers underneath her school uniform. I had to manage the situation. I wouldn't be seen as a good parent if she went in wearing an AP biker bikini on her first day."

Wearing micro-sized glamorous adult clothes is something Cora got used to quickly. "When I was small, Vivienne used to make me mini versions of her clothing. And I very much remember they had all these drapes and things, and I used to get dressed in them when I'd go to meet her at the theatre or somewhere and I used to have my head in an armhole or something." Serena continues: "She had some beautiful things made by Vivienne given for birthdays and Christmas which she hated because they were tight and little people don't like tight things. There was a lot of complaining at the time, but she understands now how special it was."

Images of Corré's debut Westwood catwalk appearance, aged four, show her alongside legendary supermodel Veruschka; both are wearing a celebrated 'Tiger' dress. A portrait of Cora wearing it, accessorised with a matching bonnet and holding hands with her grandmother, is on display at the National Portrait Gallery in London. It's not the only photograph of her there – another shows her as a baby wearing a *toile de Jouy* milkmaid gown, sitting on Westwood's lap. The clothes worn in formative years are often only cherishable in retrospect. Serena remembers a particular childhood outfit Bridget made her wear:

"My mother dressed me in black patent Mary-Jane shoes – and crocheted me a suit with a wide-leg pant and a sweater top; the outfit was turquoise, yellow and dark brown. Ugh. And in addition,

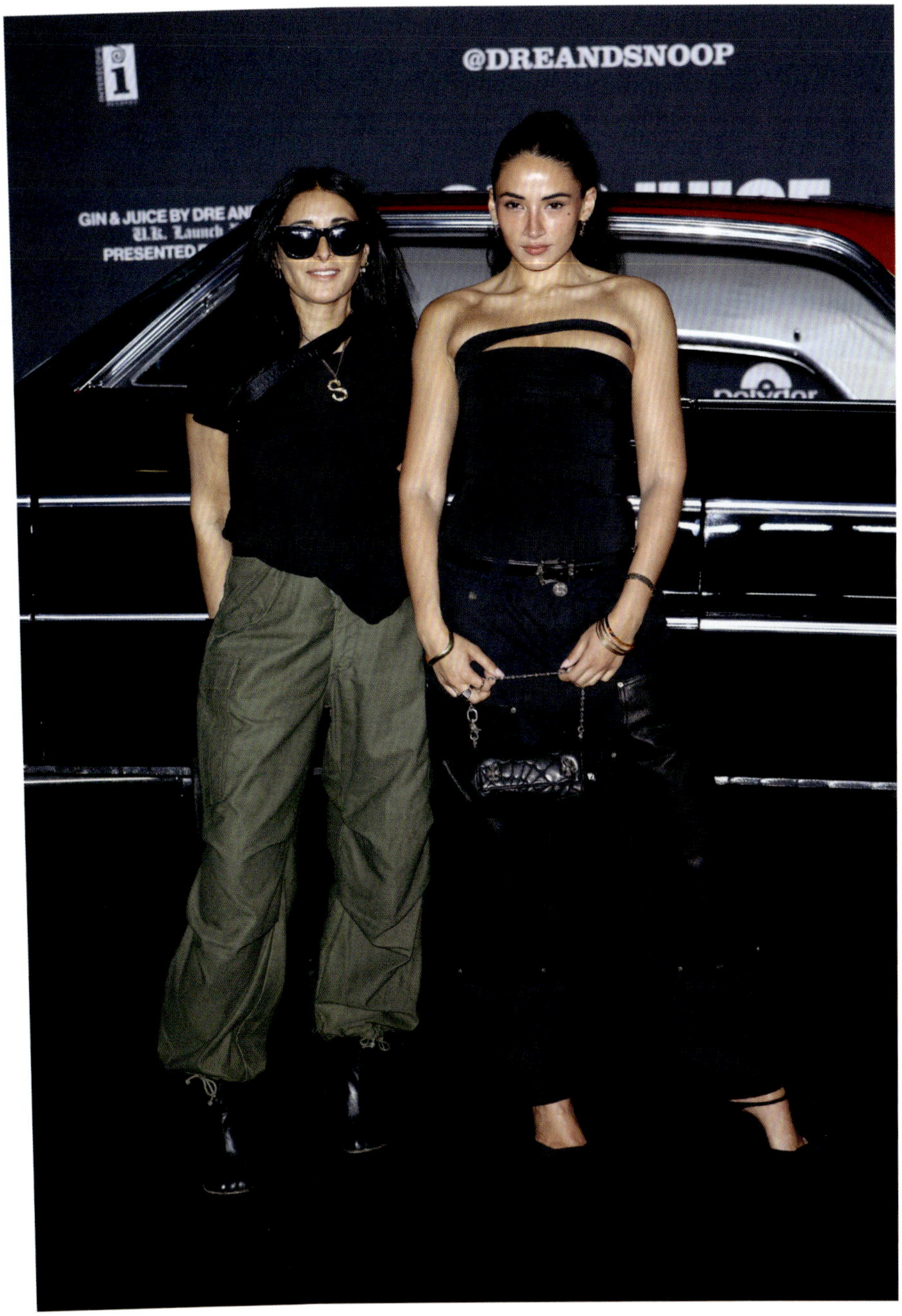

"My mother instilled a sense of self-confidence in me. I had a very grounded upbringing and was always seen and heard. My feelings meant something. This gave me a confidence to have conviction in my own taste."

Serena Rees,
2025

she had made a big brown beret which I refused to wear so I'm holding it in the picture she took. I don't think I've worn such a statement since. We had so many arguments about clothes that in the end she gave me an allowance and let me buy what I wanted."

Serena, meanwhile, dressed Cora in retro deadstock, which her daughter found equally strange at the time. According to Cora: "I wasn't very happy about it, but when I look back at pictures now, I think 'thank God I wasn't wearing horrible plastic flashing trainers', which I think was all I really ever wanted instead of these cute gingham 1950s frocks my mum dressed me in." Today, it's the craftsmanship of clothes and the longevity of fashion that appeals to Corré:

"When I'm modelling on shoots or in a show, I want to celebrate what the atelier has made. If I wear something beautiful, I try and carry myself with the knowledge that so much time has gone into creating it and honour that. In the last few years before Vivienne died, we worked together on her foundation, and I saw for the first time in a long while that she felt so much joy and excitement in what she was doing. Watching her creative process was wonderful to see but it very much came from one of her slogans, 'Buy Less, Choose Well'. She was someone who would layer pieces and I think that's something I've learnt to do in the last few years. She had this very sweet, knitted waistcoat she'd wear in the summer by itself but in the winter over something warm. She definitely opened my eyes to the way you can adapt and wear things through the seasons and that was very much envisioned in the collection she made for the foundation. She didn't want to have seasonal collections, as the way she styled herself wasn't like that. She built and added to what she wore or stripped back, depending on the time of year, and it's definitely something that I do now, too, and something I learnt from her."

Serena is as equally charmed with Cora's wardrobe as Cora is with hers and Vivienne's: "I think what's interesting is watching your children grow in the different phases and styles, and the experiments they go through. I'd say Cora has a very good idea of who she is now, particularly with what suits her, but she's not afraid to try different things. I think she looks fabulous."

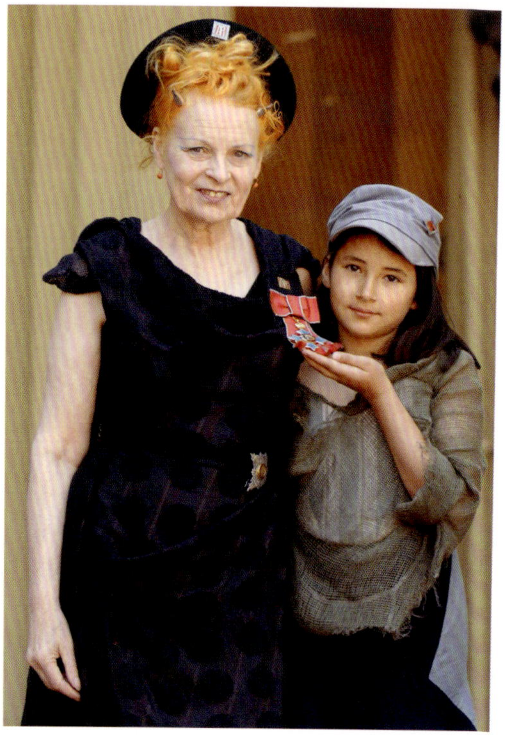

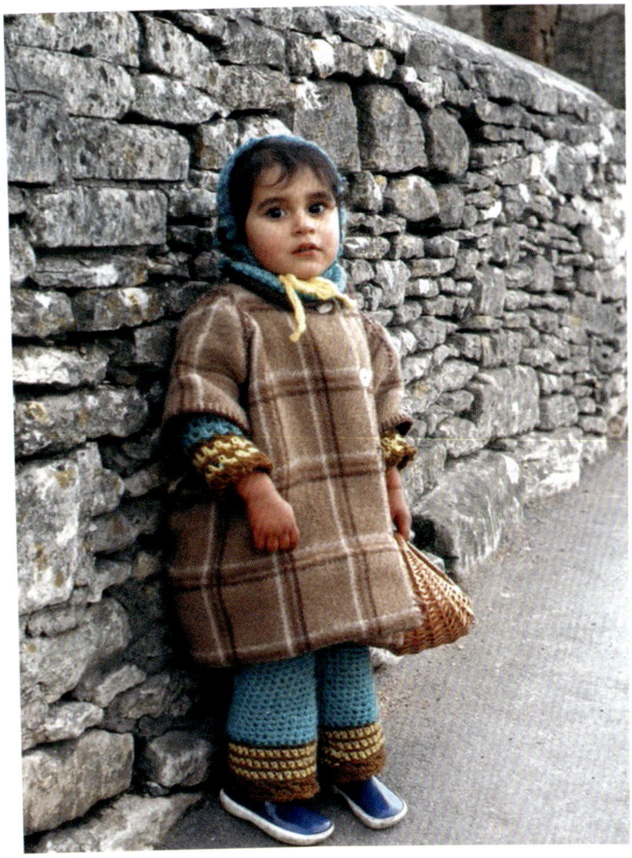

Serena Rees, two-and-a-half years old, early 1970s.

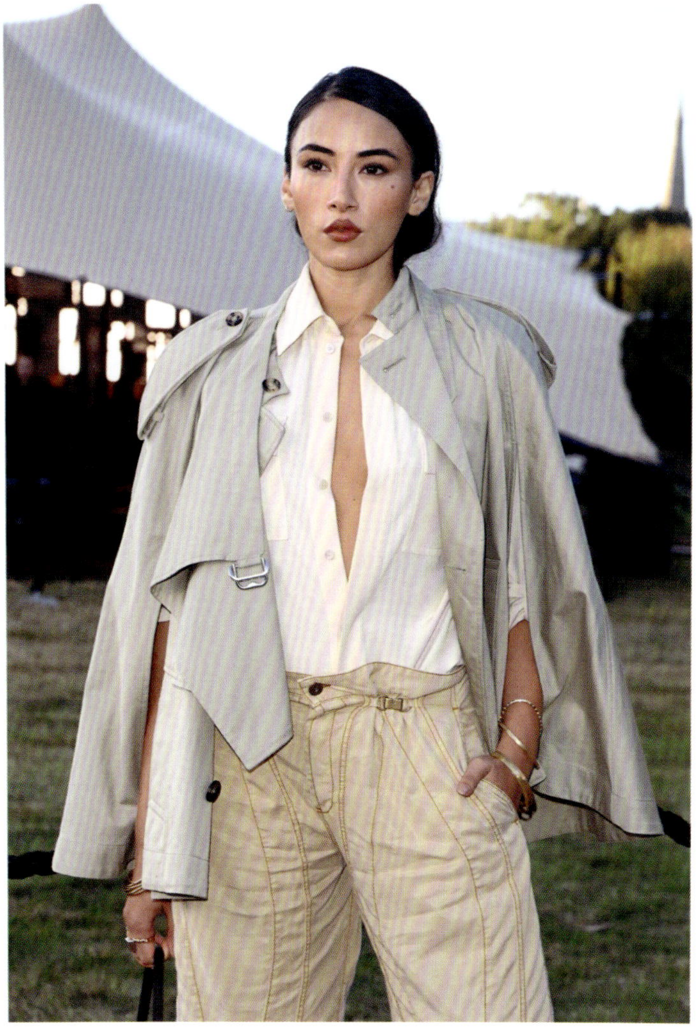

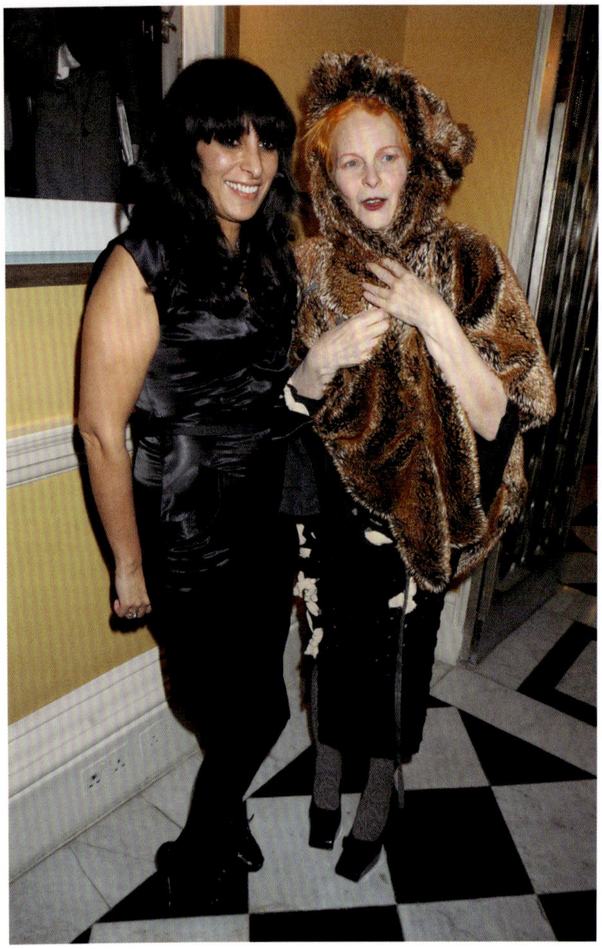

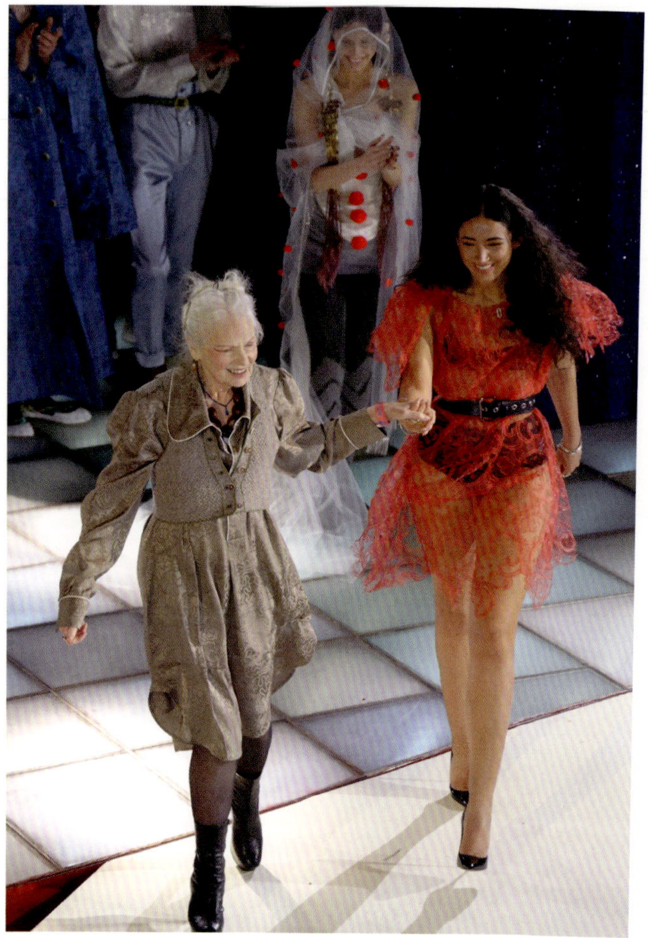

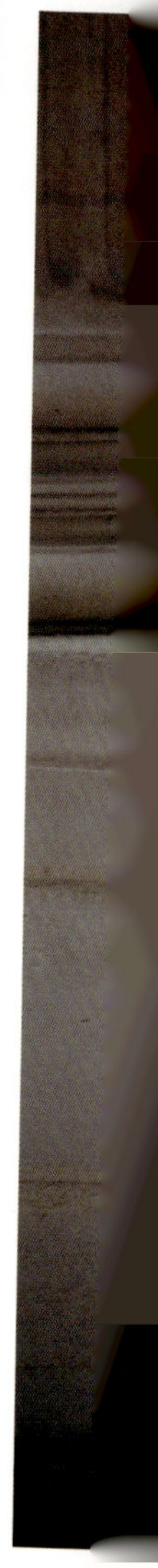

"When I'm a mum and have kids of my own, I'd be very, very flattered if they want to wear my clothes."

Cora Corré,
2025

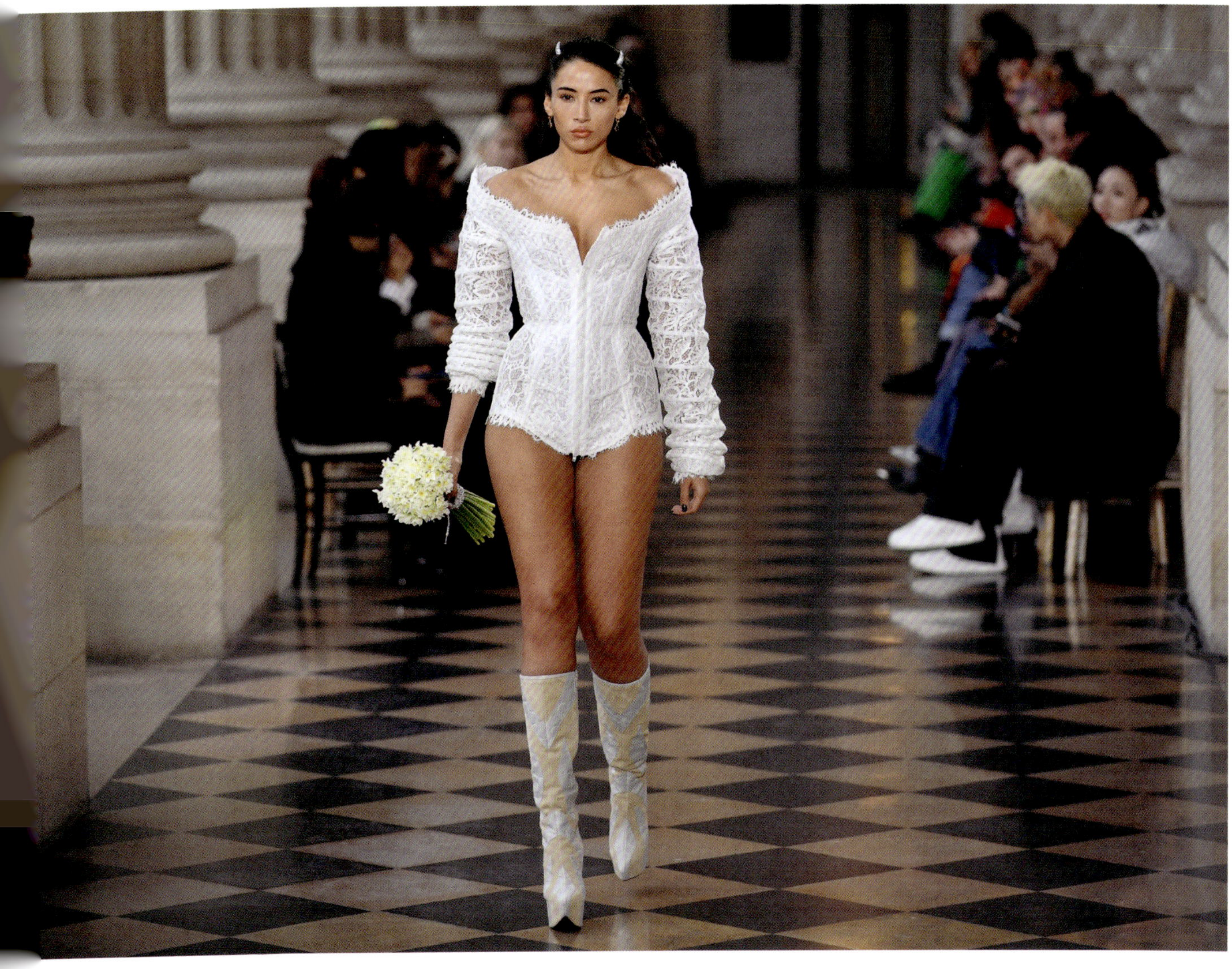

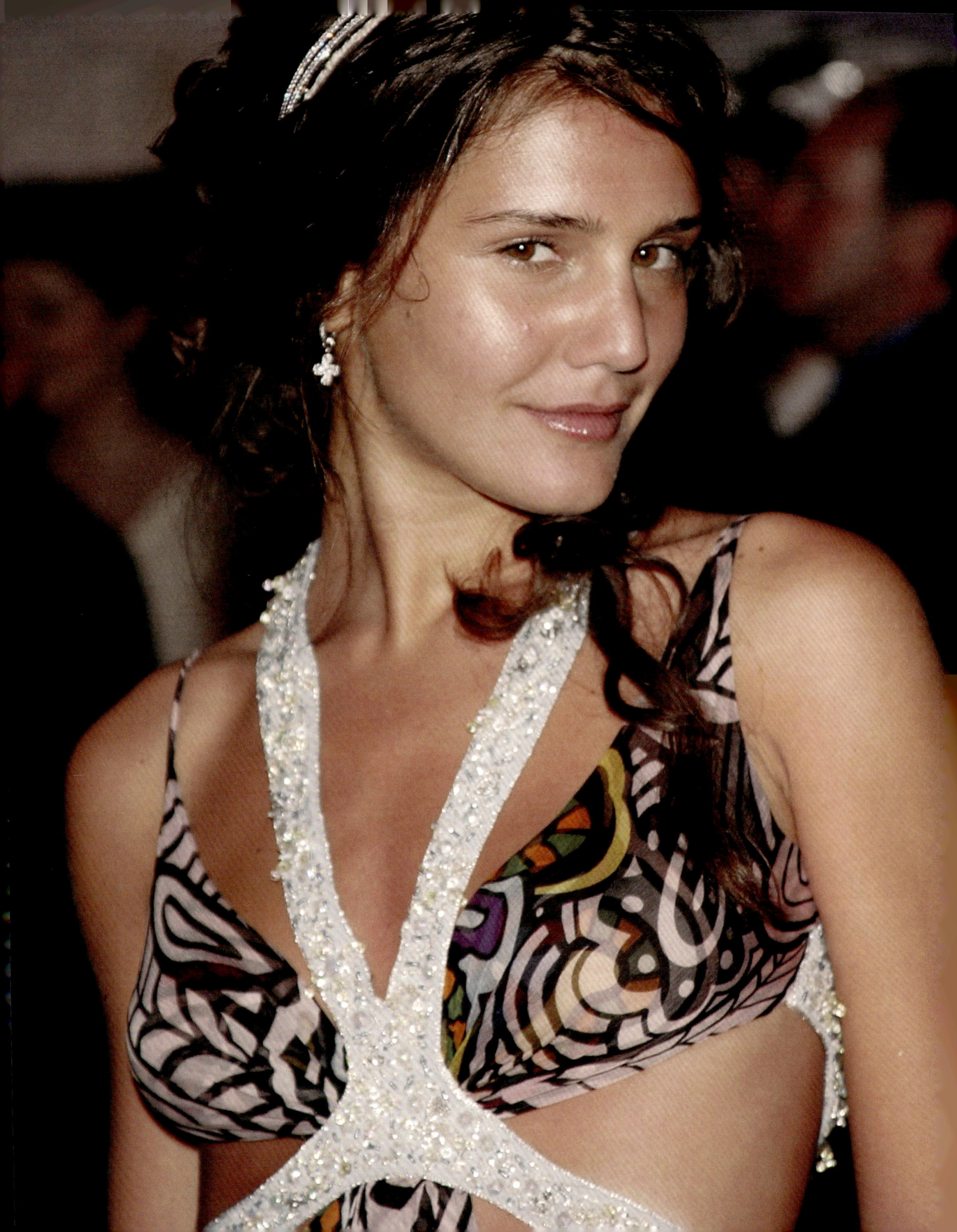

Rosita, **Angela** and Margherita **Missoni**

★

The House of Missoni, along with its signature chevron knitwear, has a unique place in fashion history. From Diana Vreeland to Anna Piaggio, the greats of style have always appreciated the originality and pace of the luxury Italian fashion brand. Founded in 1953 by Rosita and Ottavio in Italy's textile capital, Gallarate, near Milan, it has been dominated by three generations of women, who have pioneered an artistic approach to business and fashion. The Missoni ladies and their clothes tell both a personal and collective story.

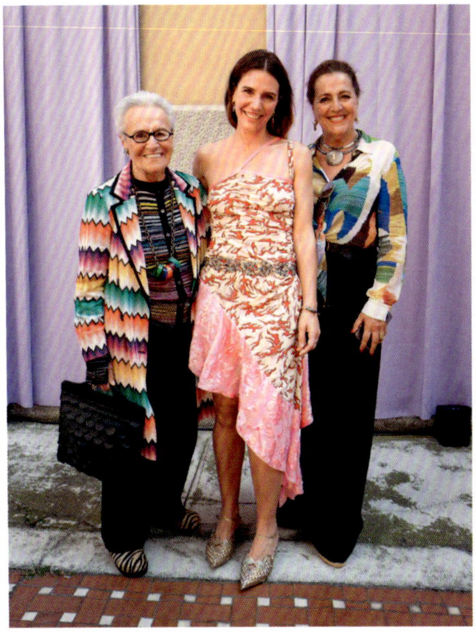

Angela Missoni, daughter of Rosita and mother to Margherita, is president of Missoni and an archetypal bohemian mama. In her mid-60s, she is an unaffected beauty and arrives for an interview with her hair long and flowing, wearing a smock top, vintage rings on her fingers and a smudge of mascara. She grew up in a female-centric family where life was open to possibilities, and what she chose, at the age of 23, was to become a young mother. "It was nature, I remember first telling my mum when I was 15 that I was going to have a child at 18 and she almost fainted, but she didn't try and dissuade me. I was driven, and while it was my rebellion to become a parent, it was also a very natural thing to do coming from my environment which was so non-judgemental", she says. She spent time at home with her children, Margherita, Francesco and Theresa, before going to work at the family brand for over 20 years, where she ran the celebrated Italian fashion label as creative director and commercial head, developing its cultural and creative DNA with skill and integrity. "I think the fact of being a mother opened my heart to be more understanding of the rest of the world. It made me more aware of how life is."

As a child who was a teenager in the 1970s, she was surrounded by women who were unapologetic feminists and who forcefully demanded a family and a career.

> "I saw a life where you could be a mother, breastfeed and still fight for women's rights; you didn't need to choose one or the other. We were the first generation to push for maternity leave; I know I was privileged – I had a great support network and lived in a house five minutes from the Missoni factory and Rosita's house – but I was always thinking forward."

It's little surprise that her work saw her turn the 2017 Missoni runway into a women's protest march, with models wearing bespoke zig-zag knitted 'pussyhats' with pink cat ears, in support of the Women's March that had taken place that January, following the first presidential inauguration of Donald Trump: "When I have a show, my voice is louder so I can use it for a good cause."

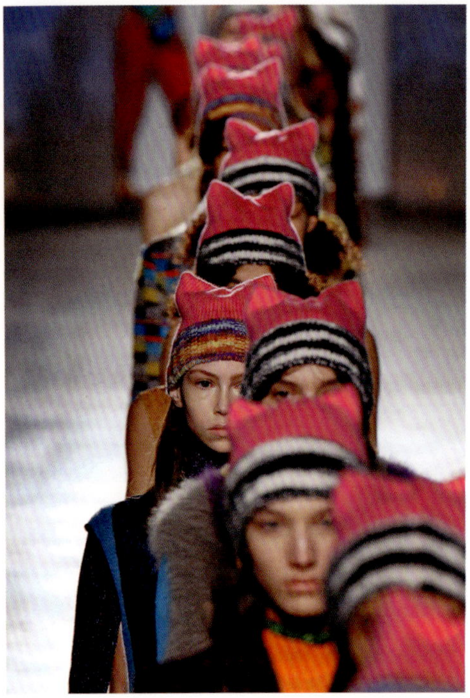

In the early 1980s, when Angela was pregnant with Margherita, she showed off her growing bump, championing her own femininity at a time when many women's maternity wardrobe was restricted to voluminous, silhouette-hiding dresses. Instead of pyramid-shaped smocks and bijou sailor dresses, Angela explains: "I wore skinny body suits, belts and oversized earrings and people were shocked. I decorated my belly with bells. I thought I was elegant!"

The family has always had their finger on the cultural pulse, and when Margherita was born in 1983 they were collaborating with legendary illustrator Antonio Lopez. It was his great sense of style that infused the Missoni advertising campaigns, sketching the progressive clothing the brand conceived and family wore so well. Their collections were aimed squarely at the fashion-forward and, although not designed as such, worked well as part of Angela's maternity wardrobe, with expandable striped knitwear fitting all sizes. One of Angela's favourite stories that has been handed down the generations is of Rosita wearing the legendary Missoni chevrons:

> "The story takes place when I was just 13. It was 1972 and the American store, Neiman Marcus, gave my mum an award. She decided to wear something very beautiful and elegant – soft palazzo pants decorated with a mauve zig-zag, a long cardigan and an art-deco inspired belt: all very 1920s inspired. It wasn't a look that the American PR, who was wearing a puffed up, typically American ball gown, appreciated. As she checked the seating, she saw my mum and told her that as it was almost time for the ceremony, could she please go and get dressed properly! Rosita's vintage look was too much for her."

Mother and daughter's styles are singular, and Angela reflects:

> "The way I have dressed is very different to the way Rosita wore her clothes – I was [from] a different period. She was linked to the 1940s and I always say she was born with a low heel, and I was born with a high heel! I had my first heels from the age of 16 when I bought my first pair of Fiorucci platforms. After that I wore heels for 30 years in a row, apart from when I was pregnant with Margherita."

Angela's look, however, has always been infused with the influence of Rosita, who made custom-Missoni pieces that she wore as a child: "When I was about nine years old, I had a Missoni bathing suit, tank top and mini skirt. I also had a blue-and-red-trimmed jersey dress with a Nehru collar in shiny cream fabric. I loved it and I remember that Monica Vitti, a very famous Italian actress, was photographed wearing it, too, which thrilled me." Something that has united all generations of Missoni mothers and daughters, though, is a love of vintage:

> "When Rosita was alive, we all went to flea markets in London, and even today it's the family hobby, and my grandchildren love it too. Saturday or Sunday morning is flea market day. I remember my mum buying a little 1930s Lanvin coat for Margherita so she would know what real quality was like. We all loved it. That's what we are all like."

argherita (left) and
ngela Missoni attend the
NMI Sustainable Fashion
wards during the Milan
ashion Week, 2025.

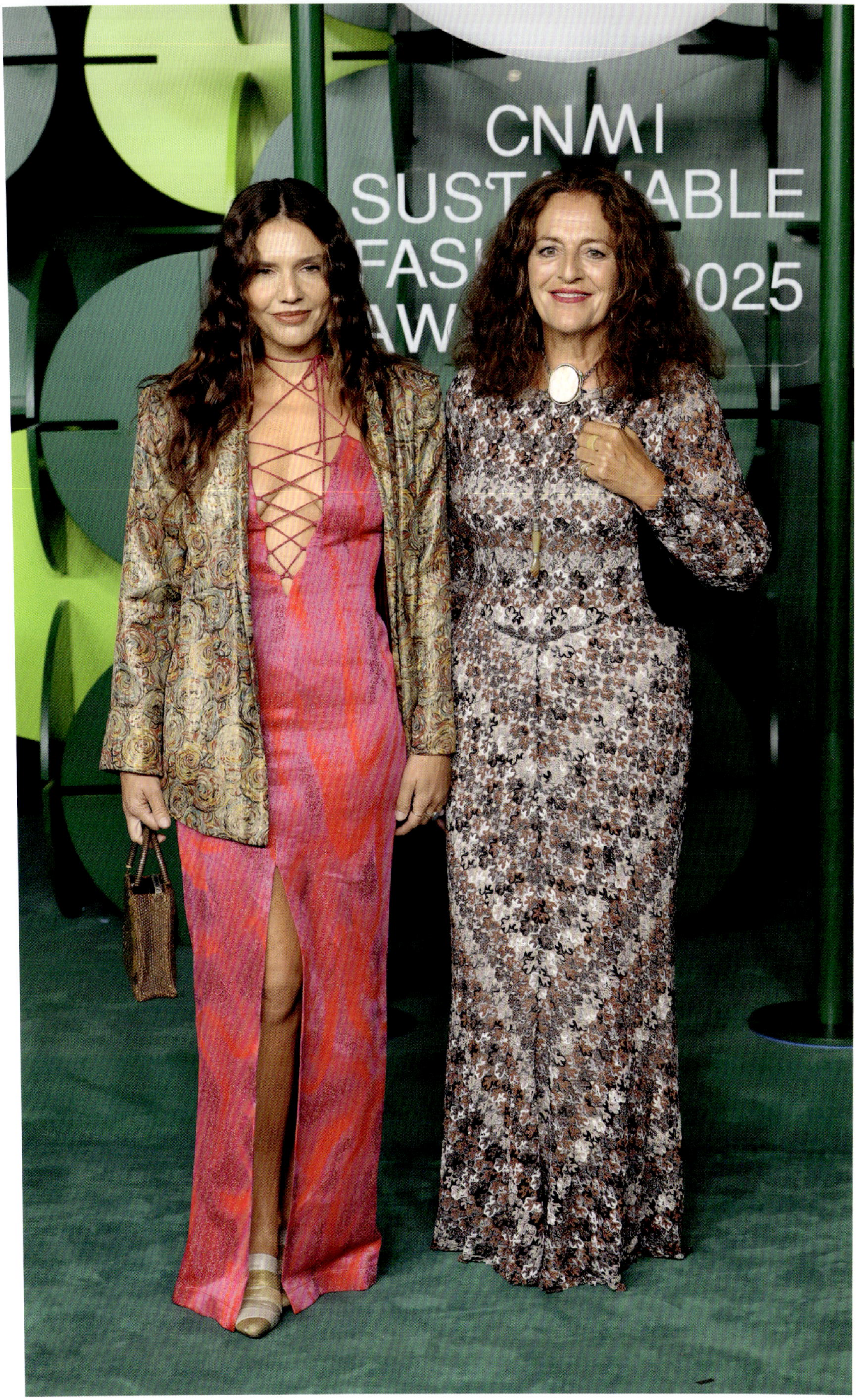

Margherita with Rosita, 2010.

"Women have been the voice of this family."

Angela Missoni,
W magazine, 2021

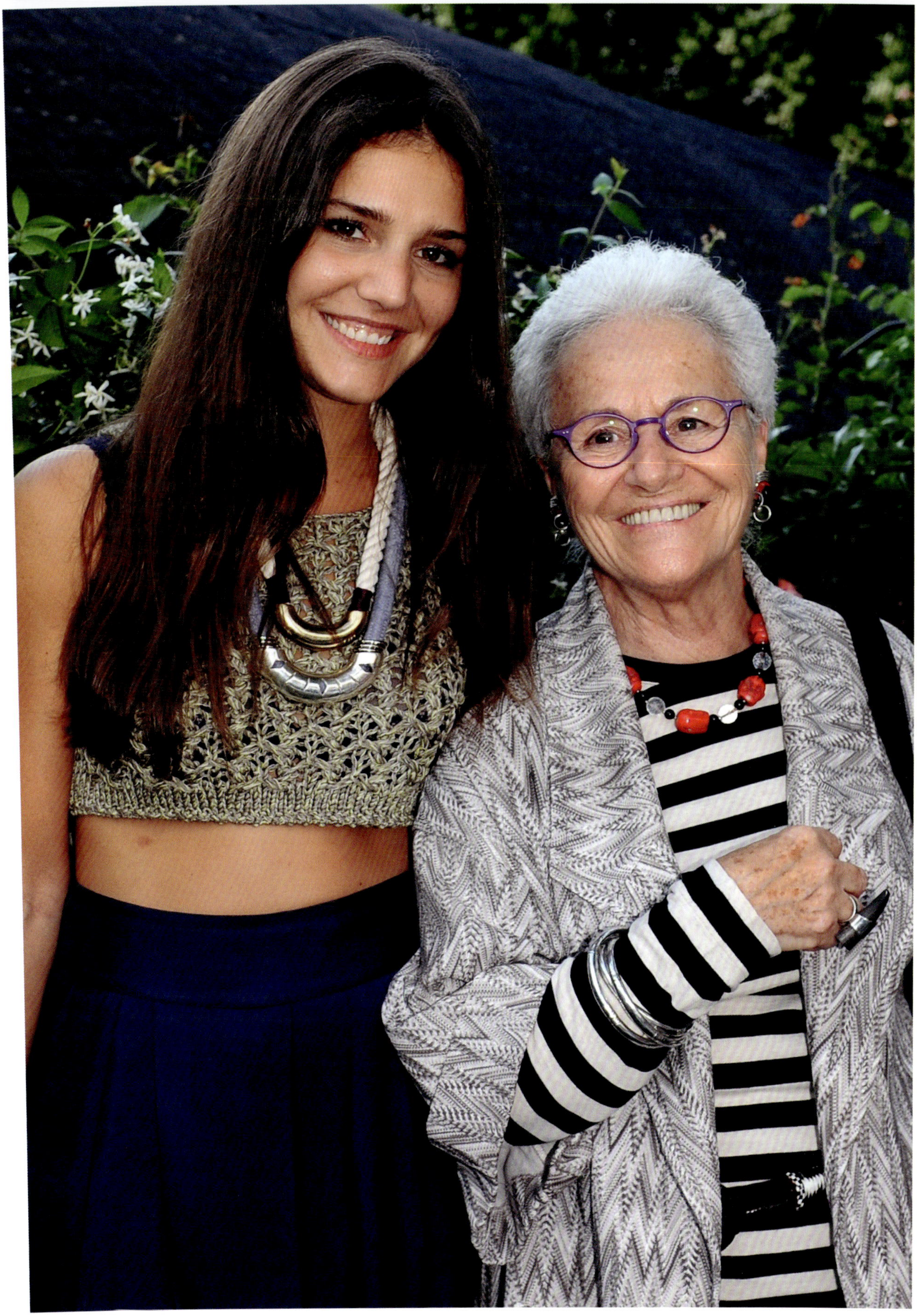

Margherita Maccapani Missoni, Angela's daughter, launched her own fashion house in 2023, and although it is a side-step away from the family legacy, it still feels resonant with its creator's attitude. "My work designing Maccapani feeds into my love of vintage, and my Missoni heritage is very relevant as we as a family are about loving what you wear, sustainability and storytelling." Recognising the reflexive familial sway, she says:

"I don't dress like my mum, but a lot of my references come from her – style is emotional; it resonates because of experiences. Today, I'm wearing a pair of cowboy boots that used to be my mum's. We both treasure old things – they get more value – especially an emotional value. A lot of what I like I wear for over 30 years, and then I feel like they truly belong to me, and even better if it's something that has a history and that once belonged to my mother."

When Margherita was six years old, her parents, Angela Missoni and Marco Maccapani, divorced. In protest, she changed her wardrobe to the complete opposite of how her parents dressed her.

"I rebelled against my fashion background and instead became quite conservative and wore smock dresses; I just wanted to fit in with what other children wore. I didn't know anyone whose parents had separated so I started to go to church and tried to become a good Catholic and resisted in that way. I asked my other granny to take me to a shop in Milan to buy navy cardigans. But by my last year of primary school, when I was 10, I fell in love with clothes again. I would wait for my mum to come back from trips around the world, and she would give me things to wear. Grunge was my earliest fashion moment; I got a plaid shirt when I was 11. In 1993, my mother started her own collection. In 1997, she took over Missoni as creative director and it was this year that Tom Ford staged his debut collection for Gucci and Mario Testino, and Carine Rothchild did the campaign. My mum took me to the very first Gucci show Tom did and I was just dying – that honestly was my first fashion crave. Angela bought herself a petrol-blue coat – I was dying to have one of the Gucci military jackets, and by the time I was about 12 or 13, she eventually bought me one but changed the buttons."

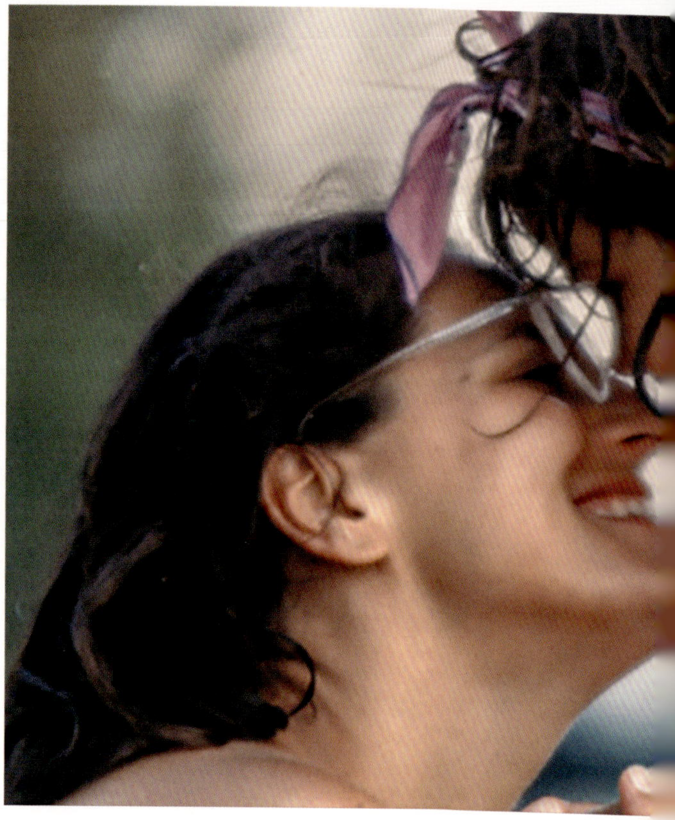

This kind of mix-and-match approach is very much evident in Maccapani's design DNA today, and the brand has even collaborated with eBay – which Margherita was introduced to by Angela, too: "I love eBay. It was my mum who told me about eBay, and I always wondered why people were surprised. Real fashion professionals use it."

Margherita's own style is contemporary, but her fashion memories are suffused with her mother's stylistic sensibility.

"I was one of those children who thought their mother was the most beautiful in the world. When I was young, I loved watching my mother getting ready. She had a huge bathroom, and I would watch her put on her make-up and I remember her wearing a lot of black and white Missoni. She had me quite young and by the time she was 32, she was divorced with three kids, but she was beautiful and she wanted to go out. She had an Alaia moment and started wearing a lot of mini skirts and jackets, but she always wore big chunky earrings and snake rings."

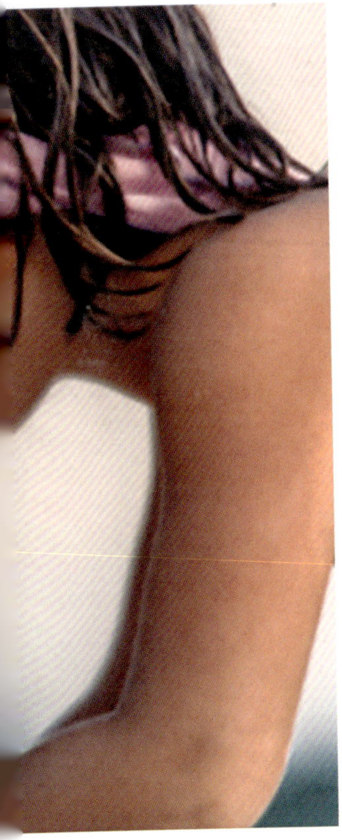

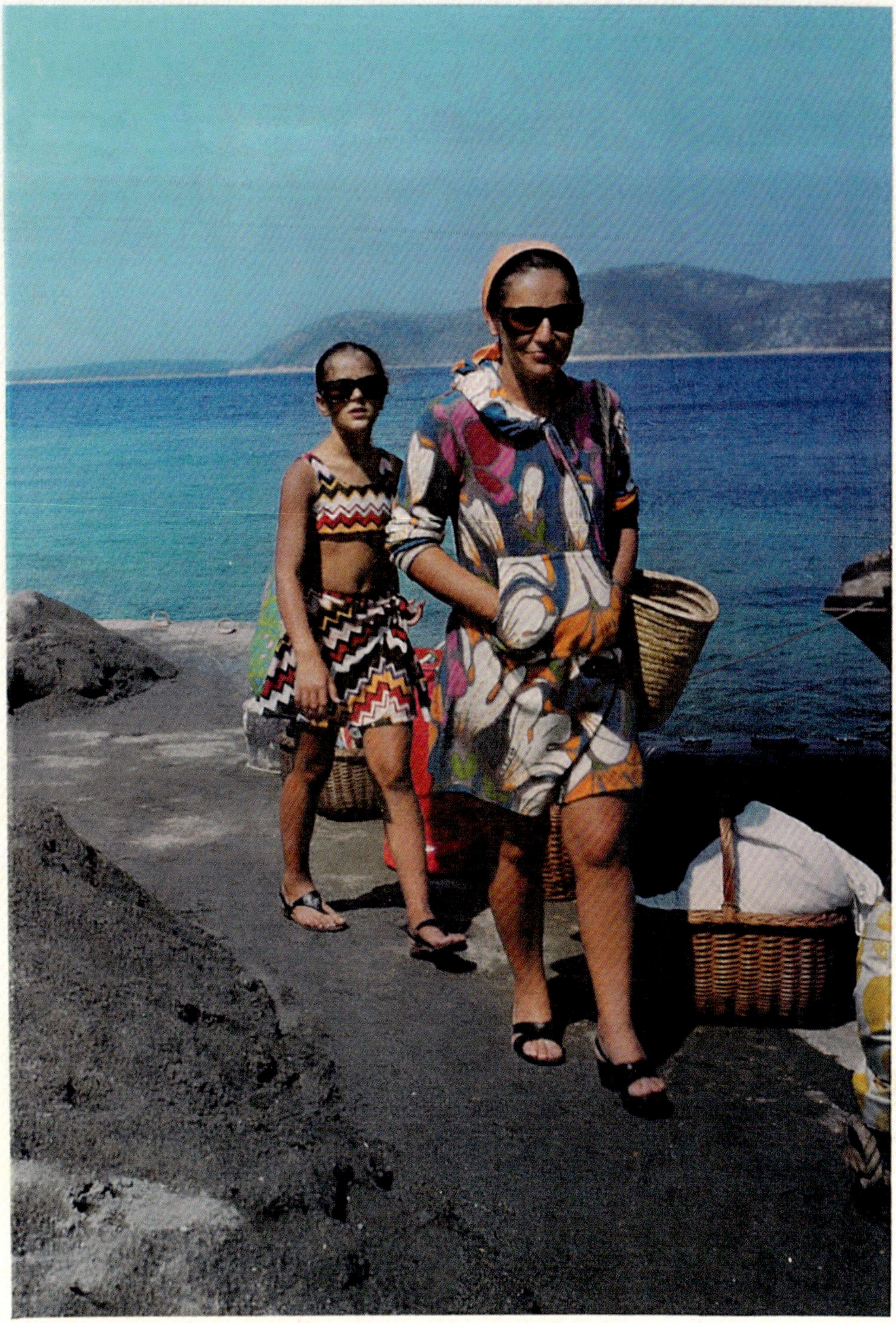

Left: Angela with Margherita, 1986. Right: Angela wearing zig-zag bikini top and mini skirt, alongside Rosita, circa 1968.

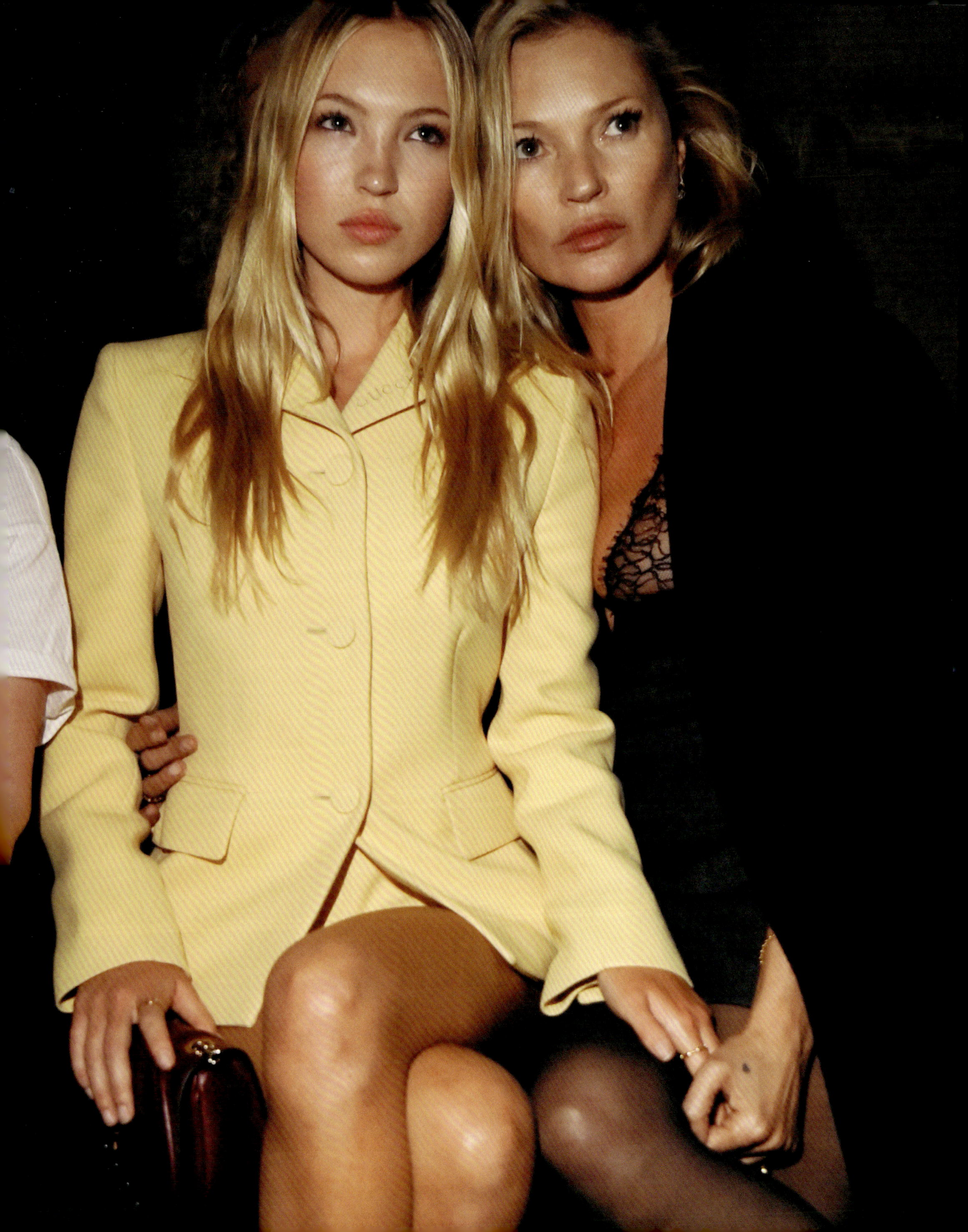

Kate and **Lila** Moss

★

> **"I'm always going into my mum's drawer and stealing her old rock T-shirts. My favourite is a Rolling Stones one I wear all the time."**
>
> **Lila Moss,**
> *Vanity Fair*, 2020

When you are the world's greatest supermodel it's easy to presume everything must be easy, but being a mum is a responsibility no one is born knowing how to manage. You find your own way and Kate Moss's way is, to date, a masterclass of chic individualism. When she was expecting her daughter, Lila, she didn't start going to bed early; instead, she got into training for night feeds by sitting for one of Britain's most famous artists: "I had an easy pregnancy. Sitting for Lucian Freud every night until two in the morning for months and months was as close as I came to 'preparing' for parenthood, although I did randomly spot a copy of *What to Expect When You're Expecting* in our library the other day, so I guess I must have read it at some point" (*Vogue*, 2023a).

Equally, some might think that being the daughter of a style icon is a tricky learning curve, but Lila Moss has risen to the challenge with grace and elegance. Negotiating a successful career as a budding supermodel on her own terms, she has appeared on high-profile magazine covers and campaigns, including for *Vogue* and DKNY. She has led an unparalleled life immersed in the highest echelons of the fashion world and developed a critic's eye of what looks good. Growing up, she had the best role model and wardrobe to plunder:

> "I was always dressing up in my mum's closet. I also looked up to my mum in the sense that I'd want her black vests from Saint Laurent, or I'd wear black leggings and all black and grey. I was so particular from day one. We were actually talking yesterday, me and my mum, about how all the arguments we had when I was younger were about clothes and me not wanting to wear white socks" (Carlson, 2024).

Fashion has clearly been a two-way conversation in the Moss household since Lila was little. While Kate began modelling for John Galliano back in 1992, today it's his vintage trench coats, found by Lila in Paris boutiques, that catch her eye. Even back in 2014, when she launched a Topshop collection and Lila was not yet a teenager, Kate disclosed that she valued her daughter's flourishing sense of style, telling *Harper's Bazaar*: "She's very good. I do trust her instinct" (quoted in *The Daily Mail*, 2014).

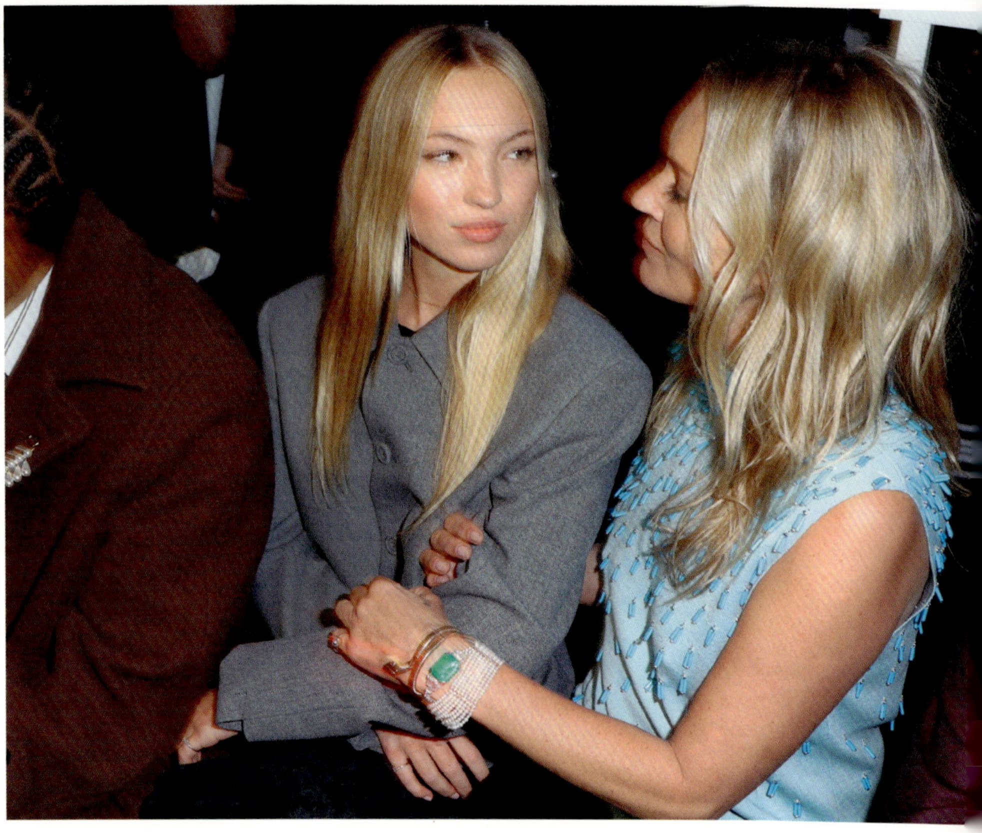

Yet, before she became a parent, Kate's legendary rock-and-roll aesthetic was provoked in part by a close friendship with the late fairy godmother of bohemia, Anita Pallenberg, with whom she would go second-hand clothes shopping. According to Kate, "she had such an amazing knowledge about fashion, and taught me about Fortuny and Schiaparelli" (Krentcil, 2024). Pallenberg's style expertise is almost as celebrated as Kate's, and both women have blazed an artfully alternative vision of what a mother is traditionally supposed to look like. They have inspired others, interrupting the status quo of mum-jeans and re-translating them into tiny cut-offs worn at festivals and fashionable front-rows, in turn influencing legions of women, whether mothers or not. Kate's signature clothes – spaghetti-strap dresses, leopard-print jackets and skinny black jeans – are similarly collaged by Lila, whose 21st-century take subtly advances the family fashion gene.

**"I'm a mum.
All the time."**

Kate Moss,
Vogue, 2008

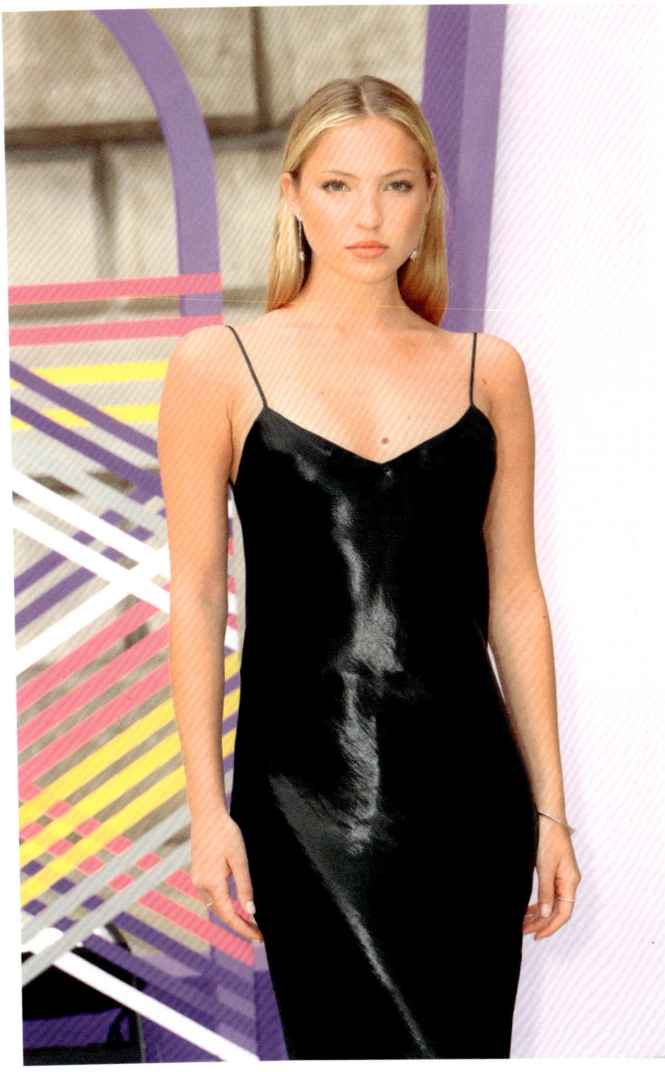

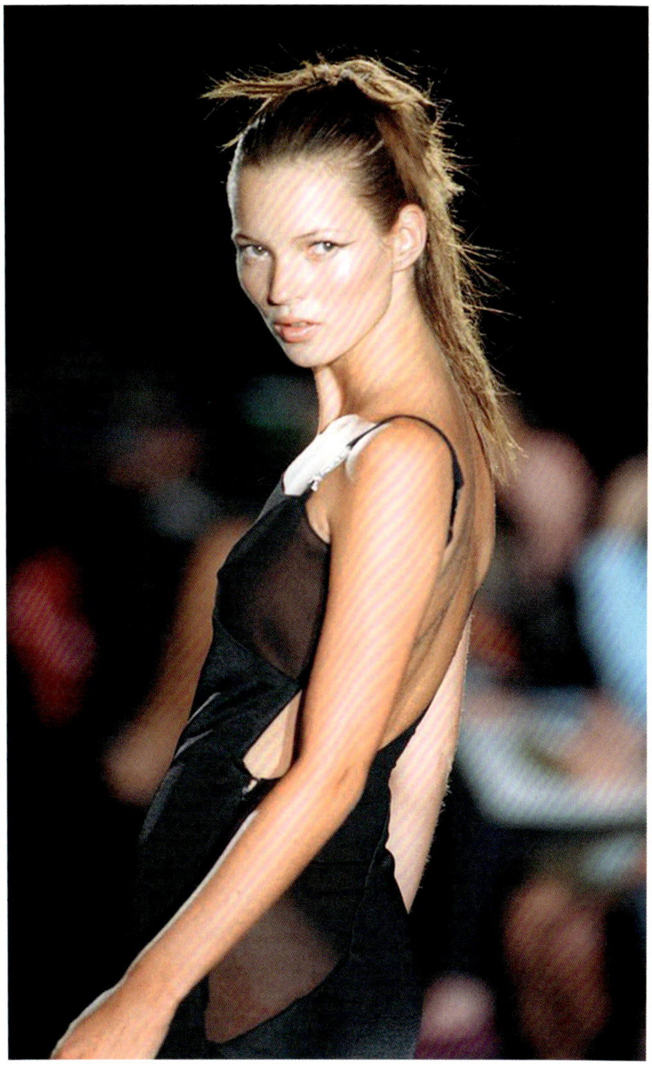

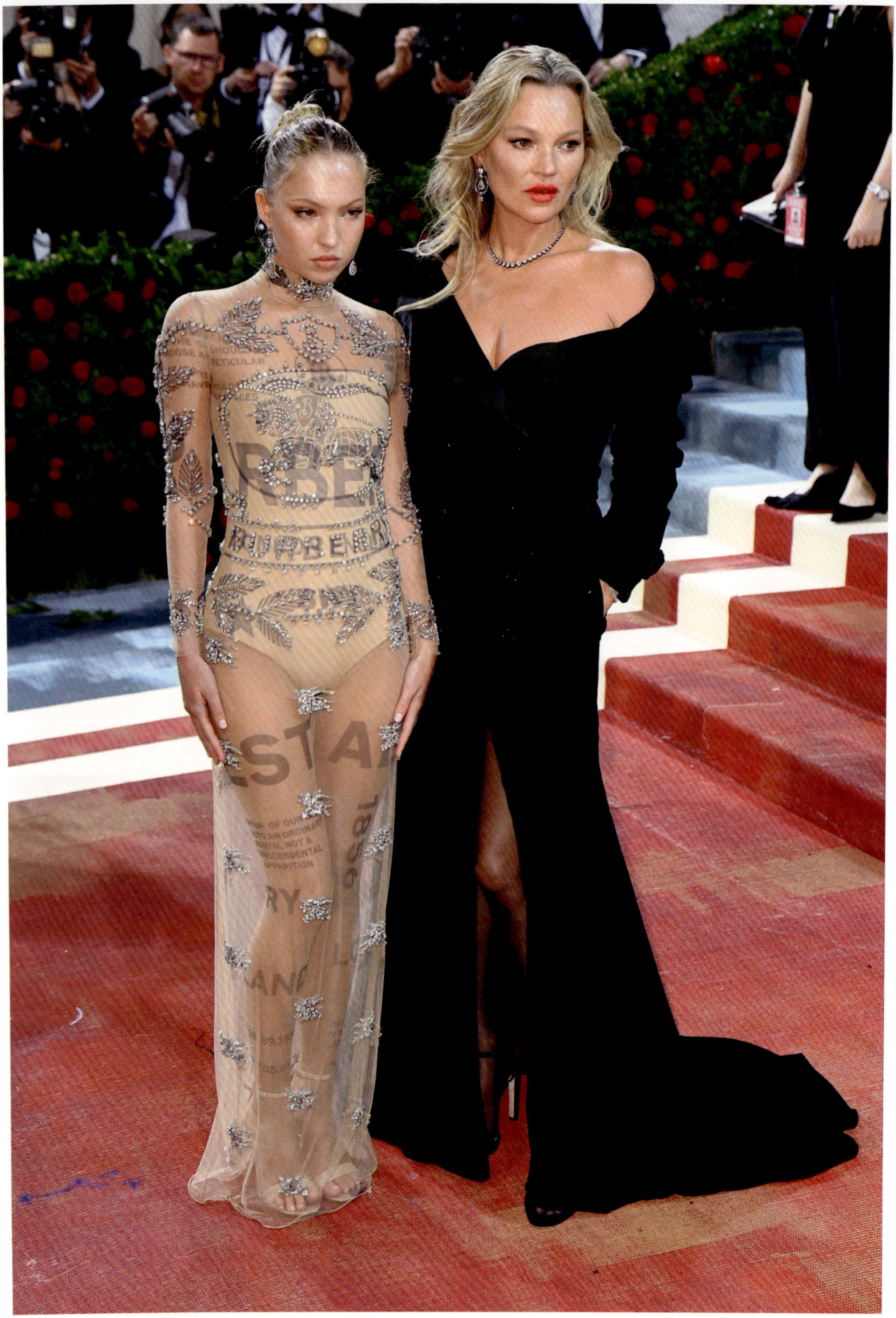

"'Oh, your mum's Kate Moss!' You don't really have a filter when you're that young and I was like, how do you know who she is? She's old! She's old and boring."

Lila Grace,
Vogue, 2022

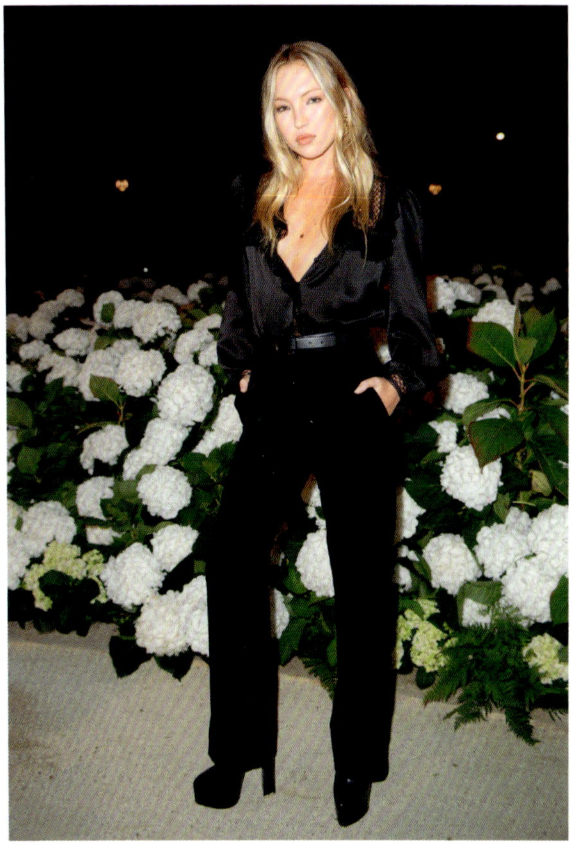

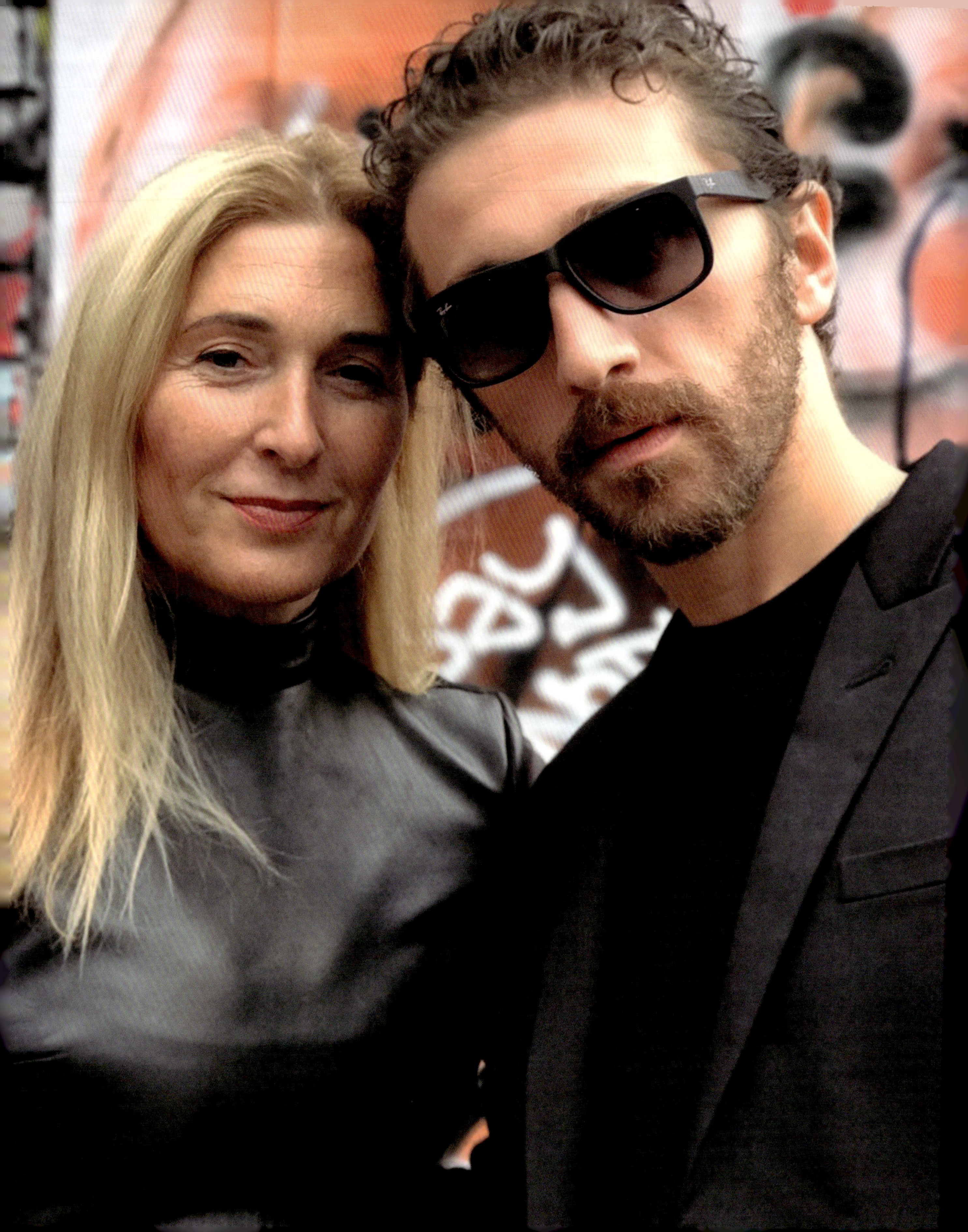

Lali **Dzhinikashvili** and David **Koma**

★

David Koma's trajectory as a designer feels written in the stars. After studying at the Russian Academy of Art in St Petersburg, he gained a place on the BA Fashion course at Central Saint Martins and moved to London in 2002, subsequently studying for an MA before launching his eponymous label and first standalone show in 2009. He was the creative director of the House of Mugler from 2013 to 2017 and appointed head of Blumarine in 2024 – milestone achievements all realised before the age of 40. However, his impressive CV wouldn't be the same without the help of his mother's own style input: "Looking back, I realise how much my mother has shaped my own perspective on fashion. She taught me that true style is about authenticity – about balancing practicality with statement pieces and making small yet bold choices that make an outfit feel personal."

David's mother, Lali Dzhinikashvili, was born in Tbilisi and studied to become a geologist at Georgia's largest university, the Georgian Technical University. She had David in 1985; then in 1993, during the Georgian–Abkhazian War, the family moved to Russia where they settled. It was a time when post-Soviet states were opening to the world and Western designers became accessible. Koma's favourite fashion memory of Lali is when she bought a Mugler suit in St Petersburg in the early 2000s. It was made from technical scuba-diving fabric and featured an "impeccably tailored, crisp, front trouser pleat" detail. It was not the normal thing she'd wear; Lali typically opted for something a little more relaxed. It was, however, a perfect choice and the teenage Koma thought that, in that very special outfit, "she looked like superwoman". His admiration for her fashion sense is enduring and tender, and he reminisces on how "to this day, she is very self-confident and reflective with her fashion choice – her style really represents her personality". Although the clothes she wore were "rooted in comfort", they were something to be enjoyed.

Over the years her footwear choices, too, have captured his imagination, and looking back at his mother's wardrobe, Koma reflects:

> "While comfort was Lali's priority, that didn't mean she avoided heels – she wore them often. But at a time when heels were the norm, her collection was built around an array of cool designer sneakers. That was what I loved most about her style – it was her signature: effortlessly cool shoes, always with an unexpected twist."

Although trained in the sciences, Koma recalls that Lali "always had an artistic side". He explains:

> "I don't ever remember her following trends or conforming to cultural norms, whether we lived in Tbilisi or St Petersburg. Later, when she had the time to explore her creativity, she became interested in painting and, most impressively, knitting. She wore lots of her own knitwear creations – she was absolutely incredible at it. When I was 14, she knitted my designs for one of my first-ever fashion shows, and it didn't stop there. Even during my BA at Central Saint Martins, she helped bring my vision to life, knitting a piece for my final collection. She has always been one of my biggest supporters and being able to showcase that collaboration was an incredibly special moment."

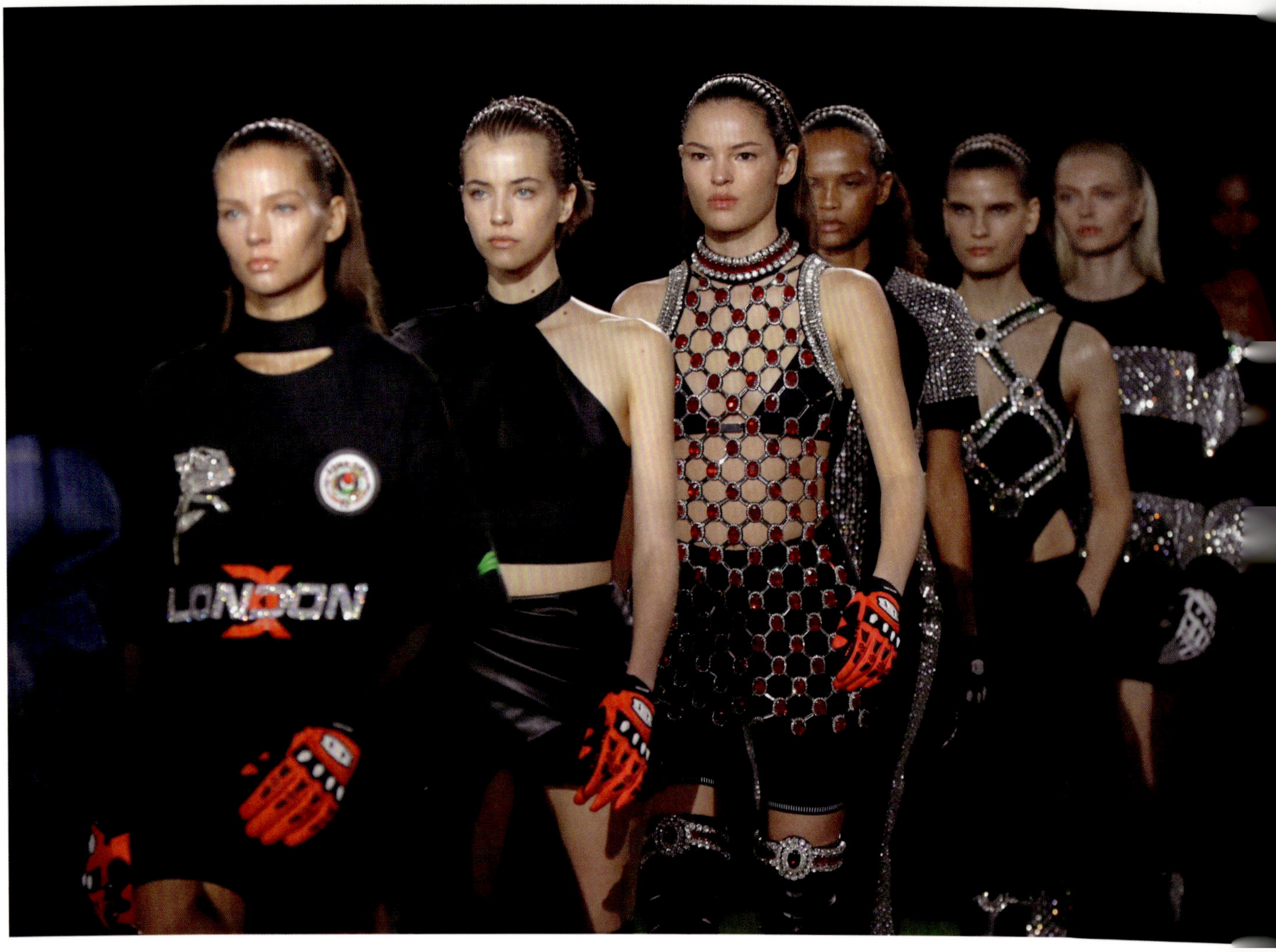
LONDON

Now living in London, Lali is a faithful presence at David's shows. "It wouldn't be the same without her", insists his head of communications, Maria Tkachenko. And whether dressed in classic Koma or off-duty model jeans and T-shirt, Lali has forever embodied her son's sense of beauty.

> "She was always a cool mom – whether in fun jeans or a mini skirt that showed off her great legs – but never in a way that felt forced or overdone. She took care of herself with a quiet confidence, embodying self-love and self-respect without any sense of excess. She was never into make-up, but she was dedicated to skincare, and she's aging beautifully because of it. That's one of the greatest lessons I learnt from her – how to respect and take care of yourself."

A strong appreciation of elegance is something David demonstrated himself from an early age. He began sketching the female form when he was just eight years old, and instinctively learnt how to structure clothing: today his work is often compared to wearable sculptures. At 12, he remembers becoming obsessed with a House of Mugler archive runway show on the fashion and lifestyle channel, FashionTV. Shortly after, he created his first collection and became convinced of what his vocation would be. "I was about 15 then, already deeply passionate about fashion and determined to become a designer. Thierry Mugler's work was already very exciting to me, but I had never seen his clothes worn by anyone I knew." David explains how the suit his mother had worn became a touchstone: "Years later, when I became the creative director at Mugler, that moment came full circle. I borrowed the suit from her as inspiration for a piece in one of my own collections. It remained just as powerful to me then as it did when I first saw her wear it."

Koma's commanding success stems from a distinctive ability to fuse memories, imagination and innovation. His roots and memories of family, his mother and his hometown all drive his ability to craft a distinctive fashion world. Though he is a product of Saint Martins and London, he admits:

> "Georgia holds a special place in my heart – it's my homeland, my roots, and a constant source of inspiration. No matter where life takes me, I make it a priority to return as often as I can, aiming for at least one visit each year. These trips are more than just reunions with friends and family; they are opportunities to reconnect with the culture, landscapes and traditions that have shaped me."

Today, women the world over turn to David Koma when they want modern, energised femininity. Beyoncé is a fan and has consistently been an encouragement from the start of his career, helping to make his name when she chose a piece from his Saint Martins graduate show to wear to the MTV Awards in 2009. Since then, Queen Bey has worn his clothes on numerous occasions – catsuits at the Mrs Carter Show World Tour in 2013; a glistening, crystal-embellished jacket and leather dress to an NBA basketball game in 2021; and full custom looks during her legendary 2023 Renaissance World Tour. She loves sunglasses, and in 2022 opted to show off the on-off silver-mirrored frames Koma created two years before with New York-based designer Chris Habana, predictably helping them go viral. Koma accessories habitually include bags, boots and body jewellery, but going forward he is particularly inspired by his mother's collection of shades and shoes: "She has an incredible collection of timeless sunglasses, from vintage Valentino and Saint Laurent to classic Ray-Bans. If I ever launched a full eyewear line, she'd be the first person I'd go to for advice. There is a certain magic in finding a pair that is just perfect – and she has that talent!"

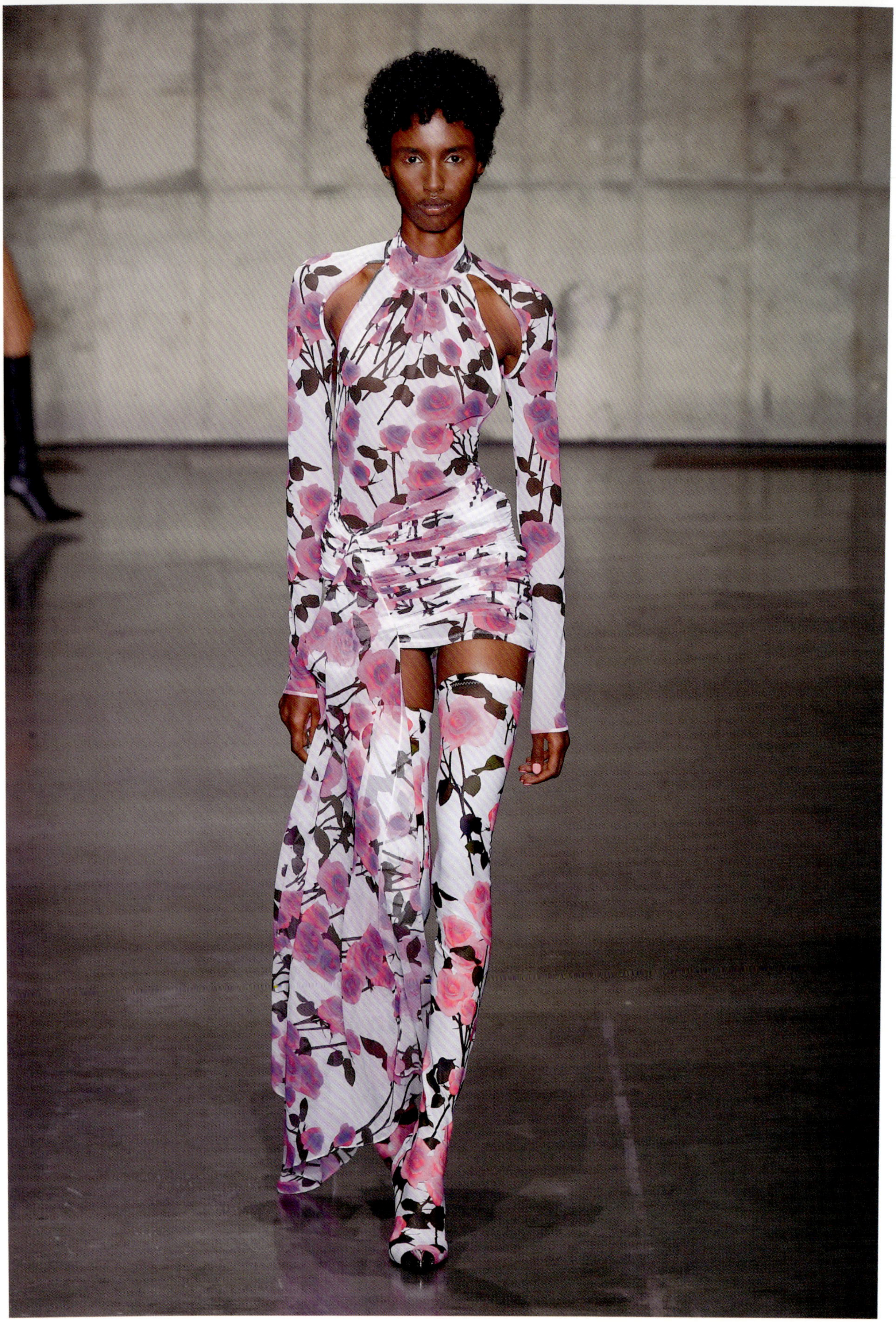

"My mother
was always
a free spirit,
a bit of a rebel."

David Koma,
2025

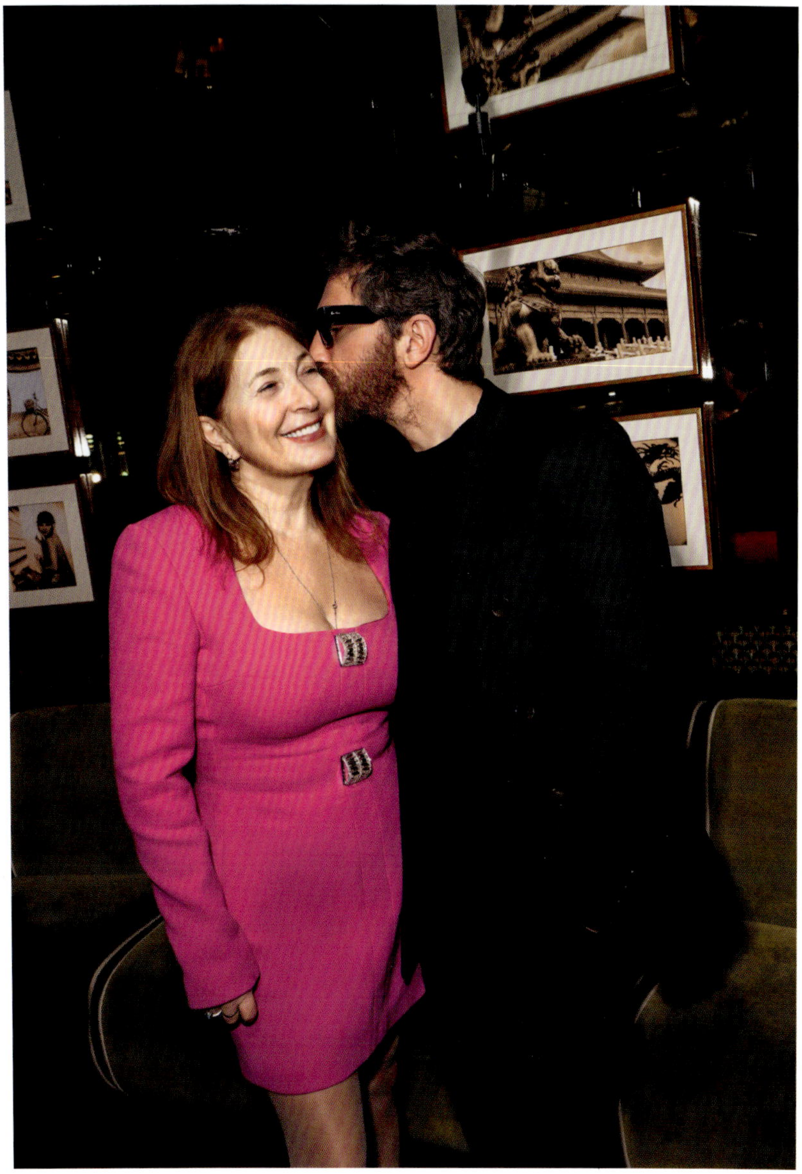

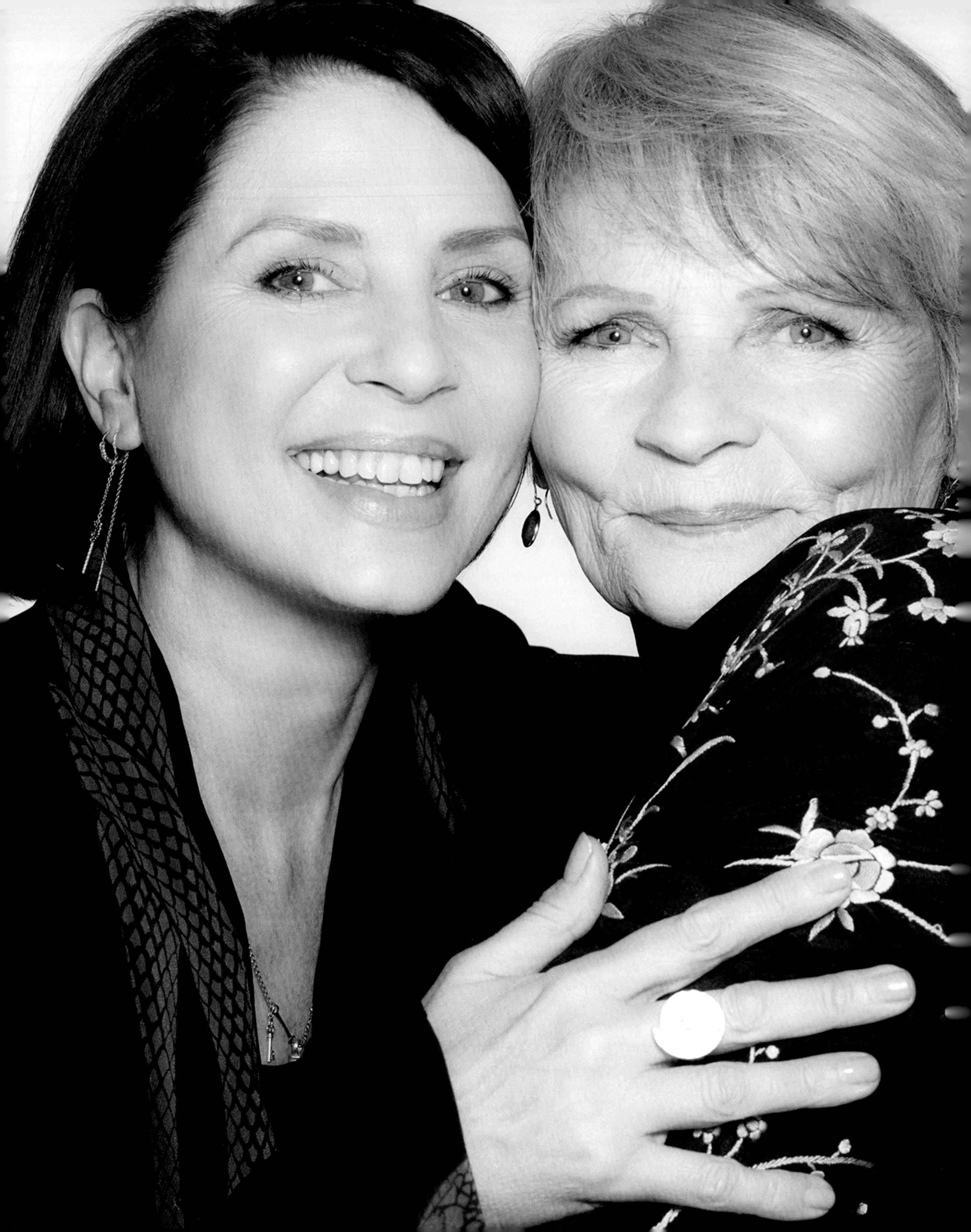

Mary Davidson, **Sadie** Frost and **Iris Law**

★

"When I think of my mum on special occasions, she'll always wear a yellow, lime and red polka-dot halter-neck dress designed by Marc Jacobs. It's a celebratory dress which she wears on her birthday with red lipstick. She says it always puts her in a good mood", reflects Iris Law, daughter of documentary director Sadie Frost and actor Jude Law. Iris has grown up around fashion: her godmother is Kate Moss, whose daughter Lila is Iris's best friend. But her maternal grandmother, Mary Davidson, is a key influence. Davidson, in turn, has keen memories of her own mother, Elizabeth Nolan's wardrobe: "I think my mum's style always stayed with me throughout my life. Although I went through many silhouette changes, from mini, to maxi, to full-on psychedelic, I would always come back to the Forties tea dress my mum would wear – and a red lip."

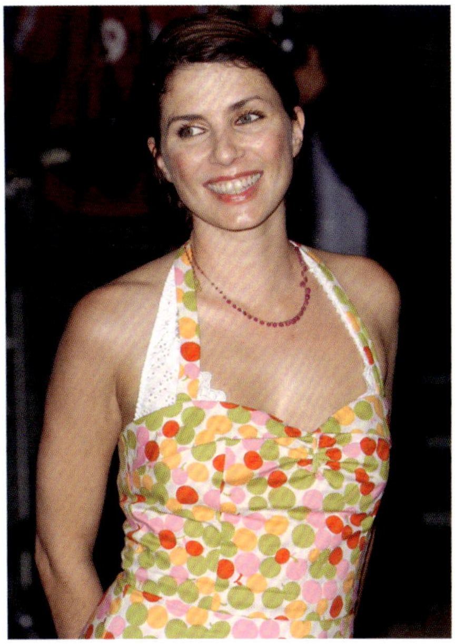

Mary has been a powerful influence on her own daughters, too. She was a 16-year-old schoolgirl when Sadie was born in 1965. She became a dressmaker, sewing all her daughters' clothes, including "dungarees studded with stars, moons and beads, and a kind of Afghani frock with lots of buttons", according to Sadie. Then there were the Victorian nightdresses that Mary bought from Camden Market where she worked. Sadie describes being really embarrassed and feeling humiliated that their clothes were second hand. "Now it's normal", she says, "but then it was different, and people would tease you". She continues:

"My mum dressed us very differently to the kids at school. The teachers were always a little bit judgy about how we turned up for class. So, I was a bit embarrassed. She called one of my sisters Sunshine Tara Purple Velvet, and we wore a lot of purple velvet. When I was about 11 or 12, I started questioning my mum and asking why she couldn't go to Marks and Spencer to buy our clothes; I wanted to wear polyester. And I remember getting a catalogue and buying my own things from

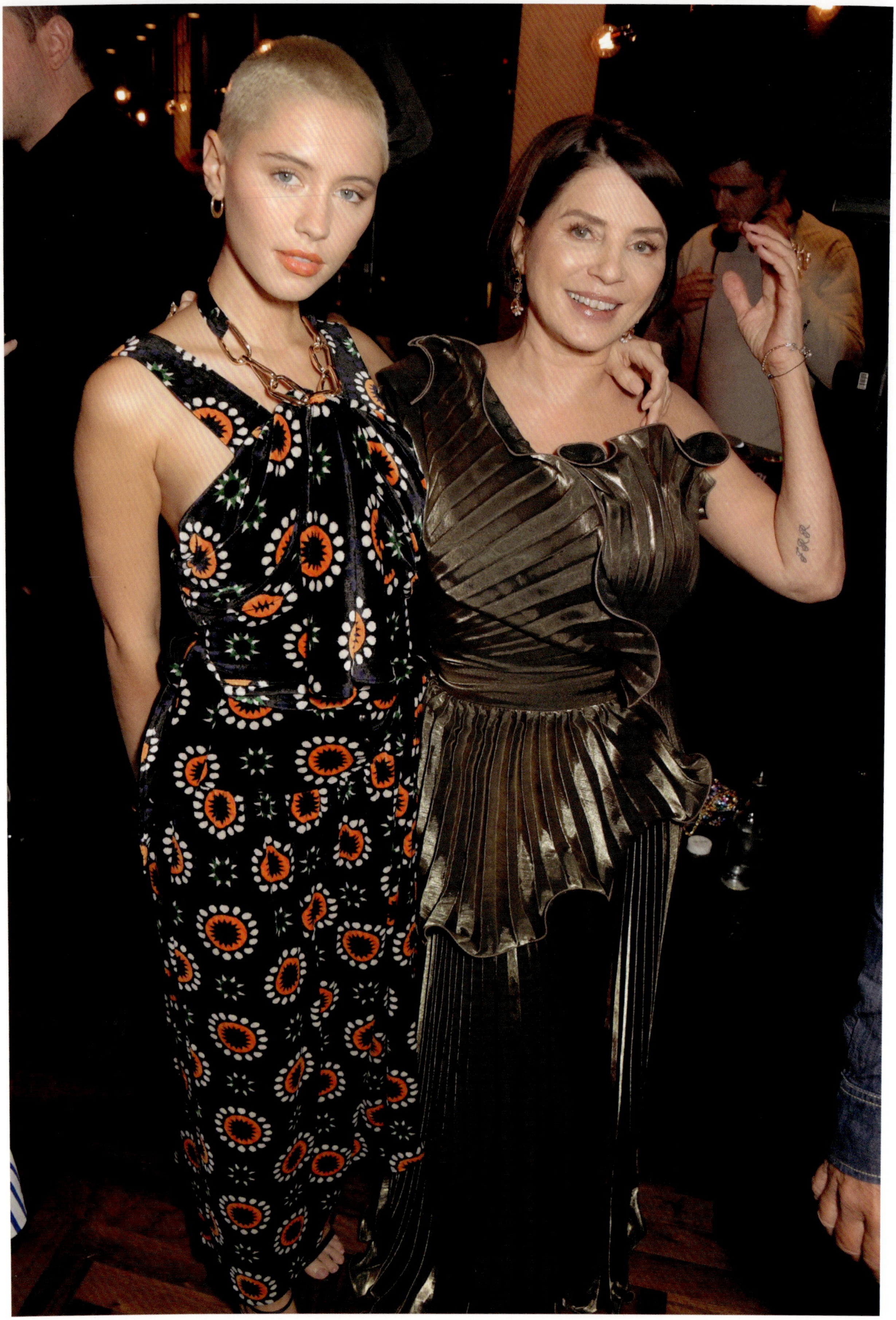

> Littlewoods. I was already acting and had my own money. I became very strait-laced and rebelled against my mum. I wanted to look like a normal girl. In fact, I started wearing a dress that maybe a six-year-old would wear, and flowery *Little Women* frocks. I used to say, 'Mum you're so weird, why can't you dress normally?' But she used to just let me get on with it."

Mary herself had a limited wardrobe of a pair of jeans, dungarees, a couple of dresses and one elegant 1940s frock in midnight blue with a V-neck and a tiny collar. She would buy all her own clothes second-hand or make them, too. Nowadays, says Sadie, Mary wears graceful, beaded Caftans, "sometimes with an overcoat on so she looks like an empress". She describes her mother as a wise woman who glows. "Her aura is so spiritual, and her clothes reflect that." Later, once she had grown up, Sadie realised that Mary had been really spot on. She had given Sadie an environment where she could be free to blossom, unrestricted by rules and, instead, encouraged her to explore life creatively.

> "Mary taught me, and I think I've taught Iris, that we all want to be comfortable in our skin and wear the clothes we want. I've never really wanted to conform to what men wanted and gravitate towards slightly androgynous clothes or easy pieces like leggings and sweatshirts that remind me of the things I used to wear when I was training to be a dancer and actress."

As a teenager, Frost attended the prestigious Italia Conti Academy of Theatre Arts in London on a scholarship and quickly became noticed as a fashion-forward girl around town.

> "Many times, I'd be walking around Camden and *i-D* magazine took my picture for their 'Straight-Up' pages. I became a punk and had my own development in fashion. I used to do crazy things with my hair and all sorts of make-up. My friends, John Dove and Molly White, owned a shop called Kitsch-22 and a label called Mozart, and sold clothes through Boy. I used to model for them when I was about 15."

In a pre-internet world, connections were often made via independent boutiques where creativity thrived. Sadie connected with the epicentre of London cool. The clothes created by Dove and White were worn by the likes of Sid Vicious before he became a Sex Pistol, along with Iggy Pop and Soo Catwoman, who modelled along with Frost in the legendary 'Boy Blackmail' catalogue produced by the duo. (In a twist of fashion fate, later in 2022 Sadie's daughter Iris would star in Danny Boyle's 2022 TV series, *Pistol*, as the punk icon Soo Catwoman – cutting off all her locks to imitate Soo's

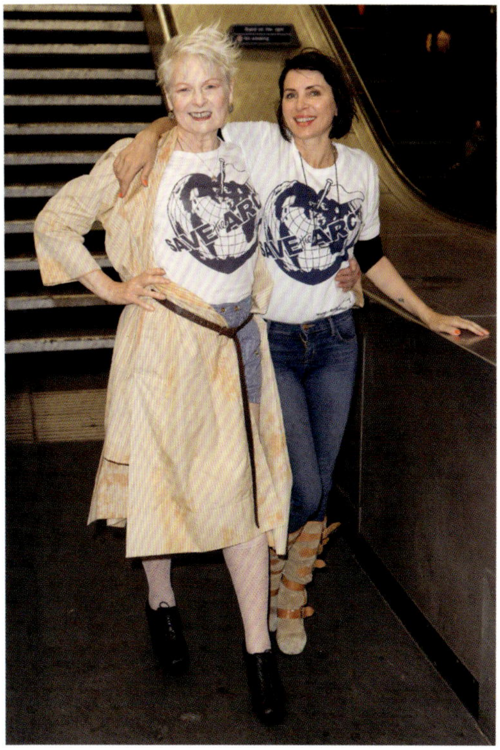

legendary double-spiked haircut.) It was around the time of Frost's early modelling career that she met Vivienne Westwood. "I was at school when I met Vivienne, and she started asking me to come and be in shoots along with Sarah Stockbridge and her band. I remember I did a couple of American shoots, and she asked me to do a few of her fashion shows. She always made me feel really special."

Westwood did indeed love Sadie; in a BBC interview the designer reminisced: "When I made the corsets, I knew everyone would go mad about them. It was Sadie Frost; she was the one that came out wearing a little coat. She was only about 16, big boobs and mouth. And the photographers just died! They said, 'Come back darling', they said!" (BBC Studios, 2009). Modelling for friends led to success and a contract with Select. "I became part of the fashion system and was told what to look like, what to wear and what

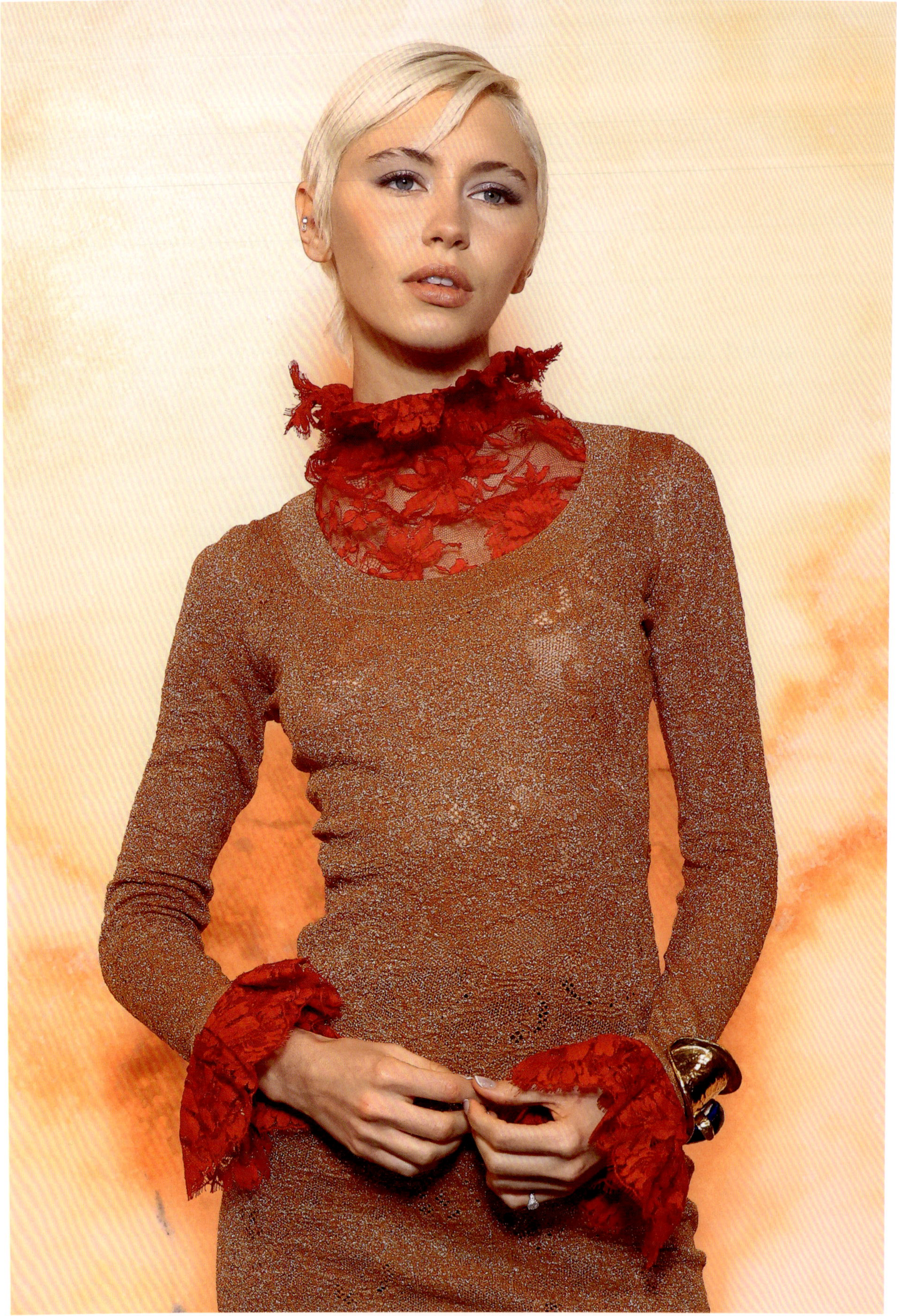

"It's so interesting when you see your daughters and their friends grow up, at first they are just these things and then become fully fledged autonomous beings and you can tell they've been obviously watching and lapping things up and emerge like beautiful butterflies."

Sadie Frost,
2025

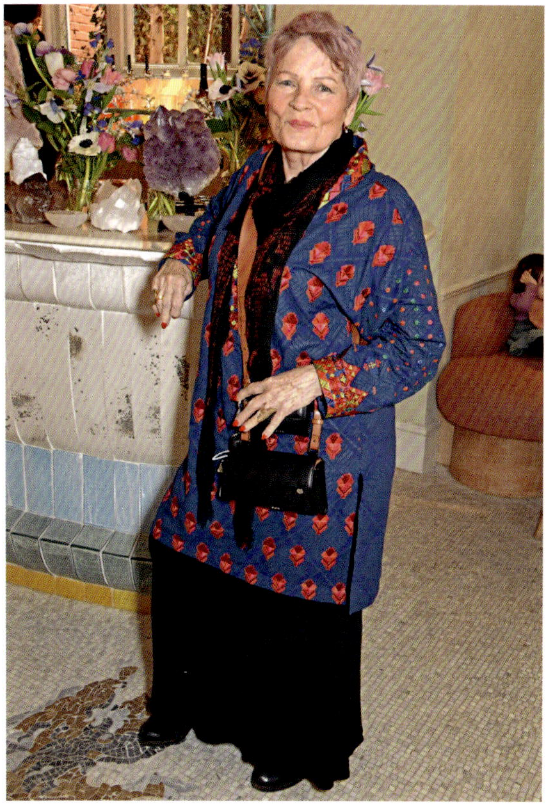

you should weigh", reflects Frost. She was thrown into the spotlight just as her acting career began to take off, after she landed a high-profile part in *Bram Stoker's Dracula* (1992), directed by Francis Ford Coppola and starring alongside Winona Ryder.

She began seeing Jude Law, who she met on the set of *Shopping*, a 1994 anarchic crime movie. It seemed that every week she and her friends were featured in British tabloids as part of the 'Primrose Hill Set', which included her close pal Kate Moss, brothers Liam and Noel Gallagher from Oasis, PR guru Fran Cutler and, of course, the man she would marry in 1997, Jude Law. Although she was profiled as a party girl, her image was something that concerned her.

> "I used to have a lot of conflict about how men wanted me to dress. I've got quite a curvy figure, and fashion can be very sexualising, and I just didn't want that – and that's why punk was great, and I felt at home with the androgyny. And then Britpop happened with musicians like Justine Frischmann and Donna Matthews from Elastica, and the DJ duo Queens of Noize later – these women dressed to be strong and powerful, and I felt in tune with that. It was about mixing up a bit of mod and a bit of punk and creating something for yourself. I was a tomboy and if I was going to wear a dress it would be my decision."

After Frost became pregnant with her son Raf, she launched Frost French with Jemima French and used it to tell fashion stories that reflected who she was.

> "We started out making knickers that talked, printed with a cat that meowed, we got lots of interesting religious artifacts and decorated the underwear with them, calling them 'holy pants', and night owl knickers that would go 'twit-too-woo'. Then we branched into dresses and made a 1940s tea frock with matching baby sling. I would always create clothes around characters and different stages of women's lives – things that were cheeky and fun, and not about dressing for men. Later, I brought out a brand called Iris and Edie, named after my and Jemima's daughters. We had some great Frost French catwalk shows; one at the Duke of York's Theatre where Kate Moss did a striptease for us, and the artist Tash Law, Jude Law's sister, did all the sets. I was just pregnant with Rudy [Frost's youngest child] by then and Iris came to the show."

Iris is still a big fan of the now-discontinued Frost French brand and explains: "I loved my mum's Frost French dresses – I hosted a *Vogue* charity auction in March 2025 and chose an old Frost French frock to put in the sale. It was a silver panelled mini dress and still looks iconic today." Sadie's fashion legacy to her daughter is keenly apparent. Iris continues:

> "I grew up with a particularly fashion-involved mother because she was in the industry with her own brand and used style as a form of self-expression every day, all the while championing comfortability and feeling that what you're wearing should make you feel good – not performative but still expressing yourself. This balance I think really influenced me because I will never put on something that's uncomfortable just to look good, but I also want to use my clothes to articulate who I am."

Nowadays, Iris is an in-demand fashion connoisseur courted by the world's biggest fashion houses. Yet, time and again, she chooses carefully curated vintage pieces to wear and has been seen on the red carpet dressed in an eclectic mix of pieces, including 1990s Chloé, Versace and Cavalli. Her signature style is born from a lineage of free-spiritedness. As Sadie explains: "Iris says to me that watching me has influenced her to feel confident about herself. She is a beautiful girl, but she doesn't feel like she has to dress in any other way than how she wants. She knows she doesn't have to conform to anything and that's what Mary taught me, too. Why do any of us have to conform?"

Today, Frost's career as a documentarian is thriving – films include work about Mary Quant and Twiggy and her wardrobe is practical rather than headline-grabbing. Her new life stage is reflected in the clothes she wears:

> "Of course, I still love clothes and have a great archive of pieces, but when I'm making documentaries and there are 18-hour days, I'm just throwing on things to be warm and functional, just to get through the day. Today, I'm not keen on being in the spotlight, probably because for so many years I was, and prefer to be behind the camera."

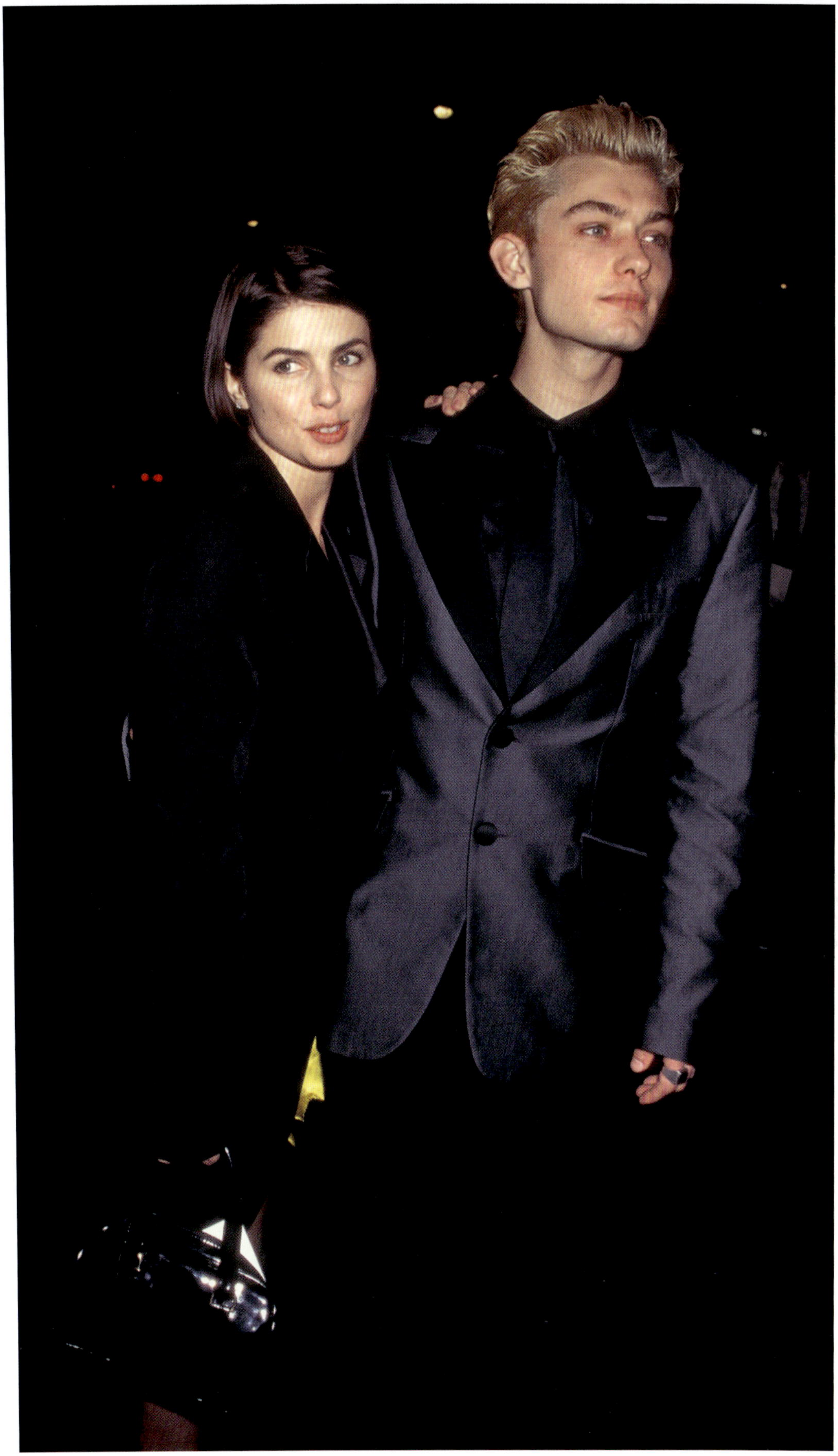

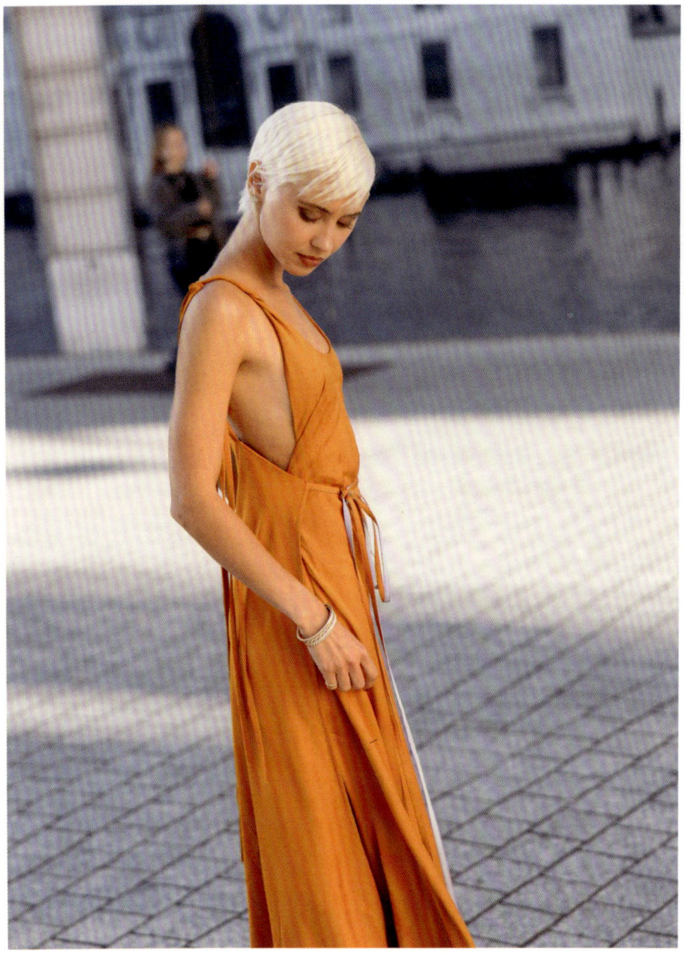

"I loved my mum's Frost French dresses – I hosted a *Vogue* charity auction in March 2025 and chose an old Frost French frock to put in the sale. It was a silver panelled mini dress and still looks iconic today."

Iris Law,
2025

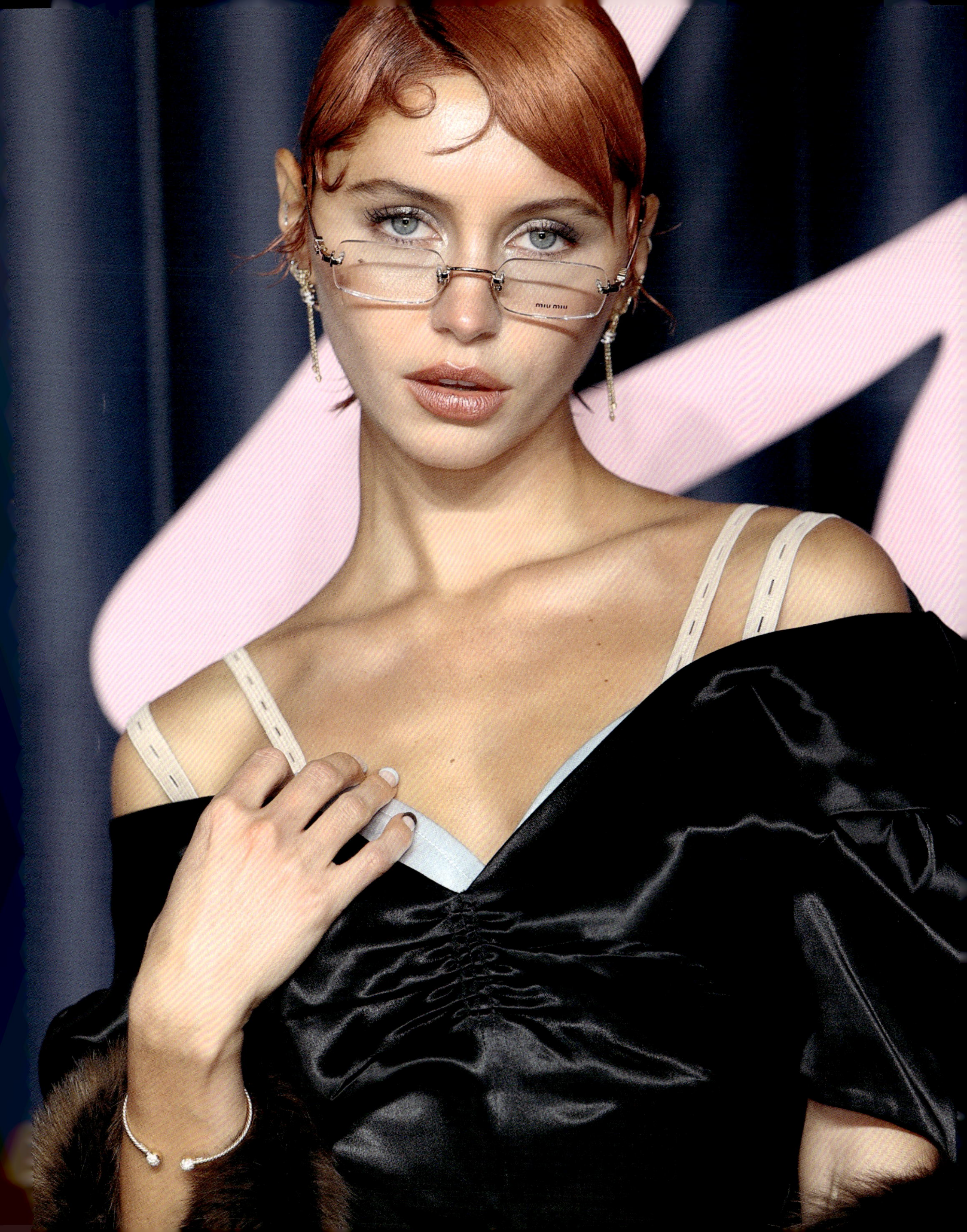
miu miu

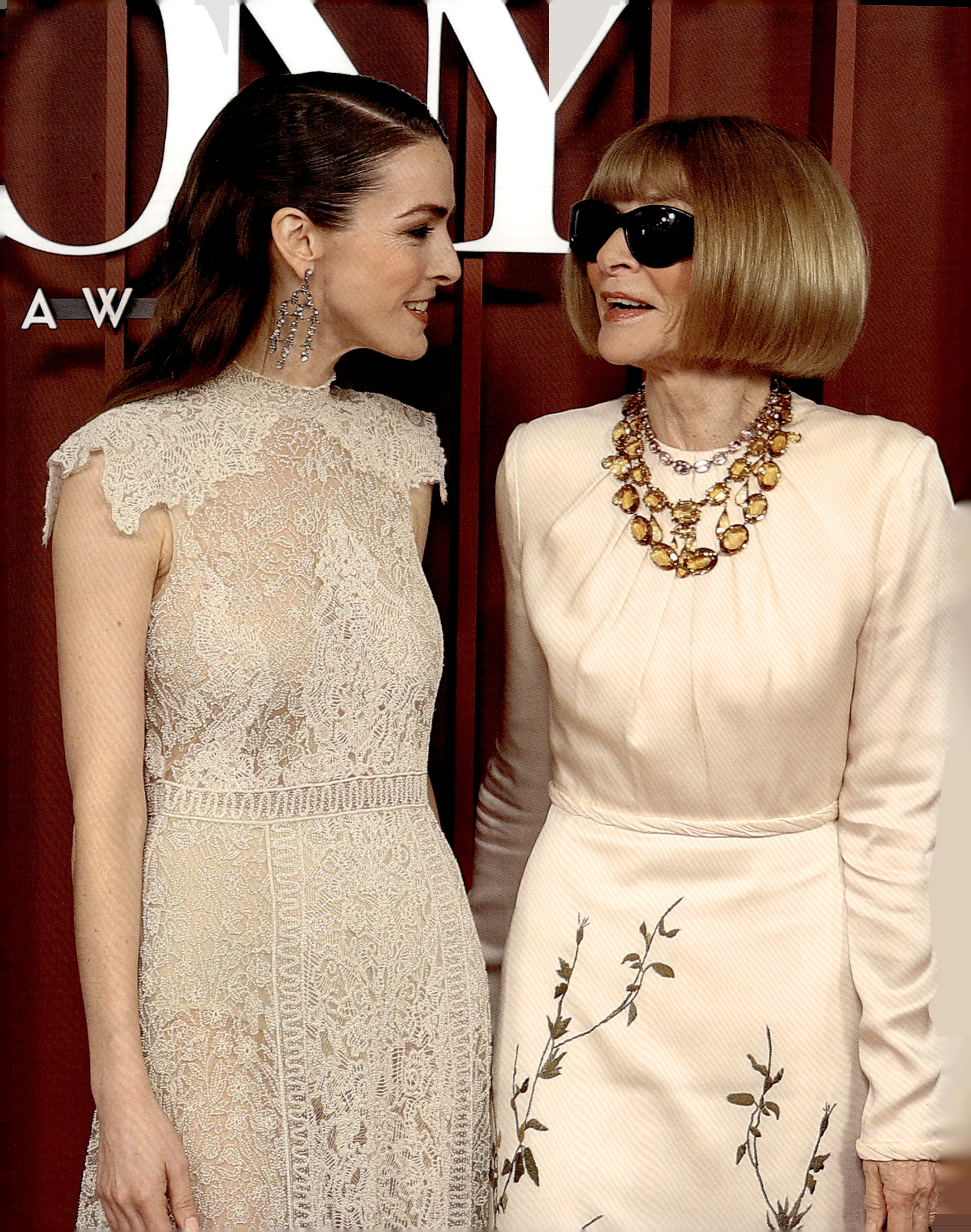
ONY
A W

Anna Wintour
and Bee Schaffer

★

Editor-in-chief of American *Vogue* for 37 years, Anna Wintour's personal style is a crisp antidote to trends: her fashion identity does what she wants it to, not what the catwalk tells her. She is hardworking and no nonsense, and so is her look. Style is about telling the world who you are, and her thick, blown-out bobbed hair, conspicuous sunglasses, Bill Blass shoulder pads, knee-length pencil skirts, confidently printed dresses and weighty jewellery have all helped broadcast who she is. Her clothes tell us she takes her job seriously, knows what she likes and is focused. Of course, the woman who became the most powerful person in fashion for decades wears only the very best labels and a nod from her is akin to a gladiatorial win, but she takes her own sartorial advice. When commenting on what a daunted interviewee might best wear, she reflected:

> "It's so interesting to me how people dress...Sometimes you feel they're wearing clothes that they just bought that morning, or maybe the night before, and not something that in any way suits their personality and who they are...You have to dress for yourself. It's the same for any job you might be going for. I think it doesn't do yourself a service to fake it" (Petrarca, 2019).

A devoted mother, she brought her daughter Bee to work with her from a young age and, albeit in the front row of fashion shows, has been photographed being openly affectionate to her. The jarring equation that you can't be a strong career woman and a caring parent is one that critically persists when you are high profile. 'Nuclear' Wintour – the devil who wears Prada – has never been celebrated for her maternal side, though she took time off and later worked from home when she had both her children, and has famously supported young designers. She has also led by example, having worked alongside editors who today blaze similar trails, such as Carine Roitfeld and Vanessa Kingori, and thus has roundly demonstrated how, in an industry that historically reveres youth, there is a place for older women, too.

Anna began honing her sartorial savoir-faire when she became a Saturday girl at Barbara Hulanicki's legendary London boutique, Biba, taking a job there when it first opened in 1964 while she was still attending North London Collegiate School – an establishment known for its driven parents and high-achieving pupils. Moving into journalism, she took a position as an editorial assistant at *Harper's & Queen* magazine in 1970 and she spent the next few years learning how high fashion worked and attending couture shows in Paris. Images taken at the time show a girl with bobbed hair, who already mirrored the mother and grandmother she is today. She bears a striking resemblance to Joan Didion, a writer who had had worked at American *Vogue* almost a decade earlier – the very magazine Anna would become celebrated for editing. When she eventually got the job as editor-in-chief in 1988 and set about revolutionising it, she had given birth to Bee less than a year earlier.

The contradictions inherent in mothering, looking immaculate and thriving in a new career, is a challenge many women have faced. Reports of 7am hairstylists post-5am tennis matches may make her sound like a machine, but Wintour makes time for her priorities: "I think it's very important for children to understand that women work and that it's fulfilling, and it doesn't mean that they love you any less or care about you any less" (Larocca, 2015). Now a working mother herself, Wintour's daughter, Bee, revealed back in 2014 that she had "never been very fashion-forward" (*Teen Vogue*, 2014). Despite this, her self-assured evening wear of choice on the red carpet and at award ceremonies include exquisite gowns by top-drawer designers such as Alexander McQueen, Dior and Erdem. She looks like the fashion royalty she is, which is no surprise since her ex-husband, writer and director Francesco Carrozzini, is the son of fabled *Vogue Italia* editor-in-chief Franca Sozzani.

Despite not connecting with the family's fashion vocation, Bee followed in her mother's footsteps by bringing her along to her workplace in January 2024. She was working as a producer for Gutenberg! The Musical!, which was playing on Broadway at the time. She invited Wintour (gamely wearing a baseball cap) onstage alongside the actress Anne Hathaway, who had previously played the assistant to Miranda Priestly, the fictional editor based on Anna in The Devil Wears Prada (2006). The audience got the joke when Wintour introduced Hathaway as her assistant, referencing the iconic film and evidencing a largely overlooked sense of humour, as well as spotlighting her relishing a motherly role while sporting her signature shades.

"I try to do the best job that I can, I try to be the best mother that I can, and if for some reason there are people that are offended by things that I've done or things that they've read that may or may not be true, I cannot spend time ... You can't be everything to everybody, and there are things that get into the public world that were never grounded in reality."

Anna Wintour,
The Cut, 2015

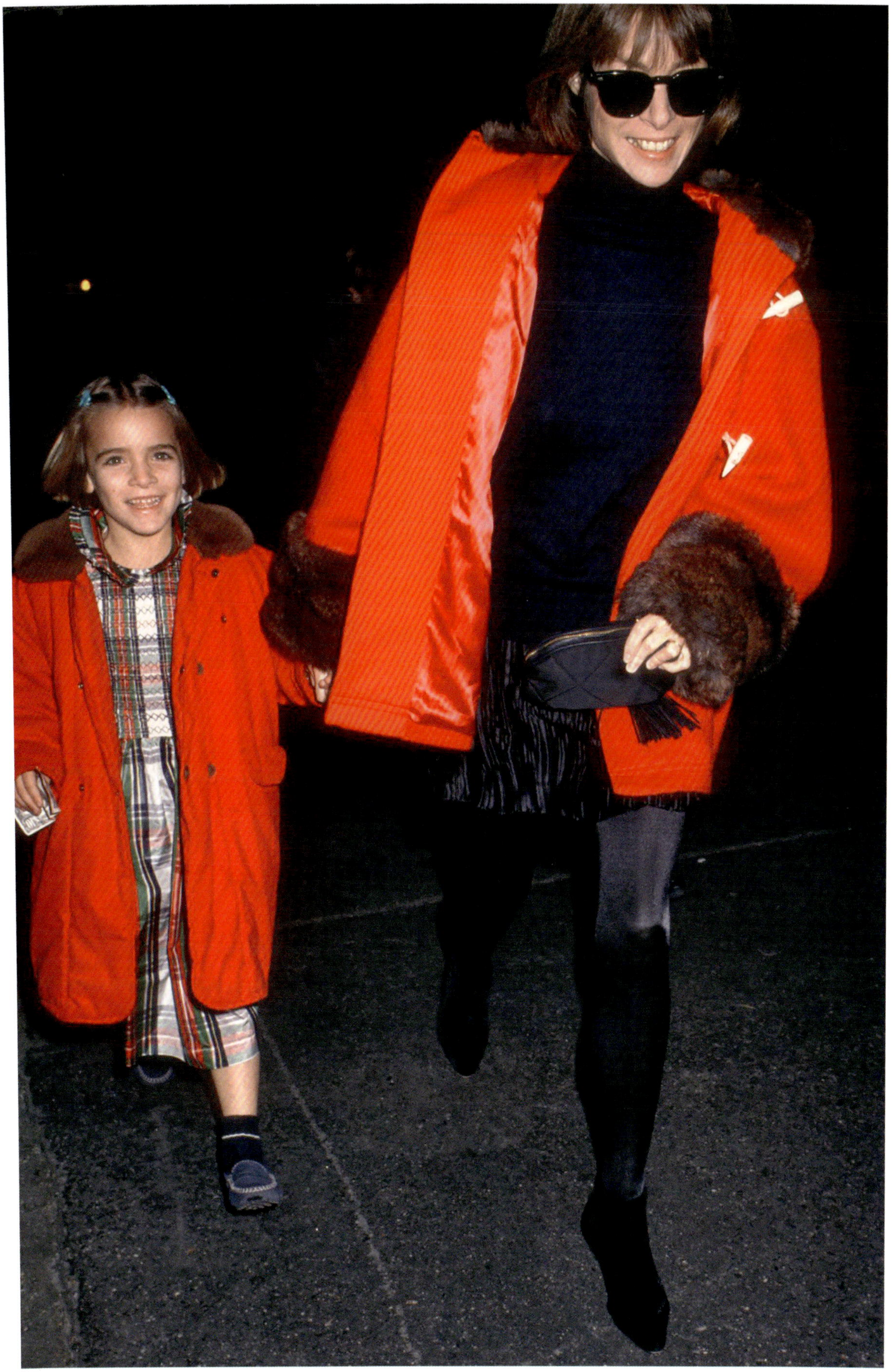

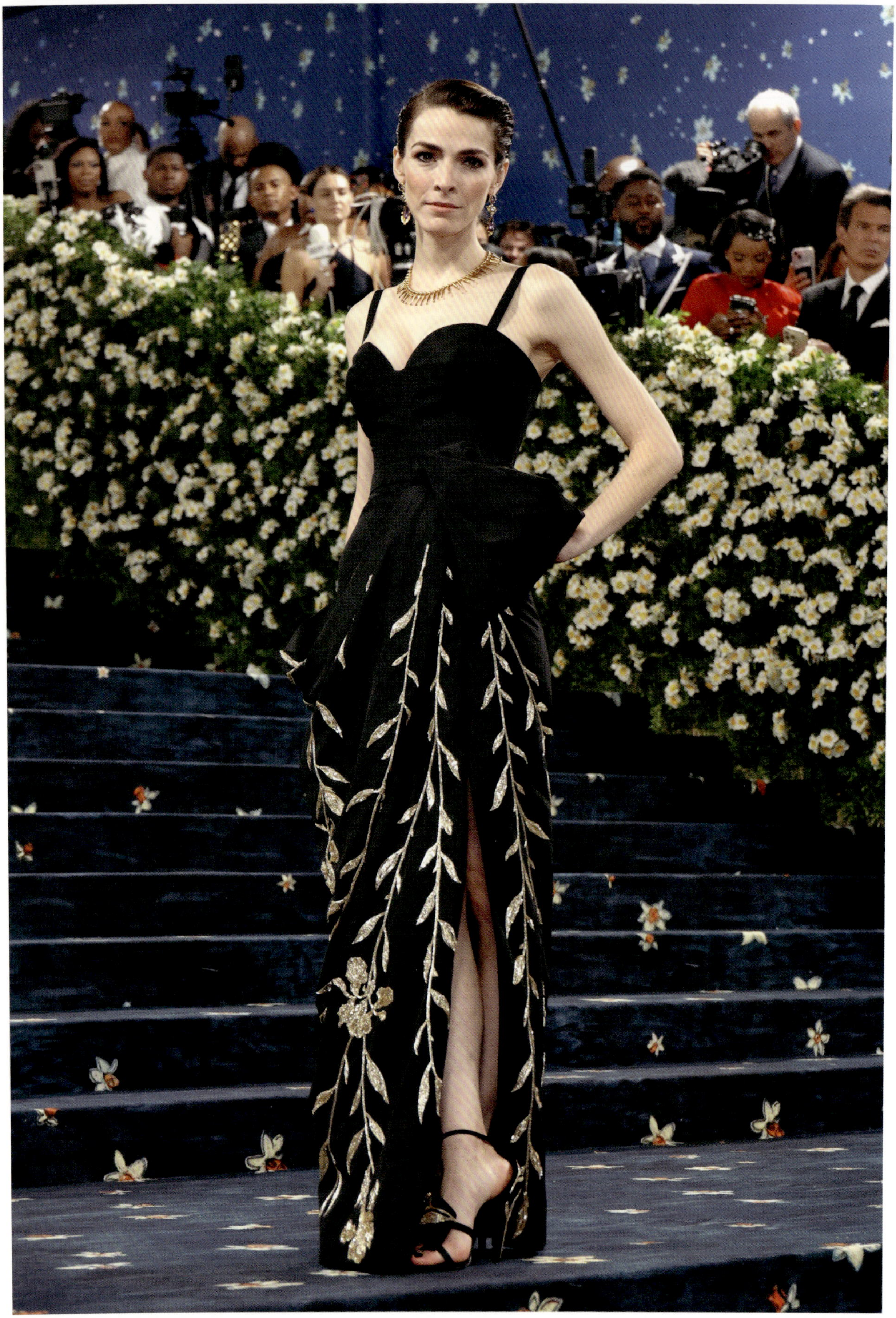

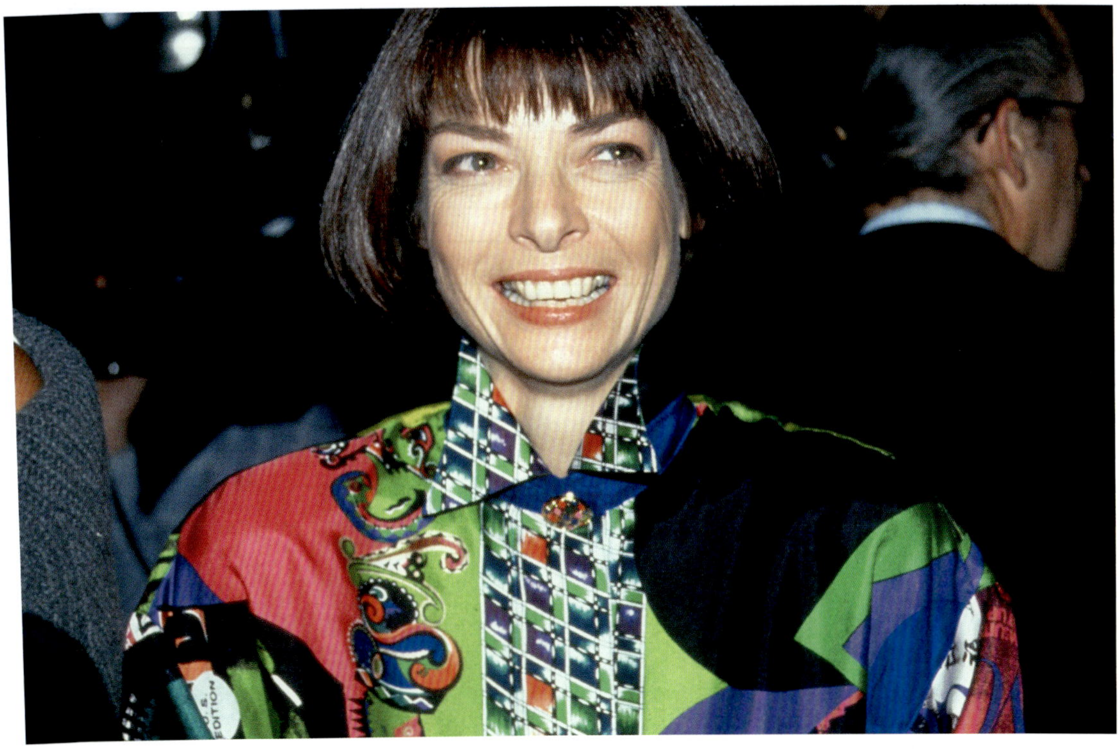

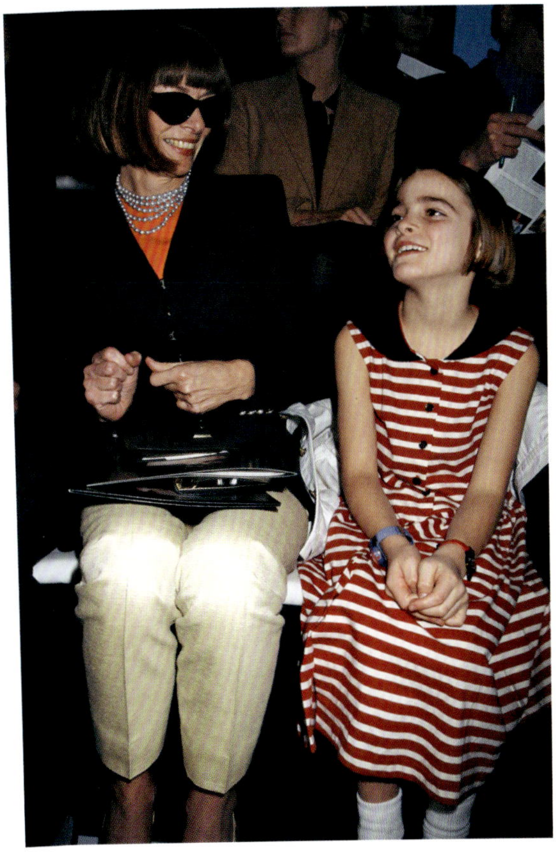

"She's the most generous person that you will ever meet. It's crazy, but she will put everyone else before herself. So, I know that that's who she is. She's also efficient, she gets bored easily and wants to get things done. But she's a boss!"

Bee Shaffer,
Teen Vogue, 2014

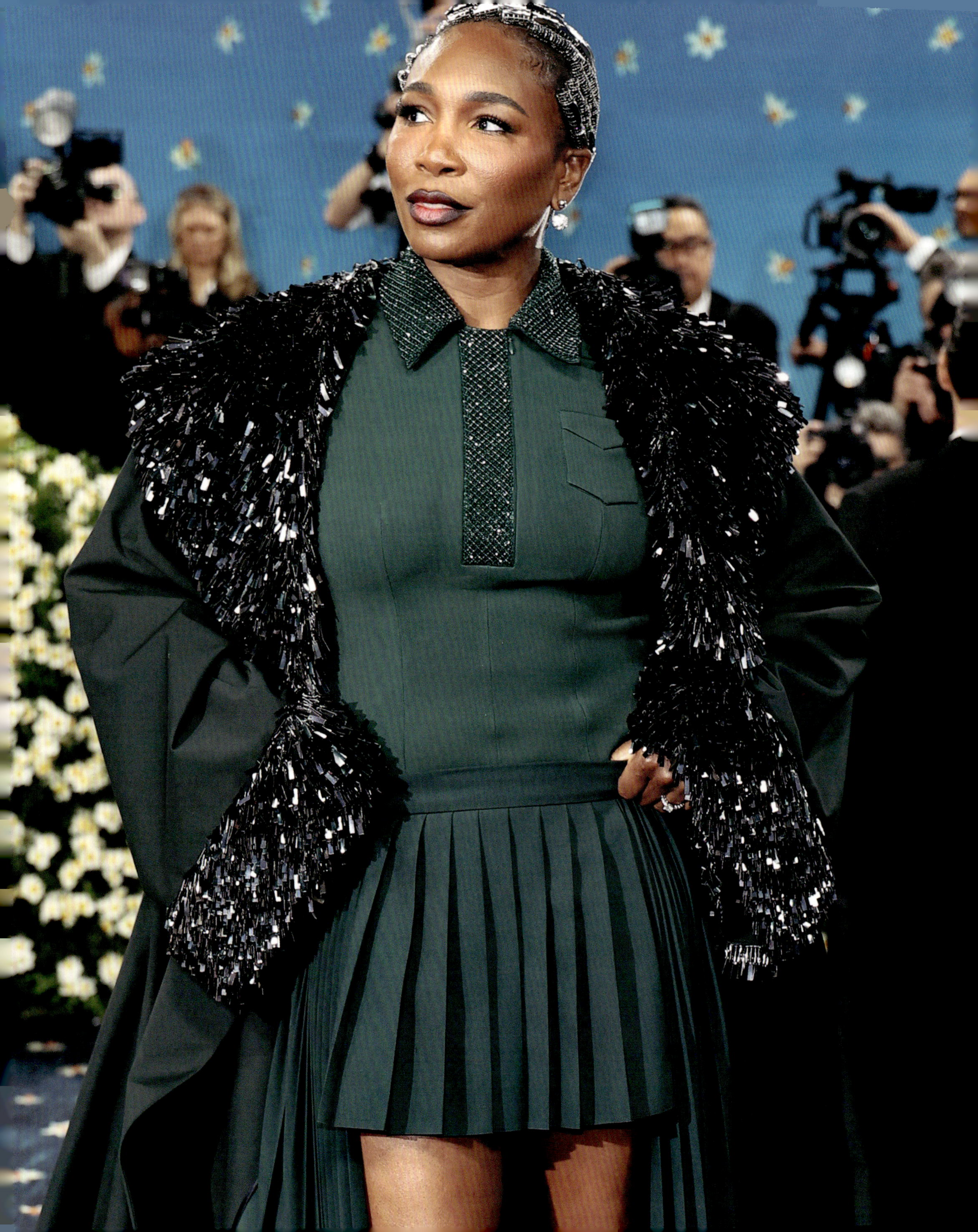

Oracene Price, **Venus** and **Serena Williams**

★

Today, Venus and Serena Williams are celebrated for being style setters as much as they are for being tennis stars. Both women have blazed an international trail of sporting success while their wardrobes on court have revolutionised the traditional silhouettes the game was known for, opting to wear corsets, denim and catsuits instead of time-honoured tennis whites. According to Serena, "seeing myself and my sister on the big stages of Wimbledon and the US Open being ourselves and wearing great outfits and looking our best, really changed women's sports—which is crazy" (Lesavage, 2024). Being themselves is something mum Oracene Price instilled at an early age. In an interview in 2019, Serena said: "We were not afraid to wear braids. We weren't afraid to be Black in tennis. And that was different" (Ford, 2019). Venus shared an Instagram post on her own thoughts, saying:

> "Wearing braids and beads, unbeknownst to us at the time as children, was an opportunity to share our beautiful and rich heritage with the world. It gave other African American women and children pride to wear their natural hair even before the natural hair movement sprouted decades later" (@venuswilliams, 2021).

Price is famous as the legendary mother of Venus and Serena Williams. She is equally famed for busting her own fashion moves and, practising what she preaches, being uniquely herself, too. Most recently, she was seen sitting front row at the Gucci Spring 2025 menswear show looking stylish in a cotton-and-lace shirt and slingbacks. She serves up chic in the same way her daughters hit the ball – by smashing it. Tennis lovers are familiar with her stand-out red lipstick and corkscrew blonde curls, often topped with many kinds of hats – from formal British bowlers to baseball caps and straw trilbys – practical and smart accessories she has donned while watching her daughters win. Her most famous accessory, however, is her signature sunglasses, à la her good friend Anna Wintour, which she candidly admitted in 2010 to Tennis Australia allowed her to go to sleep without anyone noticing.

The girls' interest in fashion, inspired by Price, began at an early age and both went on to study fashion design at The Art Institute of Fort Lauderdale. Venus told *Fashionista* in 2023: "As a kid, I remember trying to sew clothes for my doll. My mom used to sew, and I always wanted to learn. If I had more free time, or any free time, I would definitely spend time sewing" (Bossi, 2023). Serena remembers her mother's talents, too, and how she "used to watch [Oracene] put those old *Vogue* patterns on the floor and cut out the outfits" (Friedman, 2022). These early fashion tips from Oracene equipped the girls to set their own style trends, and then watch as the world followed.

In 2023, Serena was named Fashion Icon of the Year by the Council of Fashion Designers of America, saying at the time: "I explored fashion and style as a way to distinguish myself. In many ways for me, the tennis courts became my runway" (Drenon, 2023). Oracene's inclusive philosophy has helped pave the way for bright young talents to be themselves, too. In an interview with Sheinelle Jones on the *Today* programme, the tennis mum affirmed: "We are all made different. We all have different looks. And if you really look, everybody is beautiful, and one size don't fit all" (*Today*, 2019).

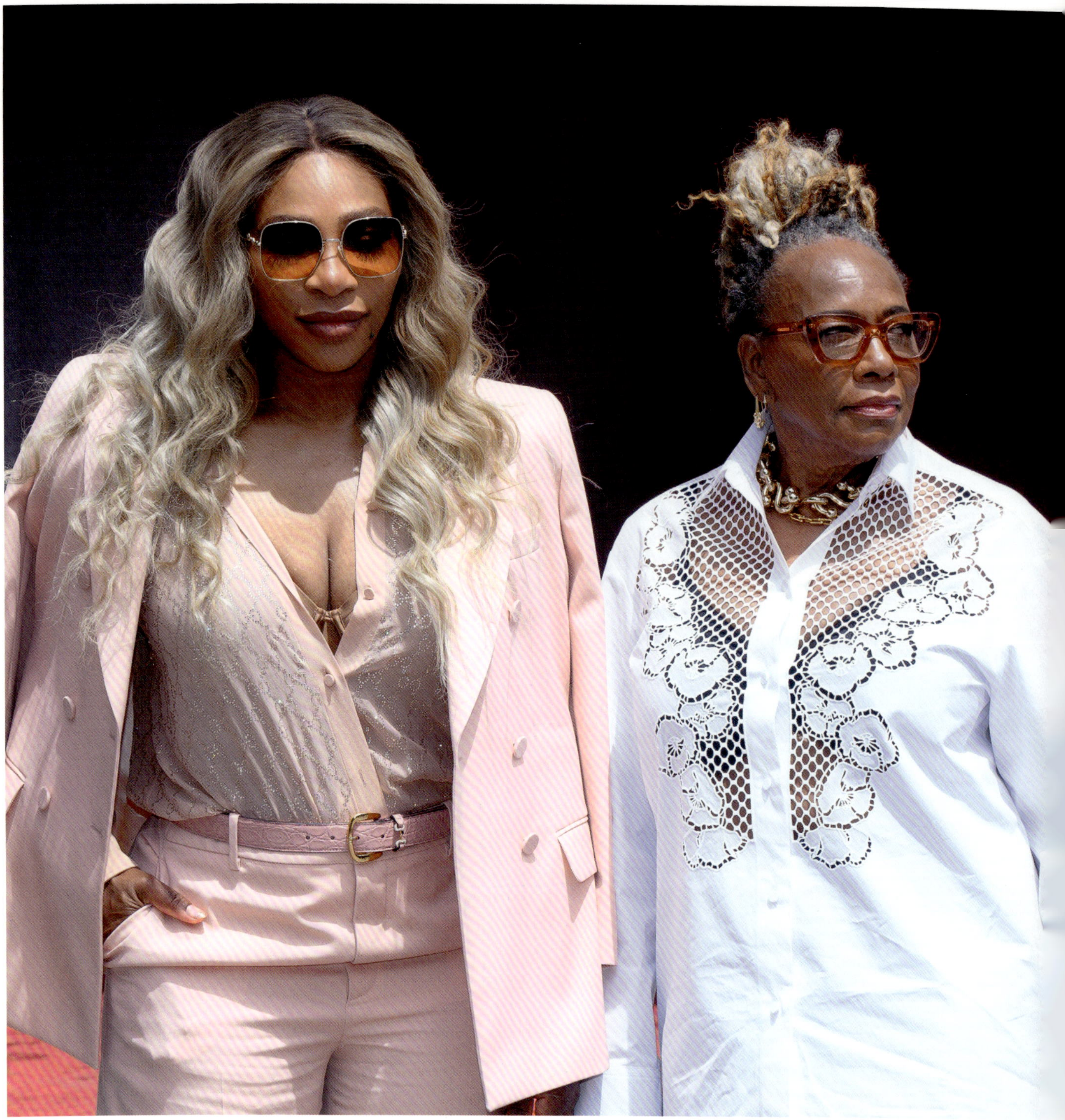

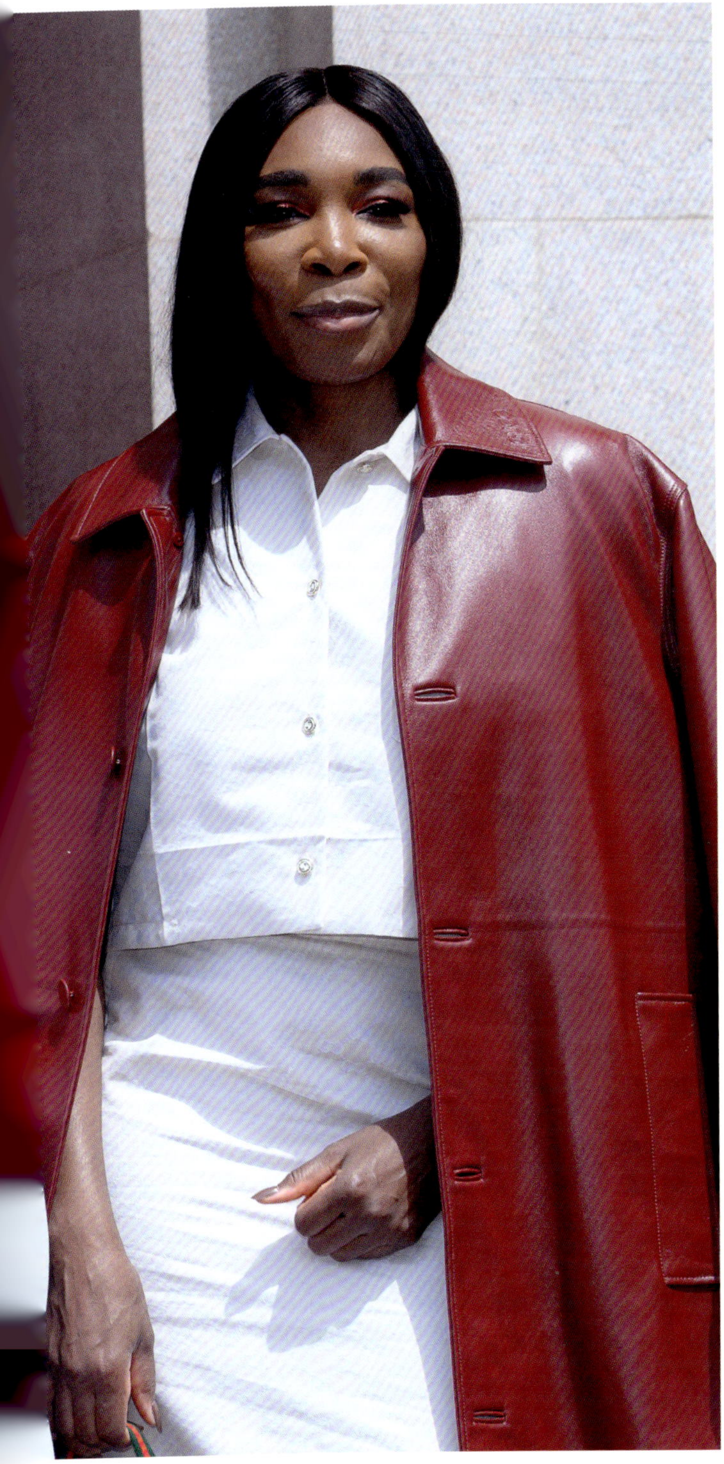

"We try to give love all year round. Every day should be Mother's Day. We buy mom things all year and tell her that we love her."

Serena Williams,
Ebony, 2023

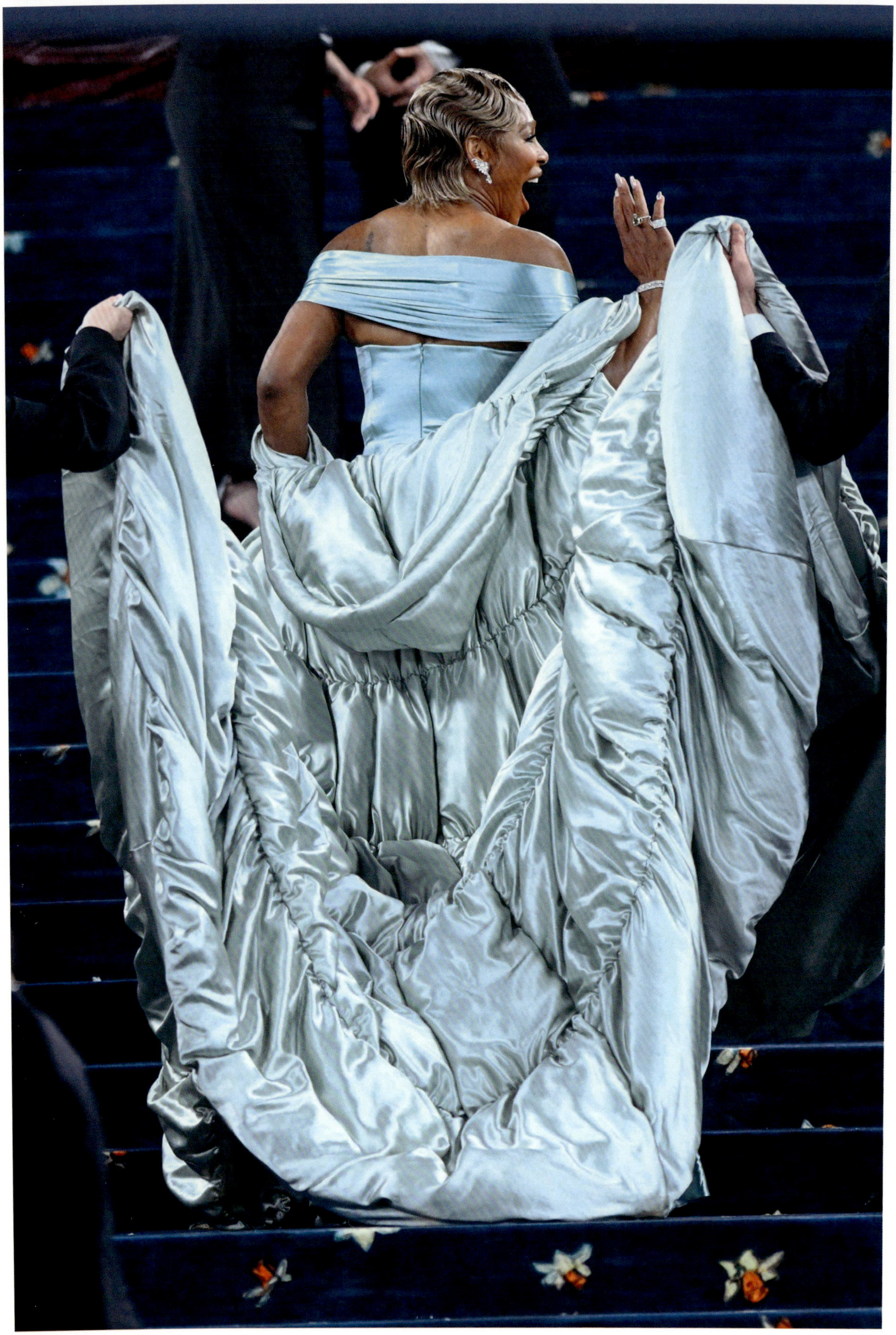

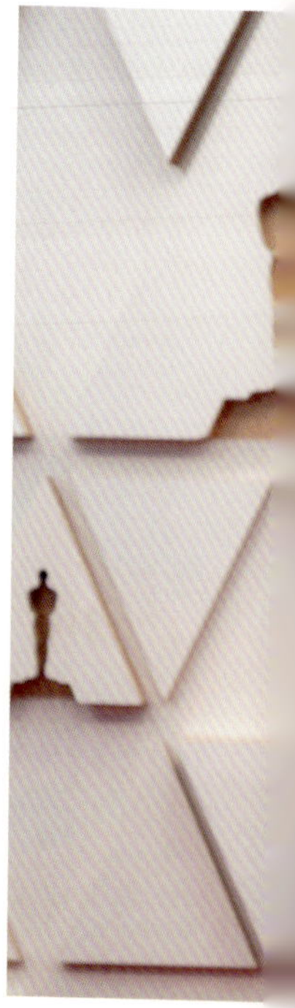

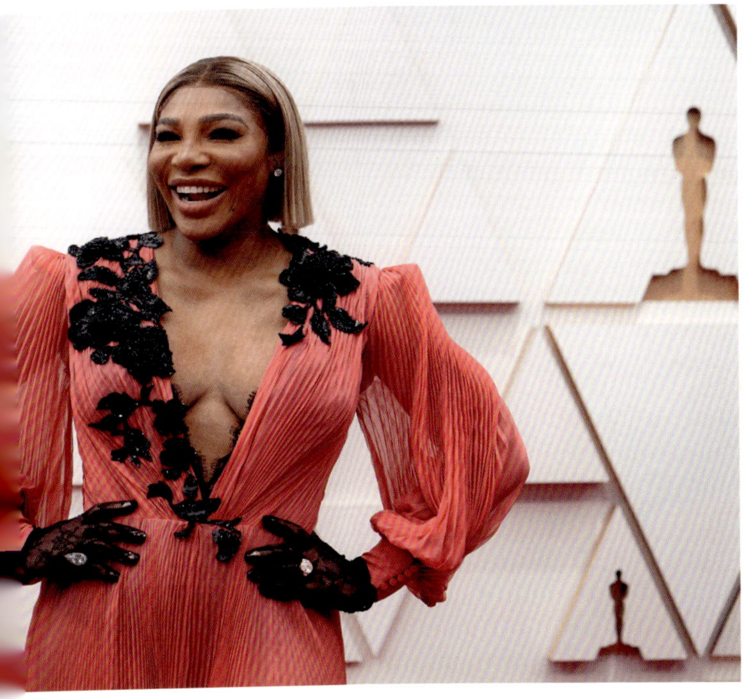

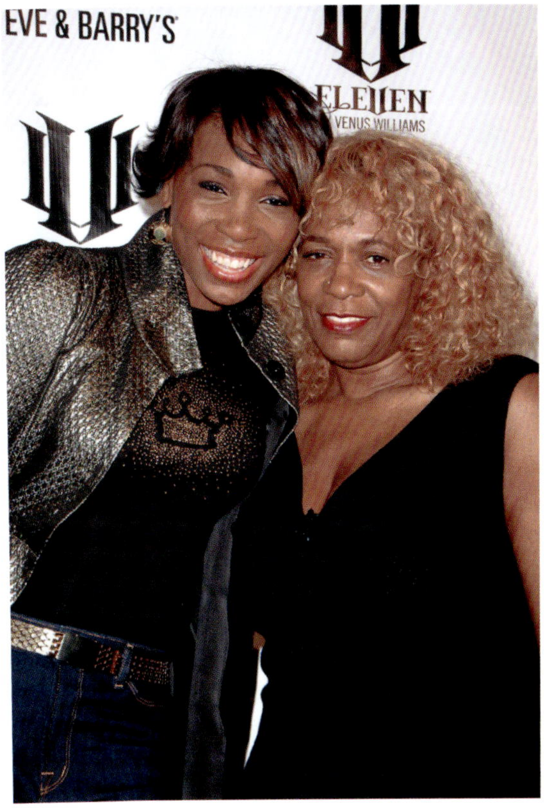

"Fashion started at a grassroots level for me. My mom ended up sewing my tennis skirts for my first professional tennis match. I still love it at that creation level. I studied fashion and it was a great experience. It taught me so much about the garment, what that means and how to create something that's entirely you."

Venus Williams,
Fashionista, 2023

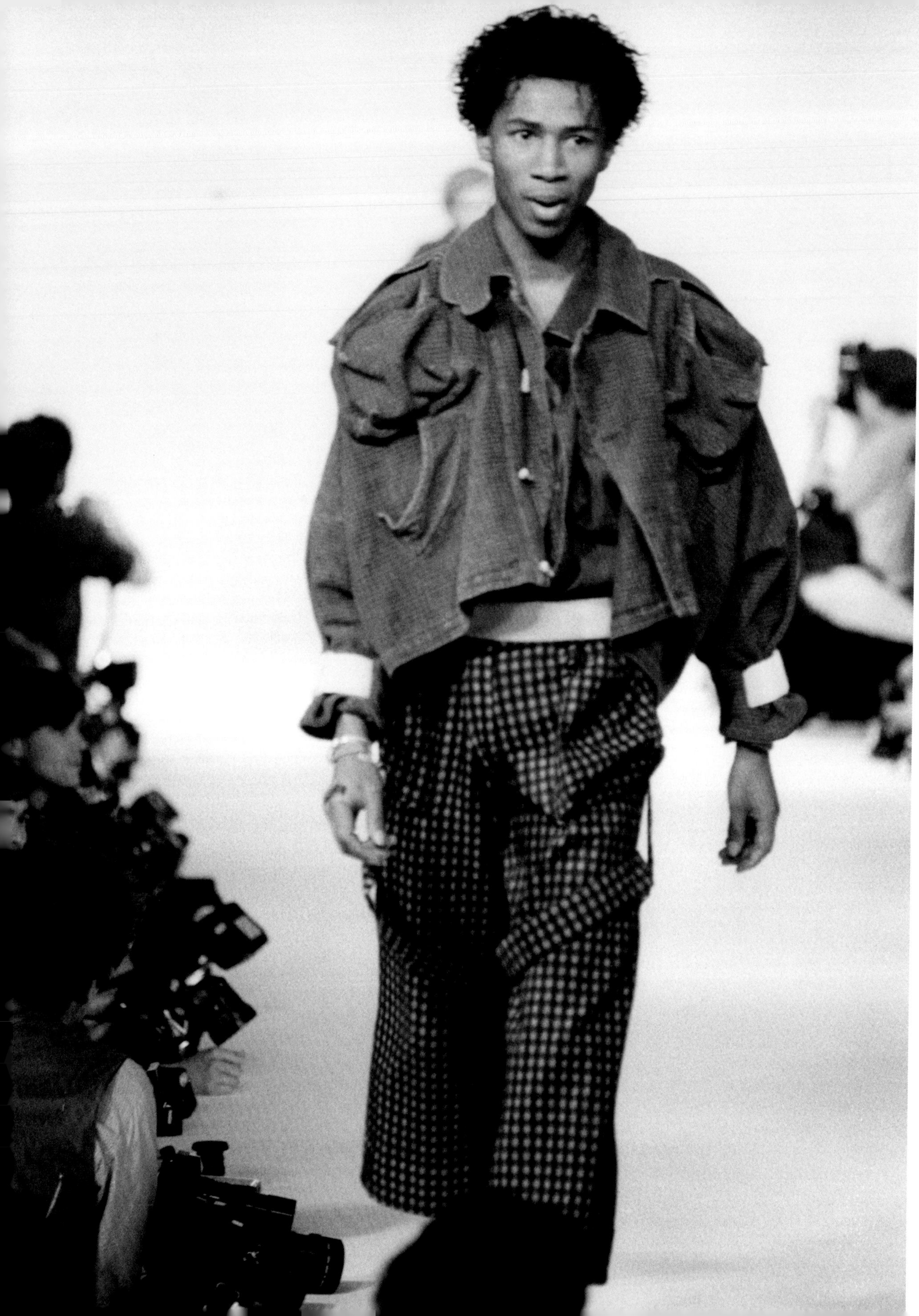

Agnes and **Herbie Mensah**

★

Born in Ghana and based in London's Notting Hill Gate, the sustainable designer Herbie Mensah started in fashion as a model for Vivienne Westwood in the 1980s when he walked her celebrated Autumn/Winter 1982–83 'Nostalgia of Mud' show in Paris. Later, he became part of the creative world she and Malcolm McLaren spun. McLaren liked Herbie's look so much that he signed him up for singing lessons with the famous voice coach Tona de Brett, with a view of him singing in a notorious band as successful as the Sex Pistols. Instead, Mensah turned to making clothes himself and building up a cult following of clients. Today, fellow creatives from the houses of Michael Kors, Dolce & Gabbana and Gucci have all bought his unique upcycled pieces. "I hate throwing good clothing away. Reimagining vintage pieces is my way of giving them a second life. One of the first pieces I made was out of old pockets."

His thrifty and imaginative sartorial sensibility was fostered as a young child, influenced by his mother, Agnes Ama Mensah. Having moved from Ghana to London in 1963 with Herbie, aged three, Agnes joined her husband, who had made the journey a year before to find somewhere for the family to live. Agnes sailed on the MV *Accra* – a passenger ship built in 1947 and named after the capital of Ghana. Operated by Elder Dempster Lines, it had been requisitioned by the military in World War II and returned to commuter service afterwards, before finally being scrapped in 1967.

When Agnes embarked on her voyage, Kwame Nkrumah was in power, the first elected president since Ghana's independence in 1957. Although welcomed at first, he became authoritarian and by '64 had declared himself 'president for life', with his Convention People's Party the only sanctioned political group in Parliament. It was against this backdrop that Agnes left the country, alongside thousands of other Ghanaians. Agnes had been a schoolteacher in Ghana and her husband a headmaster. She left her two older daughters behind to be looked after by relatives and didn't see them again until they were in their early 20s. A talented seamstress, Agnes routinely made all her clothing, although in Ghana she would usually wear a wrap skirt and shawl made from brilliantly coloured, hand-woven cloth. For ceremonial and special occasions, outfits were created using Kente fabrics that featured vivid symbolic patterns, checks and designs. Chieftains would have their own decorative fabrics and one of the treasures Agnes brought to London was a piece of Kente that had belonged to her father, a village chief in the Ashanti region, which Herbie treasures to this day. In England, she used her tailoring skills to great effect and not only made her living creating clothes but also dressed her son: "I still have two tailor-made suits from when I was about six", admits Herbie, going on to reflect: "The clothes my mother made me were really what made me first love fashion."

When Agnes arrived in England, the Race Discrimination Bill had yet to be passed, and prejudice was not only legal but casual and common in the UK. The famed Bristol Bus Boycott of 1963, which campaigned to overturn a ban on employing Black or Asian bus workers, was integral in passing the Race Relations Act a few years later in 1965. Living with her husband and Herbie in a single room, Agnes was determined to move somewhere bigger, so Herbie was sent to live with a white foster parent in Croydon, so that

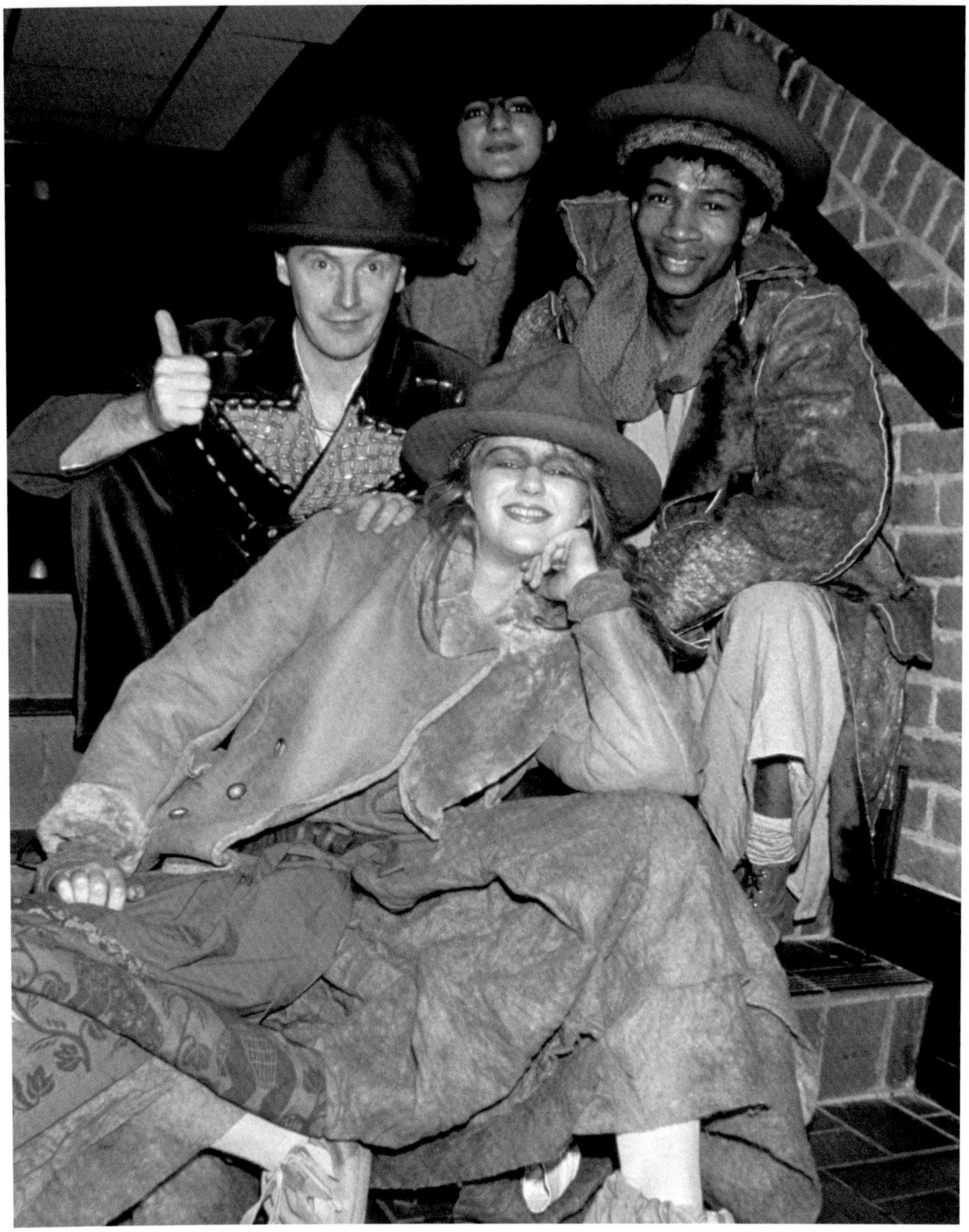

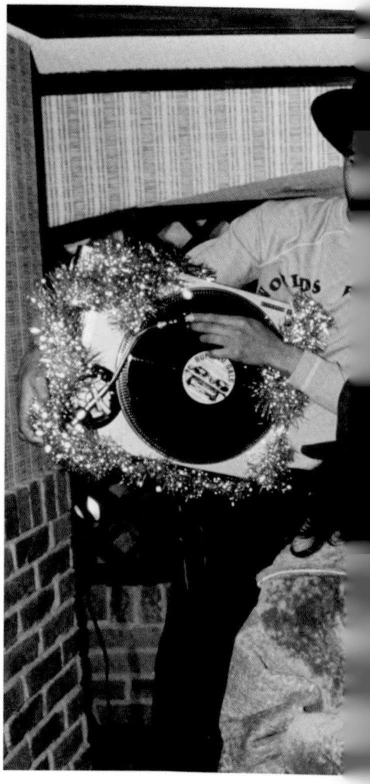

Left: Herbie poses with Malcolm McLaren and other models, wearing outfits from Vivienne Westwood's 'Buffalo' collection, London 1983.
Above: Herbie with American hip hop radio show duo The World's Famous Supreme Team and Malcolm McLaren, London 1983.

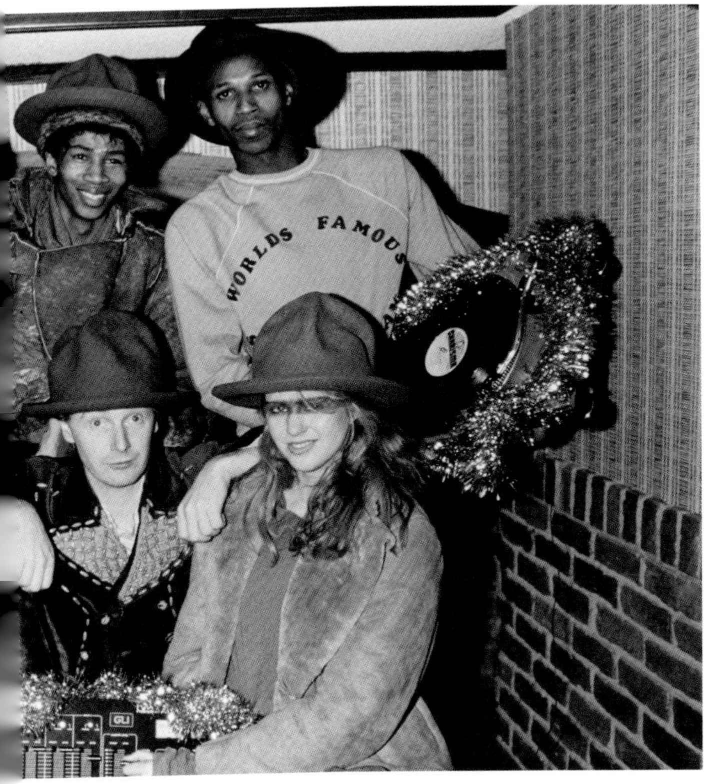

Agnes could work full time (private fostering was common then). Flexing her talents, she was soon employed by Cecil Gee, the Jewish tailor who helped reinvent menswear in post-war Britain, and whose slogan was 'Forget the Blitz, here comes the Ritz!'. In the '60s, his menswear was sought after and worn by sharply styled mods, and he began a custom suit-making service that benefitted from Agnes's expert needlework. Like the fashionable mods she helped look stylish, whatever circumstances prevailed she always looked polished. She spent regular evenings at the Commonwealth Institute dances, wearing variations of favoured shift dresses. Herbie remembers:

> "We often visited the tourist places in London. When we went to Madam Tussauds she wore a Ghanian outfit she made herself and really stood out! She loved exploring the capital. My favourite outfit when she wasn't wearing Ghanaian pieces was when she took me sightseeing to Buckingham Palace in a bracelet-sleeved, pilgrim-collared, white mini coat, carrying a snap-shut frame bag, with chisel-toed buckle shoes. She loved looking smart."

It was a feeling that Herbie channelled in the 1980s as a soulboy teenager, going to London's clubs and dancing the night away wearing baggy trousers and oversized blazers. "I didn't look anything like the guys who hung around with Vivienne and Malcolm," he confesses, "but after learning about clothes and living in London with my mum, I was ready for an adventure."

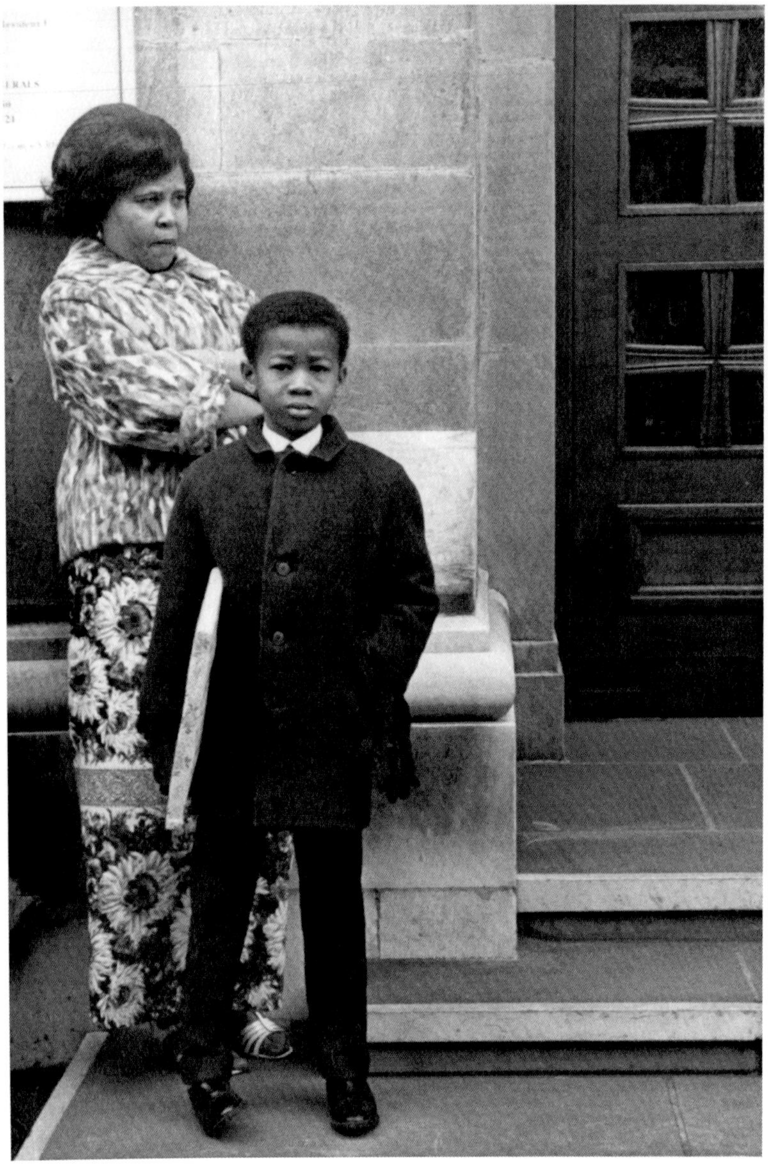

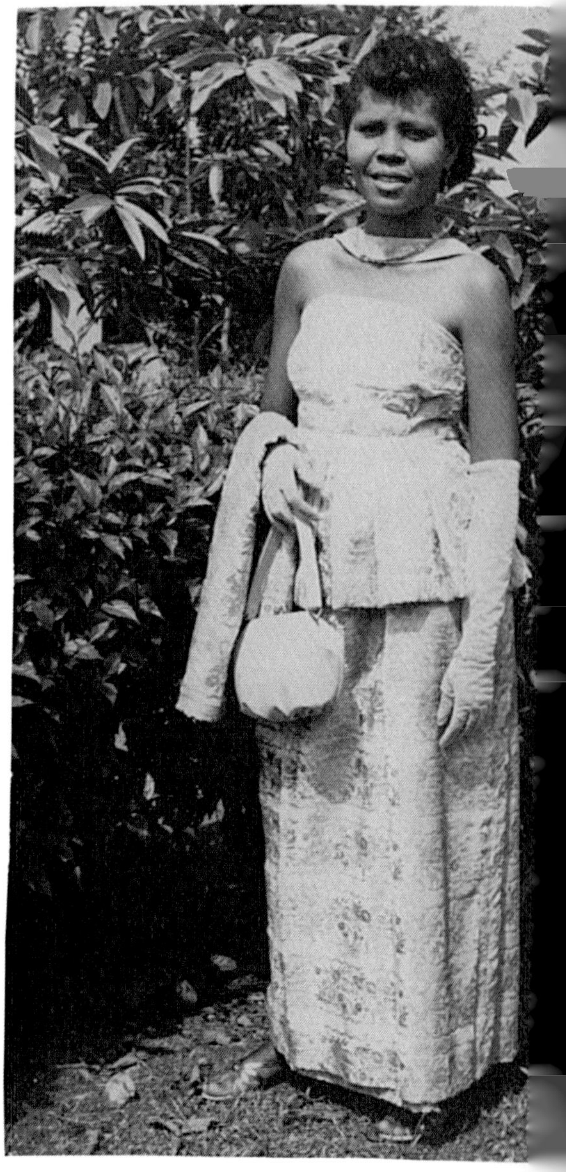

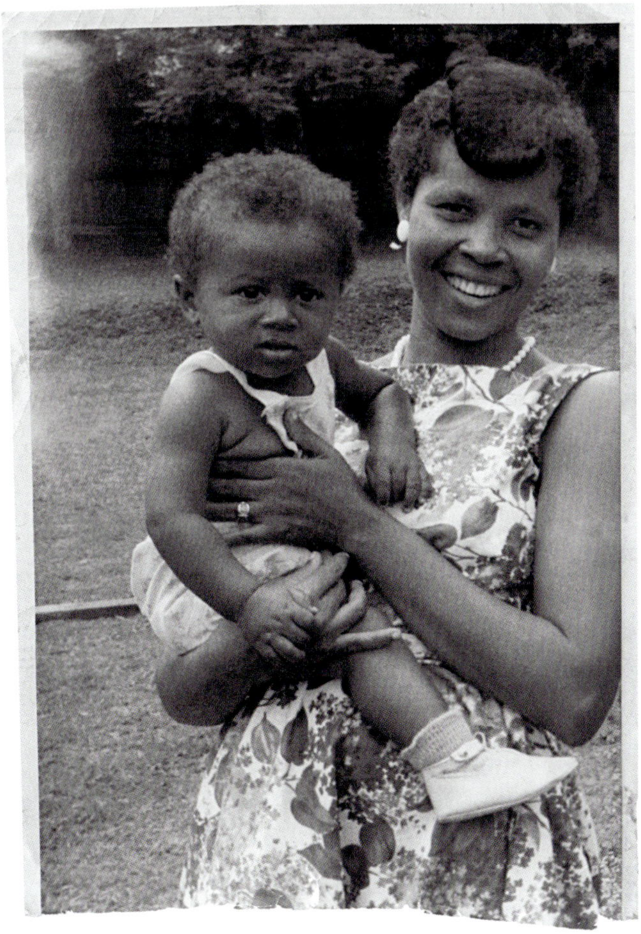

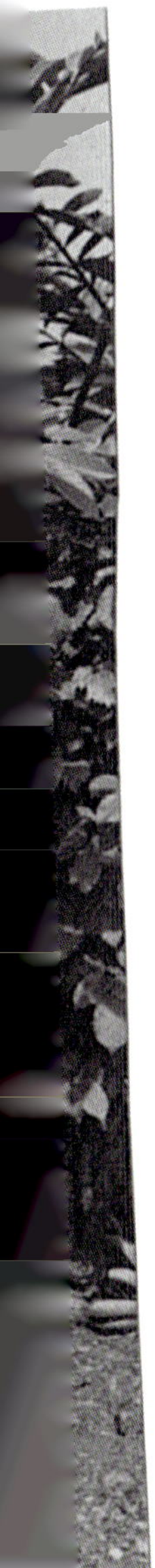

"We often visited the tourist places in London. When we went to Madam Tussauds she wore a Ghanian outfit she made herself and really stood out!"

Herbie Mensah,
2025

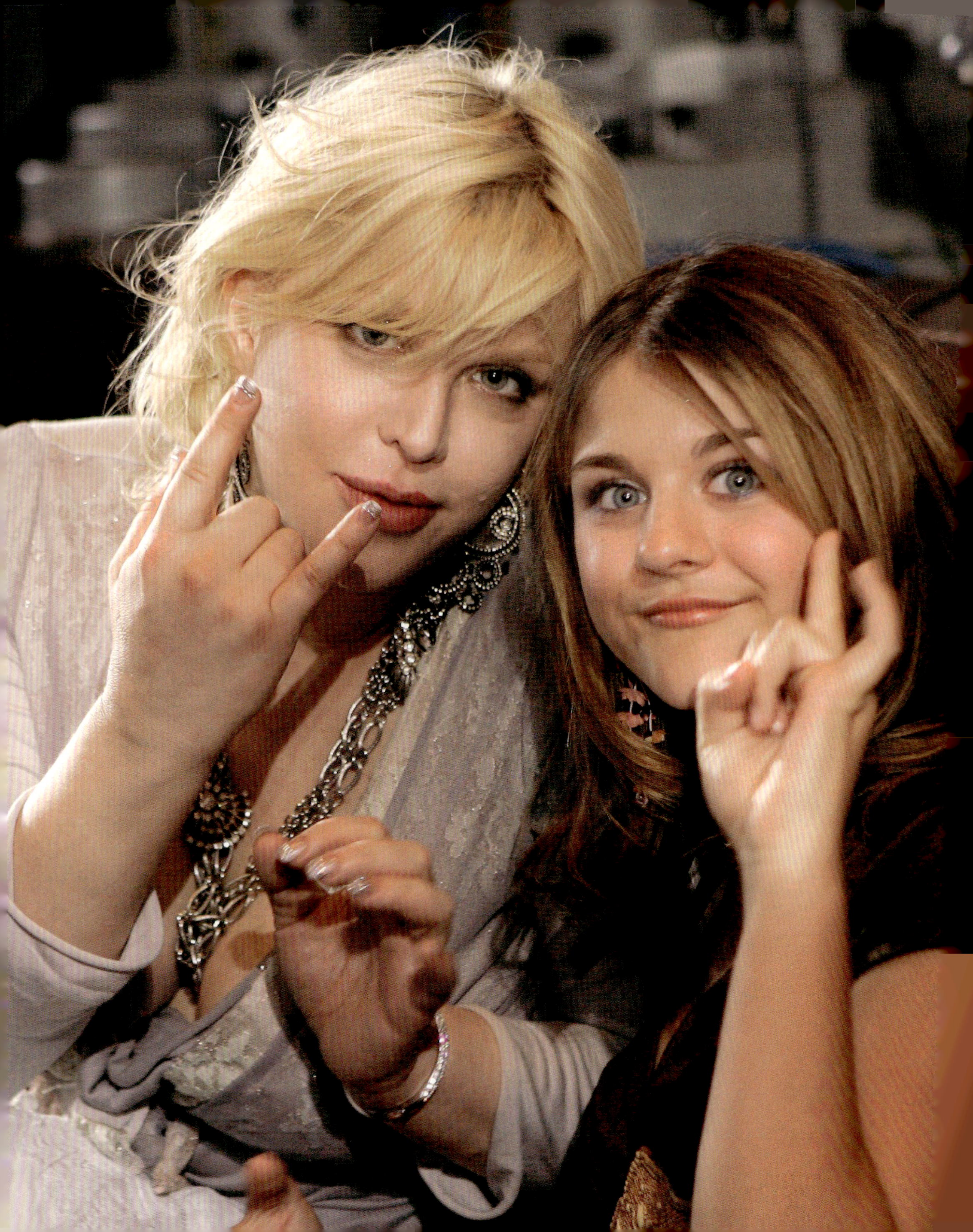

Louella Risi, **Courtney** Love **and Frances** Bean **Cobain**

★

Courtney Love's fashion legacy captures the unruly intersection of feminist self-expression, identity and the subversive power of style. She is also the only mother to date to tread the red carpet accessorised with her baby and a feeding bottle. Style, for the award-winning musician and actress, has never been superficial; instead, it's a lens through which she navigates character and cultural storytelling. Her impact on both high and outsider fashion is equally unique, yet she admits that her daughter, Francis Bean Cobain, has "fought really hard to not be influenced by me because she wants to do her own thing. So, if I say something's a really bad idea, she's sure to do it".

Love became known for her deconstructed wardrobe and defiant self-expression when she was a teenager playing in bands like Faith No More and Sugar Babydoll before going on to front Hole. She honed a thrifty avant-garde look living in Liverpool, England, when she was just 17, standing out from the crowd in upcycled Edwardian bobbin-lace gowns while those around her dressed in Bauhaus-inspired clothing sourced from Army & Navy Stores. Although Love's look has been described as chaotic, she insists it's "all planned" and, looking back, there has always been a consistent authority about her approach to clothes that remains unerringly unadulterated. Moving from place to place, she remembers having a capsule wardrobe long before it became a lifestyle choice:

> "I had a kit. It included Revlon's 'Cherries in the Snow' lipstick, Chinese slippers, Mary Jane shoes – because I can't play in f*****g heels and I didn't want to play in ballet flats – this indigo-dyed slippy dress thing, floral long johns, seven pairs of underwear – because I'm not going without clean underwear – a trench coat, a cardigan and one big, big sweater that I'd kept because it belonged to a pop star whose granny had knitted it for him, and I kept that f*****g around for a long time. It was actually a better sweater than anything from the Row, in my memory. Living in squats you had to be able to leave, like De Niro says in *Heat*, in 30 seconds."

Her famous love of Mary Jane shoes was fostered when she started school in New Zealand:

> "It's why I liked Peter Pan collars later, too, but I was first given those shoes from my rich grandmother, Louella, and my mother would want to throw them out the window because her whole thing was the opposite. I think my mother's single contribution to American culture, and this is nothing to be proud of, is that she ordered these German shoes with the name of Birkenstock. And that's what she sold at the Saturday market alongside people with crystals, homemade granola and Nancy's yogurt. I believe that she was the first, and I blame her. I blame her for all of them."

Despite the complexity of her relationship with her own mother, Linda Carroll, Love relishes a favourite memory of her hosting a cheese and wine party for Gloria Steinem. The legendary feminist left a lasting impression on the fledgling Courtney: "I thought she was a movie star. Like, the way she moved around the room in her mini skirt at this cocktail party where all the other women were like, so f*****g anti the male gaze."

Throughout her life, Love found motherly mentorship outside of her blood family. Sharon Stone offered advice and support early in Love's acting career, and emphasised the importance of women supporting women. But, indirectly, her maternal grandmother's taste and lifestyle influenced her sense of fashion, too. Good friends with Hubert de Givenchy, Louella shopped regularly in Paris, so it was as a child that Love consequently came into contact with the couture pieces her grandmother bought. Later, Love worked with Bernadene Mann (the mother of her then-boyfriend Jeff Mann), who was a costume designer at Paramount Studios. When Bernadene took Courtney under her wing, her appreciation for the artistry of handmade pieces and the mythology surrounding the wardrobes of what she calls "old-school movie stars" consolidated. "I was supposed to throw out the dry rotted stuff from the 1920s, but I didn't throw any of it out. I just wore it 'til it fell off, which was usually that night. Most things did not fit because those people were a lot smaller. I did come across Lauren Bacall's shoes, though, and they fit me!"

She learnt from Bernadine an appreciation for precision, patience and craft: "We measured everything in millimetres, over and over, from the size of wrists to the distance between nipple and clavicle", Love recalls. She also discovered from one of their most famous clients, Faye Dunaway, how carefully curated fashion could convey power and confidence, whether in film or everyday life. One of Love's favourite finds was a gossamer-thin muslin dress once owned by the film star Frances Farmer. She would wear it onstage and off – and chose it as the gown she would wear to marry Kurt Cobain in 1992. When she and Cobain hit the VMAs red carpet in 1993 with their daughter, Frances Bean Cobain, she chose a simple satin bias-cut dress and a vintage romper for her baby. "I just wore vintage all the time and, you know, a white dress is the easiest thing to put on", Love explains, admitting that that iconic moment of mothering was very spontaneous: "I didn't think about how to present myself at all. I mean, I never thought about that as anything, even minorly, like subversive, ever. It's so weird."

Today, Frances is grown up with a child of her own and, like her mother, has identified a look that is distinctive. According to Love:

> "She's really stylish, but she has her own vibe. She's living in and out of LA at the moment. And she has a baby, and she surfs, and she skates, and she can drive. And she does this kind of hippie-cool. But you know, don't forget, to be clear, she grew up in Beverly Hills and had a very, very, very fancy Irish pony and was doing dressage to keep her out of trouble. I had Keith Richards Blu-Tacked onto my bedroom wall before my mother legally emancipated me and I moved out. Frances had ponies on hers."

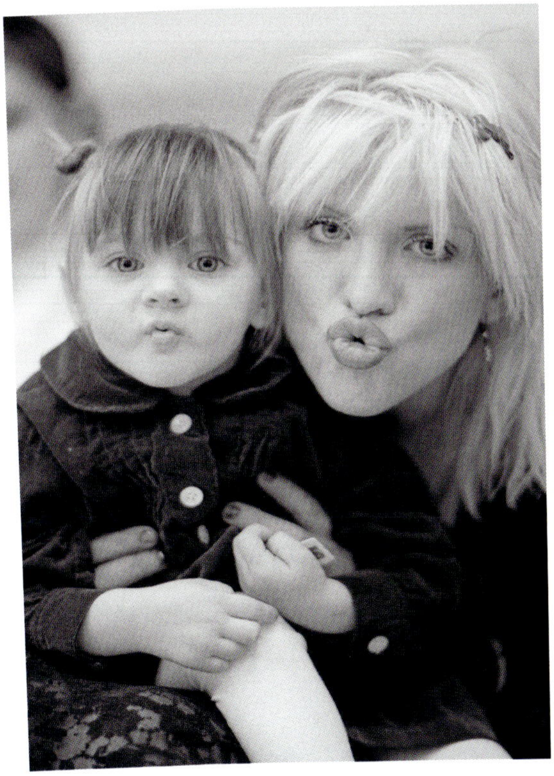

"No one's parents are cool for them. Like, it's just the way it is."

Courtney Love,
2025

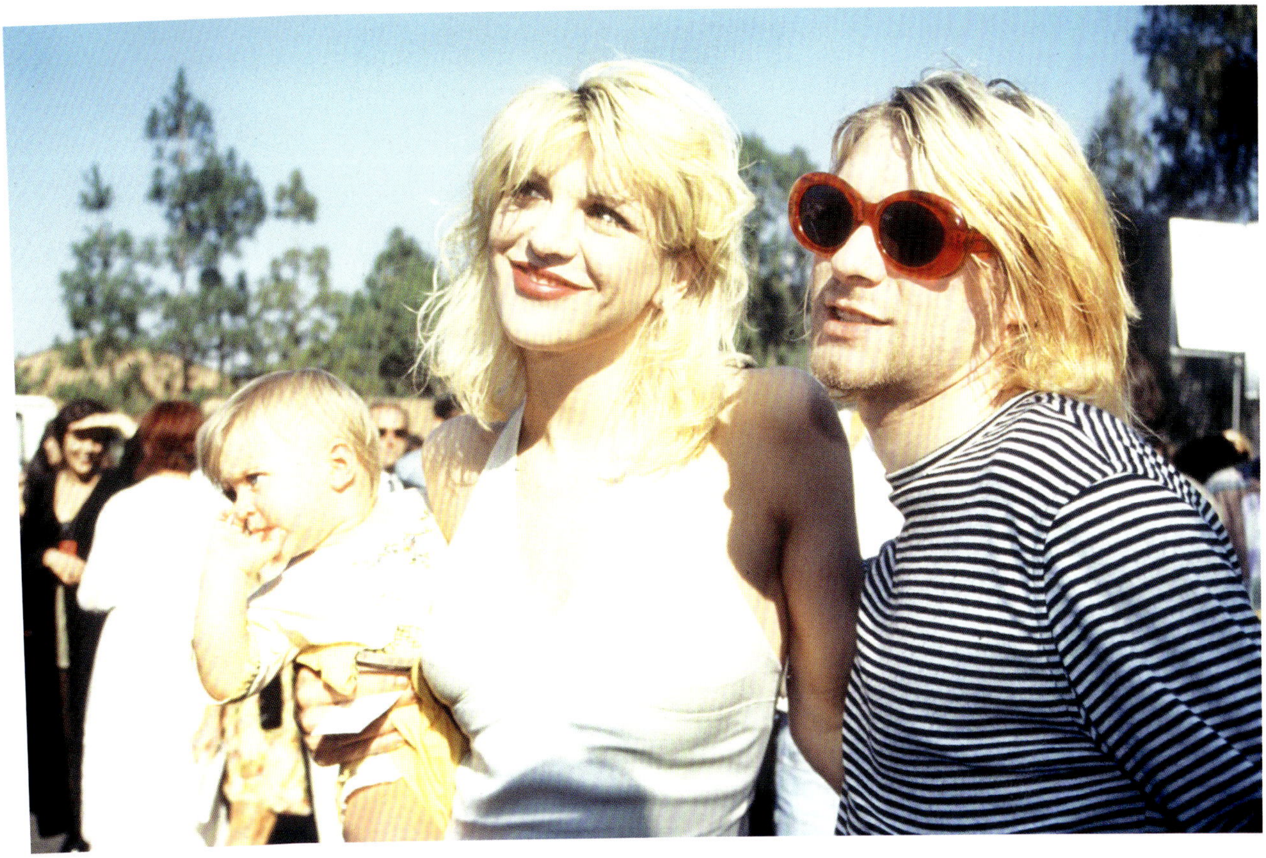

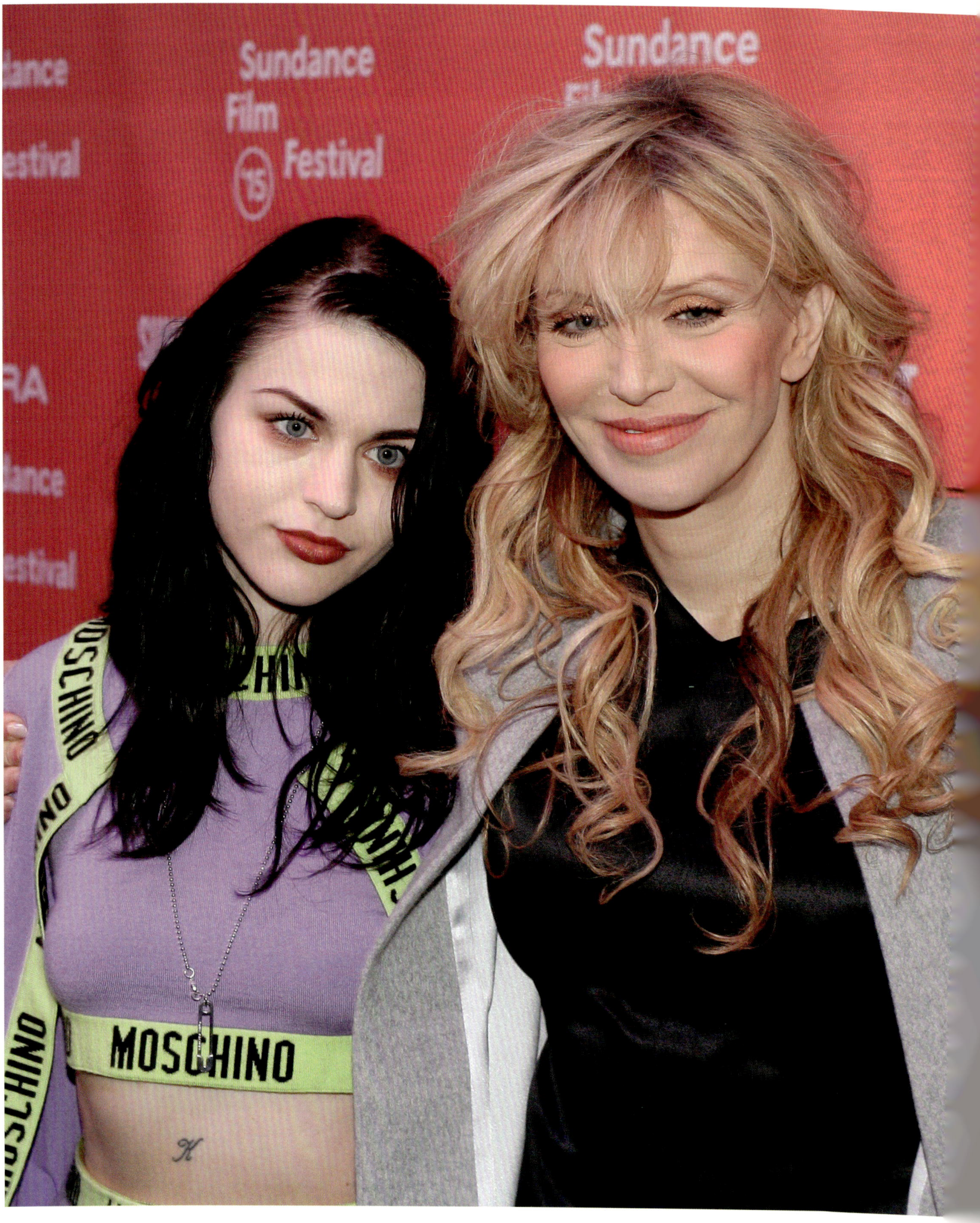
Sundance
Film
Festival
Sundance
MOSCHINO
MOSCHINO

"If this is going to be an interview about maternity wear it's going to be the shortest ever."

Courtney Love,
2025

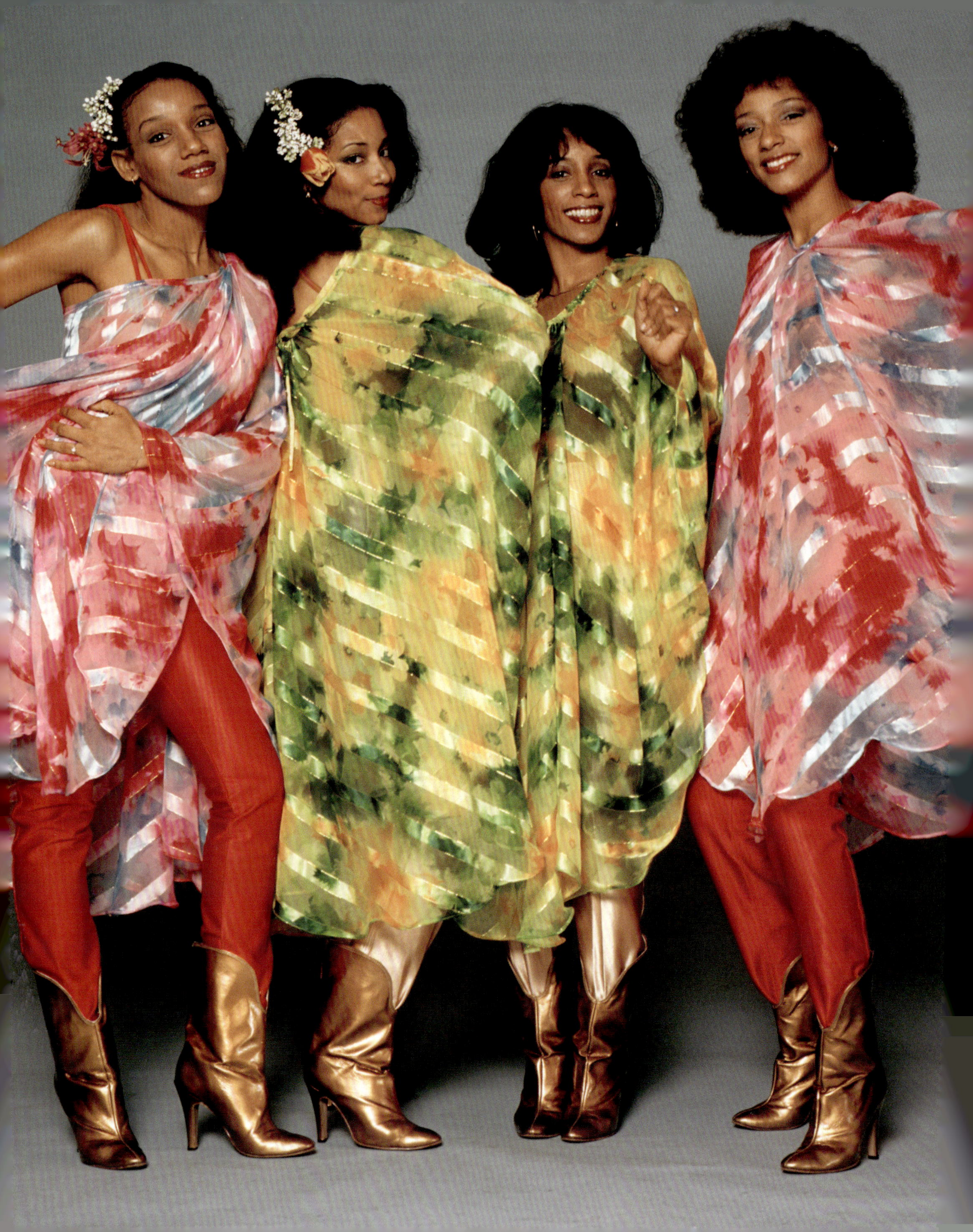

Kathy Sledge and **Kristen Gabrielle Lightfoot**

★

Kristen Gabrielle Lightfoot, Kathy Sledge's daughter, has warm memories of her mother's clothes. "First, I'll say this: growing up and seeing my mom and my aunts in concert – they coordinated. They'd wear the same outfits in different colours. When I was about 16, my cousins and I would always look at their old videos and wonder, 'Where are those pants?'"

Sister Sledge's stage wardrobe of the 1970s and '80s consisted of harmonising Lycra leggings and vivid chiffon tunics teamed with boots, which embodied club-land fashions of the day. They wore pulsating pieces that were created to move in. Spandex was the fabric *du jour* – it stretched and allowed the girls to ballet-kick, twirl and boogie. "I'm not sure if you know this, but Sister Sledge was one of the first girl groups to wear pants on stage. Before my mom, The Supremes – they'd wear dresses, never trousers, and even now people can be funny and say you need to wear a dress when you're performing. But that's so not my mom", reveals Kristen.

The silhouettes Sister Sledge wore have since become retro-style souvenirs of a moment when the world was lost in music. "I did eventually find a pair of my mom's pants. They are black and tiny! I used to wear a lot of her clothes when I was in my early 20s", admits Kristen. Another treasure she will never let go of includes a cherished tank top made from metal rings. "I don't wear it, but I will keep it forever", she explains. It's a memento of some of the clothes Kathy used to discover on her trips to London's Kensington Market, a legendary destination for style-watchers where independent creativity thrived. It opened in 1967 and, closing its doors in 2000, spanned just over 30 years of subcultural fashion history; it was a little chaotic and a little underground, but if you made a pilgrimage, you'd always find something a little ahead of the style curve. Kristen remembers visiting it with Kathy when she was just 13, and buying a reflective fluorescent orange coat, "like workers wear", along with "a pair of chunky white sneakers. They weren't popular back home, but I wore them to school and got so many compliments", remembers Kristen.

It's easy to forget that Kathy herself was just 12 in , when she and fellow sisters Joni, Debbie and Kim signed to the record label Money Back and released their first-ever single, 'Time Will Tell'. A year later, they moved to Atco, part of Atlantic Records, where they recorded 'Mama Never Told Me' (1973), which would go on to be a smash hit in the UK in 1975. Sister Sledge's sweet soul songs helped define the funky R&B sound of Philadelphia. Later, their global disco classics, including 'We Are Family' and 'He's the Greatest Dancer' (both 1979), dominated disco dancefloors – tunes that, to this day, the world continues to sing along to.

Their legacy was celebrated again during the Covid-19 pandemic, when their 1984 song 'Thinking of You' became the theme tune to DJ D-Nice's 'Club Quarantine' sets, bringing a sense of unity and hope to lockdown. Since 2020, Kathy and Kristen's Instagram Live show, *FamilyRoom*, has broadcast via and has created a space for friendship and much-needed joy during difficult times. People leant into the vibe. It was a revelation to Kristen, who realised for almost the first time what a loving and strong relationship she and Kathy enjoyed, and how unusual that was.

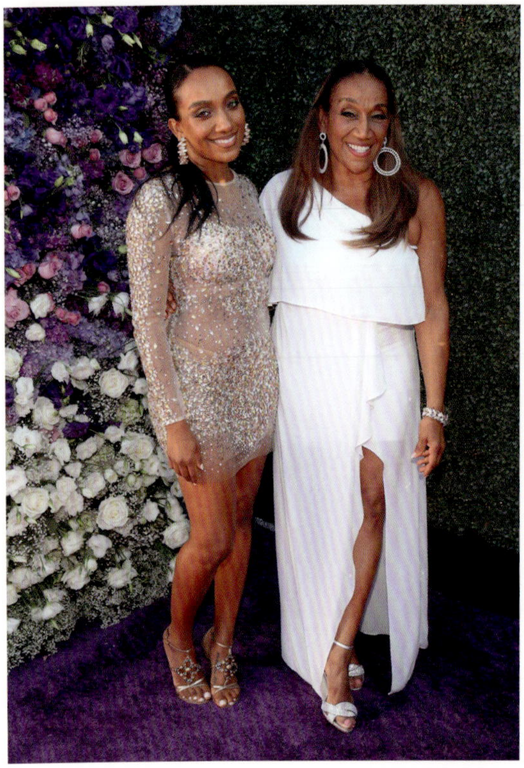

"Whether that's denim cut offs and a customised T-shirt or an evening gown, my mom says you have to be able to serve it and one thing I can say that my mom has always been good at is serving what she's wearing."

Kristen Gabrielle Lightfoot,
2025

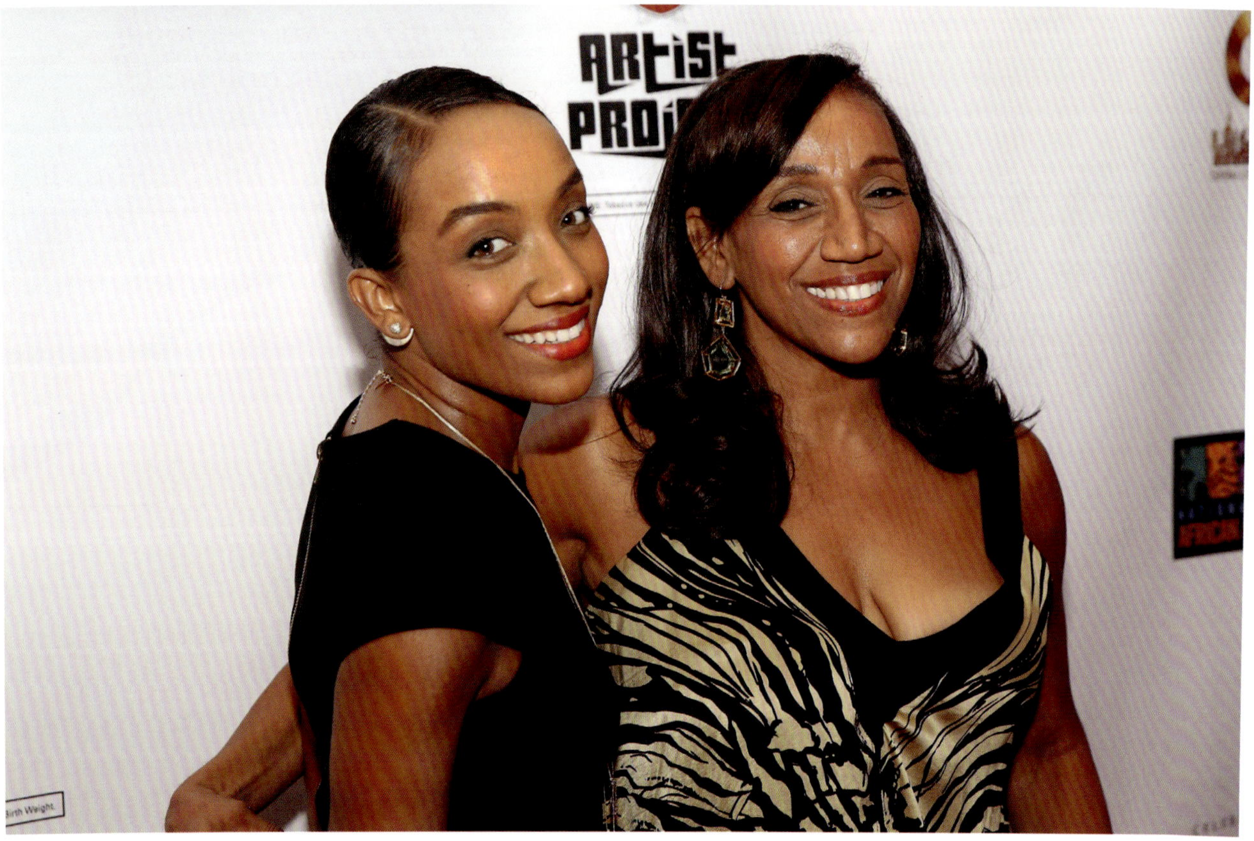

> "Honestly, we were like, let's just jump on here and talk, and it impacted people's lives and we didn't even know that that's what we were doing. We keep in contact with so many people. We get messages daily; it's very rewarding because we've been able to use our brand, 'We are Family', to bring so many people together."

Today, Kristen and Kathy work jointly on projects and although their relationship is inspirational, Kristen is pragmatic: "It's easy, but it's hard, because we have the mother–daughter dynamic. We also have the sister dynamic, and we have the best-friend dynamic, and all of those together – sometimes it can be crazy." Family is indeed central for Kristen, who has a fashion label called Florez, named after her maternal grandmother, who was both Sister Sledge's manager and an actress and singer in her own right. Florez Sledge's mother, Viola Williams, was likewise talented, and established a career as a well-respected opera singer. The Sledge sisters' melodic harmonies were honed as children when they were members of the Second Macedonia Baptist Church's choir in Philadelphia, performing as 'Mrs Williams' grandchildren'. Together, each generation of Kristen's family have instinctively supported each other. In 2007, following the death of her mother, Florez, Kathy told the *Philadelphia Inquirer* how she "and her sisters were always singing. We sang when we jumped rope; we sang when we played jacks. Our mother and grandmother taught us four-part harmony and encouraged us" (Sims, 2007).

Today, friends who know Kristen and Kathy say they are 'identical'. Describing their clothes taste, Kristen confesses:

> "On a day-to-day, we both live in Lululemon, but when it comes to getting dressed, I think that she is inspired by me, too. Her style is effortless. I've seen her wear denim shorts, maybe like an oversized sweatshirt, some slouch socks. Very cool. We both encourage each other. I think that my mom's look has shaped me, and it's shown me that sometimes less is more. You don't have to overexert. You can be who you are and just exude confidence. It doesn't necessarily have to be pretty in pink in a dress."

She goes on to reflect on their similar but different approach to fashion, revealing:

> "A lot of my fashion sense is drawn from her style back in the day, but I wear her look with a relaxed twist of my own. For example, my mom wears sneakers a lot on stage. We've talked about maybe even doing a sneaker line because she wears them to perform all the time and everyone's like, 'Why do you wear sneakers?' She loves glitzy, Kurt Geiger with lots of embellishments on them, and then the rest of her outfit will be kind of more laid-back."

There's one thing, however, that's missing from Kristen's wardrobe that she would adore to own. "I'm looking for one T-shirt that I love. It's yellow and black vintage and says 'Sister Sledge' on the front. I don't have one and I've been looking online; all I have is a photo of the band wearing it."

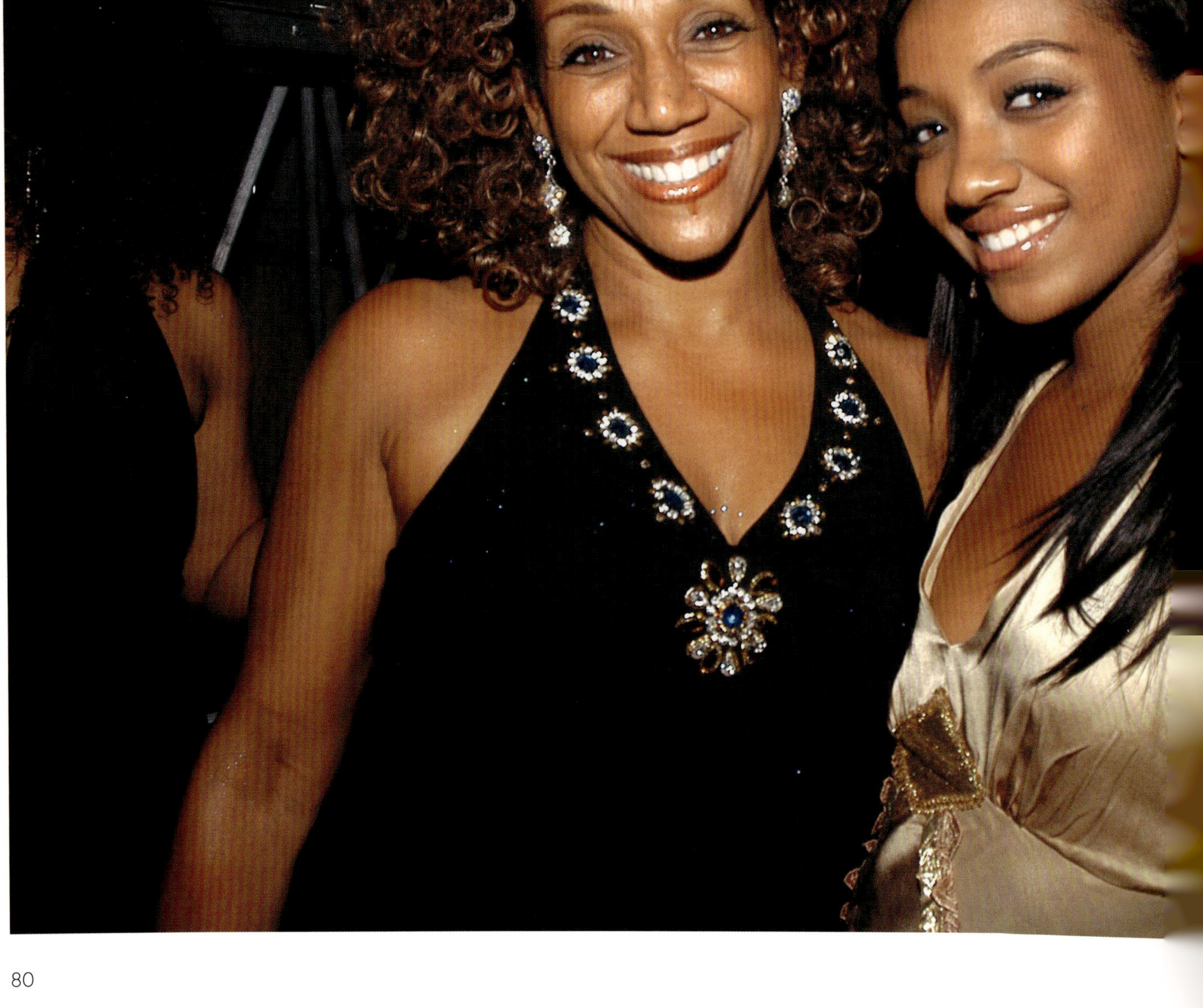

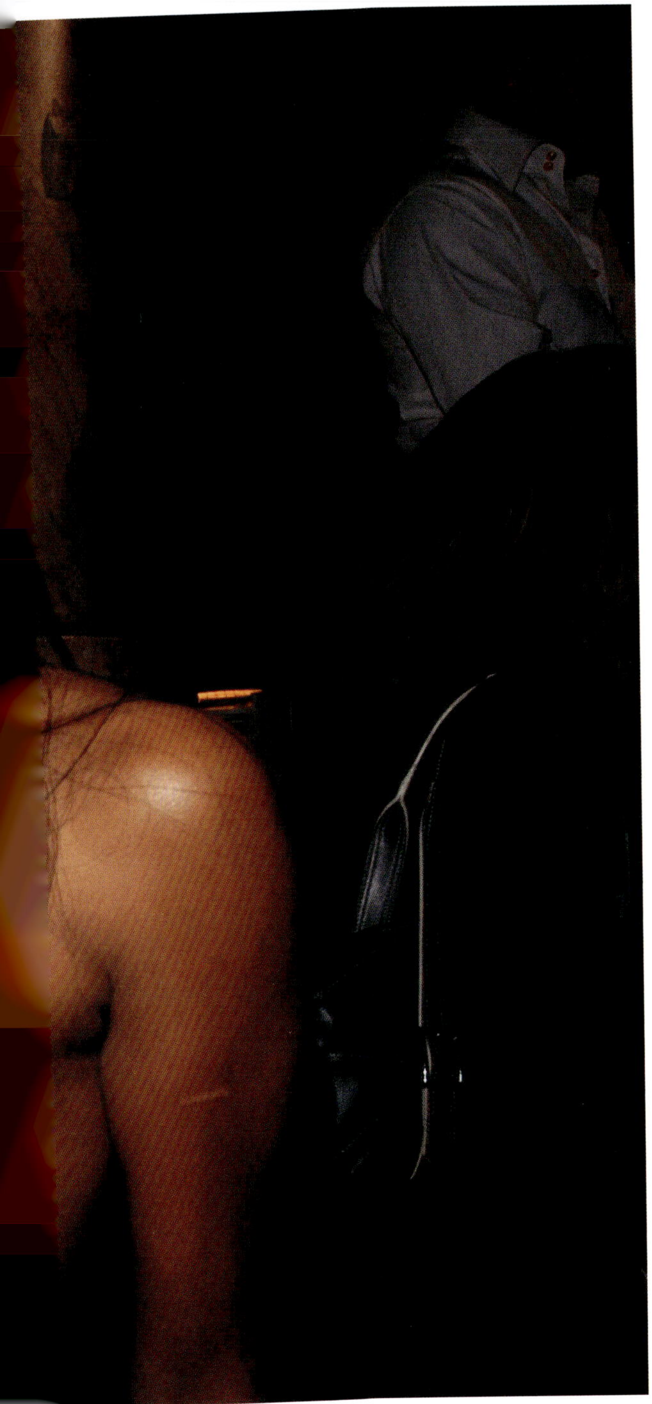

"I'm not a mother yet, but I don't think that there is a right way to do motherhood. You know, I think that you do the best with what you can and if you're showing your children love, then you're doing a great job, and she did."

Kristen Gabrielle Lightfoot,
2025

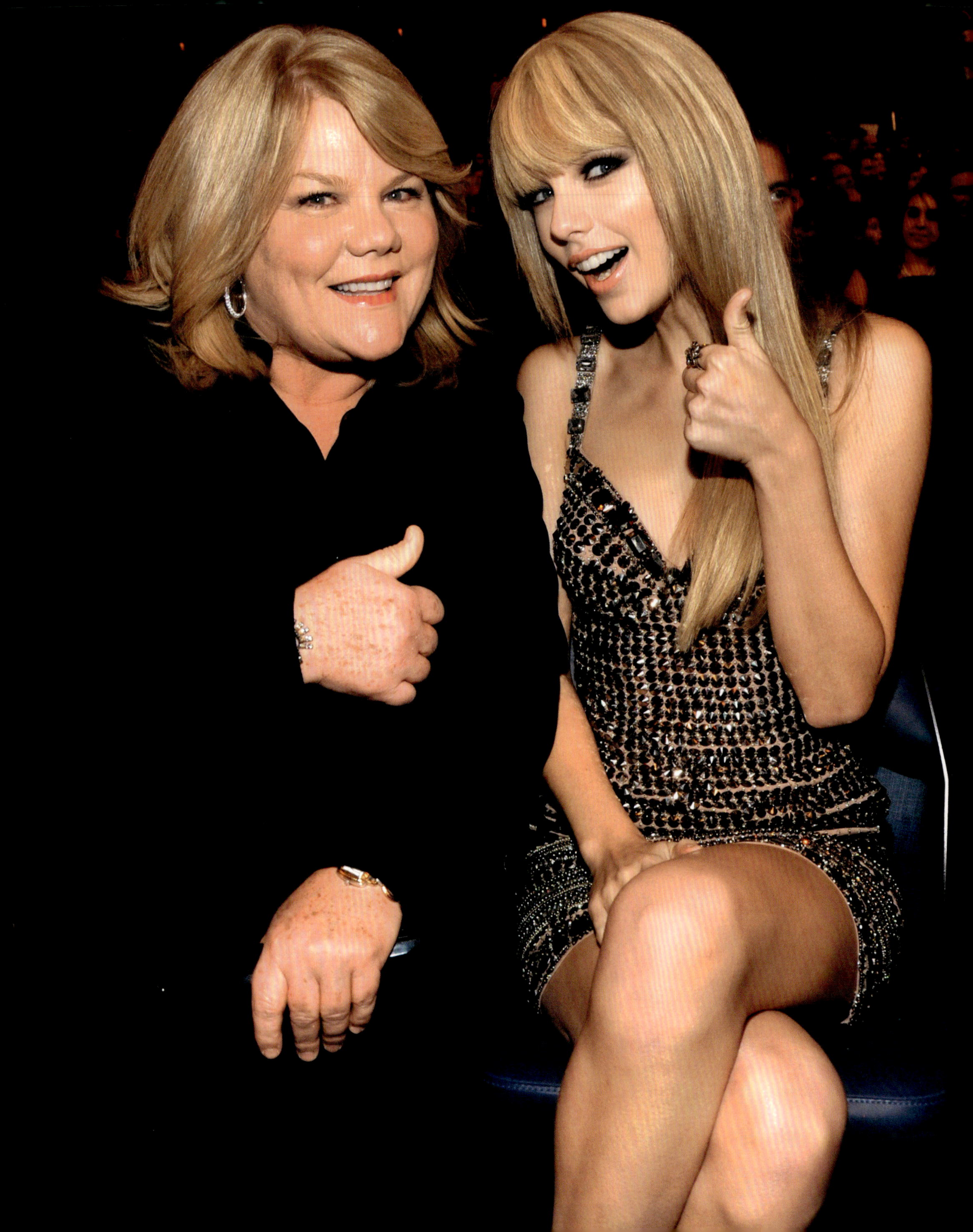

Andrea and **Taylor Swift**

★

Andrea Swift, aka Mama Swift, is known to all Taylor's fans as a wonder woman who has always been at her daughter's side, encouraging her to become the superstar she is today. She has cheered her on in all ways, and was seen enthusiastically wearing signature 'TayTay' friendship bracelets at London's Wembley Stadium in August 2024 during the blockbuster Eras Tour. Although Mama Swift doesn't tend to use her wardrobe to convey messages in the way that Taylor does, she was spotted loyally sporting a jacket embroidered with the slogan 'In my Chief's era' when she watched her daughter's then-boyfriend Travis Kelce play in a Kansas City Chiefs football game at Arrowhead Stadium in November later that year.

She has, however, honed a wardrobe that is as characteristic as Taylor's. For special occasions, she is known for dressing in minimal, relaxed chic, black separates, sometimes accessorised with a quilted Chanel handbag. Back in 2007, when Taylor was just 17 and nominated for the first time as Top New Female Vocalist at the ACM Awards, it was an occasion for Andrea to shine, too; standing proudly with Taylor on the red carpet, she twinkled in cream-satin palazzo pants and a matching chemise under a printed black-chiffon, long-line jacket.

In the video for Taylor's 2008 song 'The Best Day', created for her mother's birthday and re-recorded in 2021 as Taylor's Version, she sings: "I know you are the prettiest lady in the whole wide world". We get glimpses of endearing home movies showing Andrea sporting a fine selection of sunglasses along with a festive holiday jumper – perfect 'mum wear', especially as Taylor grew up in the fairytale world of a Christmas tree farm in Pennsylvania. It's no secret that Andrea is one of the most supportive mothers in the music business, but she has occasionally vocalised uncertainty about her daughter's style picks.

Back in 2009, before she entered her red-lipstick era, make-up artist Gucci Westman tried red lipstick out on Taylor for the first time for an *Allure* magazine cover. Speaking on *The Today Show*, Westman revealed: "So, I remember I really wanted to do a red lip on her because I hadn't seen her in a red lip before. And her mom – if I'm allowed to say this – was like, 'Well, Taylor doesn't wear red'" (Ellis, 2024). Nevertheless, the outcome is now part of pop history and it's a rare moment today that Swift is seen without what has become her signature shade. However, disagreements between the mother and daughter are few and far between. During the 2018 Reputation Stadium Tour, Taylor posted a video on Instagram where she asked Andrea: "Should I wear the Tide Pod dress or the cotton candy dress tonight?", to which Andrea casually replied, while scrolling on her phone, "I think I like the Tide Pod dress". Taylor ends the video with the quip, "So that's how we make our fashion decisions on this tour. There you have it" (@vegasetc2734, 2024).

It offered a small, charming insight: that even at the height of her fame, some of Taylor's best fashion choices are still made the same way they always were – with a quick check-in with mum.

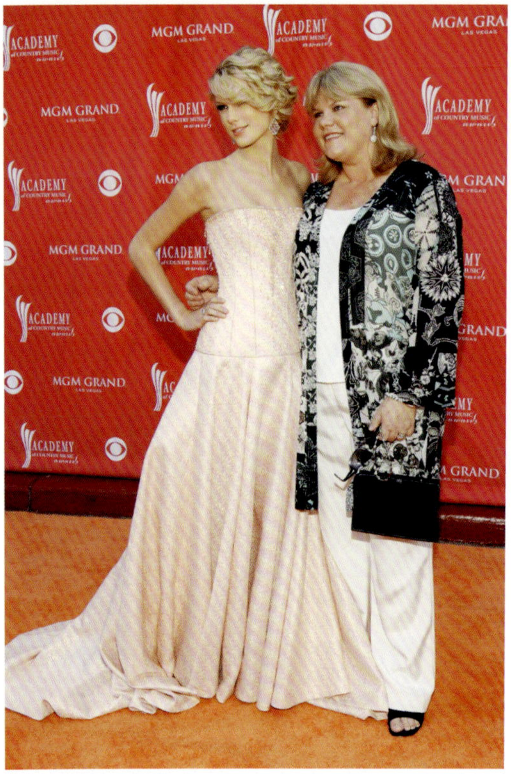

"My mom's my best friend; I'm obsessed with my mom."

Taylor Swift,
Eras Tour, 2023

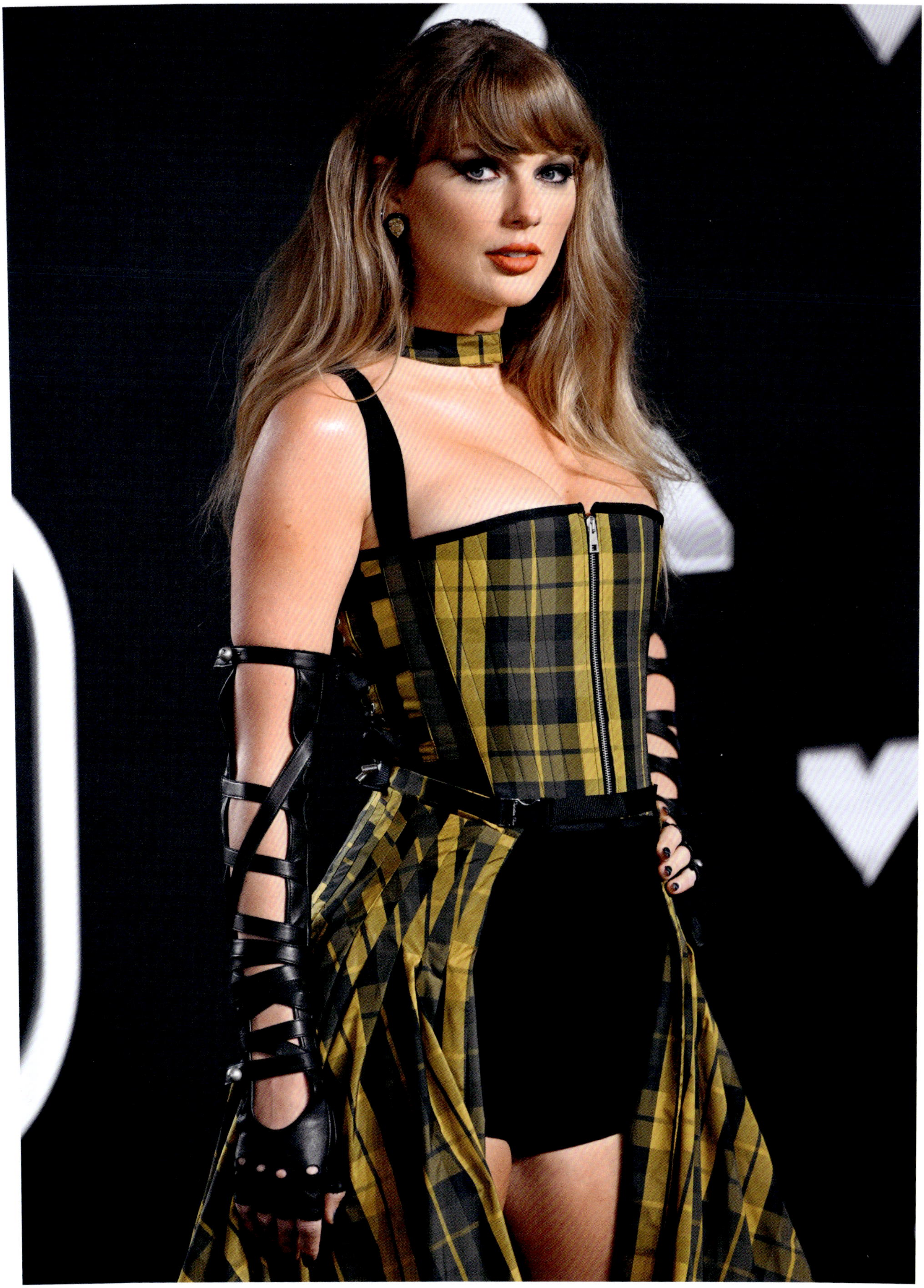

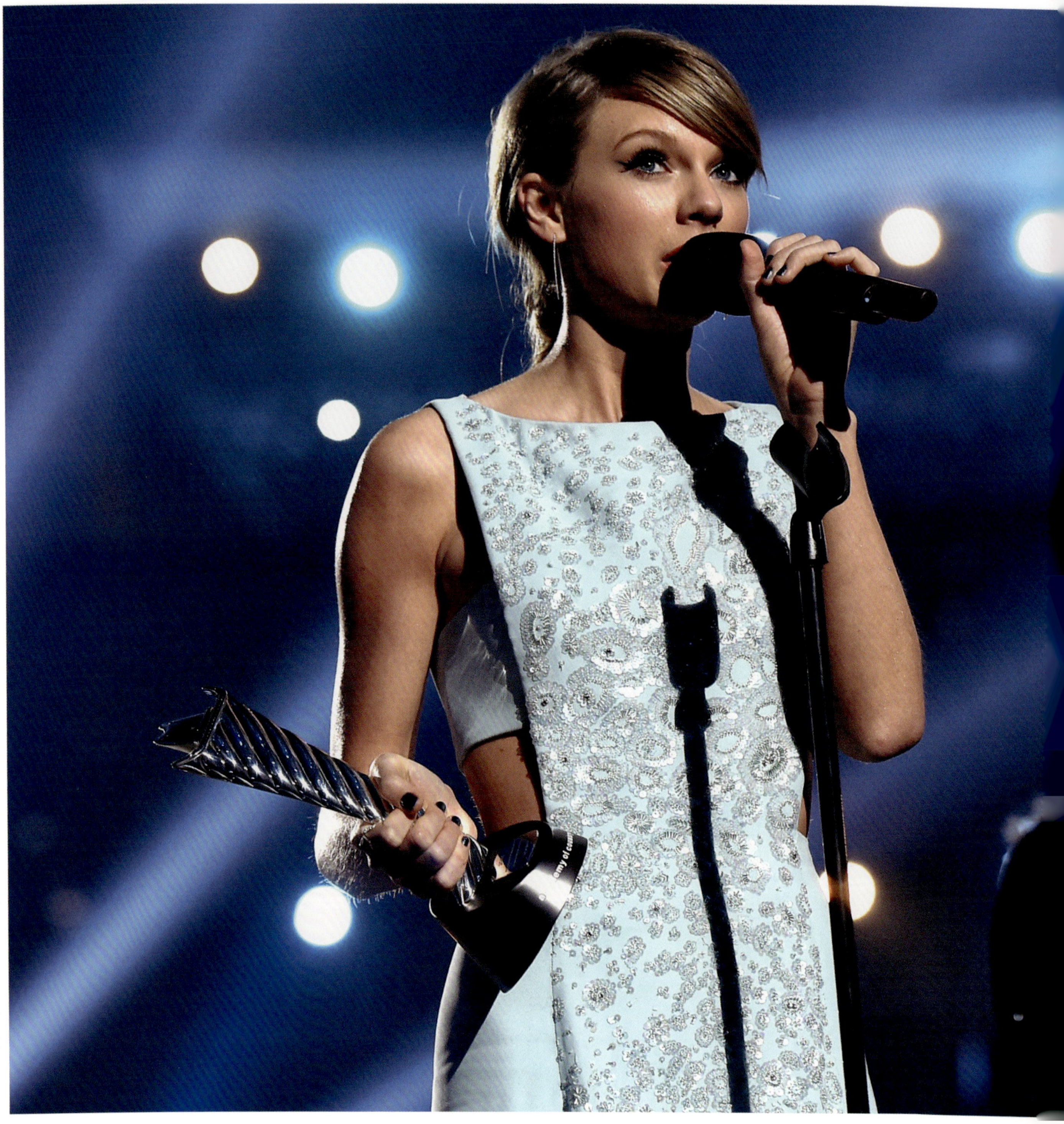

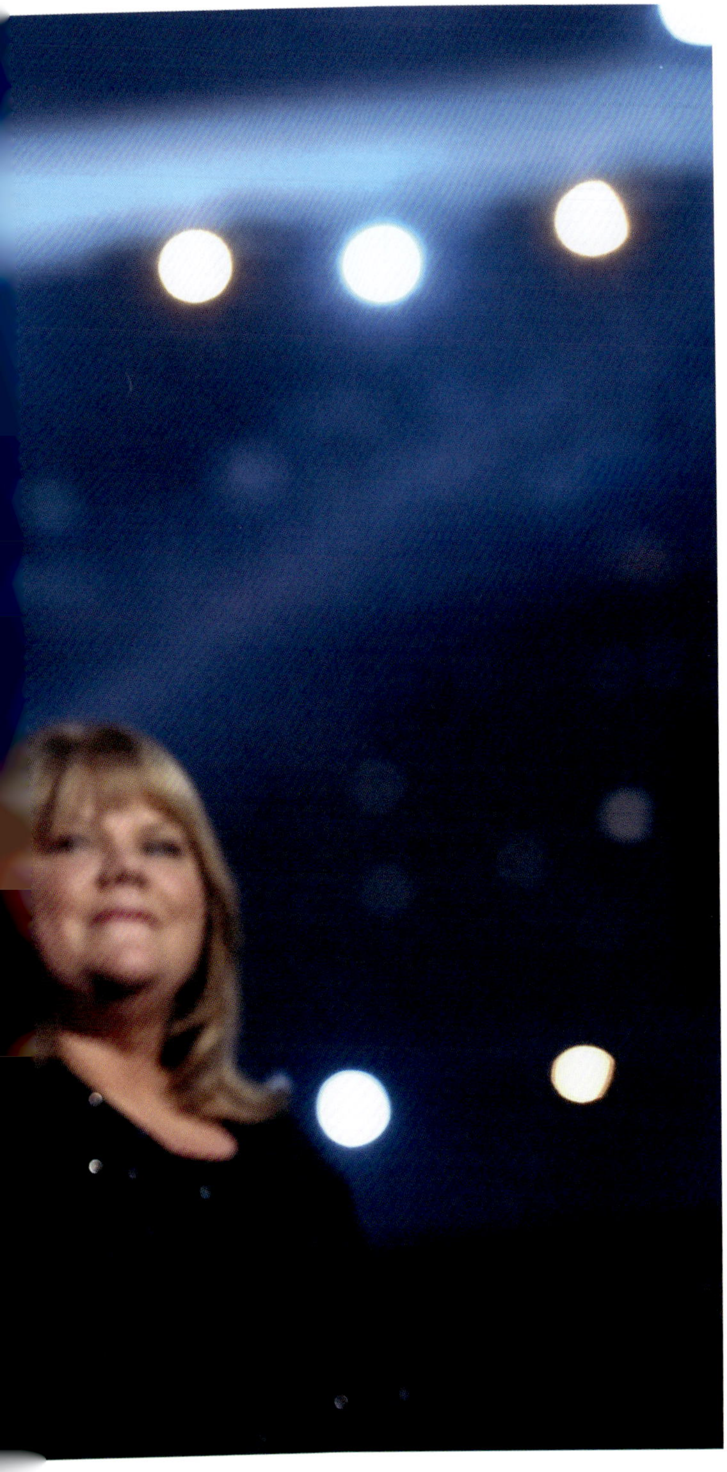

"Everyone loves their mom; everyone's got an important mom. But for me, she's really the guiding force. Almost every decision I make, I talk to her about it first."

Taylor Swift,
Variety, 2020

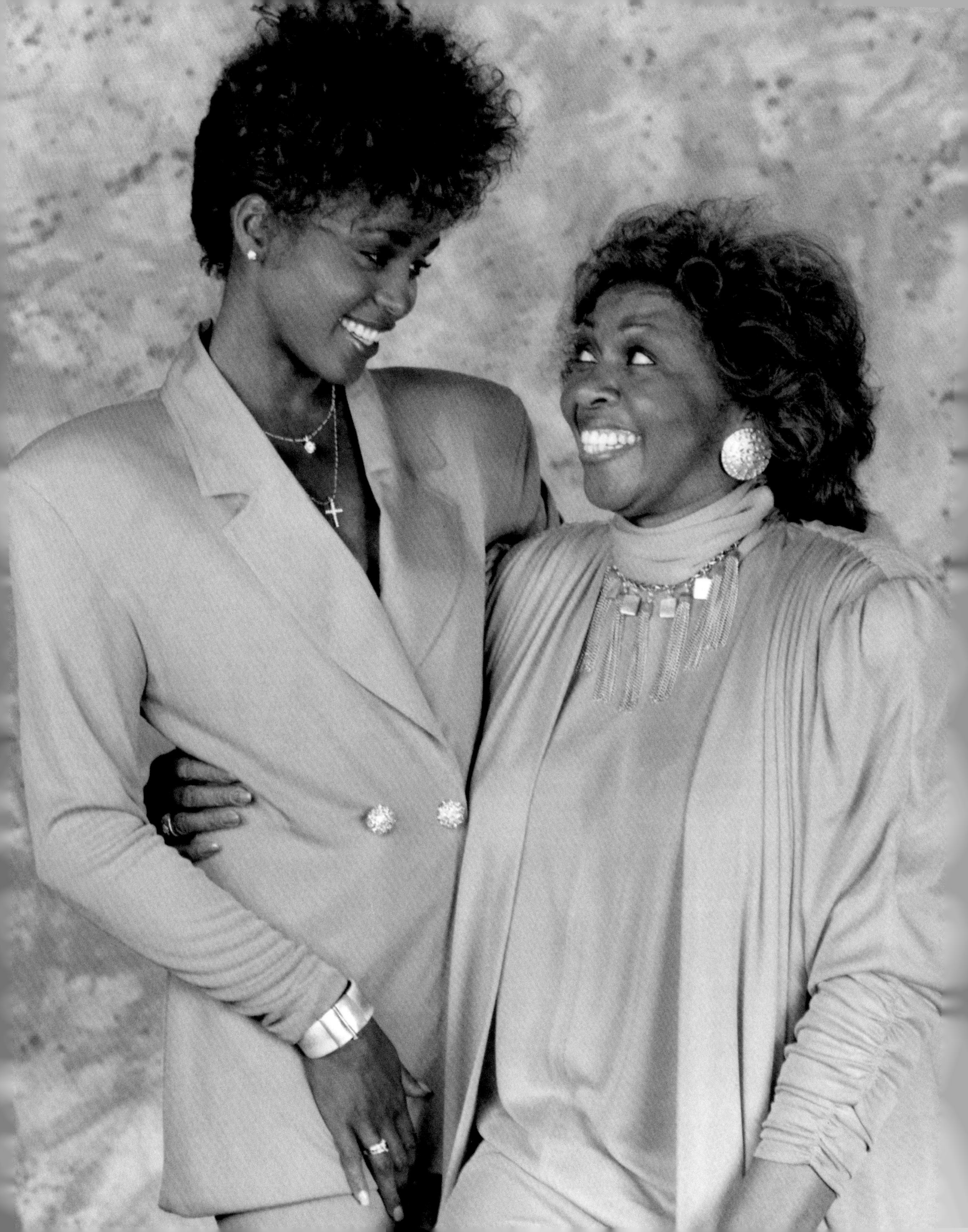

Cissy and **Whitney Houston**

★

The most crushing experience for a mother is to lose a child. Cissy Houston lost not just her daughter, Whitney, but also her granddaughter, Bobbi Kristina, Whitney's daughter. Both died in the same way: lost to addiction. Cissy's life was never the same afterwards, but she survived with dignity and fortitude. Part of her sustenance was music. When Cissy passed away in 2024, she had lived and breathed music for 91 years. A double Grammy Award winner in the Traditional Gospel Album category for *Face to Face* (1996) and *He Leadeth Me* (1997), she had begun her career at the age of five as a member of her family group, The Drinkard Singers, going on to perform with them at Carnegie Hall when she was 18.

Born at the tail end of the Great Depression in 1933, she had witnessed the intricacies of gender, race and class politics that existed in post-war America through to the Civil Rights Act of 1964 and beyond. For most of her lifetime, being talented, succeeding and enjoying the visibility of her talent was a win for a young Black woman. In 1967, Cissy founded an R&B group, The Sweet Inspirations, and signed with Atlantic Records. She and her fellow vocalists, Sylvia Shemwell, Myrna Smith and Estelle Brown's smart matching outfits were part of the quartet's appeal. Cissy wore shift dresses in block colours, go-go boots and Peter Pan collared frocks, with her hair pressed and curled. Cissy and her band hit the charts with their own recordings but also famously sang back-up for legends including Aretha Franklin, Dusty Springfield and Van Morrison. In 1970, Cissy launched a solo career, and her debut UK album cover shows her hair styled naturally, wearing a psychedelic printed tunic over a cream polo neck and accessorised with gold drop earrings. Her clothes traced society's cultural changes, aligned with the natural-hair movement and its message of a confident celebration of Black beauty.

Cissy's daughter, Whitney 'Nippy' Houston, born in 1963, was seven years old when Cissy went solo. By the time Whitney was a teenager, she would be joining her mother on stage at clubs in Manhattan and growing as a singer in the same mould. Whitney's cousin, Dionne Warwick, reflected in a 2022 interview: "Cissy had an incredible voice and that transferred to her little baby, Whitney" (McNeil, 2022). Cissy's parenting technique, however, was never insistent and she candidly admitted after Whitney's death in 2012: "A mother I don't think ever expects for their daughter to be as successful as my daughter has been...You don't think about it actually. There are some stage mothers as they're called; I'm just not one of those. I just wanted the best for all my children" (The Whitney Houston Platinum Club, 2024).

Whitney would go on to sell over 220 million records in her lifetime and dazzle the world with her powerful and soul-stirring voice. She always looked fantastic and although often seen in her signature sequins, ruffles and sparkles, she was just as at home in jeans and blazer or a white tracksuit and Nike trainers, as evidenced at the 1991 Superbowl when she sang to an estimated global audience of 750 million listeners. Despite all the glitz and glamour, she stated that she'd "never found anything more fulfilling than being a mother" (Norment, 1995). Whitney gave birth to Bobbi Kristina in March 1993, and less than a year later took her new baby to the American Music Awards, where she won no less than eight trophies and wore a white outfit that matched with her daughter's.

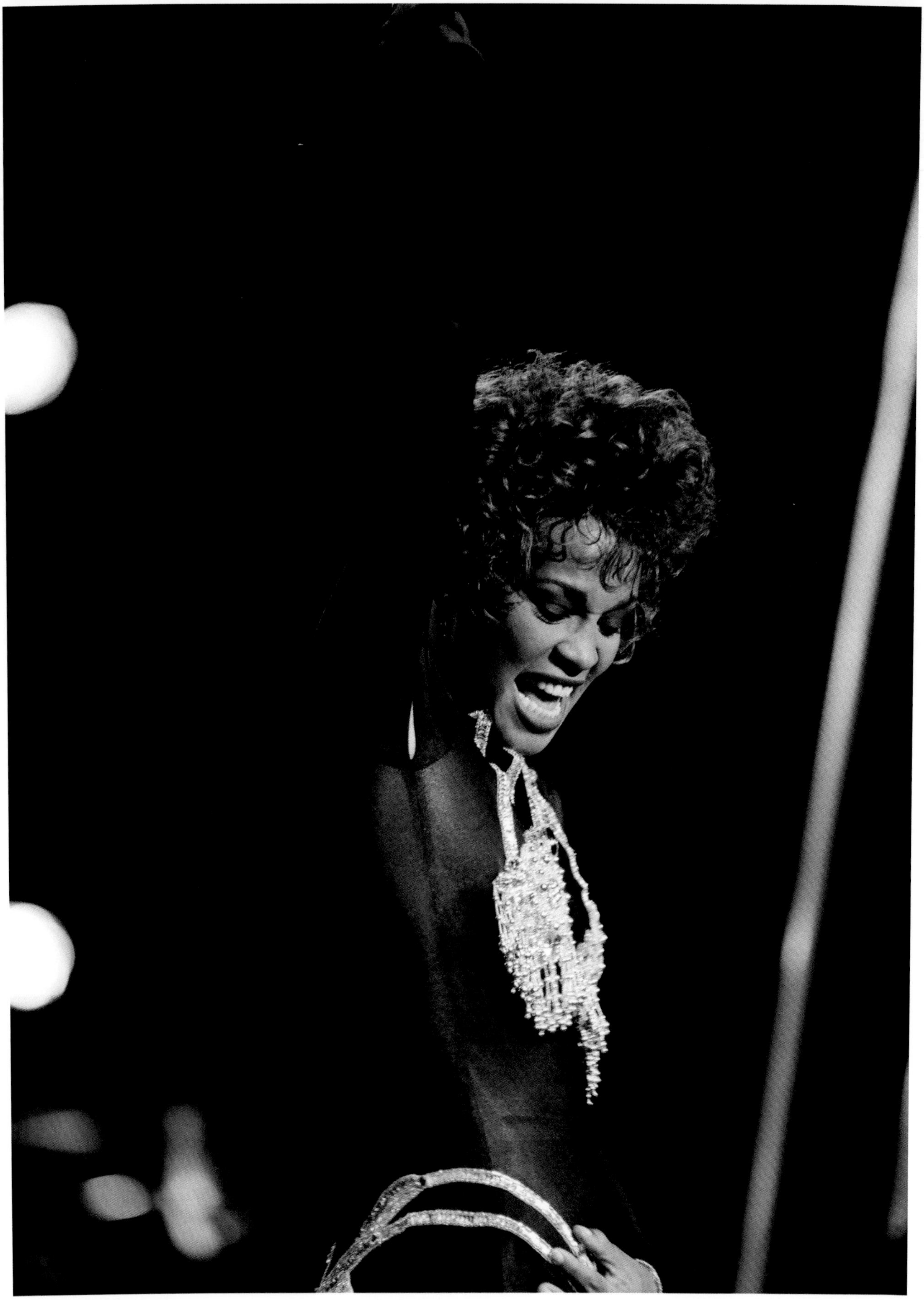

"It's all coming from inside me. What I feel is what I sing."

Cissy Houston,
The New York Times,
1983

As Whitney spun brighter and faster, Cissy would often be seen with her daughter, offering her unconditional support. Cissy had lived her own life in the spotlight and understood how to dress up and show up. She might not have been a pushy stage mother, but she was always stage smart. At award ceremonies and red carpets, Cissy showed her love and encouragement in many different ways, often wearing an outfit of a tonally similar shade that harmonised with her daughter's clothes. In 1986 on the MTV holiday show in New York, mother and daughter can be seen wearing complementary black-and-white outfits. Then, in 1990 they attended the 21st annual Songwriters Hall of Fame Induction Ceremony, harmonising their outfits once again in gold and bronze. Five years later, in 1995, the pair colour-coordinated in green frocks at Soul Train's 25th Anniversary awards ceremony.

A year after Whitney's passing, interviewed by Whoopi Goldberg and Sherri Shepherd, Cissy mused: "Nippy was the sweetest girl you've ever seen. She would talk to people on the bus...she was friendly and beautiful" (*The View*, 2013).

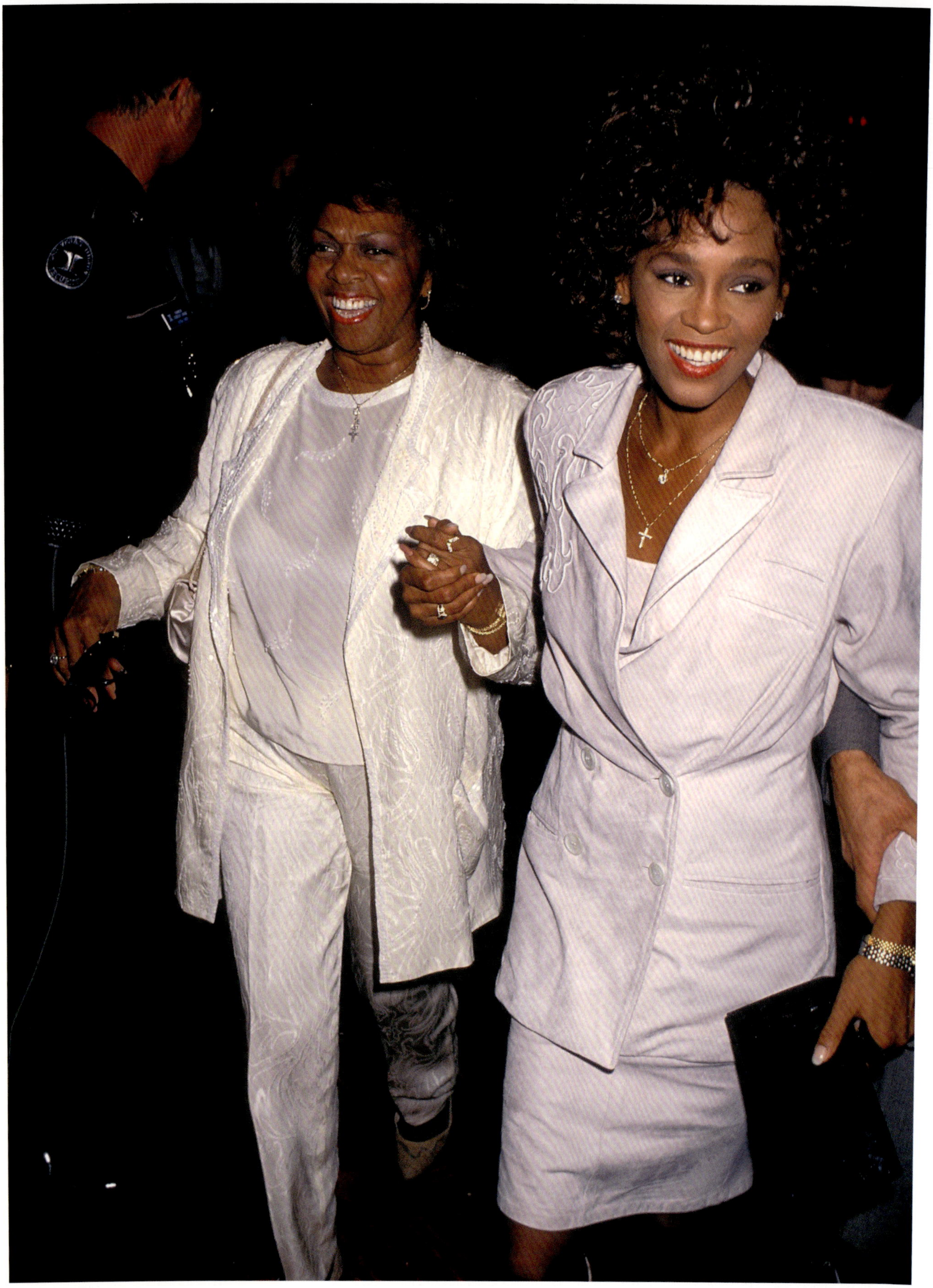

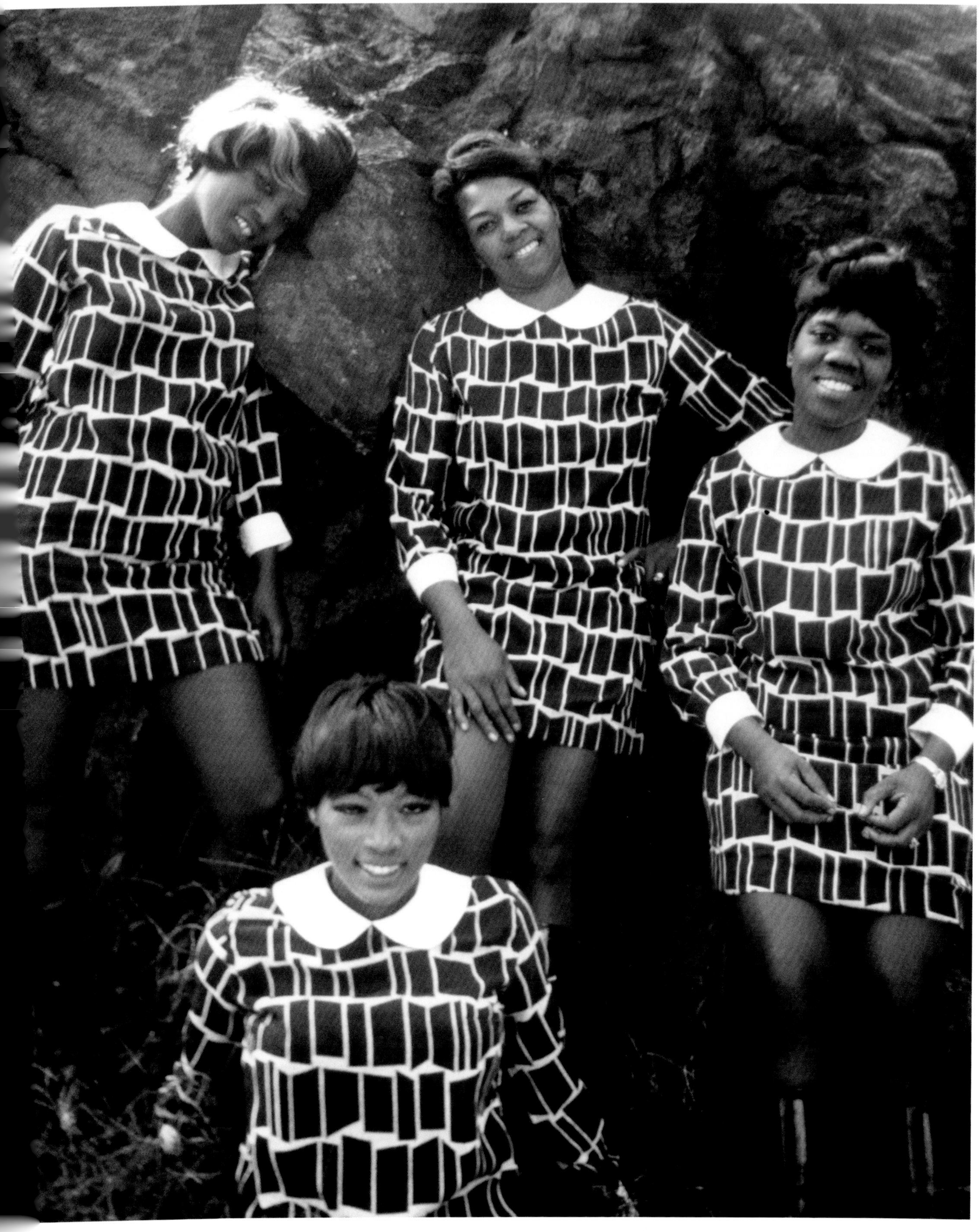

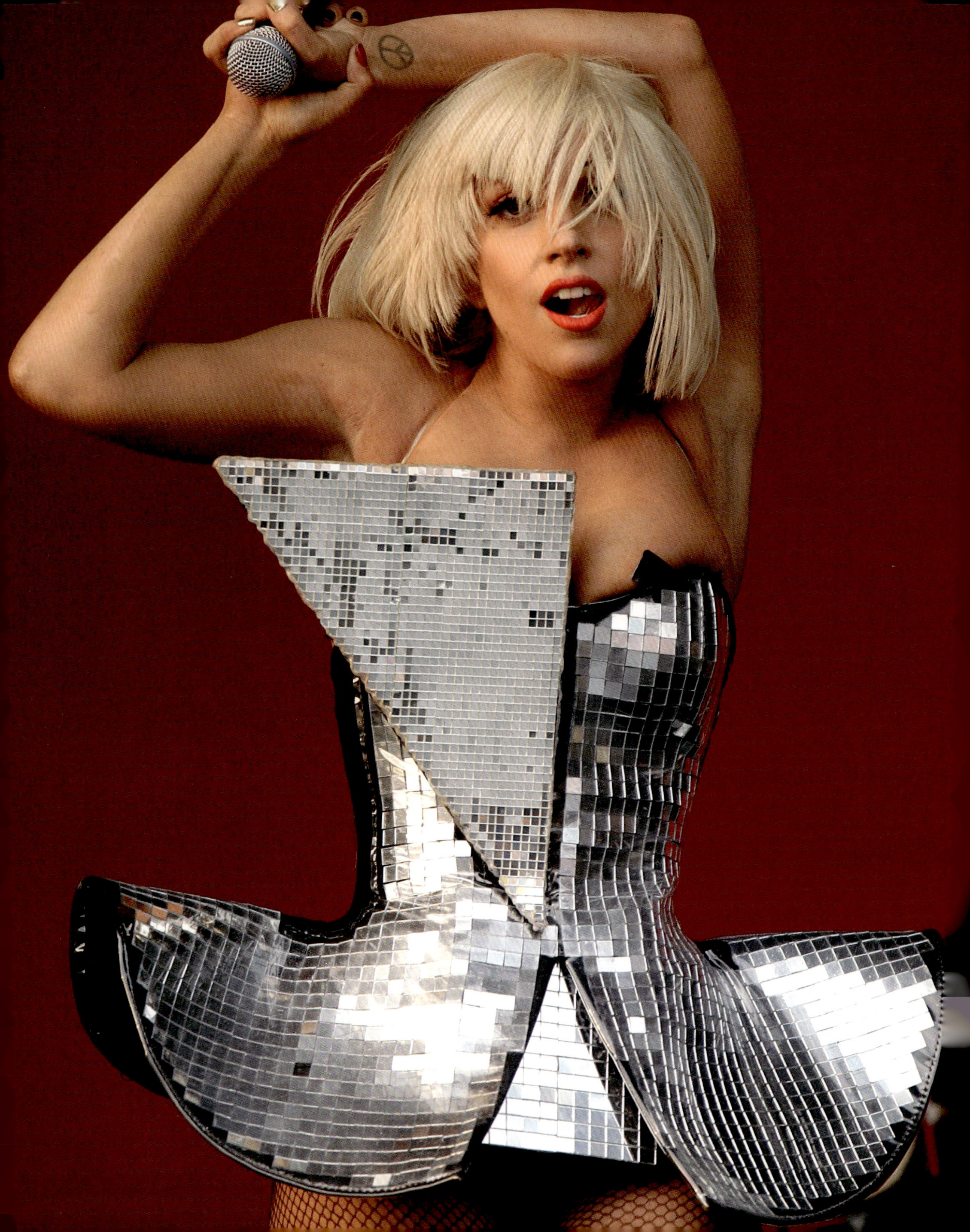

Cynthia Germanotta and **Lady Gaga**

★

When Lady Gaga was cast as Patrizia Reggiani in Ridley Scott's 2021 film *House of Gucci*, she told the film's costume designer, Janty Yates, that she wanted to look like her mother, Cynthia Germanotta. Yates revealed:

> "I was kind of nervous about talking to LG about this because I know her taste is wide and huge, but on the very first Zoom we did with Ridley...she said she wanted to dress like her mother. It was wonderful because, obviously, her mother didn't wear meat dresses, and her mother is 100 percent Italian" (Fraser, 2021).

Yates described Germanotta as a mother who "carried a certain flair...a woman who'd wear something, just to shop" (Nofi, 2021). This is translated in the film, which is set throughout the 1970s and early '80s, with a series of outfits that are powerful, glitzy and glossy. Lady Gaga's own dress sense has equal flair, and her wardrobe doesn't just speak of fashion but identity and values. At the 2009 MTV Video Music Awards, Lady Gaga performed her track 'Paparazzi' in a jewel-encrusted white bra, briefs and towering boots, every inch the architect of her own image. As the song built, fake blood began to spill, shifting the mood from glossy pop spectacle to something far more pointed. It was a cool, deliberate evaluation of fame as a blood sport, with Gaga cast not as victim but as provocateur in control of the narrative. A year later in September 2010 she wore her infamous 'meat dress' made out of steak. It was a creation by Franc Fernandez, sharply styled by Nicola Formichetti and again transformed fashion into fierce commentary, with Gaga revealing to Ellen DeGeneres that it was her rebuke of the US military's 'Don't Ask, Don't Tell' policy (Cochrane, 2010). Gaga's principles are rooted in the ideals her mother, Cynthia Germanotta, has instilled in her and, in turn, the ideals instilled in Cynthia by Gaga's grandmother, Ronnie. Germaotta explains how Ronnie "taught me that a parent should foster their children's creativity and individuality and encourage their passions, not just their successes. And she taught me to be tough, that struggle was just a part of lif" (Germanotta, 2018).

Today, Germanotta is a youthful, chic silver-blonde, often to be seen wearing Born This Way Foundation merchandise emblazoned with its kindness-giving slogans. "The Foundation started way back when my daughter was young. She was uniquely different when she was growing up and that wasn't always appreciated by her peers", explained Germanotta in a 2024 interview with *The Project*.

With Germanotta's support, Lady Gaga's career has helped to reconstruct the rules of belonging; she is 'Mother Monster' shining a light on her own outsider status – and the 'Little Monster' fans who walk their own line, too – making it not just okay to be different, but joyous. Germanotta is co-founder of the Born This Way Foundation, along with her daughter, which began in 2012 with a mission to "empower and inspire young people to build a kinder, braver world that supports their mental health", and is work that was born out of something personal. According to Gaga:

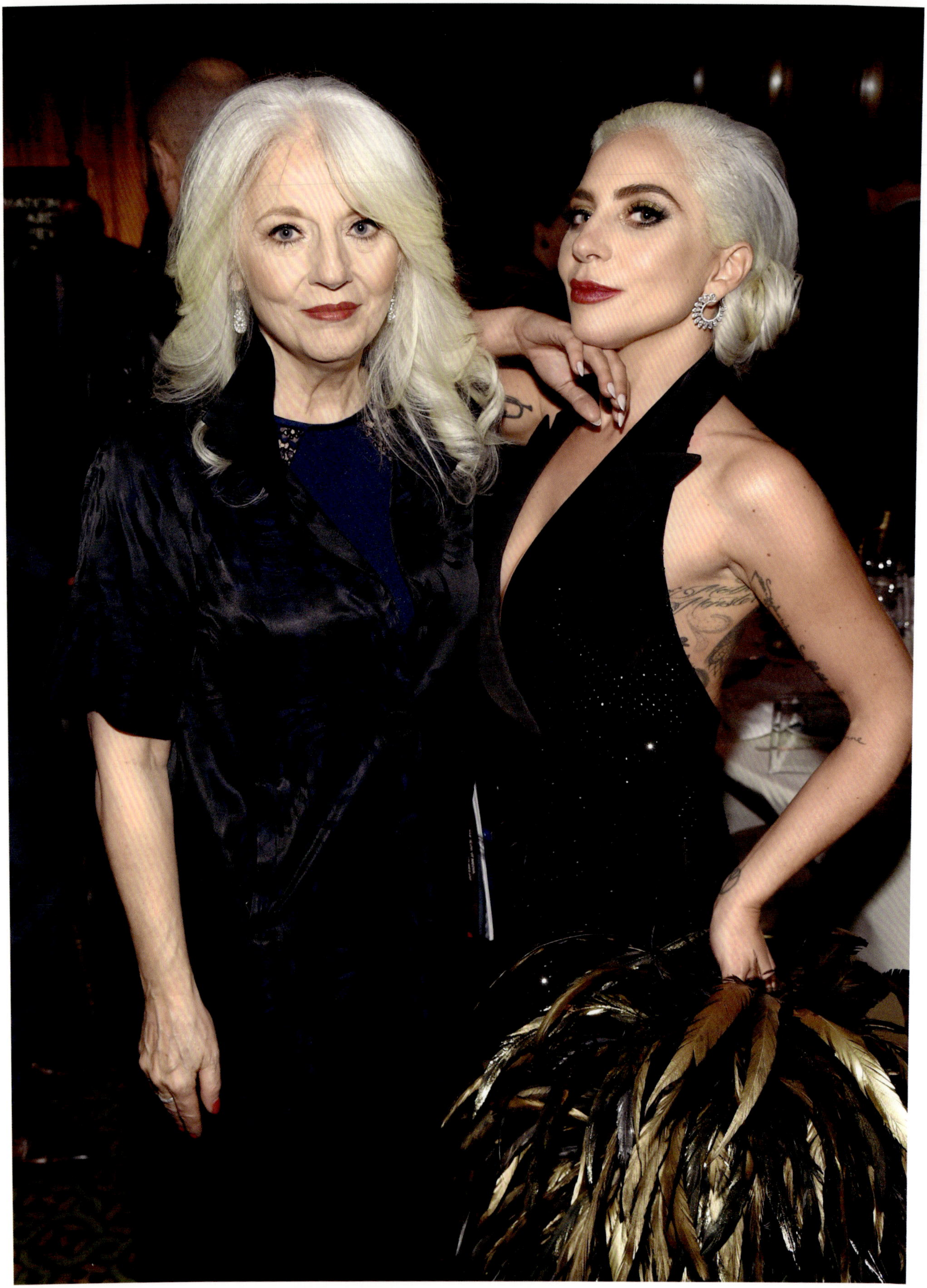

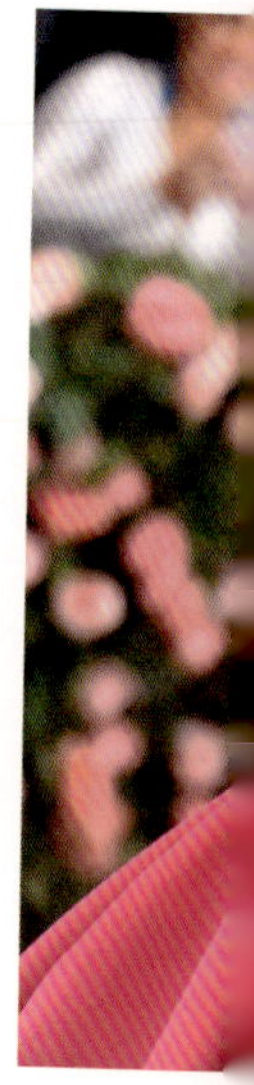

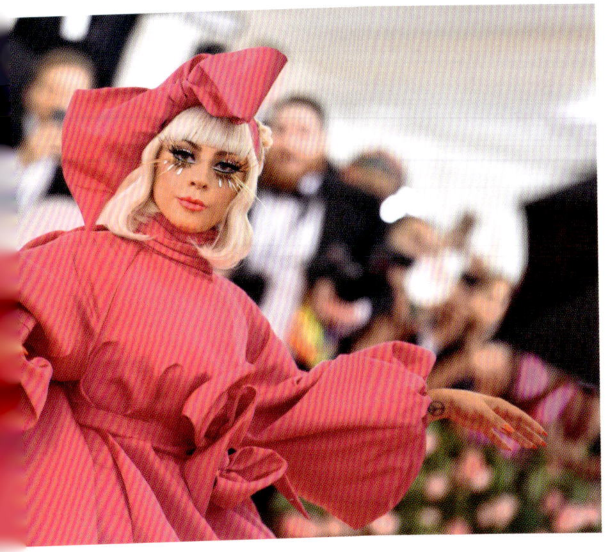

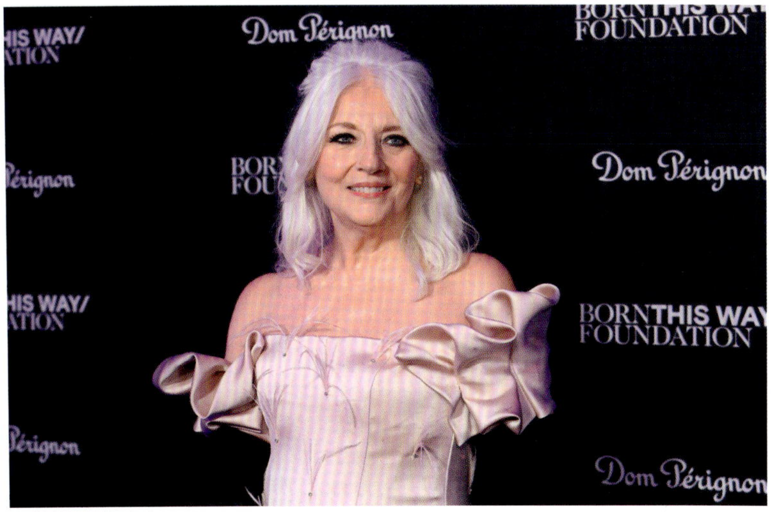

"We've always had a particular way of living and tackling life, my Italian immigrant family. Thank you for believing in me, Mom... Thank you for believing in me through thick and thin so I can fulfil my dreams. I always do what I do to make my family proud."

Lady Gaga,
National Board of Review Awards, 2019

> "I would say that my mental health always played a really powerful role in making music, because it was always when I was at my lowest that I wanted to sing. And that meant that I was feeling that way pretty often, because I sang a lot. I would write music and sing from a place of feeling lost, and it would help me ground myself and find my own voice to tell my story" (Caligor, 2025).

Her struggle was something Cynthia, aka 'Grandmother Monster', had difficulty coming to terms with, too: "As mums, we might not get it perfect every time. We have to work with the information and skills we have, shaped by our own experiences, just like everyone else. But we try, and with time and a little luck, we keep getting better. We teach our children and, in turn, they teach us" (Germanotta, 2018).

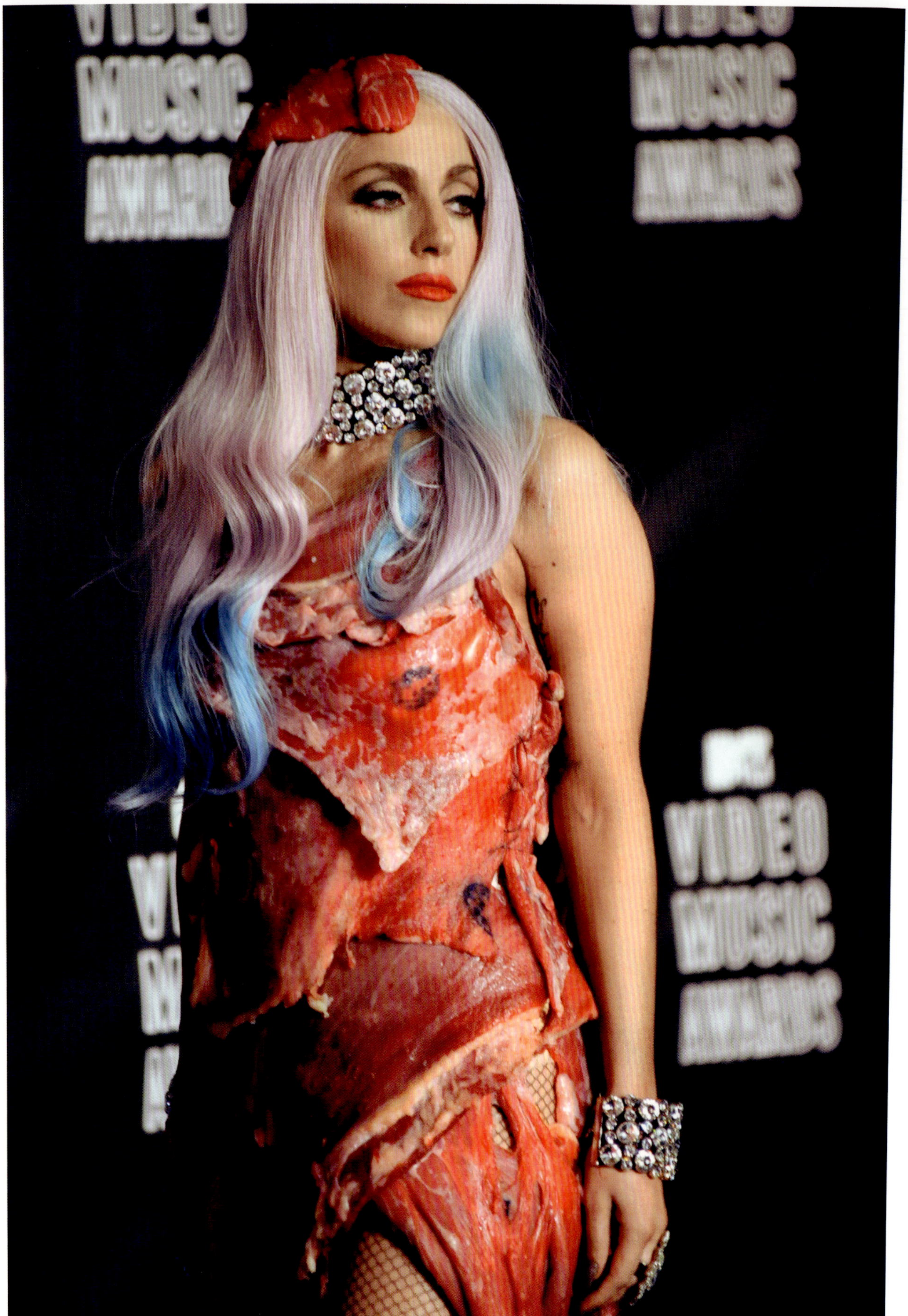
VIDEO
MUSIC
AWARDS

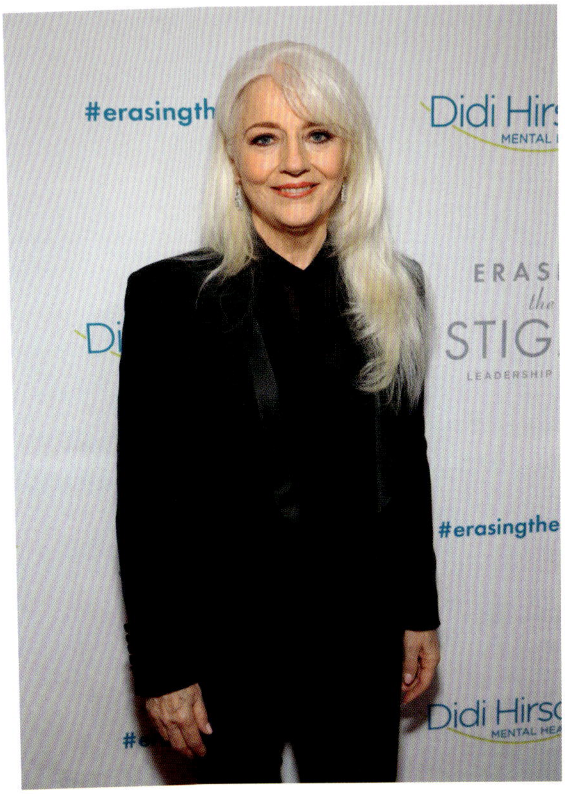

"I remember watching my mother put her makeup on every morning, basking in the glow of her power to put on her bravest face as the hard-working woman she was. I then began to experiment with makeup as a way to make my dreams of being as strong as my mother become true. It was then that I invented Lady Gaga. I found the superhero within me by looking in the mirror and seeing who I wanted to be."

Lady Gaga,
Instagram, 2019

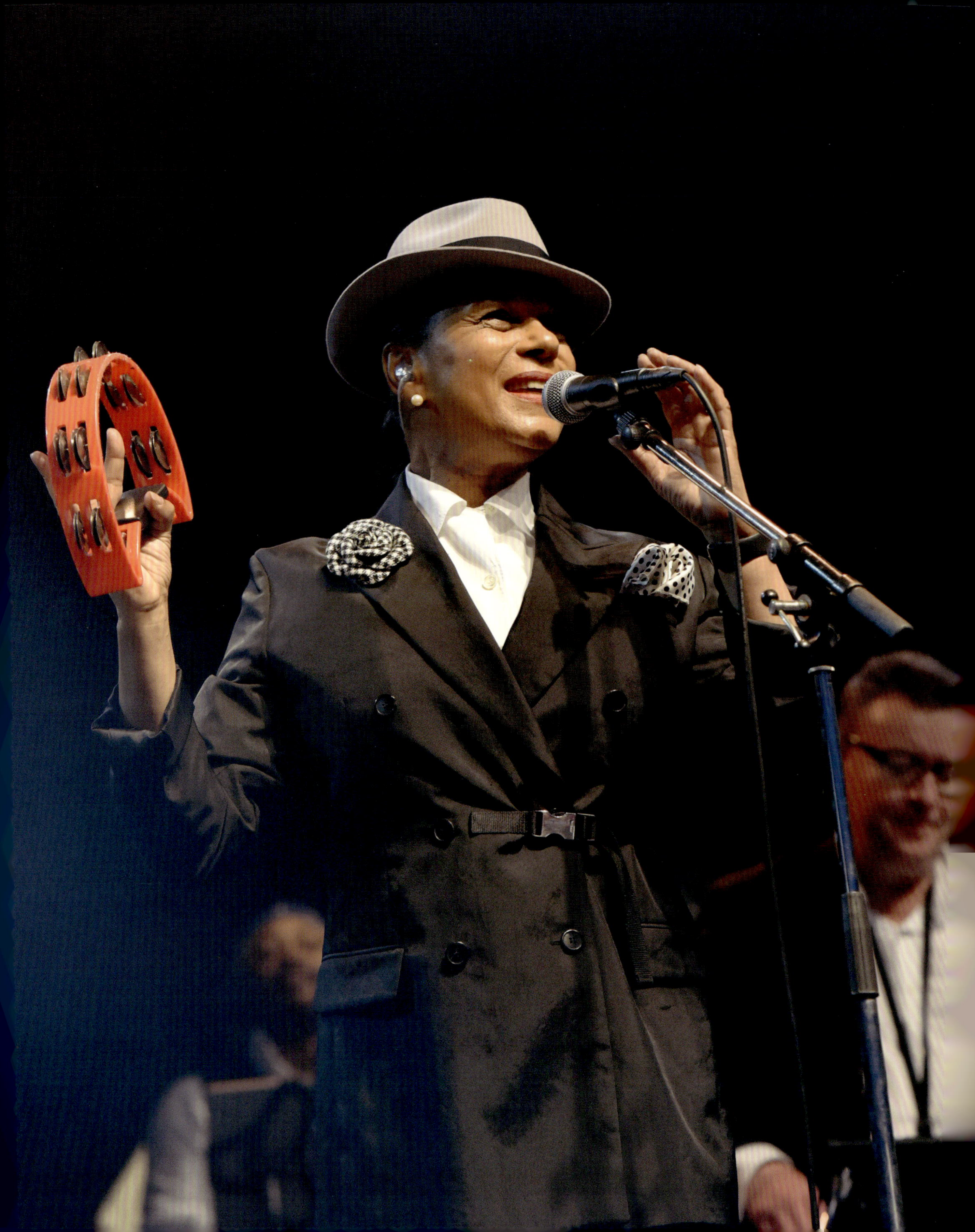

Ivy Vickers, **Eileen** Magus and **Pauline Black**

★

Two-tone music was a UK phenomenon born out of multi-cultural Britain at the end of the 1970s. Embracing both Black and white heritage, it fused punk, ska and reggae beats, and became the soundtrack for young people who wanted to rock against racism and look sharp while dancing. The legacy of two-tone was kickstarted in the Midlands city of Coventry and would go on to have a global influence, inspiring like-minded fashion aficionados such as the Japanese streetwear label Neighborhood, and multi-award-winning artists such as Amy Winehouse and Gwen Stefani.

One of two-tone's most successful bands at the time was The Selecter. Its lead singer, Pauline Black, was a fitting ambassador for the movement, as she personified the racial struggles of 1970s and '80s Britain. Born in 1953 to an Anglo-Jewish teenage mother and Nigerian prince father, she was adopted soon after by a white couple, Ivy and Arthur Vickers. It would be over 10 years before Britain's Race Relations Act of 1965 made it illegal to discriminate based on colour and ethnicity, and so Pauline grew up at a time when casual bigotry was widespread. The only Black girl in her house, in her street and in her school, she certainly felt the effects. She spent her childhood being told she wasn't Black, but 'coloured', which is why, she said, she changed her adopted surname to Black, as a way to recognise her birth heritage, "so people had no choice but to call me Black".

When Ivy passed away in 1988, Pauline kept some of her mother's clothes, including many of her 'Sunday best' white gloves: 'They smell of her even now, all these years later. She had lots of pairs, always white, sometimes lace or crocheted, and wore them when she went visiting", reflects Black. She also saved Ivy's favourite 1960s powder-blue suit: "It has an A-line skirt, and the jacket is decorated with a dainty little rosette, made of the same fabric. She always wore it with a pretty hat, like a headband that fit close to her head."

Post-war Britain was a time when elegant femininity was chic, and accessories were key. After the liberating experience for many women of working on farms and in ammunition factories wearing practical trousers, gender was once again clearly defined by clothing. Although, in many ways, the world at this time was beginning to change, for many working-class women respectability and conformity was expected. Pauline's mother, Ivy Vickers, wore a wardrobe that toed this line. A photograph of Ivy taken in the mid-1920s, when she would have been the same age as Pauline when she hit the big time in The Selecter, sees her wearing a long, dark frock, pale stockings and T-bar shoes.

But when Pauline was 26, she adopted the polar opposite wardrobe to Ivy and instead embraced what would become a life-long uniform of androgynous suiting topped with a fedora – clothes that were her armour and a symbol of belonging to the chosen musical family she became part of.

> "I met the punk icon Poly Styrene, who was the lead singer of X-Ray Spex, and she was a great inspiration to me. She wore a German tin helmet and crimplene dresses, like the ones my mother had worn, but she looked great. She owned it. I thought she was out of the box, fashion-wise, so why couldn't I do the same? I

> became who I wanted to be – a version of Bob Marley when he was in his 'Rude Boy' phase. My style grew organically with the band. I tried to look good on a budget. My mum thought stage wear was what Shirley Bassey wore and couldn't understand how my clothes computed. It was the overt sexuality of women's clothes I didn't get and as a Black woman I had two models of how to look: the Rasta thing, which was not for me, and the other end of the spectrum – the fire of Tina Turner."

Subcultural style is often defined in opposition to what has come before, and Pauline's iconic appearance evolved in rebellion to what she saw around her while growing up.

> "I just knew I never wanted to look like my mother. I wanted to become myself. But as a child the clothes I wore were defined by my class and circumstance. My outfits these days are usually monochrome as a matter of course; I call myself colour dyslexic, but back then I had a neighbour who would knit and give us things to wear. I remember a pale-lemon cardigan distinctly, that I loathed. When I got a Saturday job it meant a little bit of freedom. I would buy Biba brown eyeshadow – I couldn't afford anything else, and it was the only shade that suited my skin. I also saved and bought American tan tights for school that were the nearest tone to my brown legs. I'd browse Kensington Market, but it was all very expensive. When I moved to Coventry to study, I was very much into an earthy hippy vibe and I wore an old beaver-lamb-fur coat of my mums that had once been her best 'coming out every Christmas' coat, but I wore it with cheesecloth shirts, platform shoes and an afro. My heroes included Angela Davies. I didn't want to look like a Romford housewife."

Pauline and Ivy's relationship was complicated. "When my mother passed away, I found a couple of carrier bags of all the clippings she collected about the band. I didn't realise how proud she was of me at the time", admits Black. "I refused to go looking for my birth mother while Ivy was alive because I thought it would upset her terribly and it felt disrespectful. She was relatively easy to find though and I discovered quite quickly that someone called Eileen Magnus, who lived in Australia and had emigrated years earlier, was my biological parent." Pauline would go on to have a happy relationship with Magnus for 24 years and accepting her into her life led to a new and different kind of fulfilment.

> "I was 42 when we met, and we were poles apart. She sounded like Dame Edna Everage and wore what all Aussie women of a certain age wore: baggy pants and tops. But when she came to see me in concert for the first time, she scrubbed up well and wore a beautiful black-velvet tunic-and-trouser suit and looked amazing. She wasn't the kind of woman who went and had her hair done, but she had been stylish in her time. She was very pretty. She had something."

Today, at the age of 71, Pauline Black's identity is all her own and fuses hints of the counter-cultural, post-punk music she became famous for. There's something slightly retro about the modernist silhouette with a slight echo of the Sixties that she prefers. It's often to be reliably found in a well-cut Peter Pan-collared Prada jacket; her favourites include one made of leather and another version in white with black piping, worn in 2022 to Buckingham Palace to collect an OBE from King Charles. Ironically, this style is smart enough that it is something her adopted mother, Ivy, would have liked and likely worn, too, on special occasions.

Top: Pauline as a baby with her adopted mother, Ivy Vickers, and family, 1955.
Bottom: Pauline's birth mother, Eileen Magus, circa 1956–57.

"My mother shaped my identity when I was younger, but I had to find myself."

Pauline Black,
2024

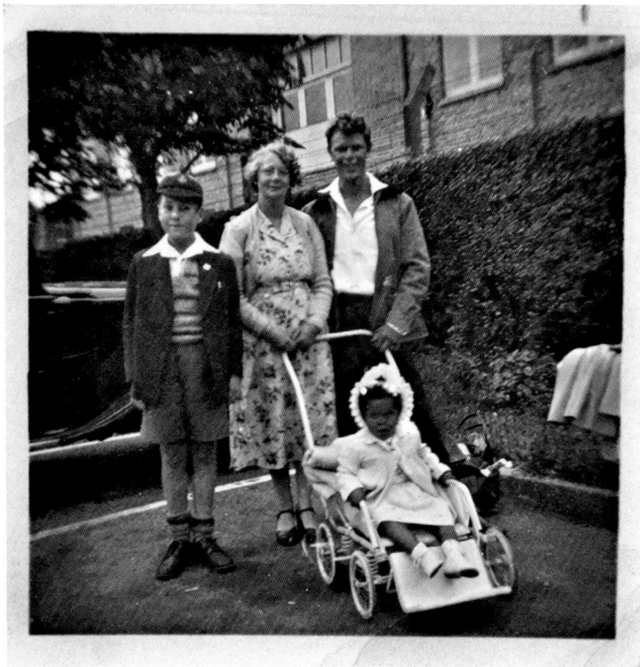

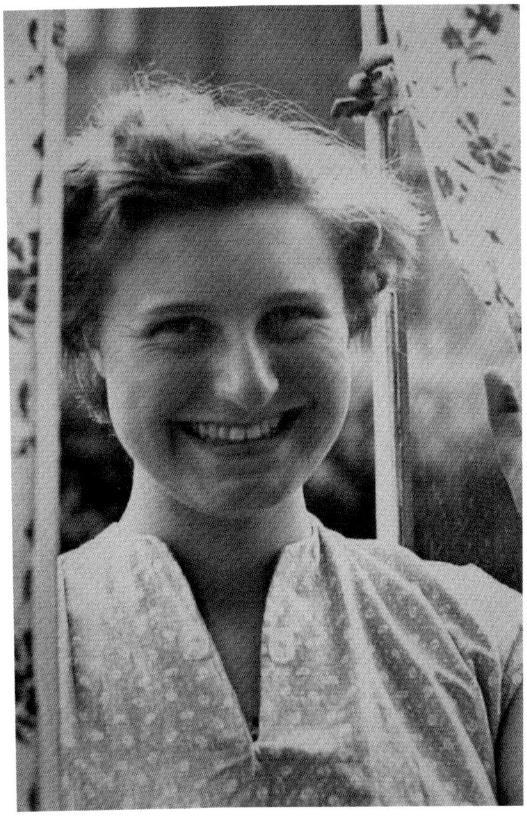

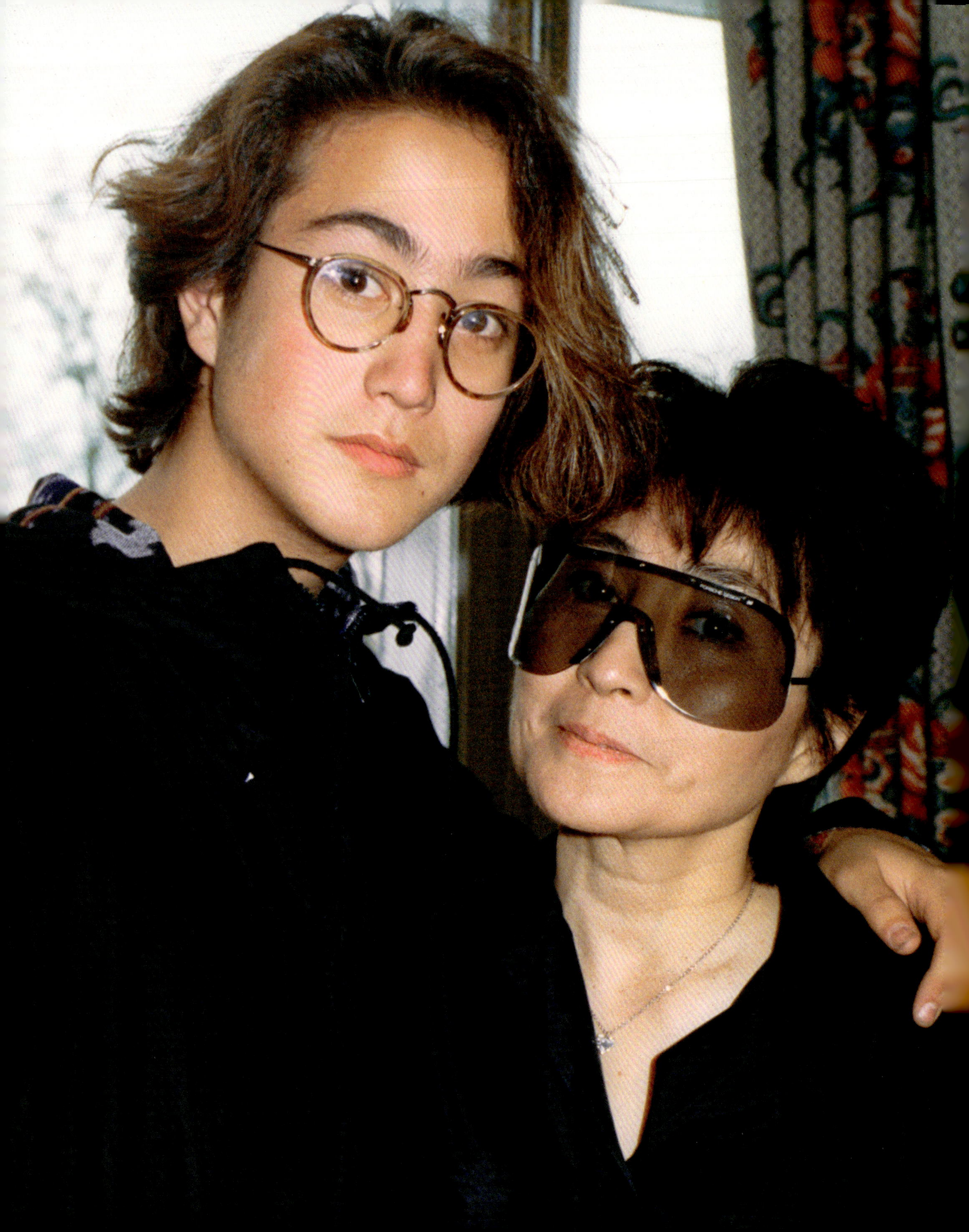

Yoko Ono **and** Sean **Lennon**

★

Artist Yoko Ono was never sure about the idea of motherhood, revealing to the journalist Caroline Coon in an unpublished interview:

> "I've never really understood the need women feel to have children – I'm not the type of woman who would feel unfulfilled by not having a baby. I was thirty when I had to make the decision to have a baby or not. People were saying to me, 'You're thirty, and after that it will be very difficult to have a child'. And I believed what they said. But at the same time, I instinctively felt that I should wait. I was sort of talked into having a child by the image society has of what a woman's goals should be" (Coon, 1974).

Nevertheless, she's compellingly qualified as one. Ono gave birth to a daughter, Kyoko, in 1963 with her second husband, artist Anthony Cox, and later welcomed a son, Sean, in 1975 with John Lennon. Her journey in motherhood wasn't without grief, however. Following a bitter legal battle for custody of Kyoko after divorcing Cox, her daughter disappeared with her ex-husband. Ono didn't see Kyoko again for 23 years: "Losing my daughter was a very serious pain. There was always some empty space in my heart" (Runtagh, 2025).

She took some time to explore motherhood at the 2004 Liverpool Biennial with an installation called *My Mummy Was Beautiful*. The installation evolved into an invitation to visitors at the Tate Liverpool gallery to write down their memories of their mother for a tribute wall of innermost thoughts that was set up. It became an ongoing art project and has since travelled the world. Yoko told *The Guardian* at the time: "This work was initially about my mother. But when I decided to do it in Liverpool, suddenly I remembered how John loved his mother, and it choked me up. So this one in Liverpool will be my tribute to John" (Ward, 2004). It was accompanied by blown-up images of a woman's breast and vulva, which were presented on banners around Liverpool, balancing the emotive release of Yoko's art with unapologetic imagery of the female body.

Both Ono's intrepid artwork and fearless fashion sense speak volumes about the inimitable spirit she is. She married John Lennon wearing a white mini

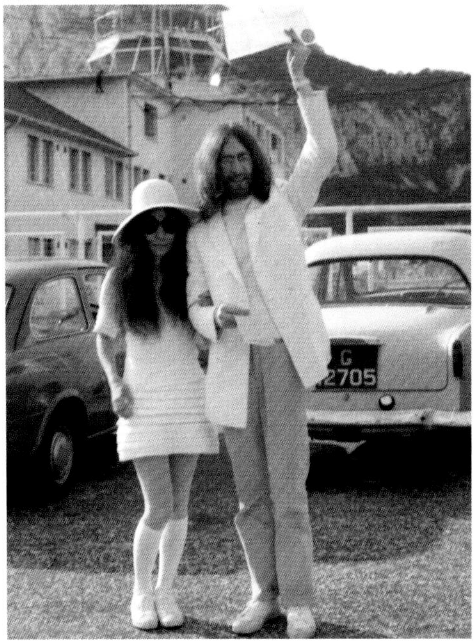

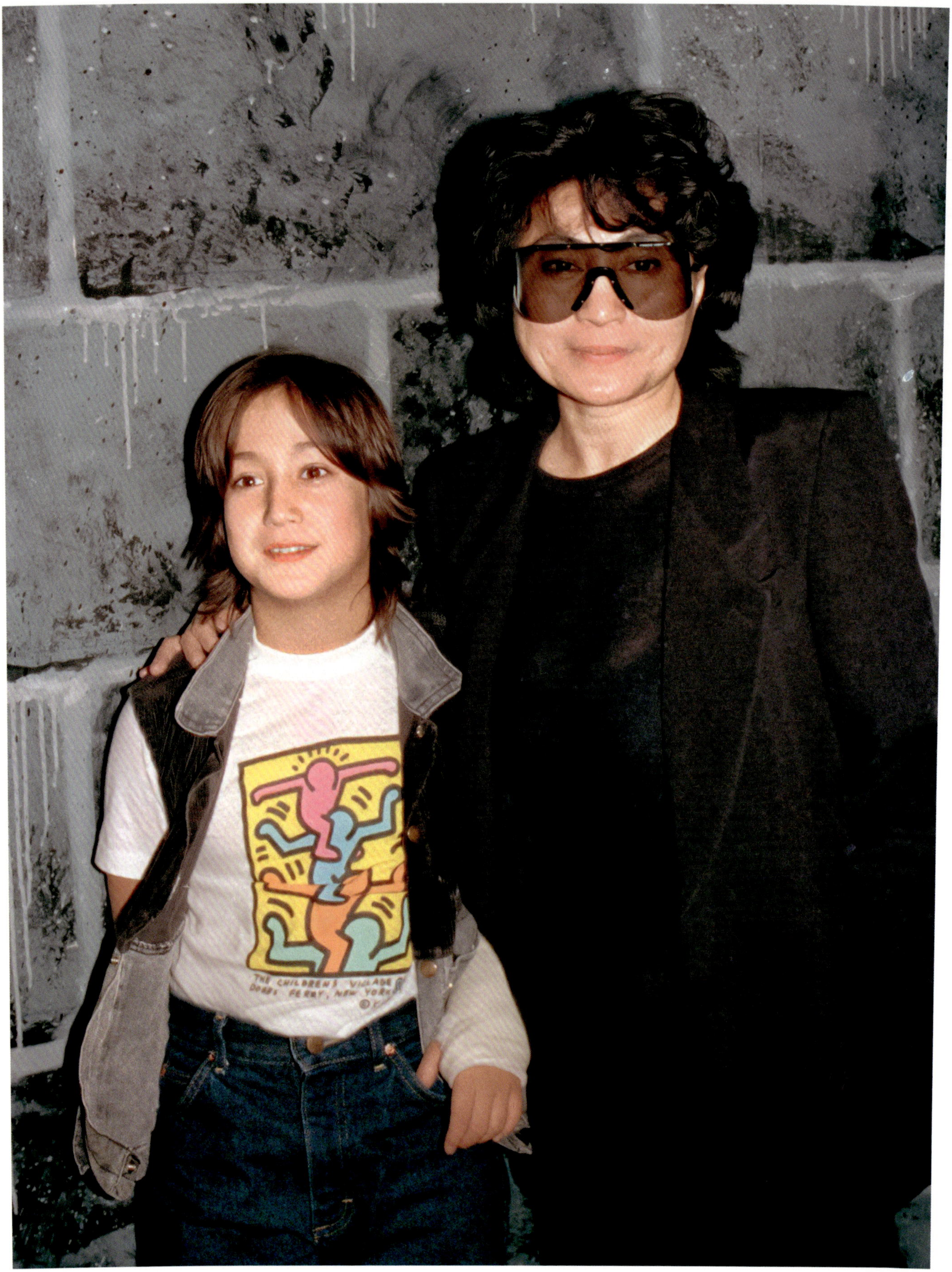
THE CHILDREN'S VILLAGE
DOBBS FERRY, NEW YORK

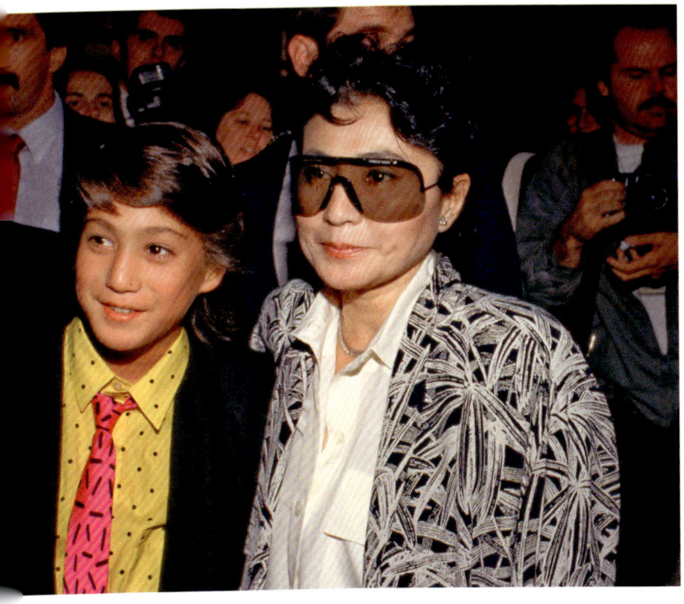

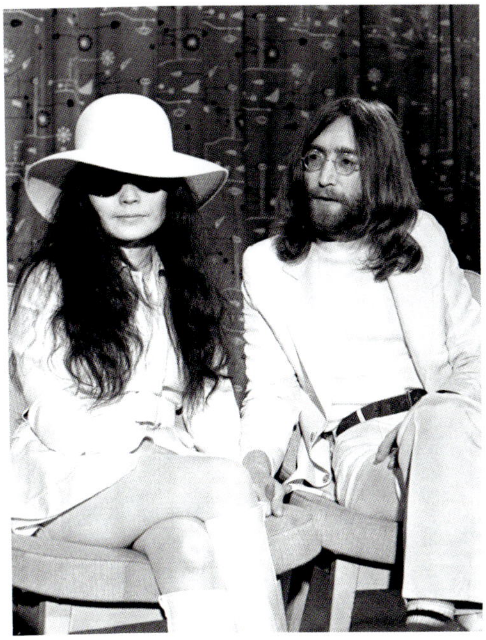

skirt, knee-high socks, a gigantic white hat, canvas trainers and big, round sunglasses that almost eclipsed her face. Clothes are as much a part of her DNA as art, and at times they intertwine. When one of her earliest performance works, *Cut Piece*, was presented at the Sogetsu Kaikan Hall in Tokyo in 1964, she wore her smartest suit and summoned the audience to snip it off her body. Later, in her 80s, Ono dressed with loose androgyny: she wore simple tailored men's clothes paired with a bowler hat, or a leather biker jacket with sheer shirts. Her art is multi-faceted and conceptual at its heart, and her approach to parenting is a bohemian revelation. Speaking of Yoko's mothering style, Sean describes how:

> "She had a very sort of postmodern, post-hippie, post-feminist way of thinking. It was very liberal, and she always treated me like an individual. She never really told me not to do anything, except get a Mohawk or a tattoo. So, there were very few boundaries. She believed that kids are individuals and shouldn't be treated like a subservient class" (Mooallem, 2017).

Yoko's experience of her own mother was less laissez-faire; in a March 2015 interview, she reflected: "I'd say that my mother was an inspiration to me – but, in a way, she was also someone I felt rebellious towards. It was two sides of a coin, I think" (*Classic Pop*, 2015). Despite this, when asked who she would most like to say sorry to, she said: "To my mother. I didn't say I loved her as much as I should have" (Greenstreet, 2014).

"Happy Mother's
Day, Mothers!
I understand the
injustice you
suffered;
I understand your
loneliness. Because
now I have been
a mother, myself.
Without you, we
would not be.
Without you and
me, the human
race would not
be here now."

Yoko Ono,
2012

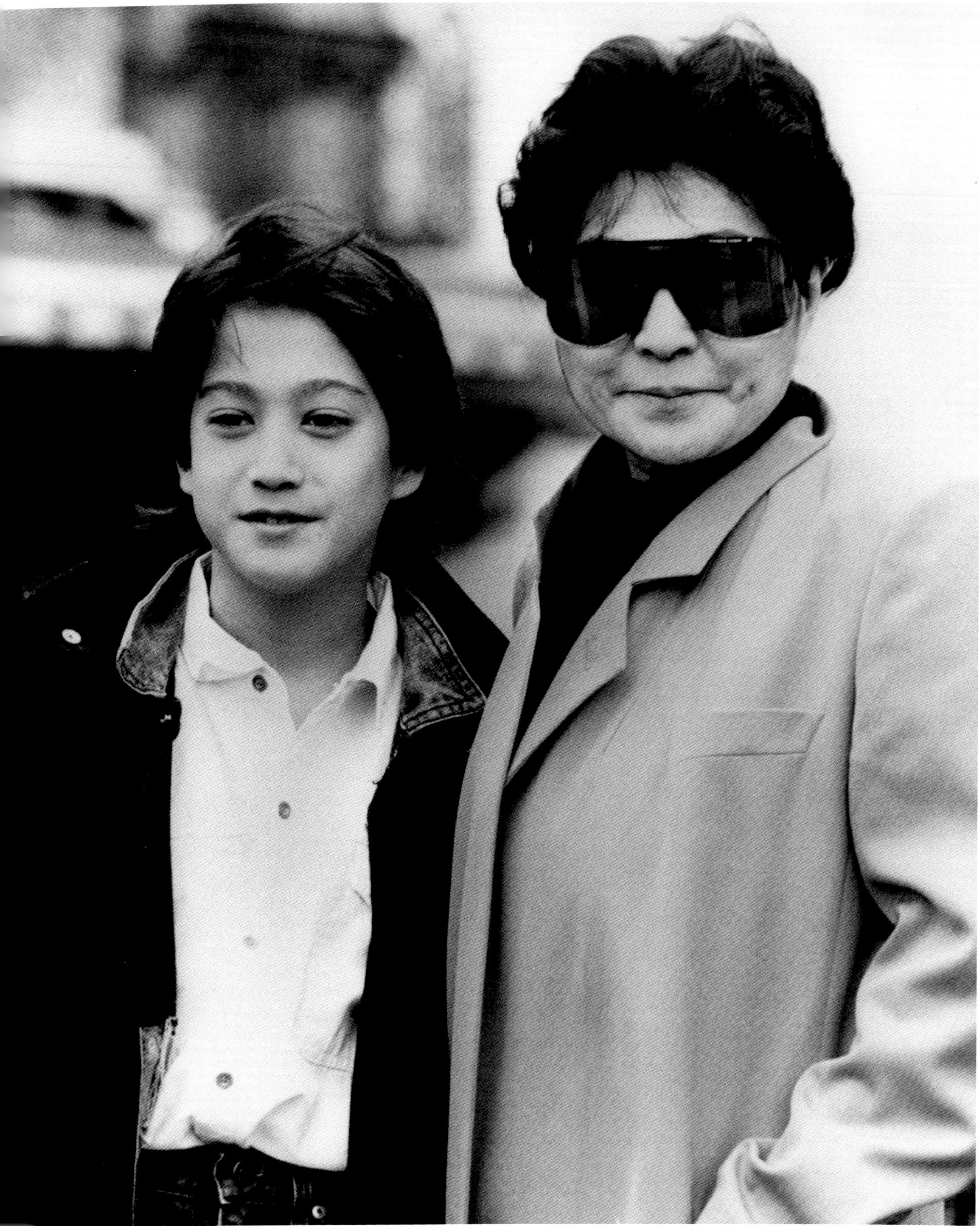

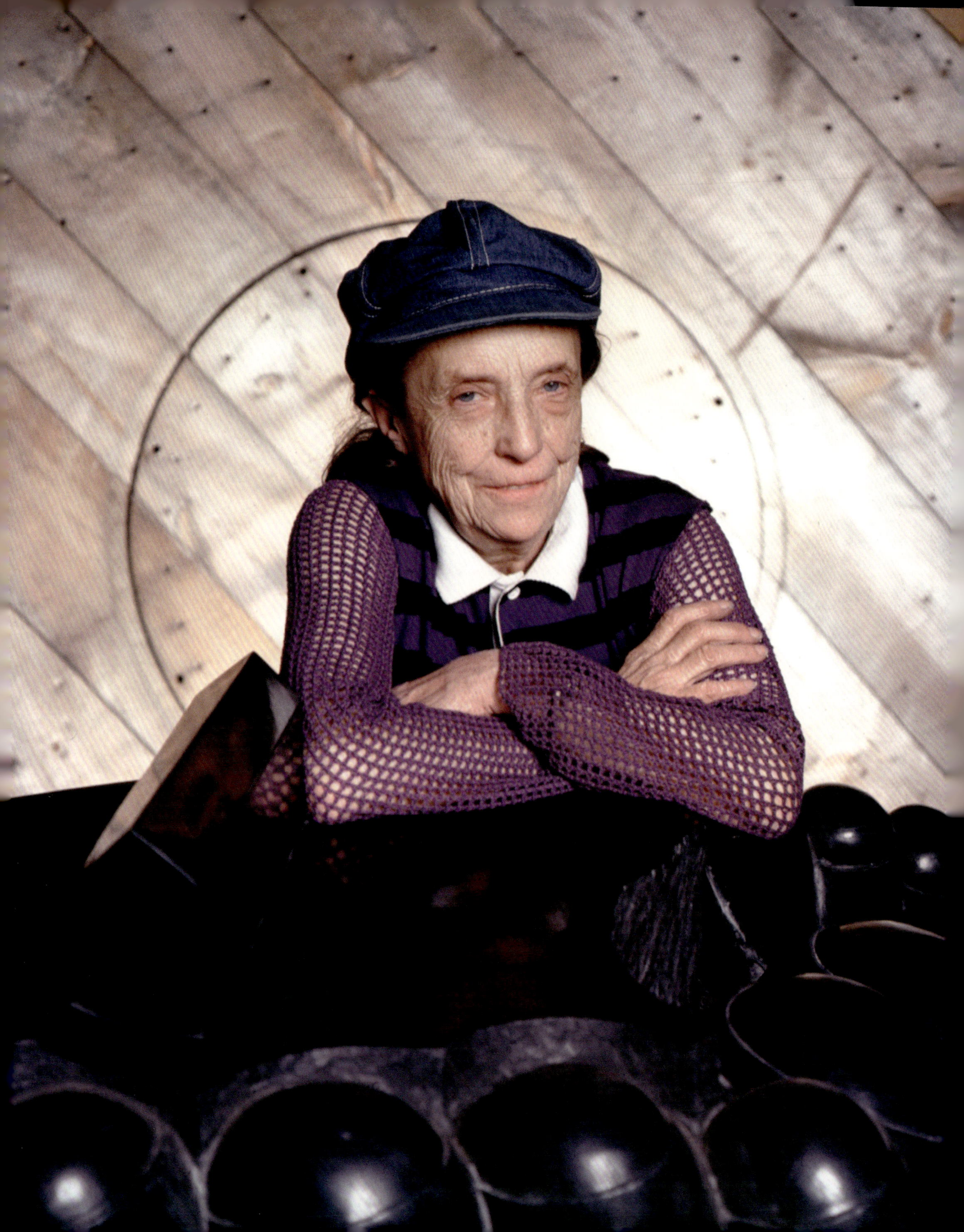

Joséphine **Fauriaux** and **Louise Bourgeois**

★

Louise Bourgeois's *Maman* spider sculptures, produced in the mid-1990s when the artist was in her 80s, are the most famous pieces she has created.They were largely inspired by her mother, Joséphine Fauriaux, who died when Louise was just 22. Bourgeois said that her mother "was a tapestry woman, and like a spider, was a weaver. She protected me and was my best friend" (Cooke, 2007). Although she studied mathematics at the Sorbonne, when Joséphine died Bourgeois switched to studying art, taking classes at a variety of schools across Paris, including the École des Beaux-Arts, École du Louvre, Académie Ranson and Académie Julian. In 1938, she opened a little gallery in a section of her father's tapestry gallery, and it was here that she met her husband Robert Goldwater. That same year they moved to New York, where she continued to paint, as well as embracing printmaking. The couple had two sons together and adopted a third.

Louise Bourgeois spent many years juggling her career as an artist with being a mother to her three boys, Michel, Alain and Jean-Louis. This combined identity is evident in her earliest shown works, with the 1946–47 series *Femme Maison* embodying the heroic contradictions of the expectations of motherhood and artmaking. It was far from easy: "There I was, a wife and mother, and I was afraid of my family...afraid not to measure up" (MoMA, n.d.).

Her mother's work as a tapestry restorer in France is imbued in the sculptural pieces Bourgeois began to build in the late 1940s, which began only when a workable opportunity arose: "Given the family setup, I worked on printmaking and painting. It was only when I encountered the roof of the building where we lived that I was able to concentrate on sculpture" (Marshall, 2007). Escaping alone to the top of the family apartment allowed her imagination to take shape and her vision was fuelled by the work her mother had wrought:

> "From the tapestries, I got this large sense of scale. I learned their stories, the use of symbolism and art history. The restoration of the tapestries functioned on a psychological level as well. By this I mean that things that have broken down or have been ripped apart can be joined and mended. My art is a form of restoration in terms of my feelings to myself and to others" (Cooke, 2007).

Bourgeois would go on to develop this theme over the course of the next 50 years. "My works are portraits of a relationship, and the most important one was my mother... The spiders, which are portraits of my mother, are large because she was a monument to me. I want to walk around and be underneath her and feel her protection" (Cooke, 2007). An image of Bourgeois on the roof of her apartment building, standing next to her sculpture *The Visitors Arrive at the Door*, shows her wearing a housewifely pinafore dress, with her hair arranged in classic Forties victory rolls. Smiling brightly in the sunshine, she looks more like a *femme maison* than the artist and fashion provocateur she would become in her later years.

In 1994, Bourgeois created a limited-edition family album consisting of photographs of her childhood, including imagery of her mother. Although she professes it as a pointed celebration of Joséphine's 'independence', her mother is captured wearing conservative clothing typical of that worn by women in the 1900s: high-necked blouses, long ankle-length skirts and practical mid-height Louis heeled leather shoes. It's a more fascinating snapshot of Bourgeois, however, who is shown immaculately clothed in fashionable Parisian labels. In a 1997 interview, she describes her installations *Blue Days* (a collection of hanging dresses) and *Pink Days and Blue Days* (which displayed her own and her family's clothes stuffed and hung on a wardrobe organiser) as referring "to a period when my mother and father would argue about who would put the best clothes on me. One would say: 'I bought her Poiret' and the other would say: 'I bought her Chanel. She is better in Chanel, and my Chanel is better than your Poiret'" (Landy, 1997). Given her perfect wardrobe as a child, it's unsurprising that the connection between Louise Bourgeois and the fashion world is passionate. She metamorphosed over time from a housewife to a style icon and then, in her very last years, for the most part to practicality. In her 70s she became friends with the photographer Robert Mapplethorpe. For one of his 1982 shoots, she is wearing a dark rock-and-roll-ish monkey-fur jacket, accessorised with one of her pieces, *Fillette* – a large plaster penis covered in latex – tucked under her arm. Mapplethorpe described the experience as 'surreal'.

Bourgeois's playful relationship with clothes, image and fashion reveal as much about this frank woman as the art she made. Everything about her kept evolving and her style never stood still. When the early constraints of family life evaporated, her look continued to develop and break boundaries in the same way as her work. In a 2008 documentary about her, *The Spider, The Mistress, and The Tangerine*, she wears an oversized, hot-pink, faux-fur coat topped with a sequinned, peaked cap and, later, a Huggy-Bear-esque pimp jumper. The clothes she chose accentuated her exuberance and engagement with the camera.

In the very last stages of life, expediency reigned. In 2003, she collaborated with another friend, the designer Helmut Lang, creating a T-shirt that they called 'What is the Shape of this Song?'. Lang recounts: "When I met her, she didn't leave her house anymore so she had comfortable clothes she would wear every day, such as a long-sleeved T-shirt with six pocket eyes. She likes to keep the extravagant pieces for special occasions such as photo shoots or when she has company she cares about" (Lang & Spero, 2007).

> **"The most important person in my life was my mother. My 'Spiders' are an ode to her."**
>
> **Louise Bourgeois,**
> 1995

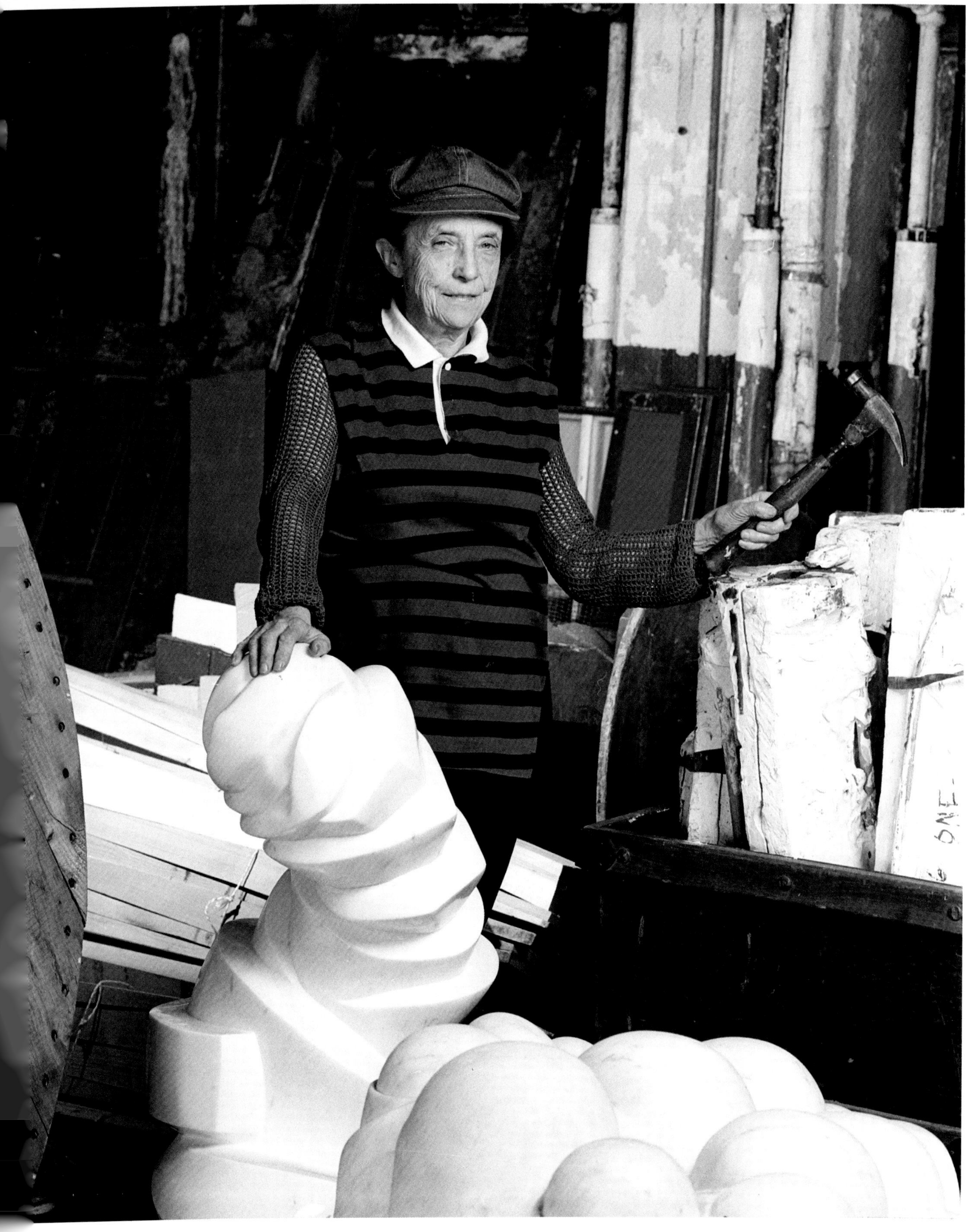

"I have the responsibility for taking care of my sons. So, when we talk about mother we are oscillating back and forth in time. I miss my mother. I am a mother. I am looking for a mother."

Louise Bourgeois,
Mary Ellen Mark, 2007

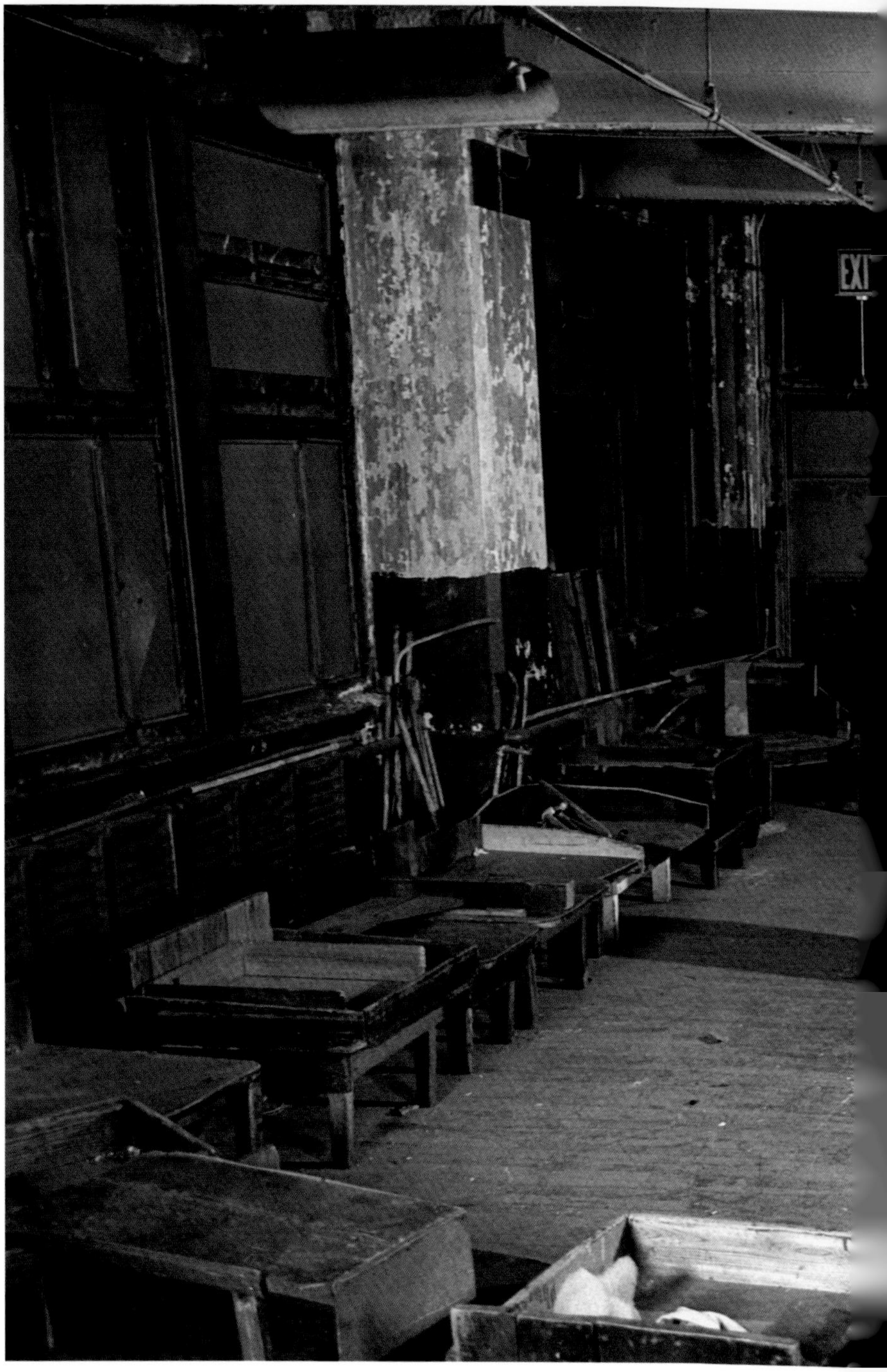

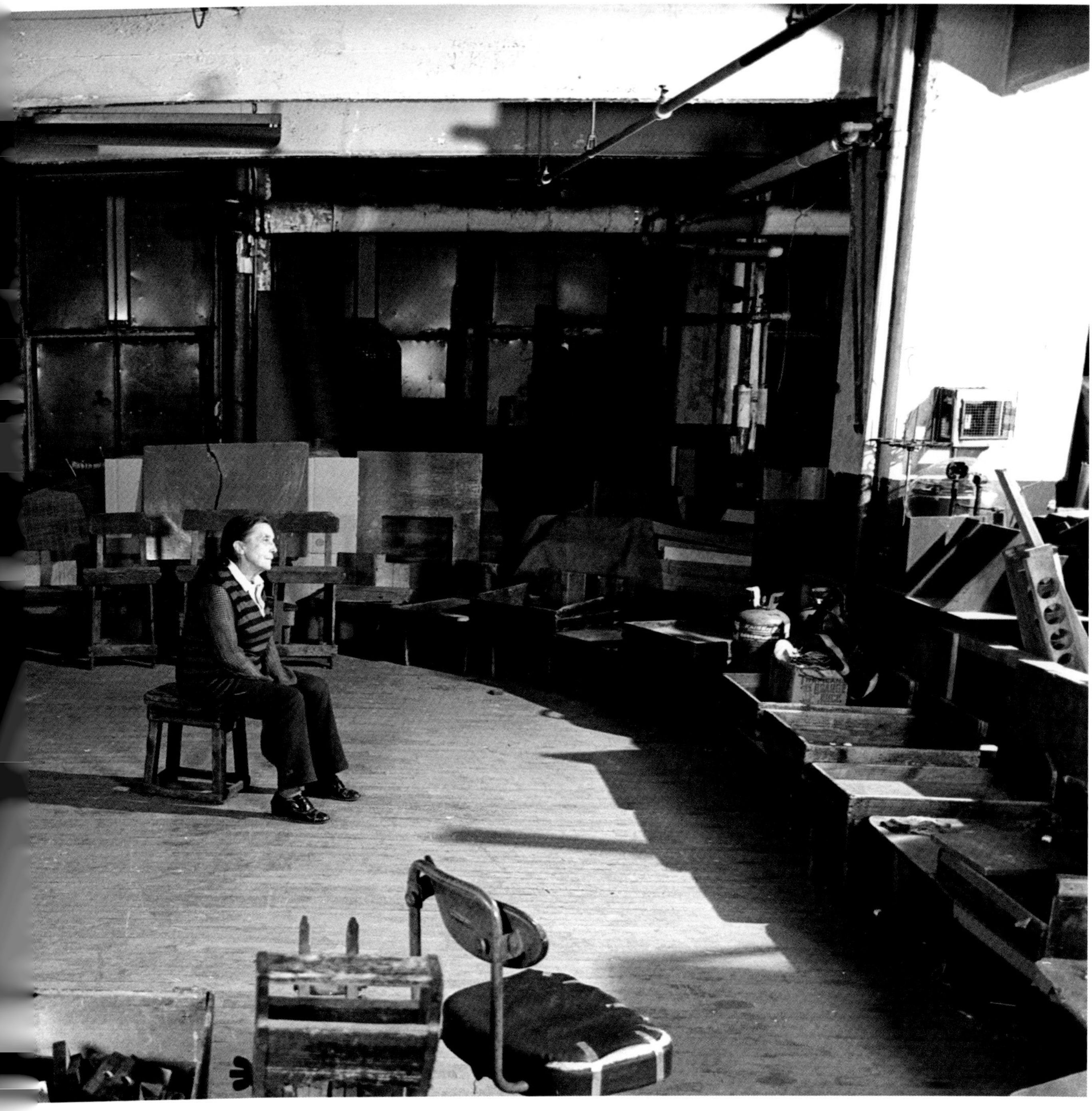

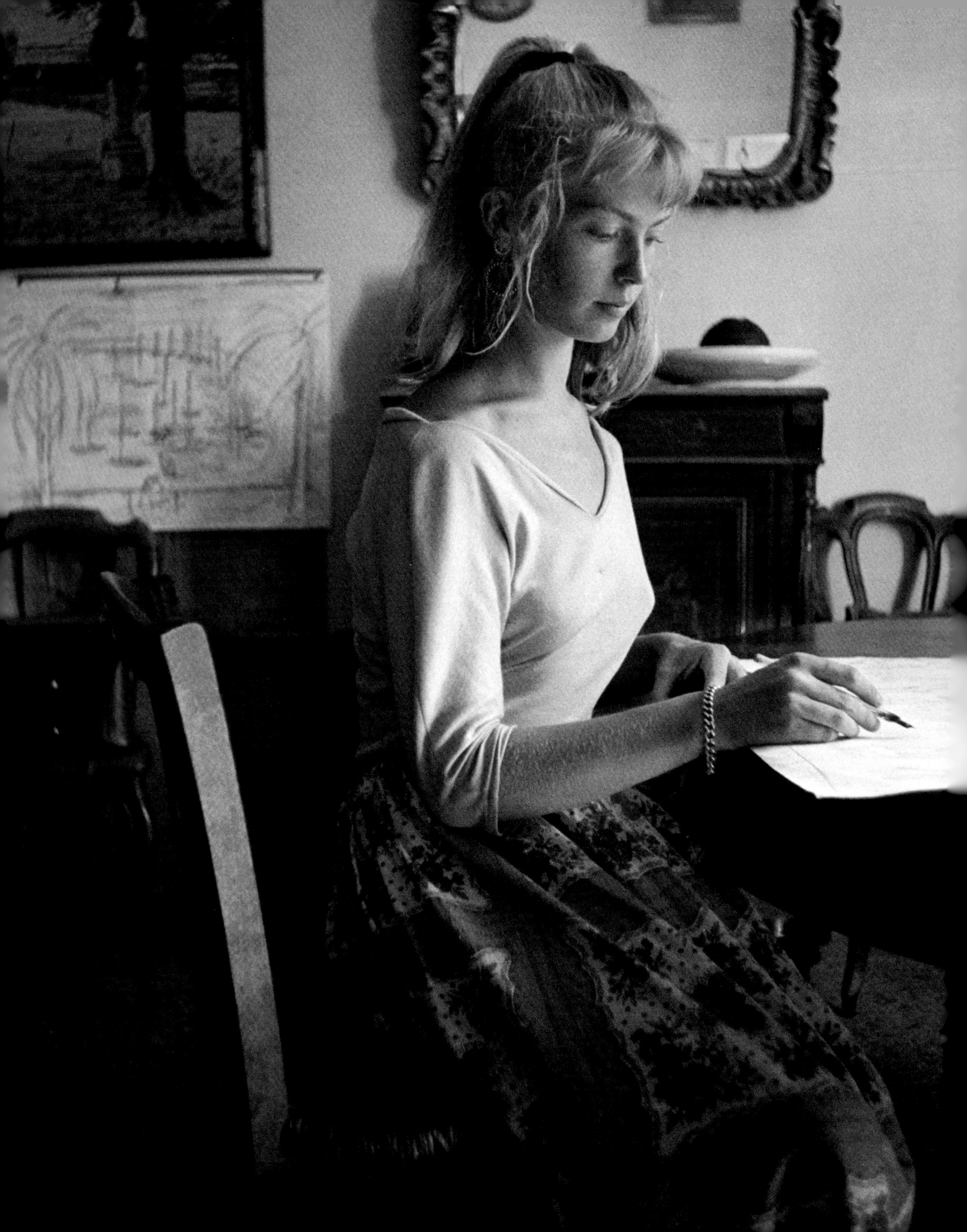

Above: Honor Gell and a baby Sylvette, circa 1934–35. Opposite: Sylvette drawing, 1954.

Lydia Corbett, aka Sylvette David, and **Alice Corbett**

The ceramicist Alice Corbett is the daughter of Sylvette David, famous as Picasso's muse. Sylvette changed her name to Lydia Corbett in the 1960s and is now celebrated in her own right as an artist. She has always been a free spirit, and her attitude to life and the clothes she wears are infused with an artistic outlook. A generational and habitual favourite in the Corbett household was a long, light skirt adorned with a traditional block print, famous in the Provence region of France.

> "When I was little, I used to wear these patterned, cotton, tiered skirts. Mum used to wear them, too. They are part of the heritage of the area and have been worn by women for centuries, but mum wore hers over trousers or leggings, or layered over even more skirts; we both had them and she still wears them. My daughters did, too."

Born in Paris in 1934 and growing up on Île du Levant, an idyllic island in the South of France, Corbett rarely wore shoes and spent her days swimming in crystal waters. "My mother, Honor Gell, sadly lost a child and ran away because she wanted a holistic cure and to live by the sea and have a healthy baby; that baby was me. I was brought up quite naturally there. Me and my younger brother were wild", remembers Lydia, fondly. Gell, a celebrated oil painter, was a devotee of the French physician Gaston Durville, who established a free-thinking community based on air and sun treatments and vegetarianism. "He lived up on the fort at the top of the island that had big steps going up. We lived further down. I never forgot all those steps, or the life we lived there. It was simple. We had very few good clothes and what shoes I did have I used for years."

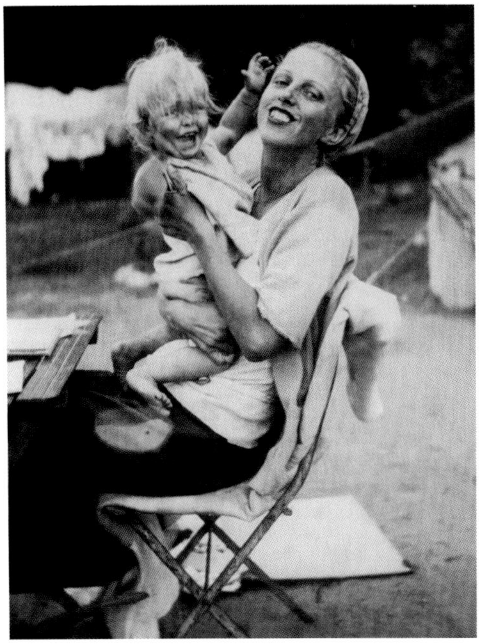

After World War II, at the age of 15, Lydia was whisked away to Summerhill School in England, a progressive environment which promises that "children have freedom to be themselves". She spent four more unconventional, magical years there before her life would take another intrepid twist when she moved to Vallauris, a Côte d'Azur seaside town, where her mother was by then living and where Picasso had set up a studio in 1948. It was early in 1954 that Lydia, then known by her birth name Sylvette David, met Picasso. She was just 19, shy, tanned, freckled and exceptionally beautiful. It was an irresistible combination for the world-famous Spanish artist who made her his muse and created a portfolio of work dedicated to her charm.

Lydia and Alice collaborating on a ceramic project, 2019.

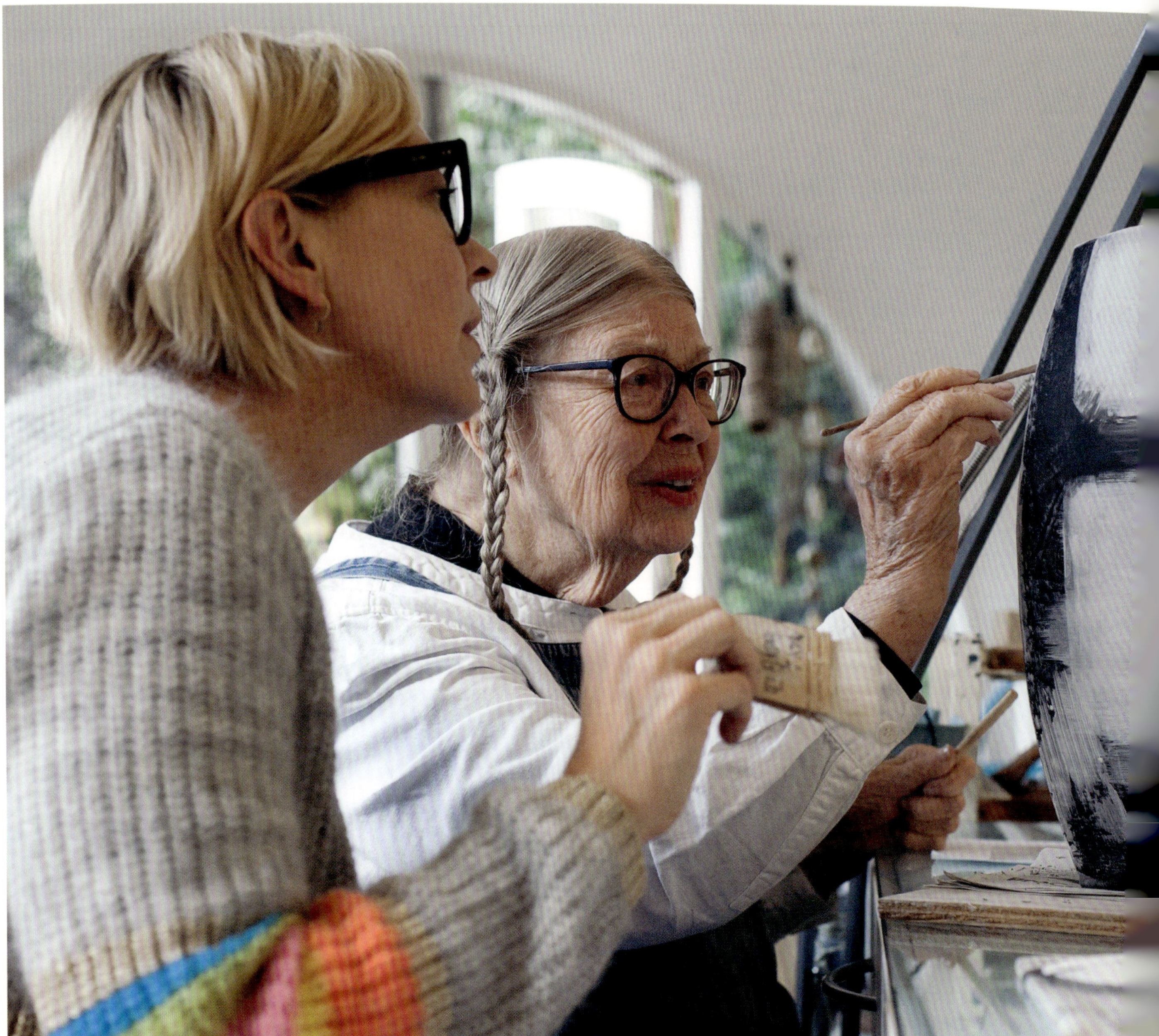

She wore her blonde hair in a high ponytail to please her art dealer father, Emmanuel, who had seen a girl with her hair in a ponytail worn in a Greek style at a ballet performance in Paris one evening. "To make my dad happy, I wore mine like that. There you go! That's why it all happened", she revealed almost 70 years later. It's a story that has transfixed the world, hitting headlines after Picasso's work depicting the 'girl with a ponytail' was exhibited later that year in Paris. The paintings, ceramics, sculptures and images of Sylvette that Picasso created impacted fashion. "Girls started to wear their hair like mine and dress like me. *Paris Match* ran stories and speculated that I was Picasso's new girlfriend", Lydia says, "but Picasso was more like a father. Very kind and respectful". He had just broken up with Françoise Gilot, the mother of their two children, Claude and Paloma, and was in love with Jacqueline Roque, who he would go on to marry and remain with until he died in 1973. Sylvette was never Picasso's lover, but she still mesmerised him.

Sylvette's style was organic, like the life she had led. She reflects: "My mother made me a black-and-white gingham skirt that I loved to wear, but I also wore a lot of old-fashioned clothes – lots of outdated petticoats and men's jackets from the 1940s. You know, I loved those. I also wore leotards and ballet slippers in all colours." It was a beatnik look that attracted the film star Brigitte Bardot:

> "I was walking along La Croisette in Cannes when suddenly Bardot saw me, and my ponytail. She was brunette at the time and afterwards went blonde and began wearing her hair like mine. A few years later she went to see Picasso and asked him to paint her, but he told her 'No; I've already painted Sylvette'."

Bardot's iconic style reflected Sylvette's; even her famed gingham wedding dress, designed by Jacques Esterel in 1959, is evocative of Sylvette's sweet Riviera chic. Looking back at the clothes she wore, they feel timeless. Lydia's love of repurposing pre-loved pieces was effortlessly elegant, and her collaged, made-at-home, pick-and-mixed wardrobe was way ahead of its time.

Alice has grown up with Lydia's love of idiosyncratic clothing, explaining:

> "Mum's my inspiration. As a child we often went together to a local shop called Revival, which is a beautiful vintage store in Totnes, Devon, and I go there now with my eldest daughter Ella – she is very much more like my mother than I am even. I grew up wearing second-hand finds and making clothes with mum. I wore them with those little cloth Chinese shoes and, as I loved tap dancing, I would always wear a hat."

The artistic streak that began with Lydia's bohemian and distinctive mother, Honor Gell, is an inheritance that manifests today. Alice's daughter Ella is a textile designer and stylist, while Alice's older sibling, Isabel Coulton, is a bronze, wood and stone sculptor. Alice and Lydia joyfully collaborate on ceramics and jointly exhibit work:

> "It began during Covid when Mum's eyesight was deteriorating. I had my first show, and we ended up working together and still do. We're very happy when we sit together doing pots; we don't have to say a word to each other and it's very peaceful. It goes back to Mum and her spiritual side. She is far more spontaneous than I am and has taught me how to work more instinctively."

However, despite their clear similarities and sensibilities, it's difficult to equal Lydia's otherworldly outlook, and Alice happily concedes: "I'm probably still much more of a suit person than she will ever be!"

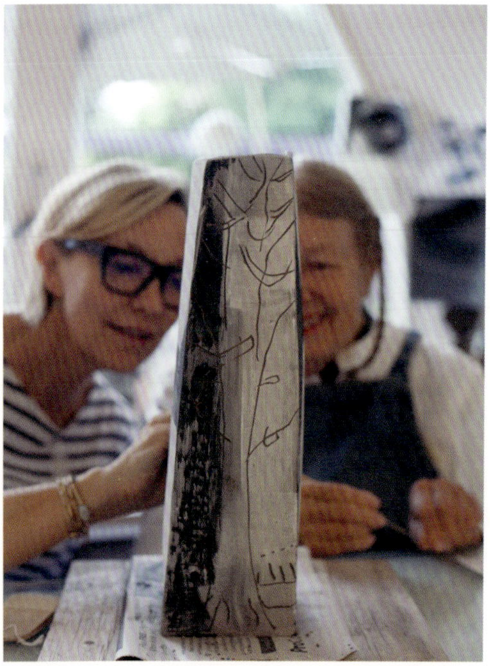

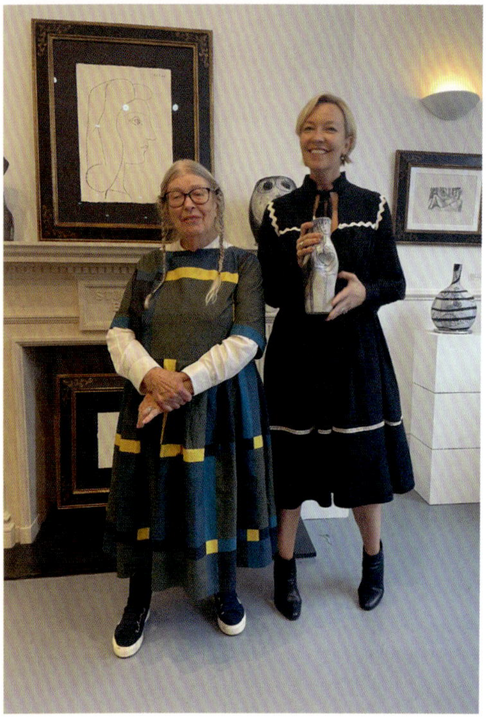

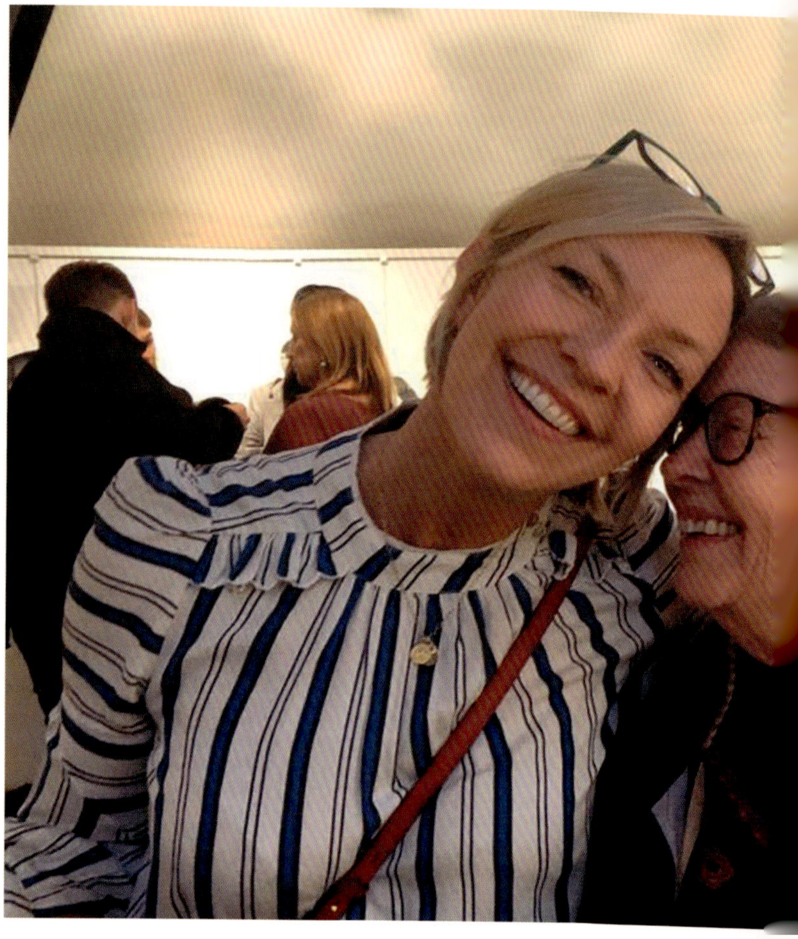

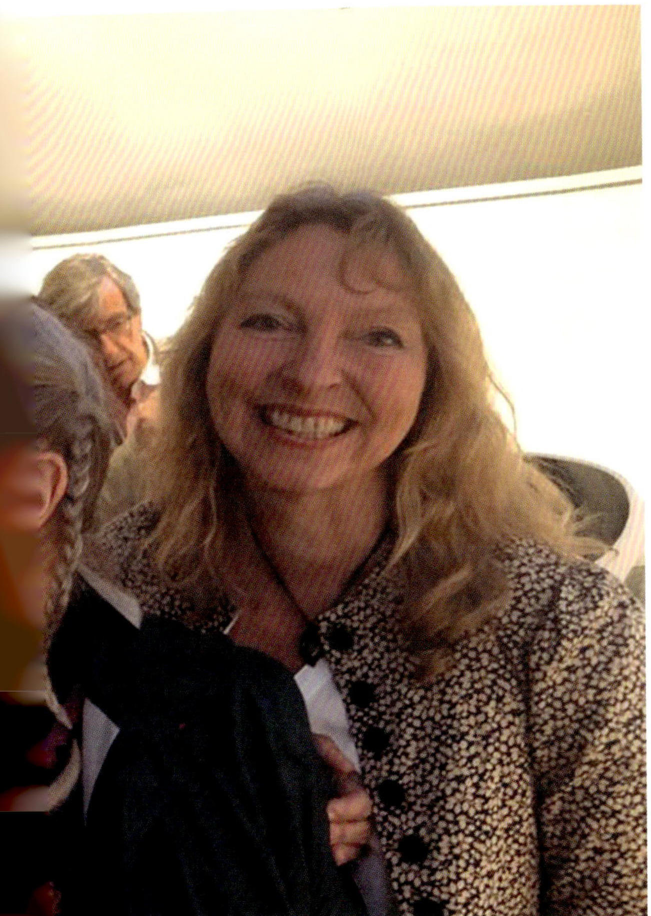

Lydia with her two daughters, Alice and Isabel.

"I've always loved everything that mum's done and never been embarrassed by what she wore. I personally went through a quite conventional phase that was very different to the way she has always dressed, but all my life she has always looked unlike any of the other mothers I knew, and it never bothered me. I'm very proud of her."

Alice Corbett,
2025

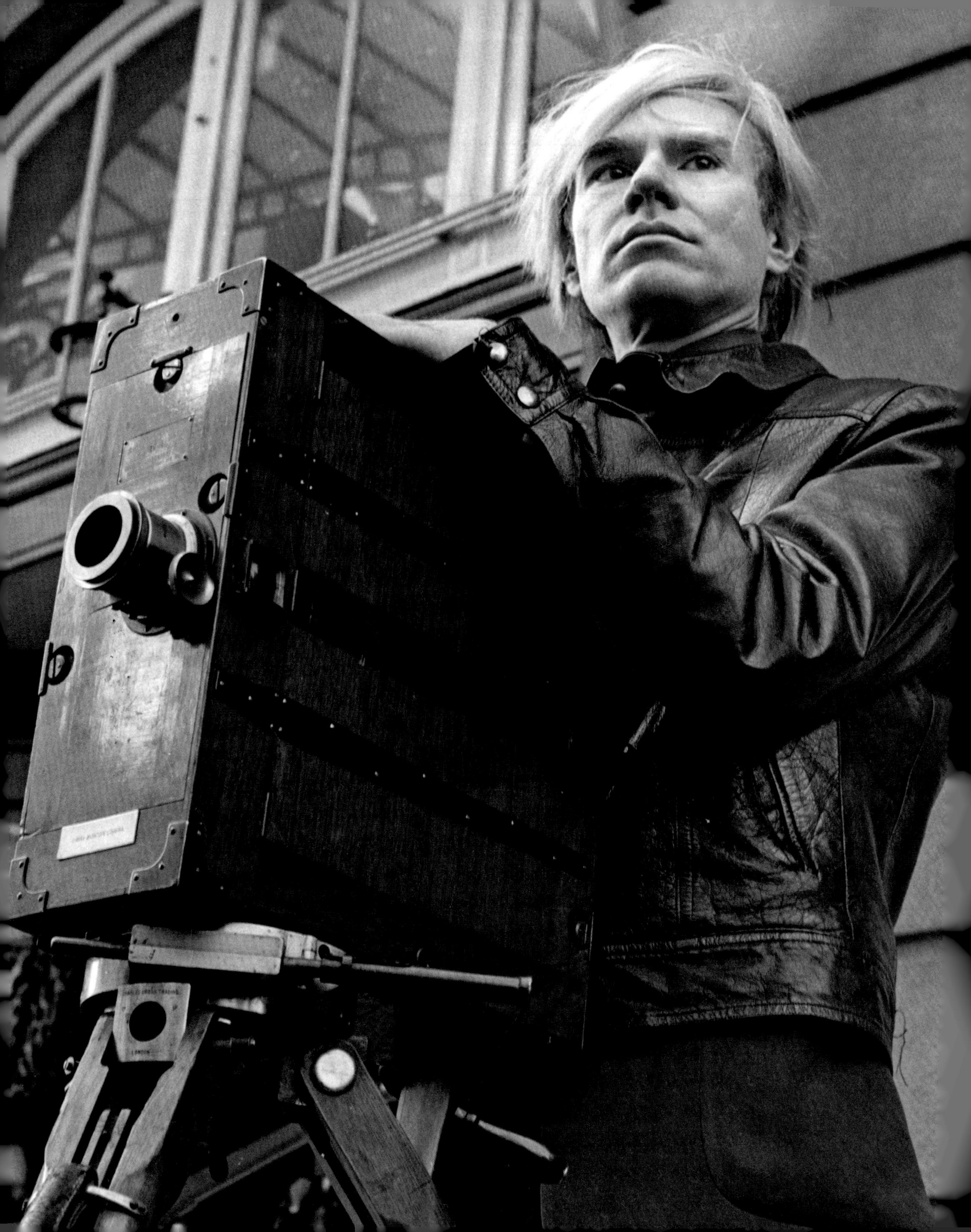

Julia Warhola and **Andy Warhol**

★

Julia Zavaczki was born in 1891 in what is now known as the village of Miková, Slovakia – a rural region that was once part of the Austro-Hungarian Empire, where bears and wolves roamed and the Carpatho-Rusyn women who inhabited the area would wear their national dress of embroidered blouses, gathered skirts, wraps and aprons for Sunday best. At 18, she married Andrej Varchola, recollecting in a 1966 interview:

> "The wedding was beautiful. I was dressed in white. I had a veil. I was beautiful. My husband had a white coat. So funny. He had a cap with lots of ribbons, three rows of ribbons. A day and a half with my mum and a day and a half with his mum. A big, beautiful celebration. Eating, drinking, whiskey barrels. Amazing food, rice with butter, sugar, bread, good bread, homemade cookies. Beautiful!" (Otriová, 2023).

In 1912 Andrej left Miková for America in search of work and in 1920, just over eight years afterwards, Julia followed, emigrating to Pittsburgh where her husband had settled. Julia's Czechoslovakian passport photo shows her wearing a high-buttoned white chemise, a folkloric black dirndl skirt and her hair covered by a headscarf tied in a neat bow. Like many of the settlers passing through, as recorded by Augustus F. Sherman, a registry clerk with the Immigration Division of Ellis Island, Julia's clothes reflected the cultural spirit of her hometown and were proudly symbolic of her heritage.

Andy was born in 1928. A grainy photograph of him with Julia and his older brother John, taken circa 1930, captures a glimpse of the young Varchola family, now going by 'Warhola', having Americanised their surname. By this time, despite the Great Depression, they are clad in American-style finery: John is dressed in a preppy blazer and tie, Andy in a smart woollen baby coat and Julia, smiling into the camera, proudly dons a fur-collared jacket, round spectacles and a voguish cloche hat. Their ambition aspired towards American glamour, but it was the traditions and customs of Miková that always drove Julia's motherly principles. This yin and yang also enriched Andy's constitution. Julia Warhola remarked that her son:

> "represents at the same time the American and European fused together, and he's very keen and sensitive to everything that goes on every day, and he registered it like... you know...a photographic plate... He has this terrific energy, and he goes out and he registers everything, and he does that everything and he becomes everything. The everything man" (Pratt, 1997).

Andy and his brother were brought up in a strict Byzantine Catholic family, and Andy would continue his faith when he moved to New York. At the height of his fame, he habitually attended church and donated food to the homeless, a custom instilled firmly by Julia who sent care packages back to her Czechoslovakian family from the moment she arrived in America, whether she could afford to or not.

Many interviews with Andy Warhol insist he camouflaged his background, telling reporters he "came from nowhere" (Higgins & Germanova, 2018). He fabricated stories and reportedly didn't tell his friends when his mother died in 1972. But if he was embarrassed by his upbringing or his mother, he

Left: Andy Warhol at the Factory with superstars Jane Forth, Jackie Curtis, Joe Dallesandro, Holly Woodlawn and film director Paul Morrissey, 1971.
Right: First edition of Holy Cats by Andy Warhol's Mother *(1954).*

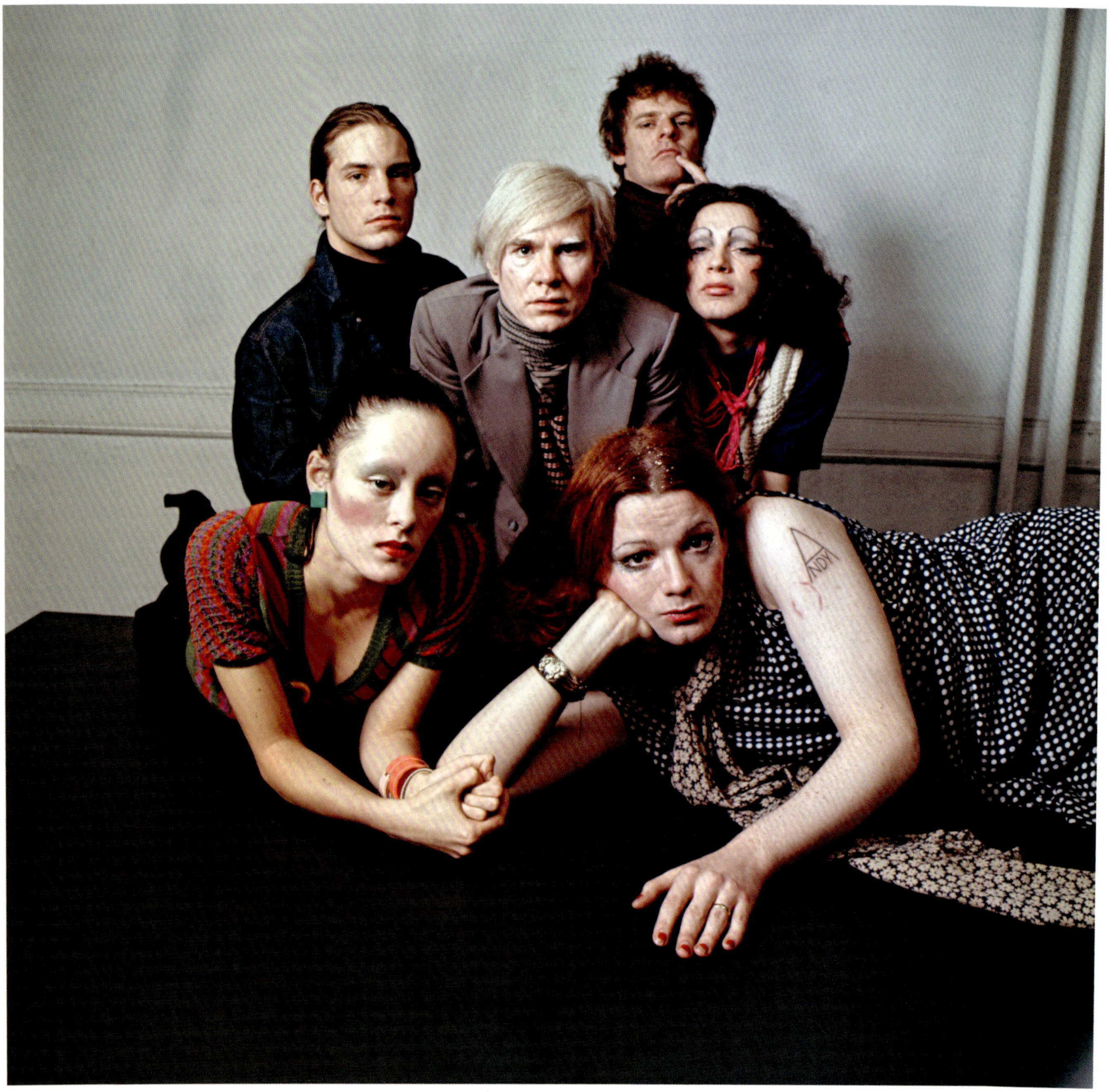

was hiding it in plain sight. Julia not only lived with Warhol in his house at 1342 Lexington Avenue near 89th Street, but he also featured her in his 1966 high-profile movie *The George Hamilton Story*, also known as *Mrs Warhol*, alongside his lover Richard Rheem and Factory star Edie Sedgwick.

Warhol never tried to shape or change his mother. An image of her going to see him in the hospital in 1968, after he was shot by Valerie Solanas, shows her wearing her babushka headscarf and glasses, sitting with 'Warhol superstar' actress Viva. Equally, in *The George Hamilton Story* she wears monochrome gingham, a pink, floral, Peter-Pan-collared blouse tied with a bow, and spectacles while cooking eggs and ironing. At times, it feels less like a movie and more like a documentary about Julia, with Warhol happy to show his mother off in all her normality. A contemporary interviewer asked: "Mr Warhol you sort of represent a sign of the times in movies, do you think you're going to go out of style?" to which he happily replied, "Oh, we're out of style already" (@thewarholmuseum, 2023).

Warhol's Factory was filled with outsiders who were on the inside, including legends such as Candy Darling and Ultra Violet, who blazed their own trail; Andy and Julia fit right in. Elaine Rusinko, associate professor at the University of Maryland, points out how the film "featured his mother speaking heavily accented English, which Warhol exploited for cinematic comedy" (Rusinko, 2022). Julia was very much a part of the fabric of her son's art, including her calligraphy, which was an integral part of his early work. As well as contributing the calligraphy to *25 Cats Name Sam and One Blue Pussy* (1954) and hundreds of his album covers, early advertisements and editorial layouts, Julia also published her own book of lithographs called *Holy Cats* (1954). According to poet and photographer Gerard Malanga, Warhol even went to the trouble of ordering a "custom-made Letraset using Julia's handwriting" (Giuliano, 2015).

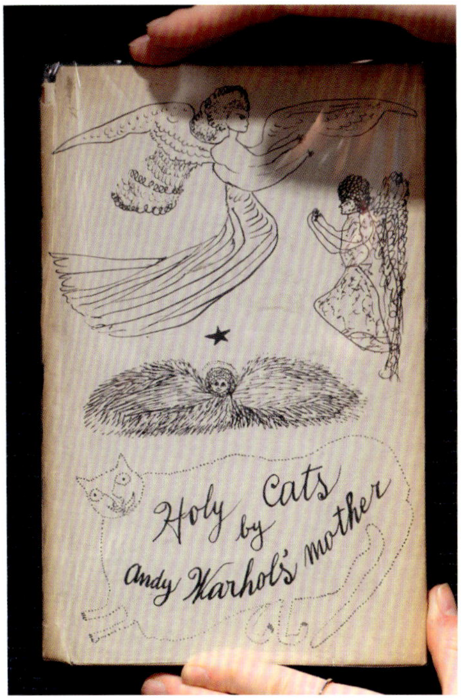

It's poignant to note that the impetus for Warhol's art began with an admiration of women's art. In a 1977 interview, Warhol says: "I always thought that most artists were women – you know, the ones that did the Navajo Indian rugs, American quilts, all that great hand-painting on '40s clothes" (O'Brien, 2019). *Mother and Child 383* from his 1986 'Cowboys and Indians' series features a Native American Indian with her child and is one of his most layered silkscreens, showing the clothes as symbolically colourful, rich and three-dimensional.

Andy included Julia's clothes as part of one of his celebrated *Time Capsule* projects, which he began making in 1974, two years after his mother died. According to the Tate, "the quantity of material, including a sizeable wardrobe filled with Julia

Andy Warhol at the age of two with his mother Julia and his older brother John, 1930, Pittsburg, USA.

Warhola's hats, blouses, head scarves and prodigious collection of housedresses, pointed to a powerful maternal attachment" (Williams, 2007). One of Andy's 1960s video-taped chronicles, *Julia Warhola in Bed, Talking*, records his mother talking in Rusyn. Translated by the scholar Rusinko, Warhol's mother discusses a hair appointment at a salon nearby, complaining about a botched perm: "It's the fault of that old boss woman, she burned my hair. For my twenty-five dollars, she burned my head with that strong evil stuff. I could have her arrested for what she did to my head" (Rusinko, 2022). She sounds remarkably like her son gossiping in *The Andy Warhol Diaries* (1989).

Warhol and his mother were the same, but different. Andy's life was of course hugely fashionable, and his inimitable look is as immediately recognisable today as it was back in the 1960s, when he emerged as a new kind of New York style icon with his platinum wigs, polo-neck jumpers and glasses with dark or transparent lenses; he was a piece of art of his own creation, born out of a fascination of high and low culture. But he was also surprisingly down to earth: "I have paint clothes. They're the same kind of clothes I wear every day, with paint on them. I have paint shoes and paint shirts and paint jackets and paint ties and paint smocks, and a great smock from Bendel's. And carpenter aprons. And paint hankies" (O'Brien, 2019). Equally, Julia's housewifely headscarves, spectacles and dainty blouses became synonymous with her identity and were unapologetically captured by Warhol after she died in 1972, with a screenprint that he created a couple of years after.

"I raise my children okay. Oh, Andy a good boy."

Julia Warhola,
Esquire, 1961

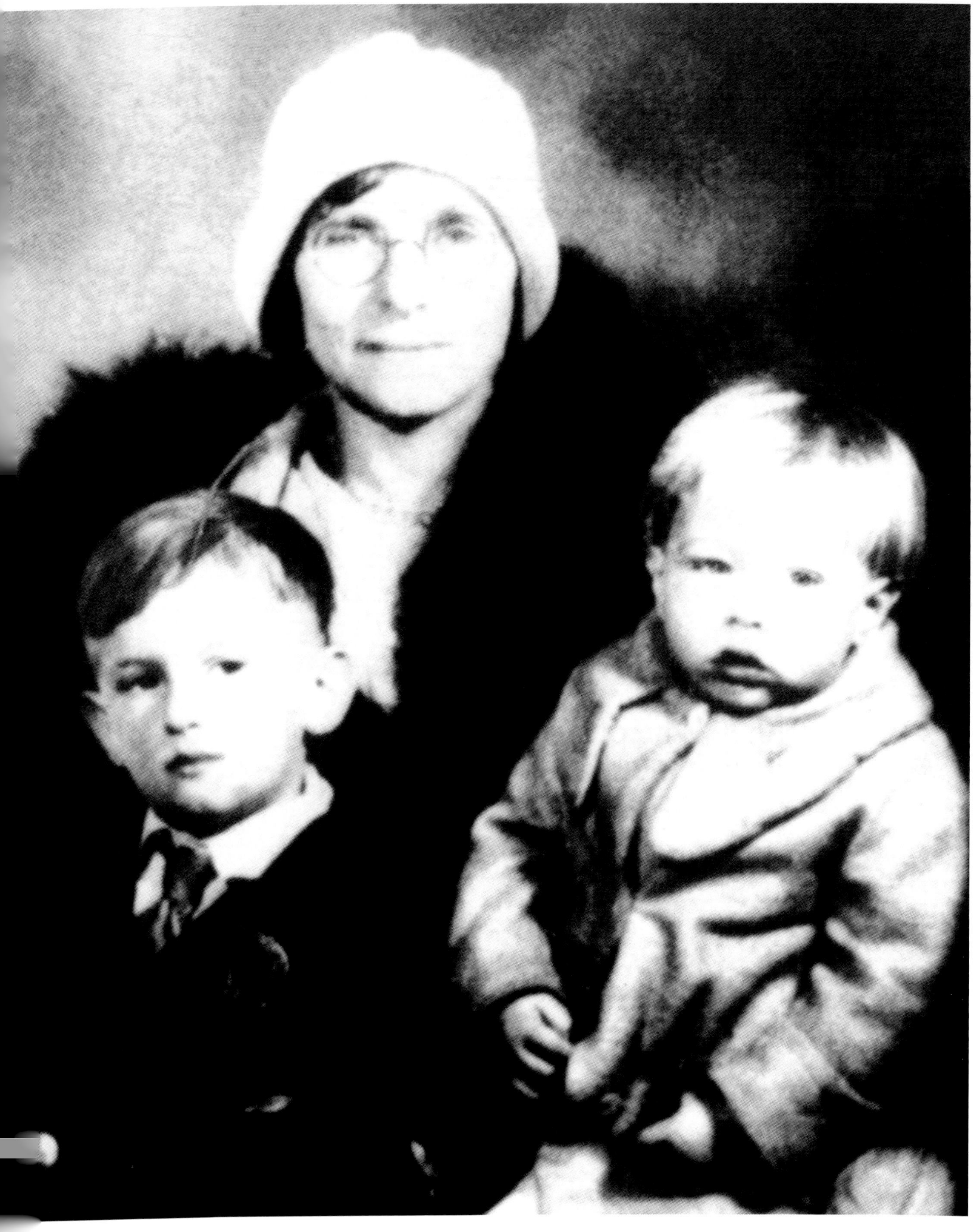

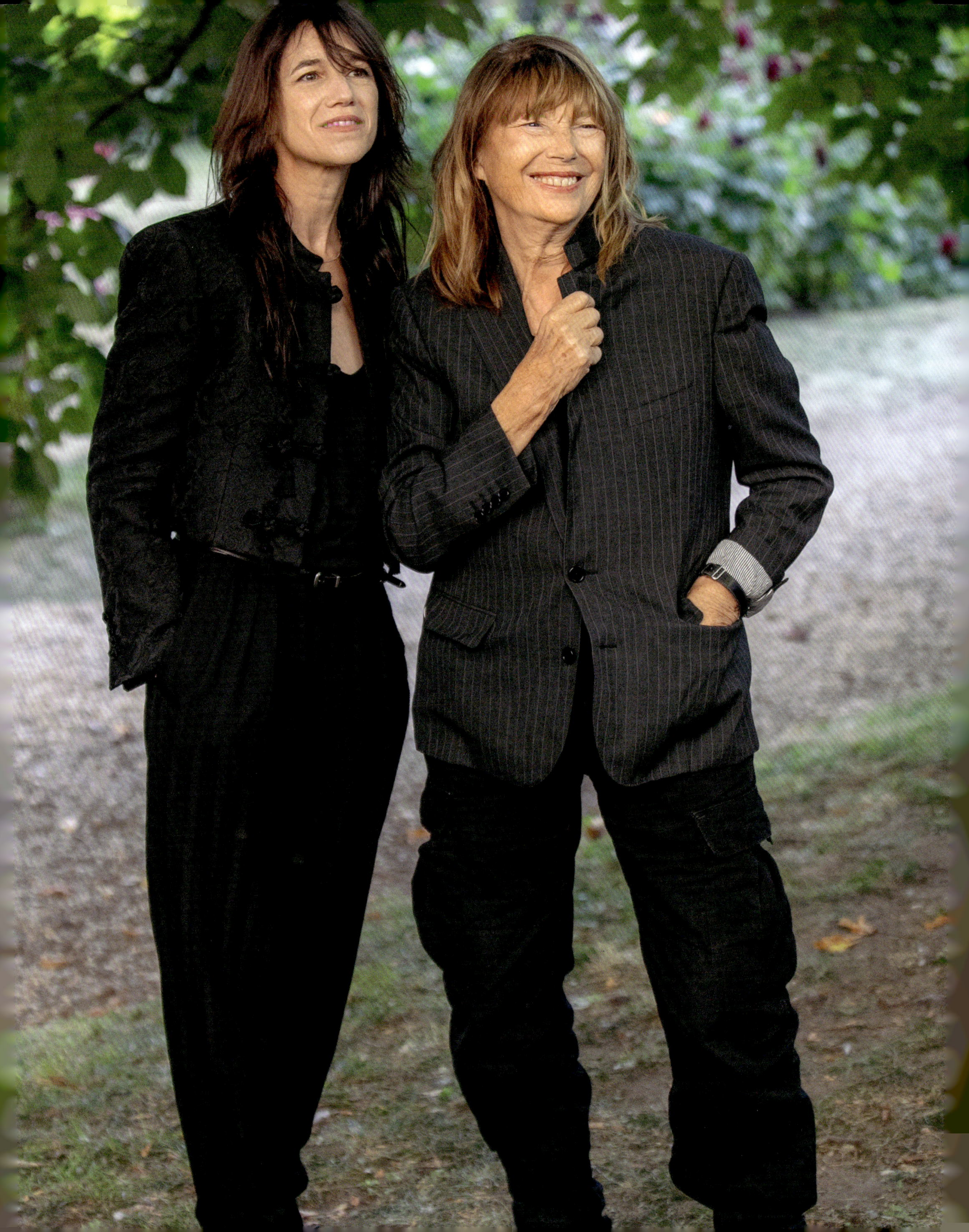

Left: Jane Birkin with her daughter Charlotte Gainsbourg. Right: The famous Hermès Birkin bag.

Judy **Campbell**, Jane **Birkin**, Charlotte **Gainsbourg** and Lou **Doillon**

★

A highly coveted accessory, the Hermès Birkin bag was designed by the luxury fashion house as a solution to a problem Jane Birkin had as a mother. She couldn't find a bag better than her signature basket to carry all the things she needed to look after her children. She wanted something practical with 'pockets' that could hold everything. It's an issue many a parent has had trouble with but, unlike Jane, few had the issue solved by the chairman of Hermès.

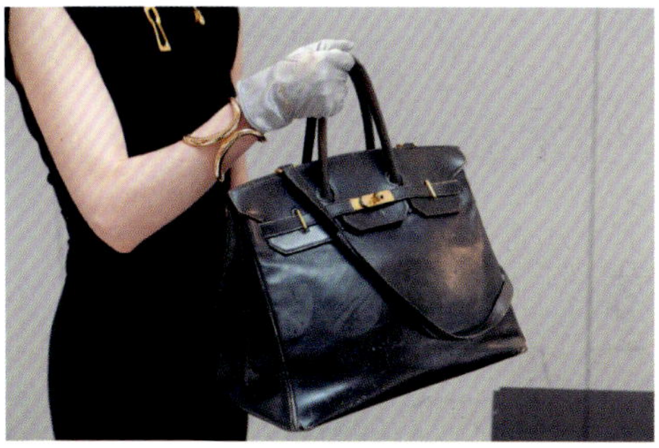

Jean-Louis Dumas, the great-grandson of founder Thierry Hermès, met Birkin on an aeroplane and hatched a plan to create just the thing. In 1984, the useful and luxurious handbag debuted. Since then, the Birkin bag has become the stuff of legends, a sought-after piece you can only seem to buy if you have a good relationship with the brand and spend good money with them. To some extent, the bag's concept is the antithesis of Jane's celebrated simple styling, as her fashion sense was somewhat anti-fashion. During her lifetime and beyond, she became the personification of not trying too hard – a dichotomy many designer brands find hard to manifest. When she passed away in 2023, the then president of France, Emmanuel Macron, called her a "French icon" who "embodied freedom". Birkin's pedigree nevertheless owed something to her distinctive fusion of London and Parisian chic, and the way she mixed and matched each culture.

Born in England, Birkin enjoyed a privileged childhood attending boarding school and growing up in the wealthy neighbourhood of Chelsea, just around the corner from the King's Road. It was the Swinging Sixties and this area of London was the epicentre of cool. Birkin's father, the grandson of a baronet, was a naval officer and war hero, while her mother, Judy Campbell, was a famous actress and singer, celebrated as playwright Noel Coward's muse. Photographs of Campbell onstage and off during her 1940s heyday paint a picture of an elegant woman who wore sweetheart-necked gowns, tidy suits and pussycat-bow blouses, all while smiling widely and showing off the distinctive gapped front teeth that her daughter Jane would also become renowned for.

Although Jane worked as a model for a while, photographed by the likes of Norman Parkinson for American *Vogue*, Jane followed in her mother's footsteps and began working as an actress in London, appearing in Michelangelo Antonioni's iconic 1966 film *Blowup*. She moved to Paris in 1969 upon meeting her soon-to-be long-term partner Serge Gainsbourg on the set of the movie *Slogan* (1969). Shortly after, she relocated to France permanently.

Today her style is still celebrated the world over, largely as the quintessence of 'French girl chic', and she is much imitated by women who crave the nonchalant, uncomplicated grace she made her own. Birkin's wardrobe of undemanding classics was,

Jane Birkin with her youngest daughter, Lou Doillon.

however, something that Lou Doillon, her daughter with director Jacques Doillon, found hard to fathom. Born in 1982, Lou said: "I had a problem with my mother growing up because I didn't understand when everyone was saying she was stylish – and she was just wearing boring jeans and a T-shirt, and the same goddam shoes every day, Converse or Bensimon trainers every day. I hated her for that" (Mower, 2009). Charlotte Gainsbourg, Birkin's daughter with Serge, more easily followed her mother's sartorial lead, telling *Dazed* magazine:

> "I think I got the comfort of clothes from my mother. [She] had a real relationship with clothes which was much more sensual. She used to destroy them – if she had a new T-shirt, she would enlarge the collar and make it big, it was about this idea of second hand. That's what I saw her do and that's what I do now – that's what she taught me" (*Dazed*, n.d.).

Birkin's poise always encompassed a *je ne sais quoi* sex appeal. In an interview in 2011, Lou said to Jane: "There was this rumour when I was in kindergarten that you wore dungarees with nothing under. I knew that you must have had a peculiar style to have children talking about it!" (Jacques, 2011).

In 2016, creative director of YSL Hedi Slimane picked up on Jane's androgynous style, photographing her wearing the fashion house's famed 'Le Smoking' tuxedo. Later that year, at the debut womenswear collection of Anthony Vaccarello, who took over from Slimane, Jane and her daughters Charlotte and Lou were front-row guests, with Lou wearing the 'Le Smoking' jacket her mother had made famous.

Over the years, the ladies in this family have been consistent about what they like to wear. In 2009, Birkin said:

> "I just did a TV show a couple of days ago...I had to make a tiny bit of effort. I'd bought a second-hand YSL suit for a cocktail in Buenos Aires and wore it with stockings and high heels and a camisole from Sabbia Rosa, where I used to buy my lingerie when I was younger. People were amazed; they're so used to seeing me in jeans.... I'd rather be dressed as a man, and Lou had found these baggy men's pants [by John Varvatos] for me in New York. As soon as I'm in boys' things I feel like I'm 12 again. I'll go on tour in a white shirt and waistcoat. Lou is my costume designer; she has all the good ideas" (Foreman, 2009).

In parallel to her mother's past fashion sensibility, and inspiring style setters today, Charlotte's relationship with Saint Laurent endures, too. Most recently, in 2024 she appeared wearing a leather blouson over a black silk chemise in Anthony Vaccarello's *As Time Goes By*, a series of short films inspired by Marcel Proust's seven-volume novel *In Search of Lost Time* (1913–27). Meanwhile, Lou has come around to the idea of wearing jeans. In 2009, she created a range for Lee Cooper and later became the face of LA denim company J Brand in 2016.

"I went to this party once, and somebody said, 'Look, it's the daughter of the bag'. I couldn't believe it!"

Lou Doillon,
Glamour, 2011

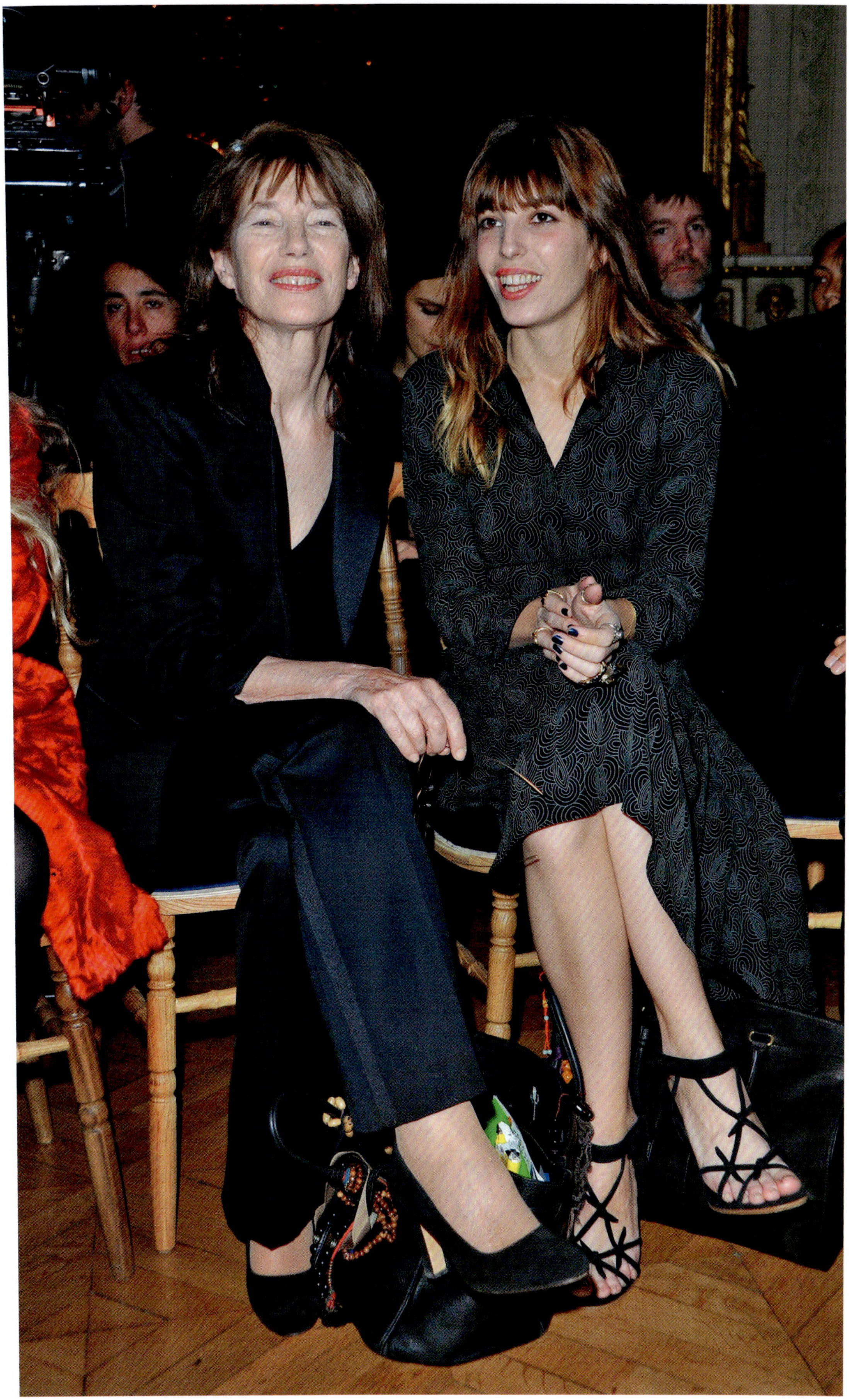

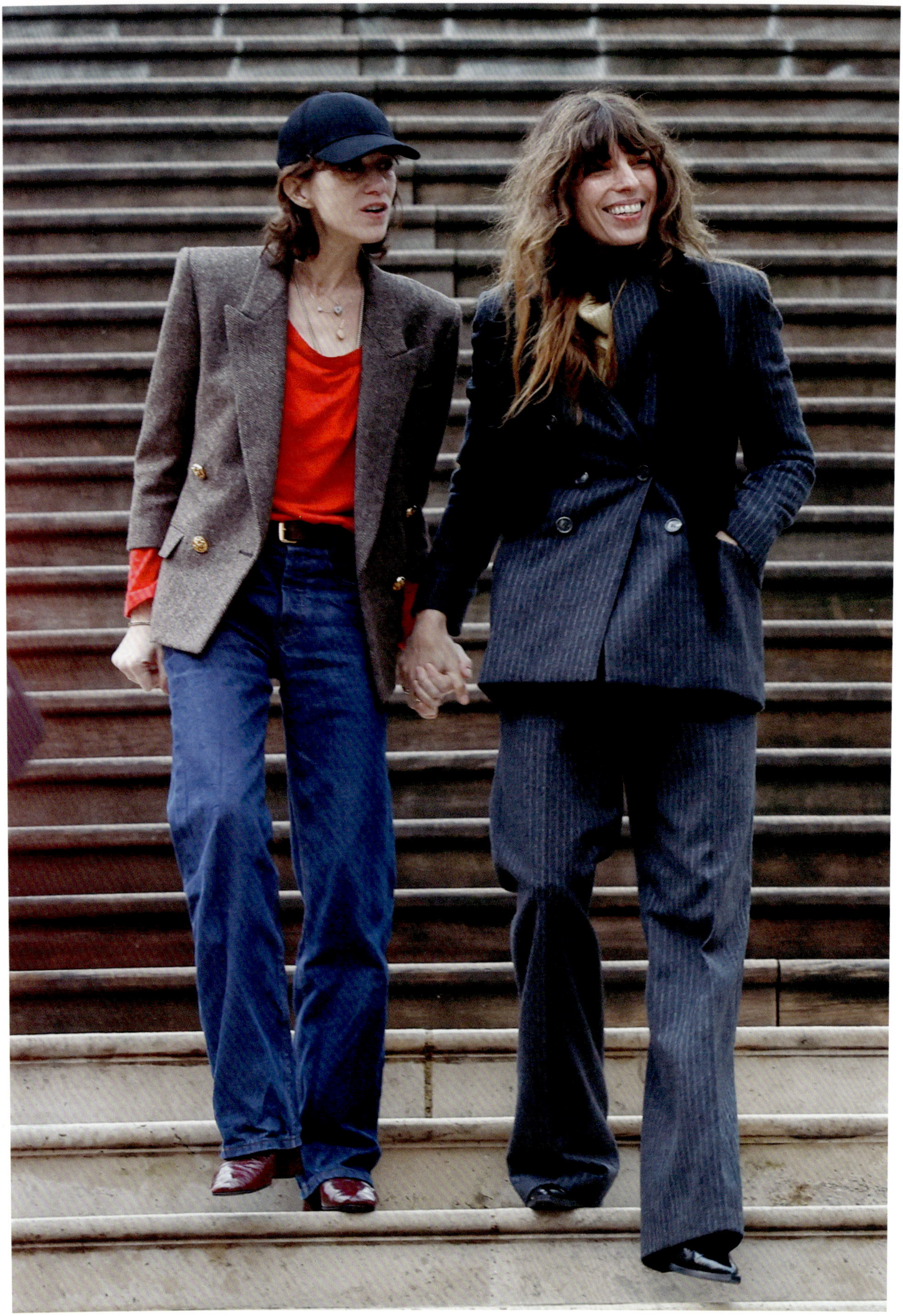

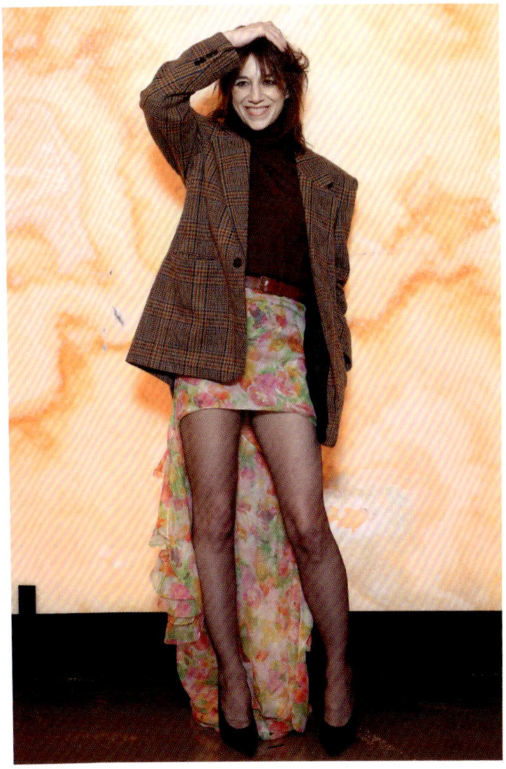

"When I like clothes, I usually wear them every day until I wear them out."

Charlotte Gainsbourg
WWD, 2014

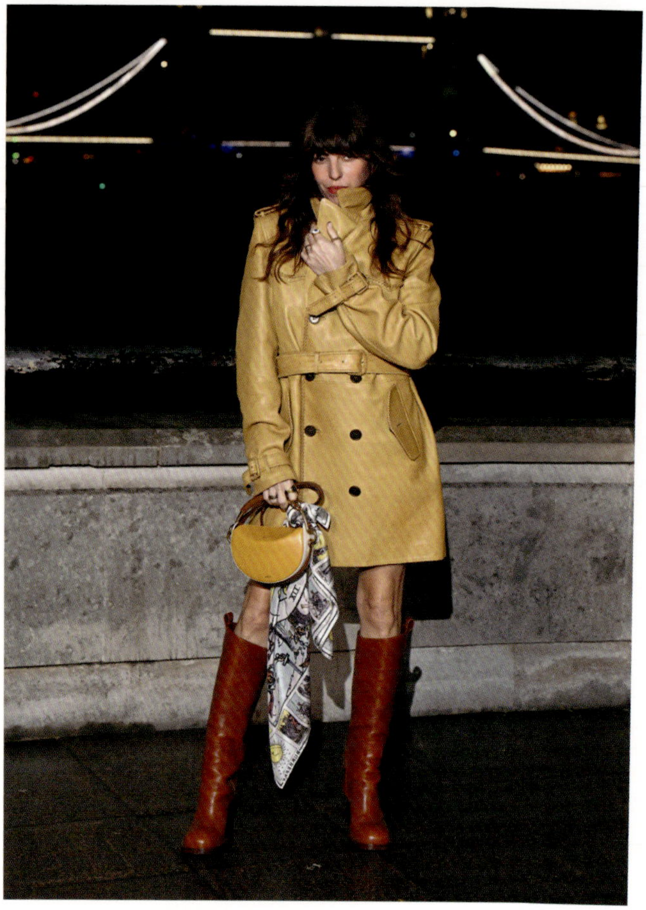

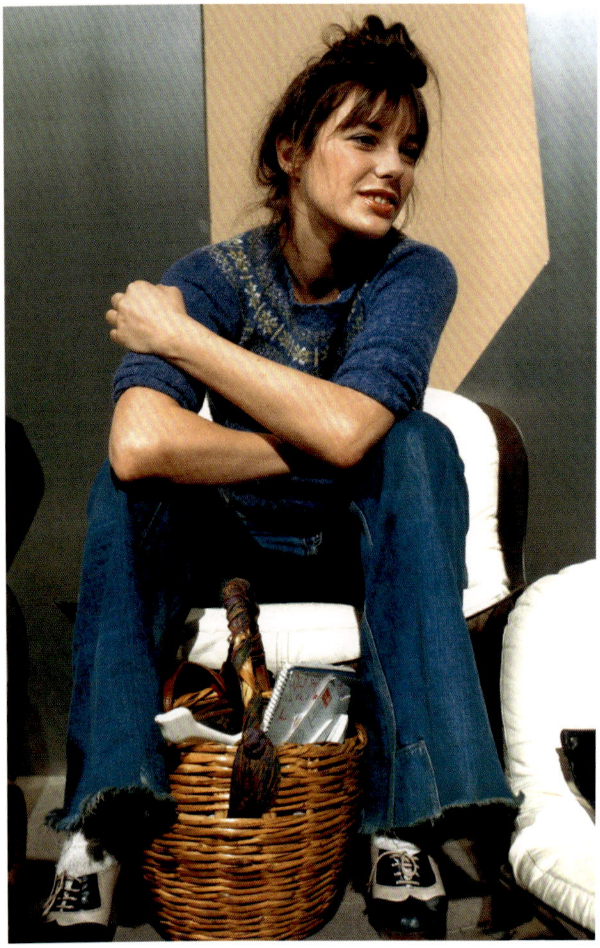

Far left: Jane Birkin in 1974. Centre: Lou Doillon models a Burberry coat. Right: Jane Birkin with her mother, Judy Campbell, 1986.

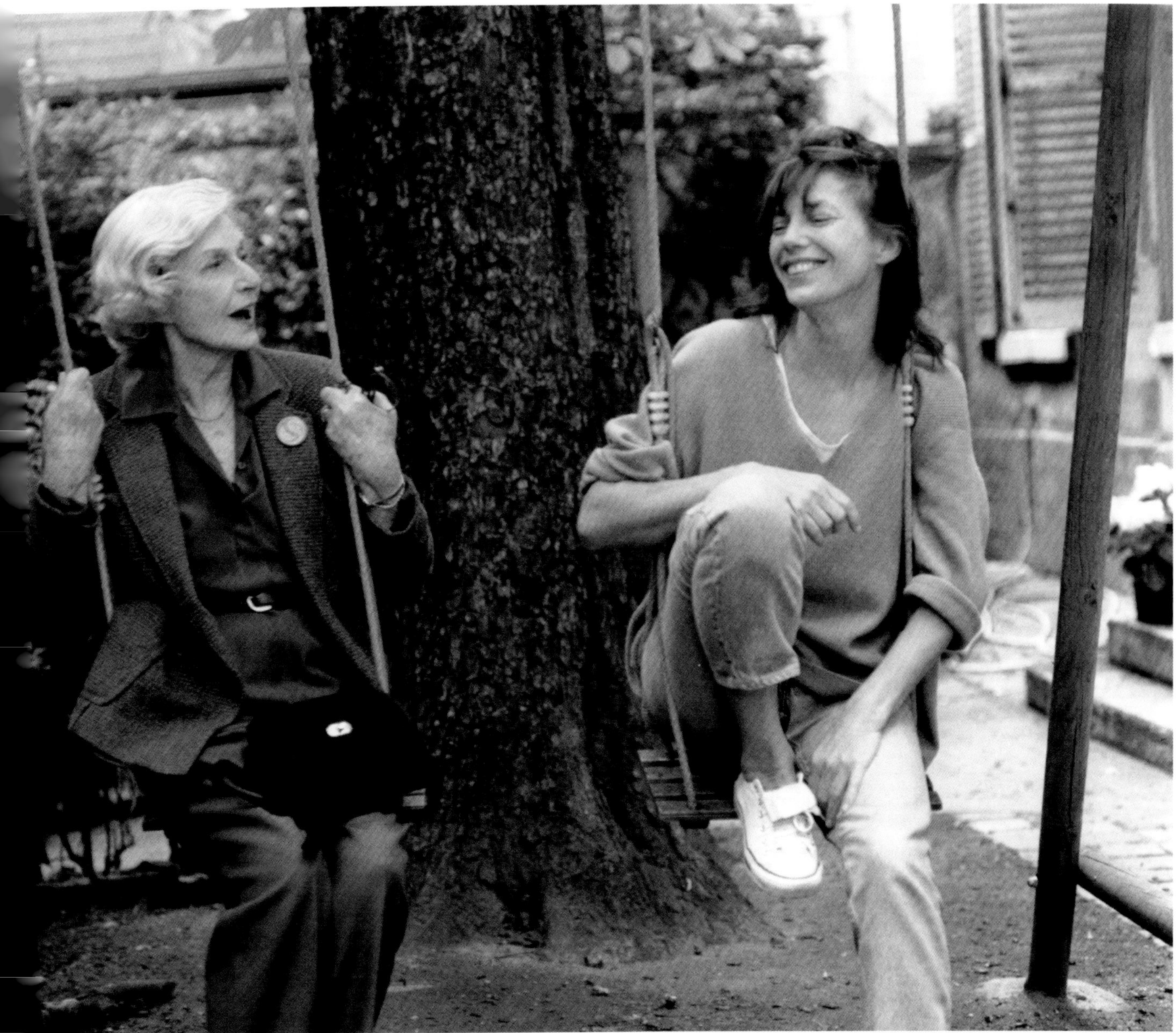

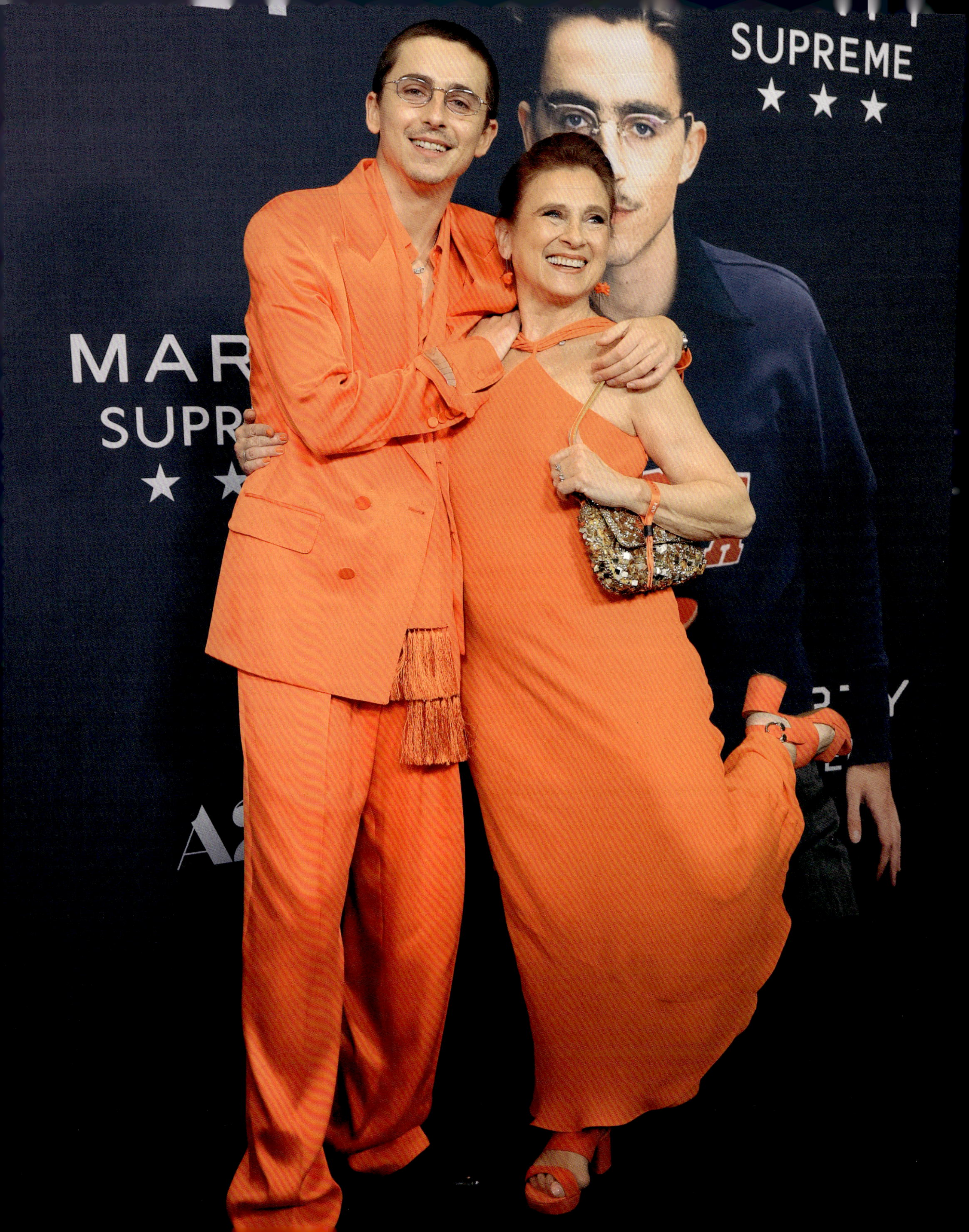
SUPREME

Nicole Flender and **Timothée Chalamet**

★

Timothée Chalamet and his mother, Nicole Flender are frequently spotted on the red carpet together, showing up and dressing up. Flender's looks are always elegant, often featuring canny and clever detailing, like the time-honoured full-length gown with a distinct crop-waist cut-out that she wore in 2018 when she accompanied her son to the Oscars. She is coolly self-assured in the beam of a spotlight, having danced with the New York Ballet as a child, as well as attending LaGuardia – a New York City visual and performing arts high school, where Chalamet also studied.

In January 2019, mother and son attended the Golden Globes together, following Chalamet's best supporting actor nomination for his performqance in *Beautiful Boy* (2018). Timothée and Nicole walked the red carpet wearing co-ordinating Louis Vuitton outfits designed by Virgil Abloh, who had taken over the helm in March 2018. Chalamet sported a bespoke sequinned harness over black tailored trousers and a custom-made shirt, while Flender dressed in a logoed vest-and-trouser set, picked from the Spring 2019 Off-White runway. Abloh's avant-garde luxe streetwear range debuted in 2012 and he quickly became known as an intellectual and artistic driving force within the fashion industry. It was a bold choice for Flender to make, and a beautifully complimentary one that felt symbolic of mother and son's devotion to each other. The media reported them as "without question the coolest mom and son duo to step foot inside the Golden Globes this evening—or quite possibly, ever" (Bobb, 2019).

More recently, at the New York premiere of *Marty Supreme* in 2025, Flender went viral when she spectacularly matched her tangerine gown with Chalamet's fluoro-orange Tom Ford suit designed by Haider Ackermann. Then, at the SAG Awards in 2025, when Chalamet became the youngest Best Actor winner, Flender made her customary appearance as his mum-date, this time wearing a daring slip dress split to the thigh, her hair wrapped in a chic black bow. As Timothée took to the podium to accept his trophy, he name-checked Nicole and her efforts, not just as a parent, but also for her work representing actors throughout America, saying: "I'll start by thanking my mother who I'm here with tonight. She has been working at Actors Equity for 40 years, the stage union."

Despite being a cool mother who more than keeps up with her son's fashion choices, practicality is clearly at the heart of Flender's mothering. In a television interview after the awards ceremony, Chalamet confessed that the first words his mother said to him after winning were entirely everyday: "She said don't forget to fold your laundry. And I was like really? At this moment? You're chastising me? When I won this award and I'm 29 years old?" (Robert, 2025).

"They had these talent shows at LaGuardia which is a high school for the arts and he had this personage that was Lil Timmy Tim and he had back-up dancers around him... we drove up to Target at 116th Street and we got sweatpants for everybody and then I had to dye them purple in my bathtub and I said okay, this is the start of something big."

Nicole Flender,
Entertainment Tonight,
2025

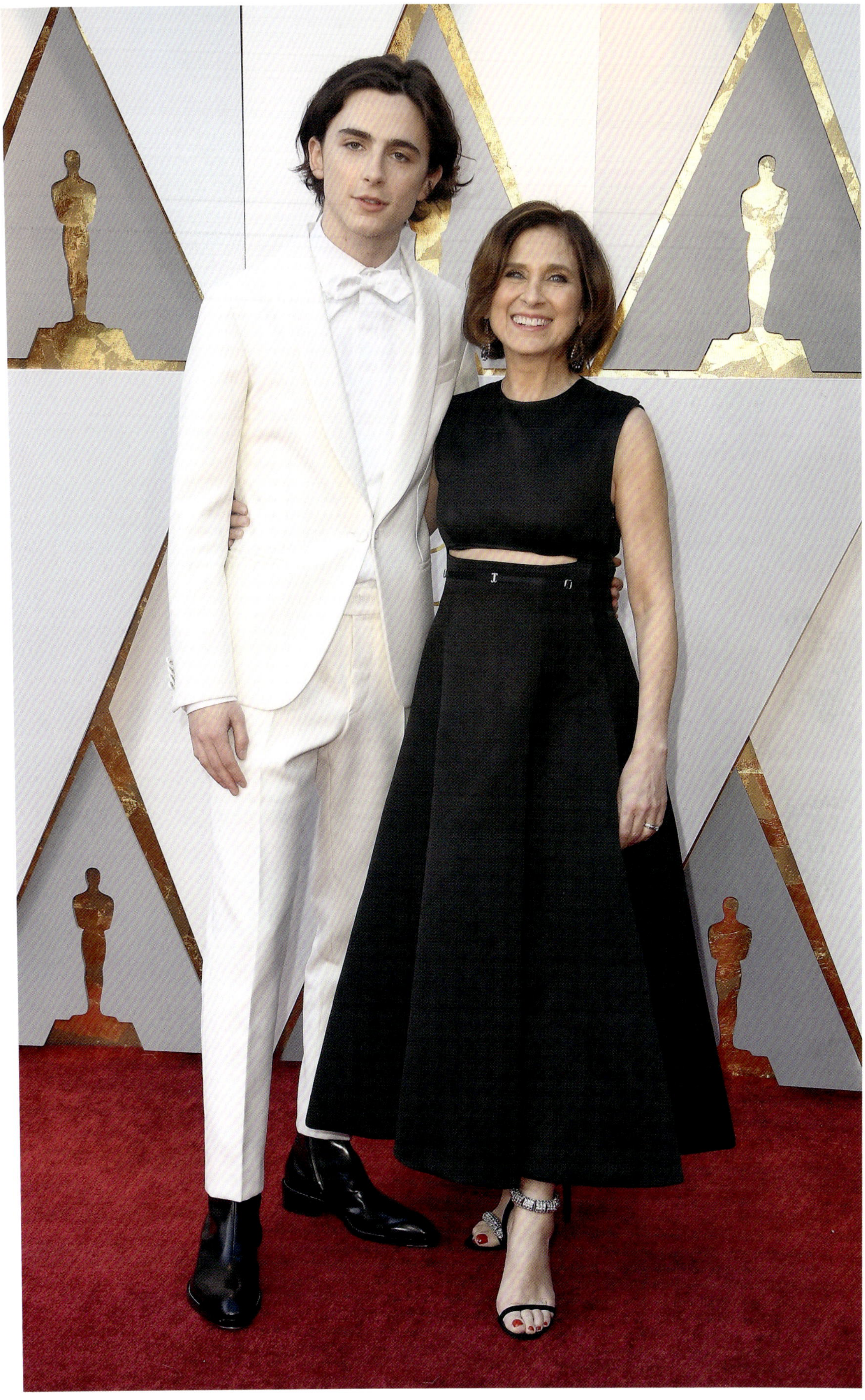

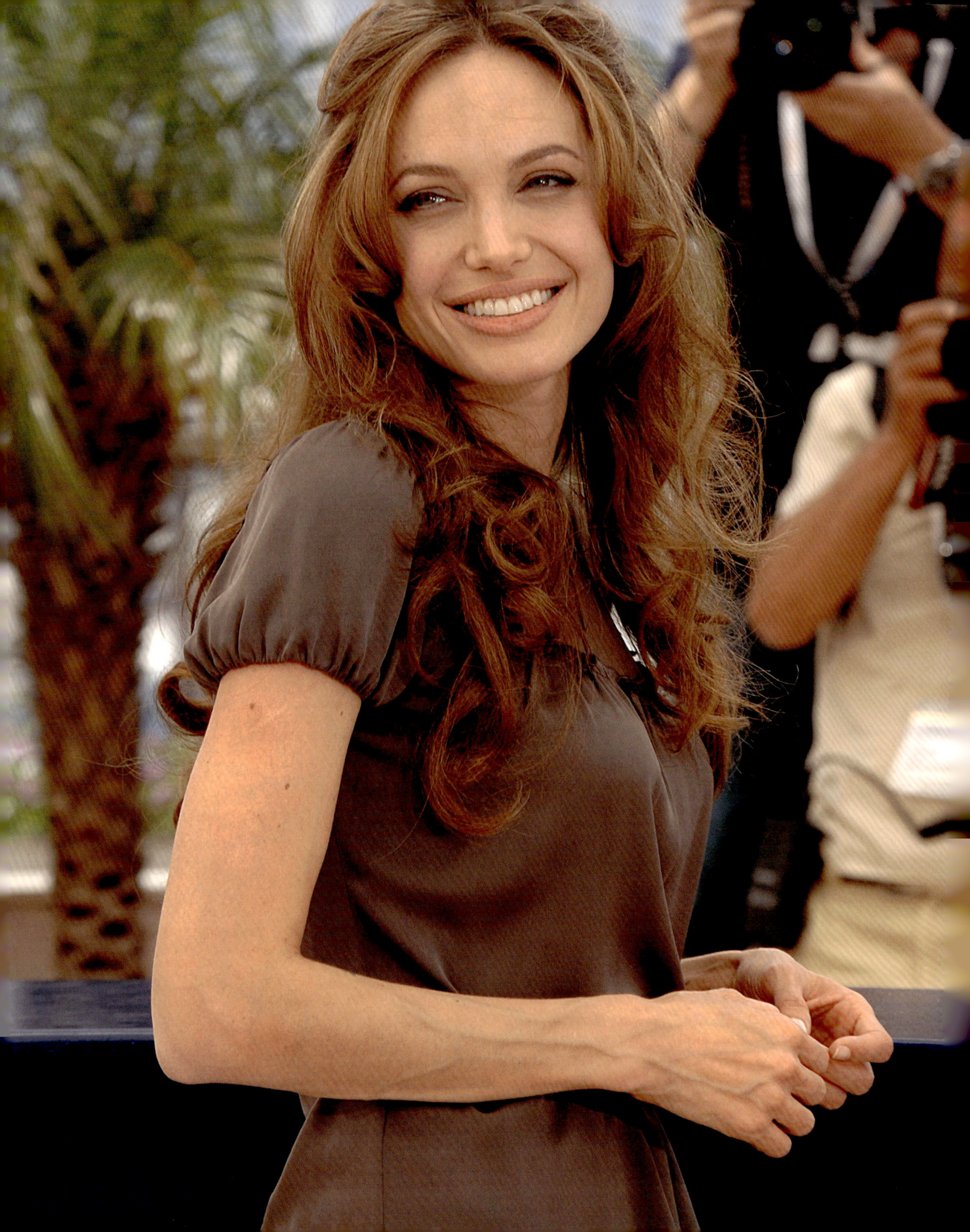

Marcheline Bertrand, pregnant with Angelina, with her husband Jon Voight, 1975.

Marcheline Bertrand and **Angelina Jolie**

★

Looking back at grainy images of Marcheline Bertrand in 1975, she was a mirror image of her daughter, Angelina Jolie's future self. Bertrand's easy cool reflected a bohemian sensibility. At seven-months pregnant she accompanied actor Jon Voight, Jolie's father, to the Oscars.

Surrounded by Hollywood stars, old and new, including Frank Sinatra, Faye Dunaway and Francis Ford Coppola, she wore an antique-rose shawl, a turquoise floor-length frock embroidered with flowers, her hair loose and long, and her face unadorned. She glowed. Angelina describes her mother as a hippie: "She called herself that, she was very proud. She didn't shop a lot. She loved her velvets and suedes. She never wore makeup, nor did she really do her hair. She wasn't a flashy person. She was elegant, natural" (*British Vogue*, 2023). In January 2024, Jolie unveiled a collaborative capsule wardrobe with Gabriela Hearst and Chloé, informed by Bertrand's style and Jolie's own childhood. It featured a black-velvet cape and a smock resembling one she'd owned as a child.

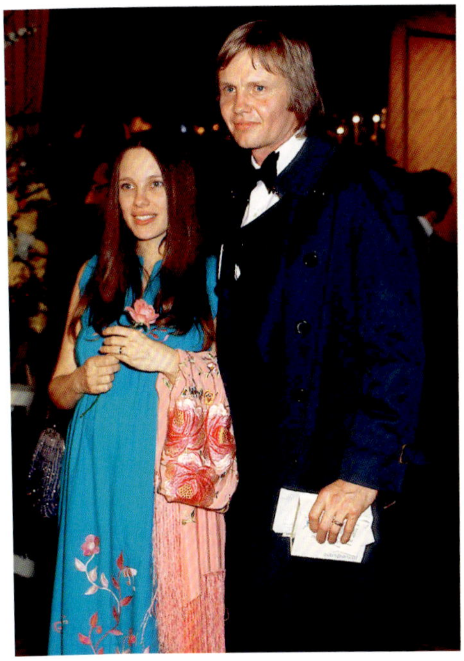

Bertrand was an actress, too, but abandoned her career after becoming a mother, opting instead to devote her life to Jolie and elder brother James Haven, born a couple of years earlier. Jolie's life as an actress segued naturally from Bertrand's ambition. In January 2025, Jolie rationalised her own vocation:

> "I did it in the beginning because it was my mother's dream. She pursued acting, but by the time my mom was 25, she was divorced with two kids, and she decided to focus her life solely on motherhood. She didn't make me feel like it was a sacrifice—she loved being a stay-at-home mom. But she really wanted me to be an actress. I don't remember making the choice. I remember it made my mom happy. My mom was my manager, and we were a team. I always wanted to buy her a house, and I started to pay the bills. When my mom passed, it was harder for me to be an actress because I realized how much of it was for her" (Hirschberg, 2025).

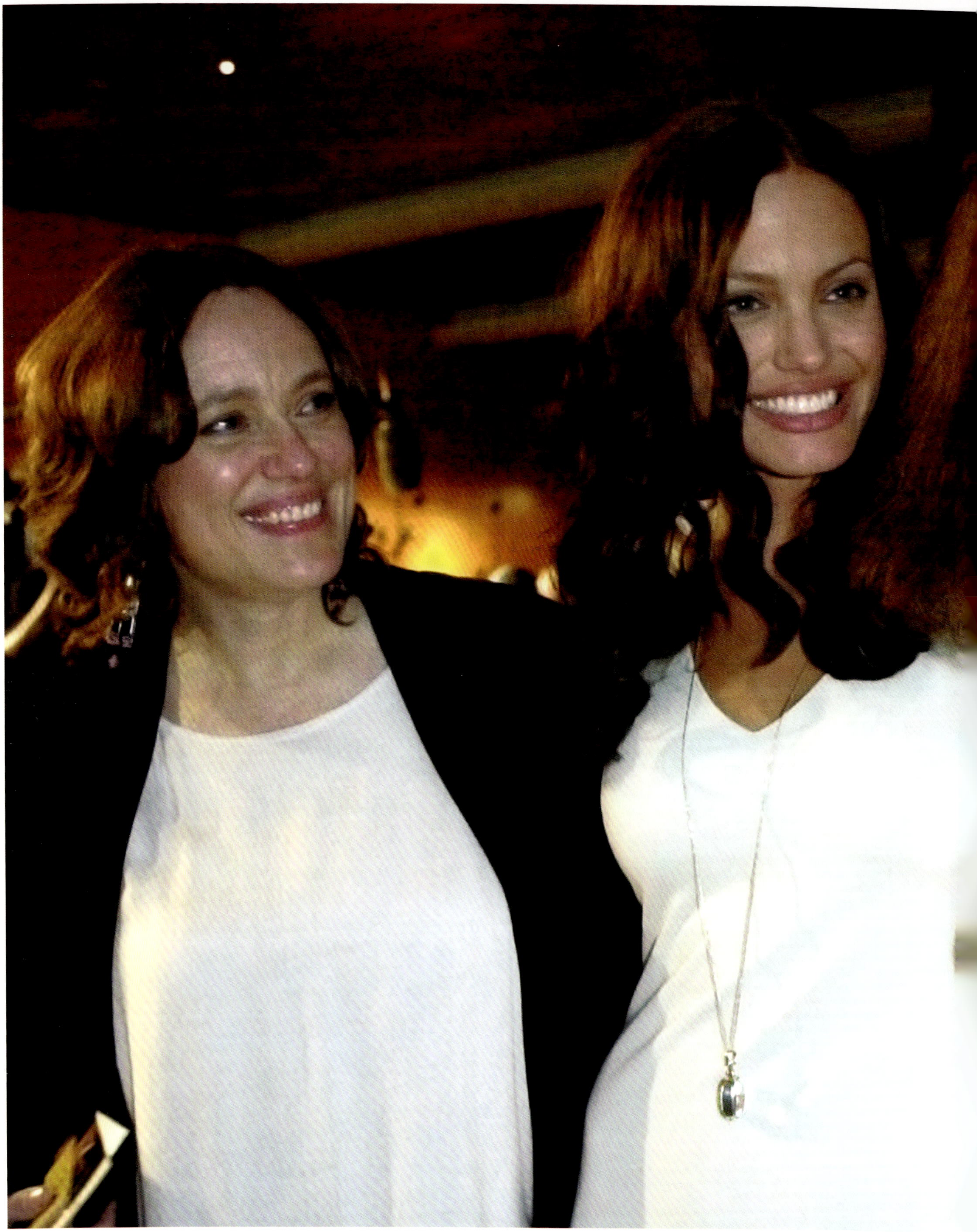

Bertrand died in 2007 from ovarian and breast cancer, aged just 56, but her legacy profoundly lives on in Angelina's world and is entwined not just with the good works Jolie conducts but her professional choices, too. In 2017 she joined forces with Guerlain:

> "It was a brand my mother loved, so I knew it from my childhood. It spoke to her, as it does to me, of beauty, history, and quality; one of the oldest perfume houses in the world, from France, a country I love and feel connected to. She was a very natural woman who never spoiled herself, never wore makeup, and wore modest jewelry, but she always had a few special items for when she wanted to feel like a lady. One of those—and I remember it because it seemed so elegant—was her Guerlain powder. I think all women have those few special things that make them feel feminine" (Rogers, 2017).

Like Bertrand, Jolie also has a strong mothering instinct. From a young age, she has wanted to adopt children: "My mom will tell you this. I've been talking about this ever since I can remember. Since I was like 12 years old. I think it's a big thing to admit that you're good enough to be a parent. It's the most important thing you could be." She goes on to reflect: "If you have tattoos and you have opinions about things and you act in very free ways then you aren't considered a person who would be a wife and mother... why is it so funny to everybody that I could be a wife and mother?" (Van Meter, 2002). That year she did indeed go on to become a parent and adopted her first son, Maddox, who was born in Cambodia.

According to Professor Nancy E. Dowd, who specialises in family law and critical theory: "Adoption creates a family that in important ways is not 'nuclear.' It creates a family that is connected to another family, the birth family, and often to different cultures and to different racial, ethnic, and national groups as well." She goes on to reflect how "adoptive families might teach us something about the value for families of connection with the larger community" (Dowd, 1994). Today, Jolie has six children and parents as a single mother. Her determination to embrace motherhood has manifested a family that has been built outside the normative values of a nuclear household and thrives.

Together, they all contribute to Jolie's most recent project: an atelier in New York, opened in 2024 and based on sustainable initiatives along with a desire to do things differently to the way fashion usually operates. It's a value system the family all seem to agree on. In 2021, at the world premiere of *Eternals*, in which Jolie played the warrior Thena, five of her kids attended wearing upcycled vintage, with Zahara sporting Jolie's Elie Saab couture dress worn at the 2014 Oscars. The consensus of individuality is a trait established by Bertrand, now inherited by her grandchildren and reinforced by Jolie: "Over the years, I've seen fashion dictated by trends and anointed arbiters of taste. But to look inward and dress for oneself—to truly express oneself with creativity and resourcefulness—is a useful rebellion in this modern age" (*CR*, 2024).

"My mother was a very globally minded, thoughtful person, who often spoke to me about injustice."

Angelina Jolie,
CR Fashion Book, 2024

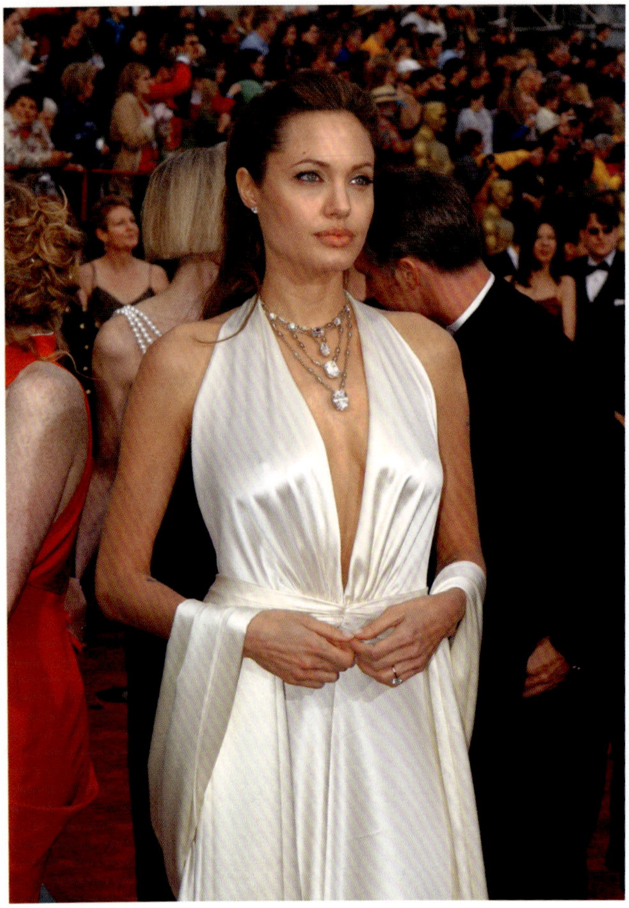

"My mother was an earth mother and the nicest person in the world."

Angelina Jolie,
Vogue, 2015

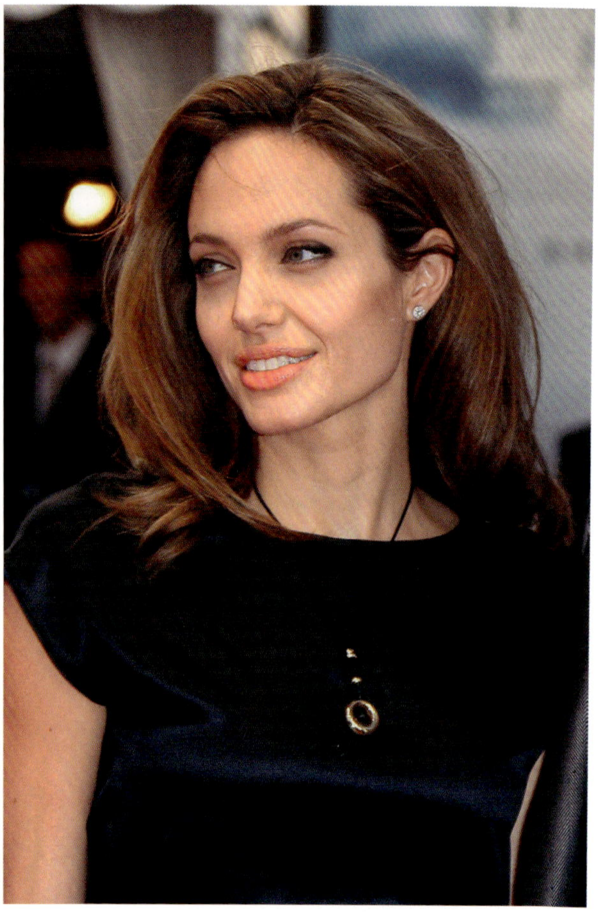

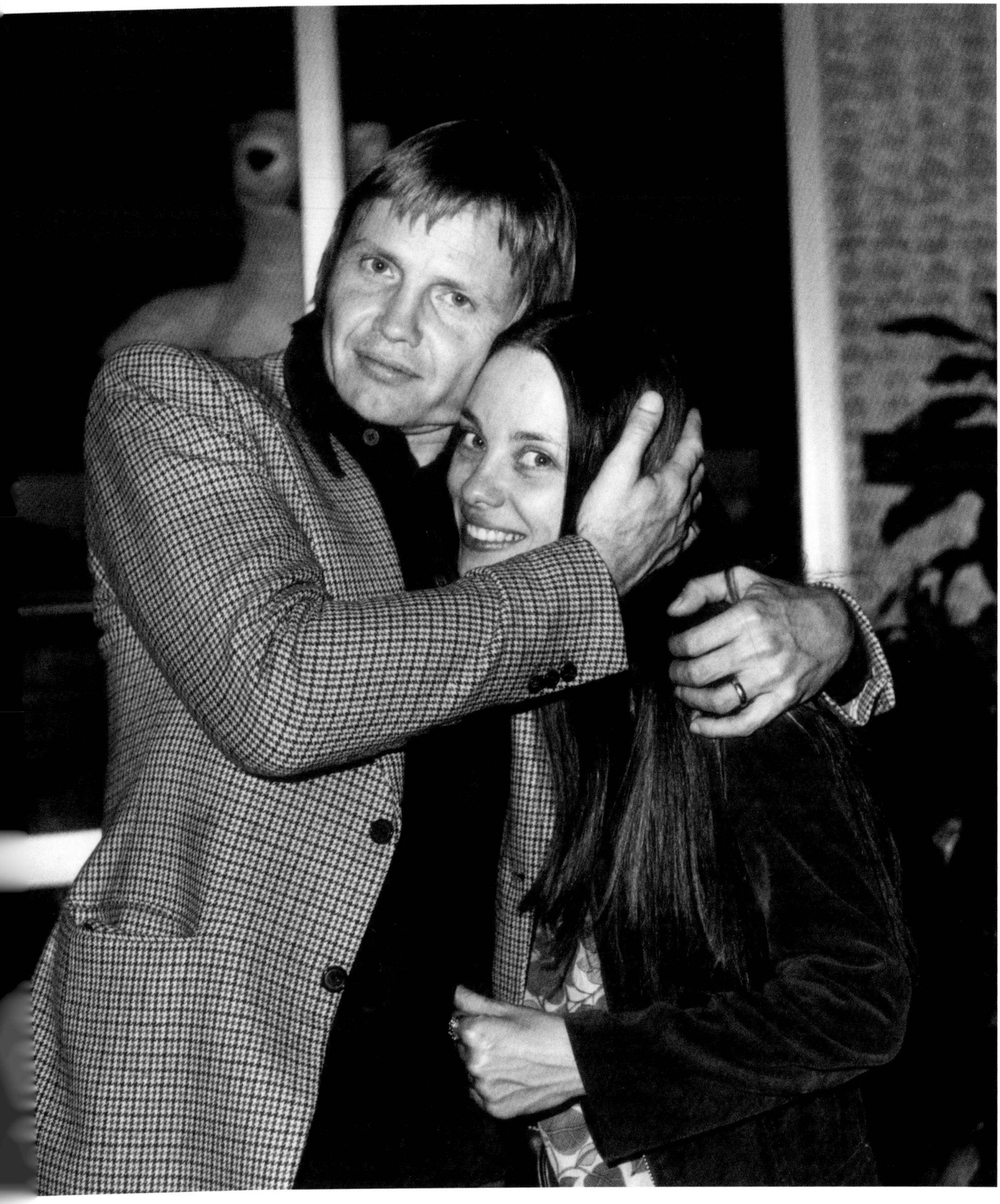

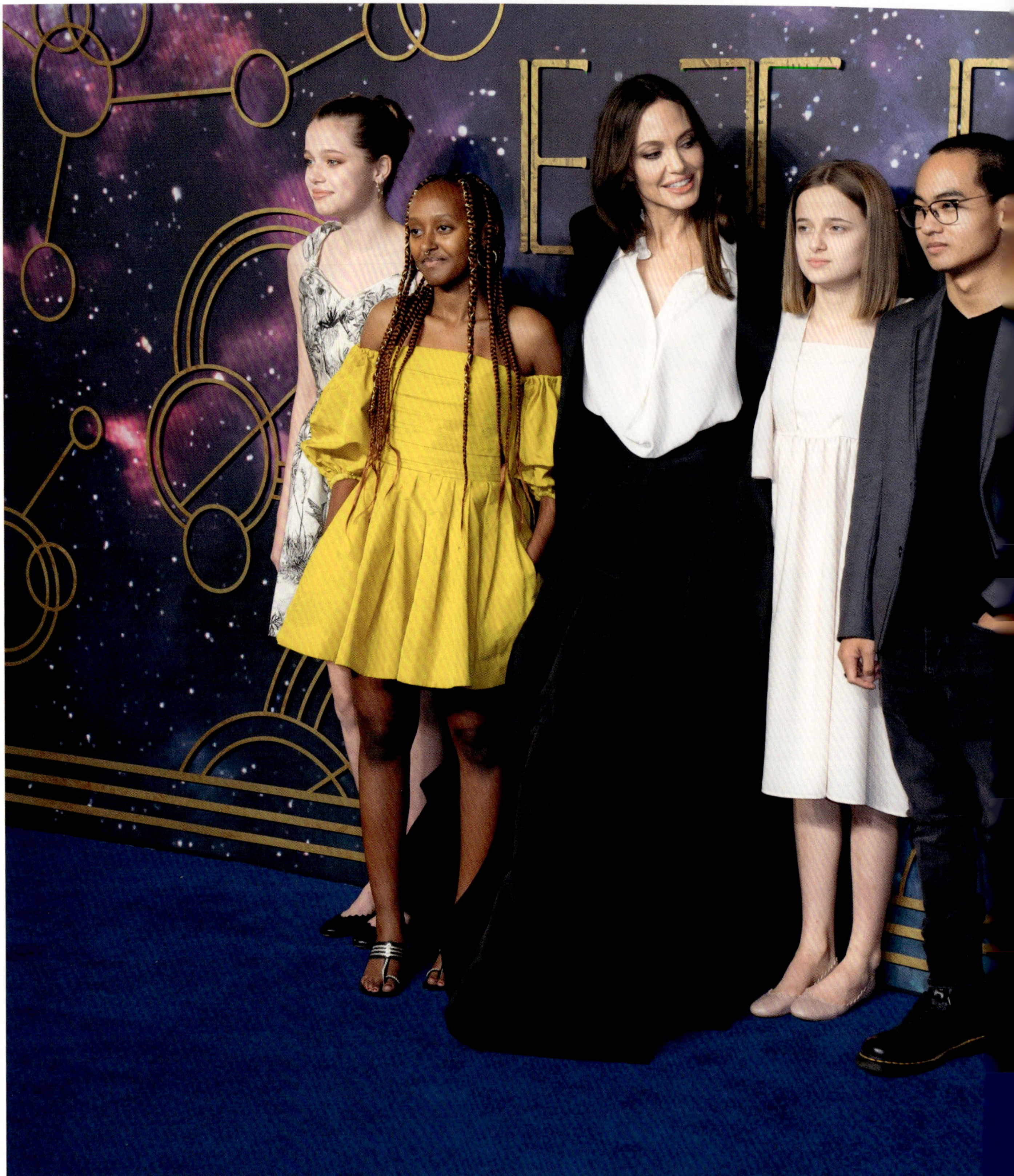

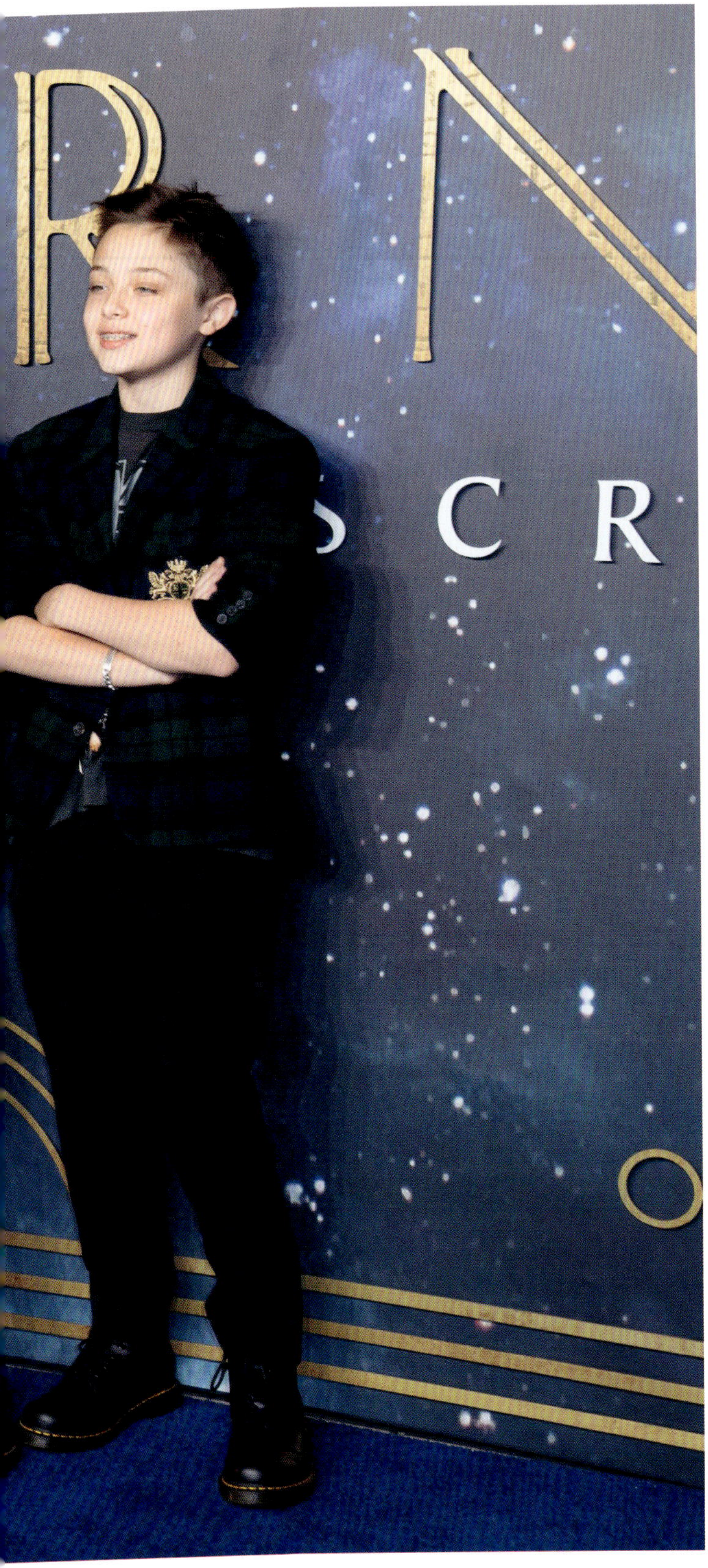

Angelina Jolie with her children: Shiloh, Zahara, Vivienne, Maddox and Knox, 2021.

"I was 26 when I became a mother. My entire life changed. Having children saved me – and taught me to be in this world differently."

Angelina Jolie,
Vogue, 2023

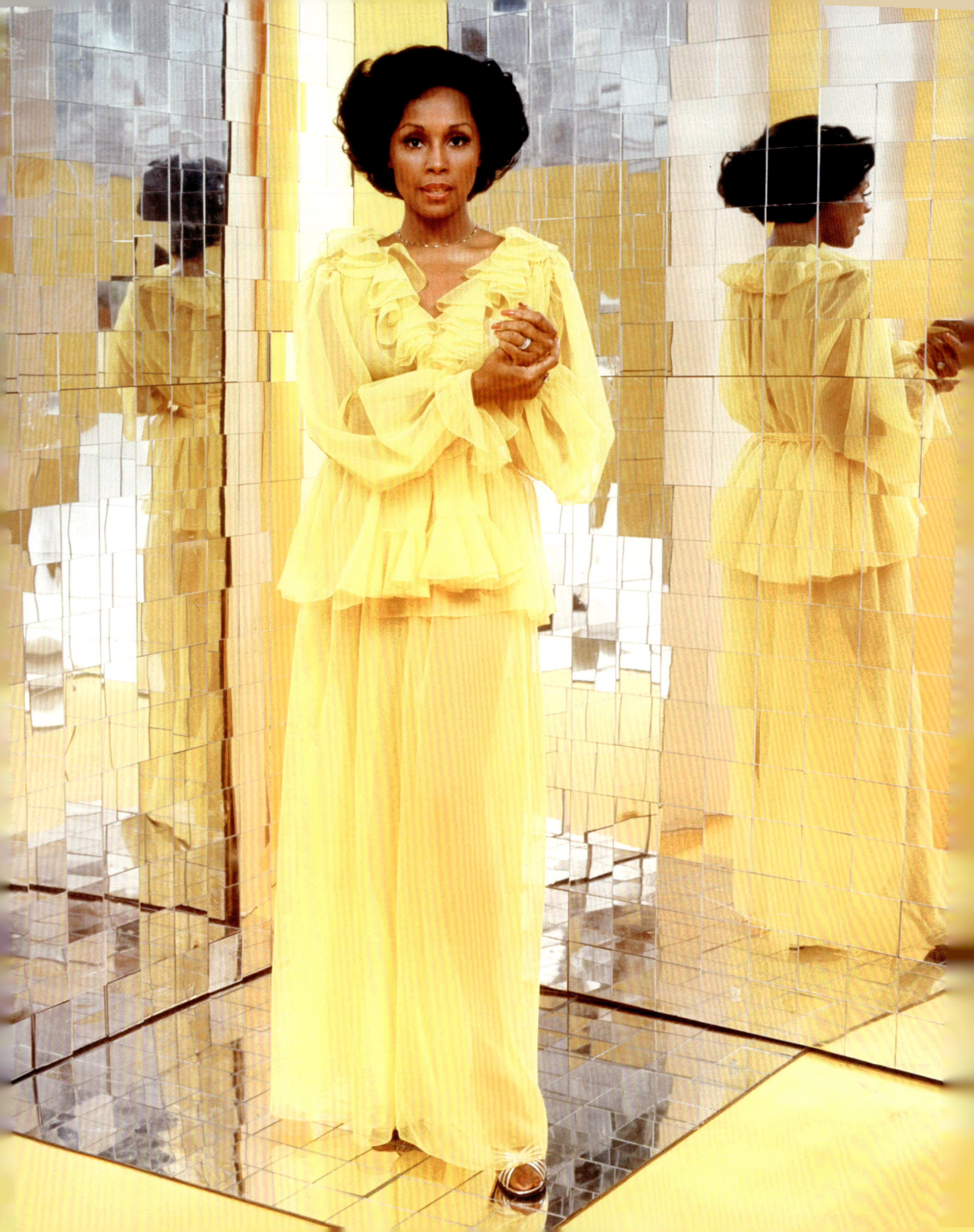

Diahann Carroll
and **Suzanne Kay**

★

> **"I think my mother proved you don't have to give up your sensuality and love of life as a mother. She had fun and never allowed others to define her."**
>
> **Suzanne Kay,**
> 2025

Diahann Carroll's legendary career was equally matched by her superstar wardrobe. The Oscar-nominated actress was a forerunner who broke so much new ground that she said, "after a while, I felt like I was the first Black woman to open a door, so I said let's drop the first Black woman, please" (*Today*, 2017). But it's hard not to overstate her significance as an important role model and a remarkable talent, who navigated life with elegance, determination and resilience while always looking impeccable. The Bonhams sale of her estate in 2020 included Chanel jackets, Bob Mackie gowns, Giorgio Armani suits, Manolo Blahnik shoes, Gucci boots, Cartier watches and diamond and platinum jewellery: all her go-to daywear.

Carroll's daughter, writer and filmmaker Suzanne Kay enthuses: "My favourite outfit of my mother's might be the pink dress she wore to the 1969 Oscars. I wish I knew the designer. She looked like an angel and the blush pink perfectly complimented her skin." That night at the award ceremony, Carroll glided onto the stage in her studded diamante gown and told the world: "Where else but in Hollywood could a girl from the Bronx come out on a night like this and introduce a boy from Brooklyn: Tony Curtis?"

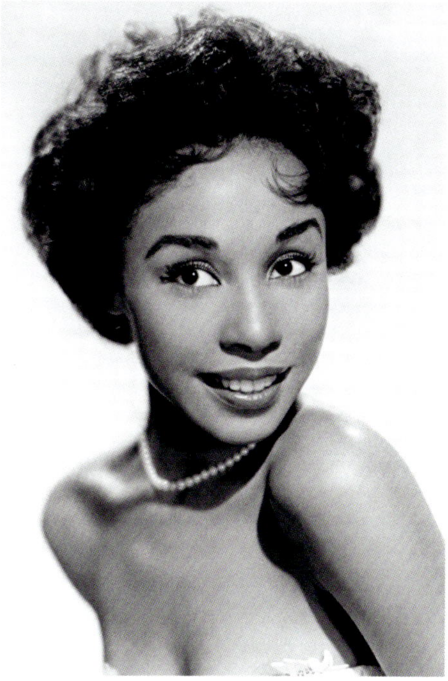

Above: Diahann with Suzanne as a baby, 1961. Below: Diahann and Suzanne with David Frost, 1973.

In 1946, when Diahann Carroll was just 11 years old, she began laying the groundwork for a life of flawless sartorial style, resilience and success. She started attending Edward W. Stitt Junior High School in Harlem, New York, with hair slickly curled, wearing neat, white ankle socks and carrying a tidy book bag. However, it wasn't a look her fellow classmates appreciated and Susan Fales-Hill, daughter of Carroll's close friend, the actress Josephine Premice, describes how her peers thought she was "too prissy, too pulled together; she was beaten up on the one and supported on the other with people saying, 'you go do what you do and represent us nicely with your pressed hair and your white gloves" (Jeff Zest, 2022). Although Carroll tried to fit in, messing her hair a little and saving lunch money to buy different shoes, it wasn't until 1949 when she was 14 and had gained a place at Manhattan's High School of Music & Art (later LaGuardia), that her conviction that she could and would become a star was cemented. Suzanne explains: "I didn't realize how much confidence I learnt from watching my mother. She owned any room she entered and showed me that no one should make a woman feel small. I inherited that sense of my own value and carry her with me wherever I go."

It was value well earned. Carroll is celebrated for many things, including succeeding as the first African-American woman to win a Tony Award for Best Actress for her role in the 1962 Richard Rodgers Broadway musical *No Strings*, where she played a Paris-based model. Later, in 1968, she took on the title role in *Julia* and became the first Black actress since Ethel Waters in *Beulah* in the 1950s, to star in her own weekly television series; it ran for 86 episodes until 1971. Julia played a widowed, middle-class, single parent who worked as a nurse – a controversial protagonist at the time. Black representation was thin, and critics felt that Julia embodied a different reality to the one many young Black single parents experienced. It was nevertheless a leading-edge show that led to Carroll's Golden Globe Award for Best TV Actress in 1968 and an Emmy nomination the following year.

Later, in 1974, Carroll played Claudine, a mother surviving on welfare with six children. It was a world away from Julia, whose chic wardrobe was smart and at times glamorous (one of her character costumes was a pink taffeta dress designed by William Travilla, which can be found in the archive of the National Museum of African American History and Culture). Instead, Claudine was exhausted and poverty stricken, and the clothes she wore were clean but shabby. It was a role that took Carroll away from the glitz of her usual appearance, with the entire wardrobe reportedly costing around $20. But she gave a performance that earned her an Oscar nomination.

Meanwhile, Carroll's own closet was the stuff of dreams, according to her daughter Suzanne:

> "I own many of my mother's beautiful shoes and bags and jewels. I've kept a few of her clothes, but we weren't the same size. I'm taller than my mother was and never loved wearing heels, so my favourite shoes are her vintage Chanel flats. Her purses were unbelievably beautiful. I inherited three Celine bags and a turquoise-skin Judith Leiber that takes my breath away. I'll just grab one and wear it with jeans and a crisp white shirt. My favourite fashion memory with my mother was when we had matching silk, pinstripe hot pants and vests made in the 1970s, and wore them out together in Los Angeles. She was dating Sir David Frost at the time, and he was our escort. That brilliant man was always so kind to me and a lot of fun.

"My mother did all of this so we could soar."

Suzanne Kay,
2025

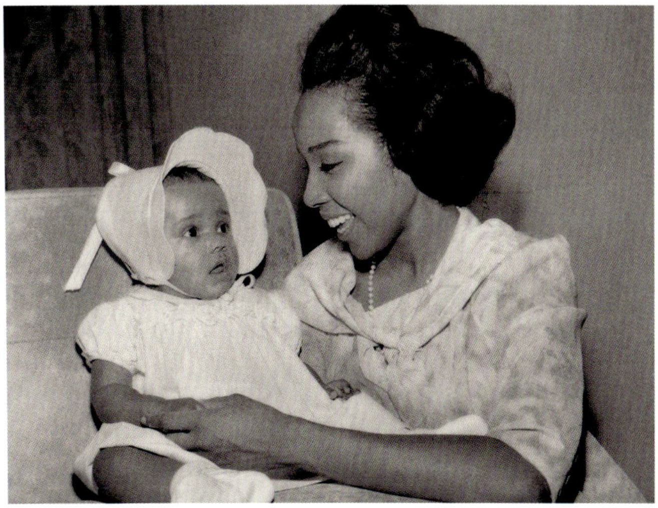

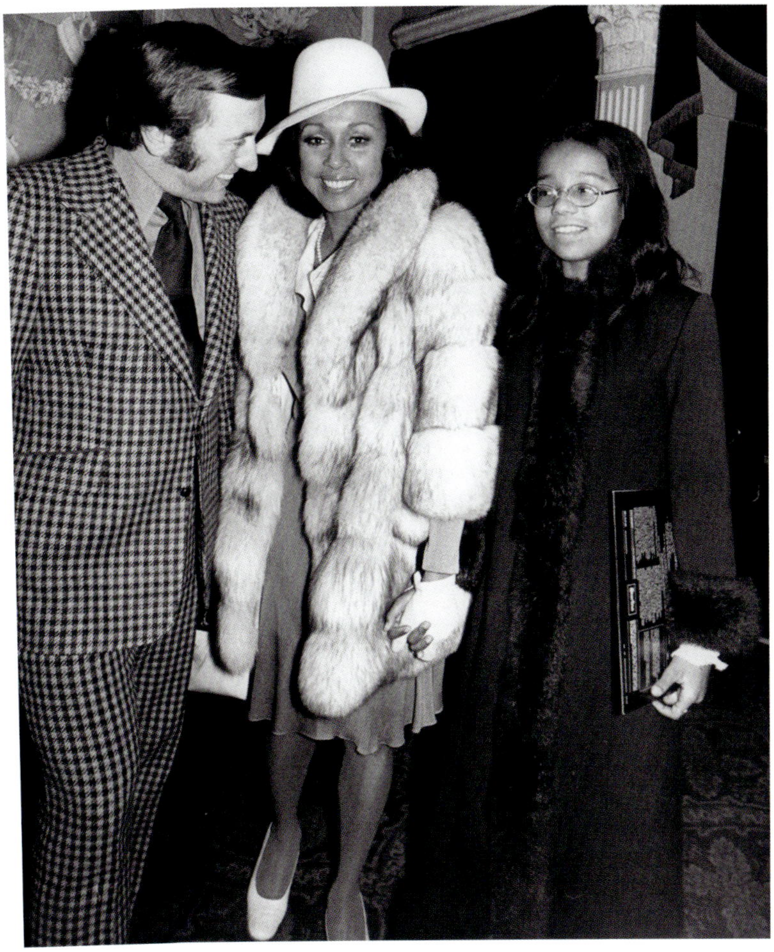

When we came home that evening, we went upstairs to the pool room and David bet me that I couldn't make a difficult shot. I hit a striped ball straight into the pocket at our billiard table and he wrote me a check for two thousand dollars! I was 12 years old and thrilled. I imagined all the toys I could buy but my mother promptly took the check from my hands and said it was going into my savings account!"

In July 1979, on the Johnny Carson show, Carroll clarified her signature style:

"Strangely, I don't like jeans. I love bathing suits around the house; love to put on my little bikini and run around the house. It's very comfortable. I don't like housecoats, I don't like rollers in the hair... Fantasy is nice, and it helps us to get through reality. Reality can be sometimes heavy and hit you in the nose. I like a little false eyelash, a little titillation; I think it makes life more... you know what I mean?" (Zany, 2020).

She leant into fantasy even more onscreen when, in 1984, she was given the part of Dominique Deveraux in the television series *Dynasty*, becoming – as she phrased it – "the first Black bitch". The clothes she wore were part of Deveraux's appeal and personified the 1980s vogue for power dressing, replete with big shoulders and a take-no-prisoners attitude. It was so popular that McCall's home sewing patterns created a line in her honour. Carroll herself brought out a line of wigs, clothes and sunglasses. It was an extension of her love for all the properties of glamour. She was a prototype influencer, not just for her adoring public but for her daughter, too.

"My mother loved decorating her homes as much as she loved clothes. I recently bought and decorated two homes. In the first, I found that my taste reflected my mother's elegance and I chose all creams and beiges and black. In the next home, I painted my bedroom a pale green and bought bold, colourful art that lifted my soul. I learnt from my mother that fashion and art and home decorating should reflect who you are. When I was in my 20s I went through a period of dressing like my mother. I even wore many of her clothes, even though they were too mature for me. It took me years to find my own style because her impact was so big. But now I'm comfortable in my own skin and I love being playful with fashion and home decorating. What I learnt from her about style and elegance, I couldn't shake off if I tried; and as I grew older, putting my own spin on that has brought me great joy."

"I grew up watching MGM musicals, Joan Crawford, Bette Davis, Lena Horne, all women who were concerned with looking smashing, not natural."

Diahann Carroll,
The New York Times, 1998

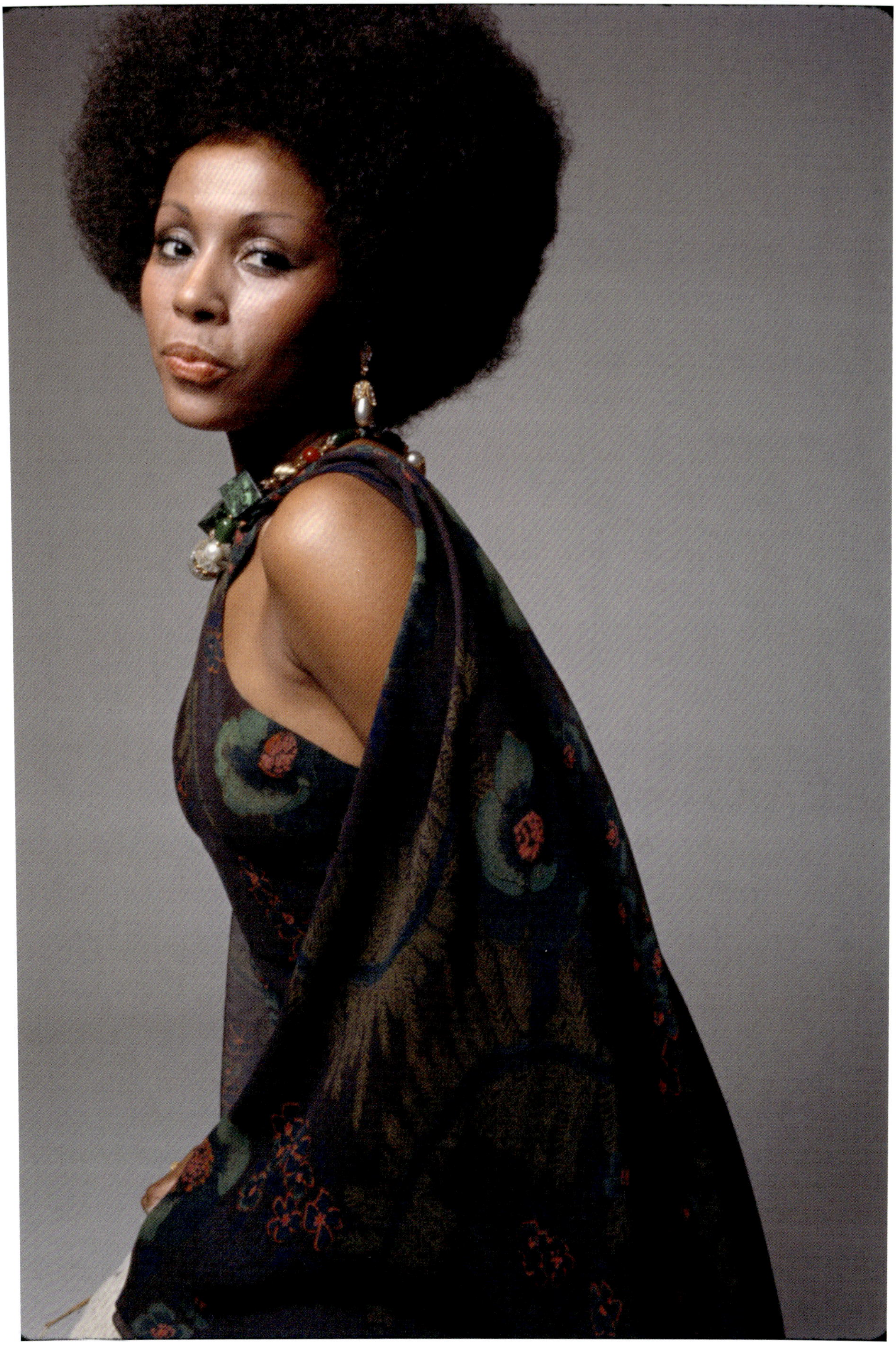

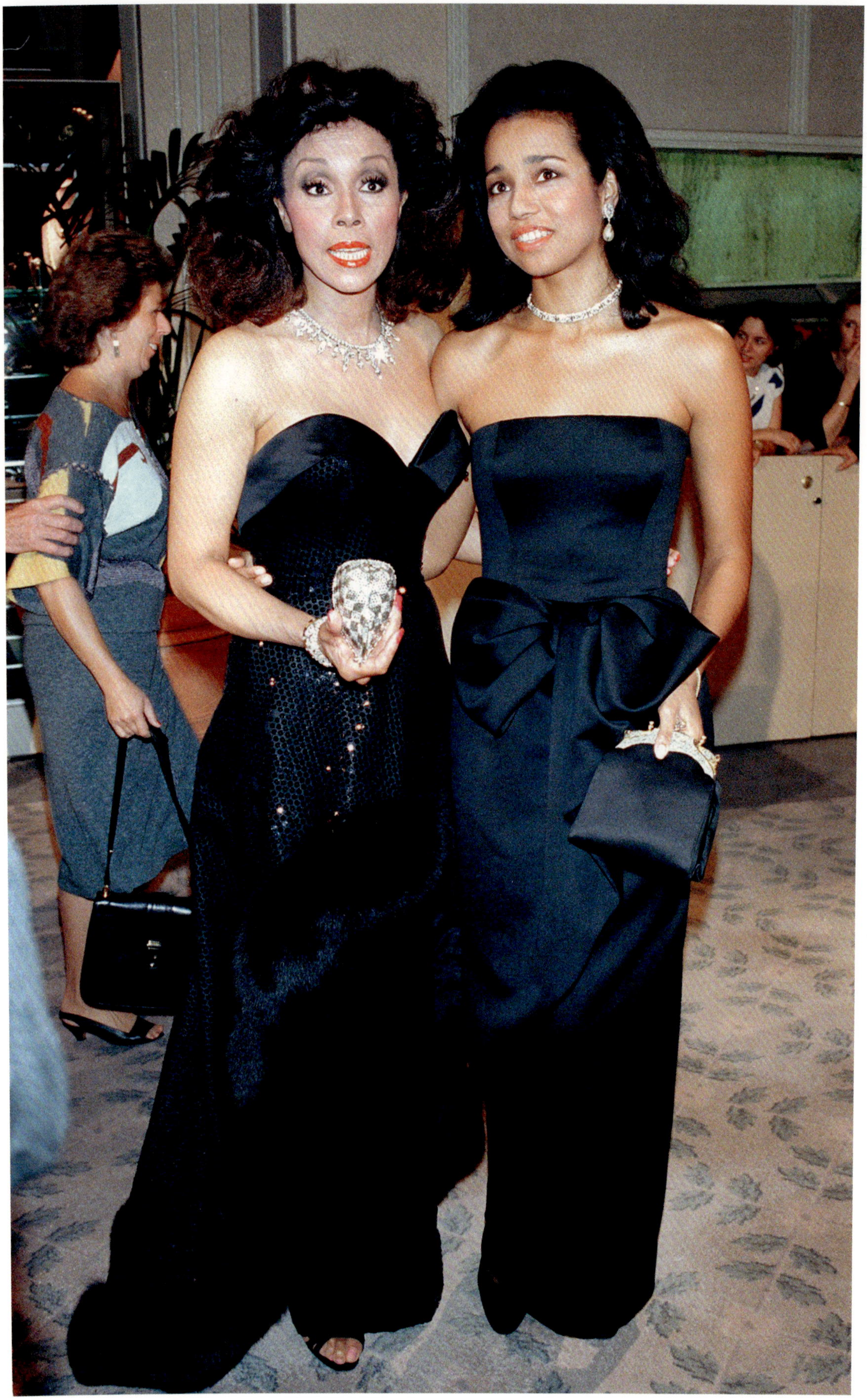

> **"I think that business of overwhelming people with your presence, and your grooming—it's not part of today. It's not important today. I cannot tell you what it meant then. I was dressed in Givenchy from head to toe. It meant a great deal during an interview."**
>
> **Diahann Carroll,**
> *The New York Times*, 2019

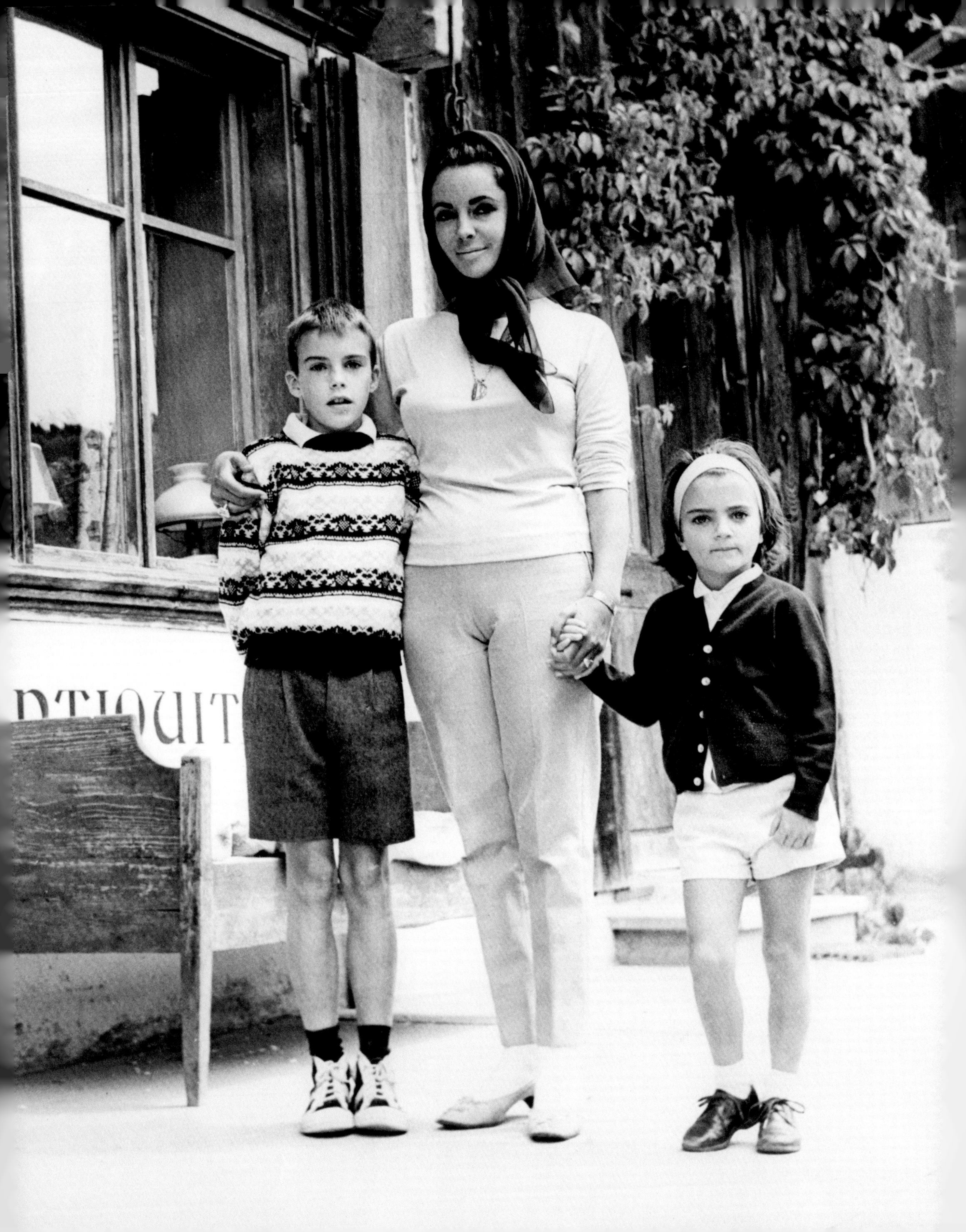

Elizabeth Taylor with her children, Christopher and Liza, 1962.

Sara Sothern, **Elizabeth Taylor** and **Naomi deLuce** Wilding

★

Naomi deLuce Wilding, a Central Saint Martin's fashion graduate, built a career as a stylist in Los Angeles and now co-runs Wilding Cran Gallery, supporting artists around the world. She grew up understanding the power of clothes. Her grandmother was Elizabeth Taylor, and as a result she learnt from the best.

> "There was probably always a divide between the in-person 'granny' and the onscreen Elizabeth Taylor. I loved both, but it was her screen identity that probably inspired me the most in terms of fashion. Also, she was younger on the screen – closer to my own age, so it was easier to identify and be influenced by her. As I grew up, I could see her physique as a template for my own. I saw what worked for her, what was iconic even; I could apply that to myself. I used to love the silhouette of the clothes from the '50s, buying vintage patterns from the charity shops near where I lived in Wales, or pick up vintage pieces when I visited London or California."

Taylor's fashion influence began when she was still a teenager. She was first shot for American *Vogue*'s November 1948 issue and modelled in an editorial headlined "Co-Stars: Elizabeth Taylor. Young Fashions Young Prices", dressed in "shirt and skirt fashion that the young love for its different every time look". She was 16 and had been acting since the age of 10, having hit the big time when she was 14 appearing in the movie *National Velvet* (1944). She discovered quickly the value of her identity, as deLuce Wilding explains:

> "She learnt from being a performer at such an early age that she could communicate the character in how she dressed for a role, and often that went beyond how the clothes looked but also how they made you move and stand, which in turn affects how you feel and present yourself. My grandmother understood that costumes existed in the social sphere just as much as on the screen or stage. When she got ready to go out, she went through a lengthy transformation. I always thought she was more beautiful without make-up, but I came to see that applying the make-up was about putting on a mask for the world, that was both internal and external; the process was part of a mental and physical preparation and transformation. What she wore was a costume and an armour to prepare herself for the scrutiny of the outside world."

Taylor's experience with the wardrobe department was vital. Tim Mendelson, Taylor's constant and loyal assistant for over 20 years, revealed:

> "She had worked with costume designers from the time she was a teenager, with Helen Rose and with Edith Head on *A Place in the Sun*. The white dress she wore in that movie became one of the most copied dresses of the '50s. These incredible women were like second mothers to her, so she had a great connection to fashion" (Bender, 2024).

Taylor's legacy is global and enduring, not just on the silver screen and in fans' wardrobes, but also within blockbuster fashion house collections. Back in 2006, the designer Michael Kors explained:

Elizabeth with her mother, Sarah Taylor, arriving in Southampton on the Queen Mary, *1947.*

> "There's always a little Elizabeth Taylor in every collection I do. For Spring 2005 we had a white dress with an Empire waist and some turquoise and jet crystal on it. It was a perfect La Liz moment. For Spring 2006 everything was based on the movie *Giant*. Sometimes when I'm working, I use shorthand [with my designers] and say something like, 'You know, it's an Elizabeth Taylor *BUtterfield 8* moment'" (Kors, 2011).

Taylor's significant connoisseurship of clothes came from years of being immersed in the world of showmanship and her confidence allowed her to experiment and enjoy her wonderful wardrobe. DeLuce Wilding describes:

> "She loved to play with clothes. I think that's what I learnt most of all about fashion from her – that it was something playful, not to be taken too seriously, and that by putting it on, you were getting to choose the version of yourself that you showed the world. What she did always communicate (and maybe in particular to her adoring granddaughters), was her love of clothes, whether she was dressing for an important event, or having friends over for Sunday lunch. She loved to try things on with us, she loved the luxurious feel of the fabrics – it was always a very sensuous experience. I used to like to run my hands along the racks of clothes as they hung in her closet, just to feel the softness."

Equally, Tim Mendelson saw Taylor's understanding of the virtue of a special wardrobe piece first-hand:

> "She certainly expressed a lot of respect for beauty and craftsmanship, whether something was designer or not. In fact, she got a kick out of finding special pieces in unexpected places. When we were in Istanbul and went to the local bazaar, she would notice the details and imagine the care that went into creating something when someone with her resources and relationships with designers might turn their noses up. I heard her argue with designers like Valentino to lower something or make it tighter beyond their comfort level. She knew what she wanted and couldn't really be convinced otherwise once her mind was made up."

"My love affair with jewellery began when I was a girl.... The first beautiful piece of jewellery I ever purchased was for my mother. It was costume, but so finely made and so gorgeous that we still have it in the family treasures."

Elizabeth Taylor,
quoted in the *Los Angeles Times*, 2014

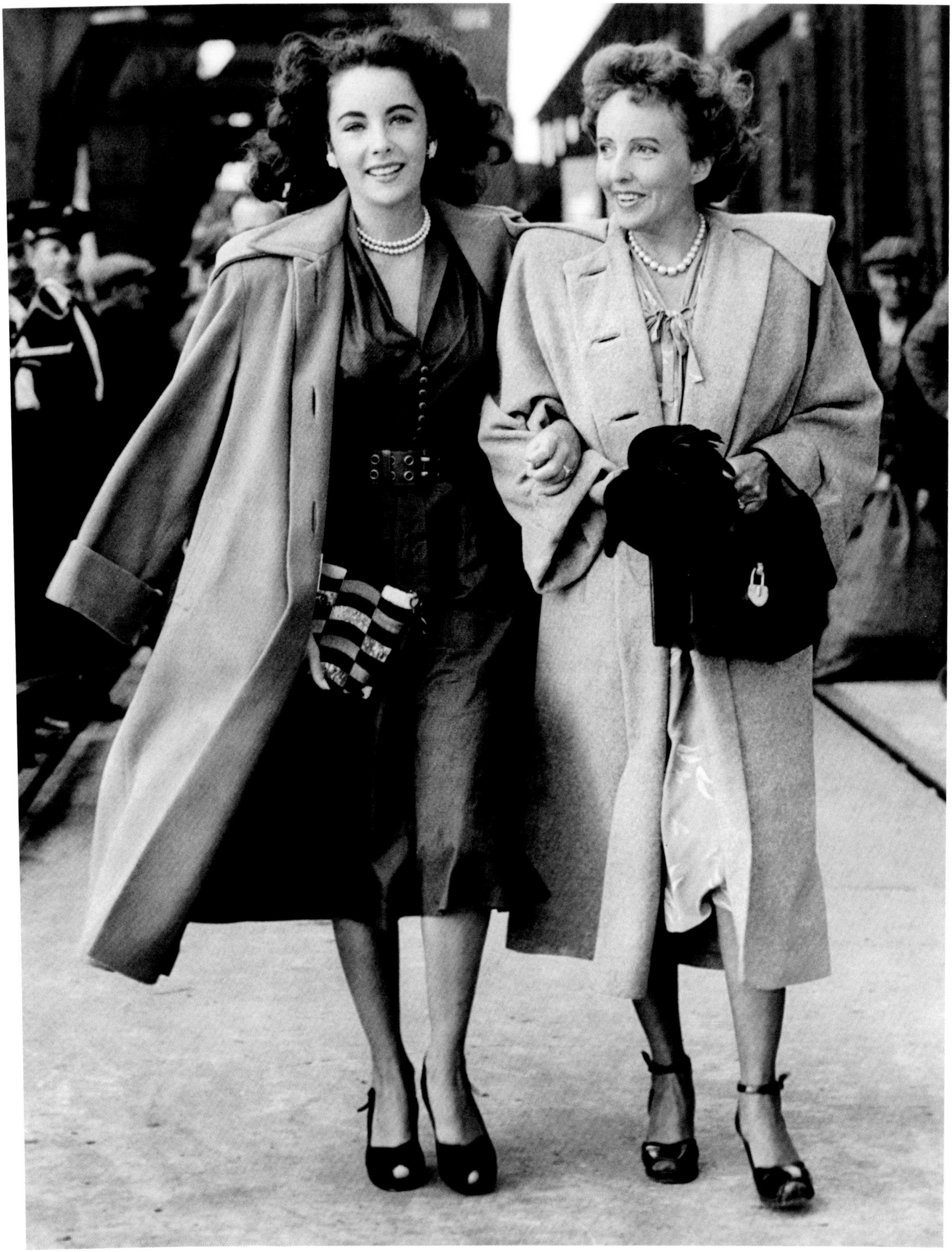

Taylor's delight in clothes can be decoded in the outfits she chose for her four children, Michael Wilding Jr, Christopher Wilding, Liza Todd and Maria McKeown. During a visit to Bertram Mills Circus in 1961, she and Liza wore matching mauve Christian Dior couture suits.

Taylor rode the dodgems and relished all the fun of the fair wearing the best Paris fashion had to offer. Matching mother-and-daughter clothes were something Taylor and her own mother, Sara Sothern enjoyed later in life, too. In 2019, Julien's Auctions sold an orange satin-lined Balmain skirt and matching top, once given to Sothern by Taylor. The two wore matching outfits – Taylor's in green to co-ordinate with the festive red – for fun on Christmas day in Gstaad, Switzerland in 1964.

Sothen and Taylor's lives and styles intermingled. Taylor relayed how: "My mother was an actress but then she married my dad, and he didn't want her to be an actress, so she gave it up. I think she lived her life through me" (BBC, 2024). The women had very similar tastes in fashion. Another outfit of Sothern's – a mint-green chiffon evening gown – went under the hammer at Julien's during the same auction. It was designed by one of Taylor's favourite wardrobe artists, Helen Rose, famous for creating Taylor's first wedding dress in 1950 for her marriage to Conrad 'Nicky' Hilton. Other iconic pieces included the white slip dress worn by Taylor's character, Maggie, in the 1958 classic film *Cat on a Hot Tin Roof*.

The clothes Elizabeth Taylor collected over the years were photographed for Catherine Opie's 2015 book *700 Nimes Road*. Opie's work shows off the poetry and scope of Taylor's wardrobe: closet after closet of lavender silk robes, row upon row of Chanel 'magnolia' shoes, boxes of diamonds and gowns, shelves of cowboy boots and sunglasses, colour-coordinated handbags, all carefully catalogued by the fine-art photographer. Taylor meticulously kept the clothes she loved and often returned to favourites. According to Mendelson: "She had a Givenchy cream-coloured, boiled-wool pullover top. It was from the '60s I would guess, and very modern looking. She was proud of herself for recognising it was such a beautiful and classic Givenchy design that would always be in style and worth holding onto for decades."

The legacy of Elizabeth Taylor lives on today. DeLuce Wilding reflects on her grandmother's work as a mother and social advocate, considering how she used clothes to project strength:

> "I often find myself wishing that I had known her more in my time as an adult woman and a mother. It is clear to me that she was very intentional about how she packaged herself for the world. A perfect example would be to see how she dressed for her hearings on Capitol Hill – addressing the government and the country on the AIDS pandemic. She knew how to dress to be taken seriously, just as the rest of the time she understood that her main commodity was her beauty, so she played it up to the fullest. She knew that, even though she was a talented actor, and later businesswoman and activist, there was power in the packaging."

She wanted her light to sparkle on through her work, as Mendelson affirms:

> "Life with Elizabeth was so busy, full of drama, fun too! Organically glamorous, she focused so much on living in the moment that the future and past played a very small part in her thinking. The only thing she really wanted to be remembered for was her role in the fight against AIDS. She was also very clear that she merely saw herself as the temporary custodian of her jewellery. That it would go on beyond her lifetime, and she hoped that it would be worn, cherished, and loved as much by others as it had been by her."

Left: Elizabeth holding her son, Michael, in her arms, 1953. Right: Elizabeth with her daughter, Liza, 1965.

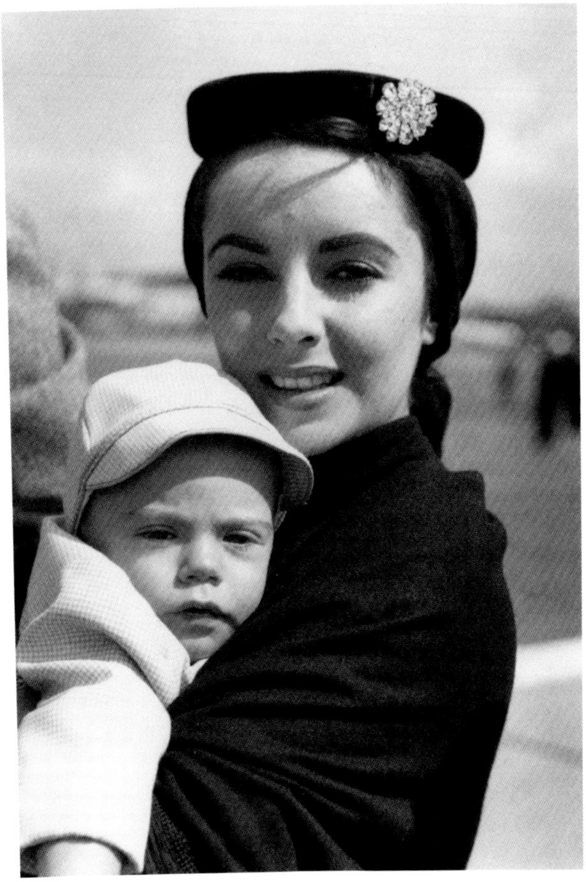

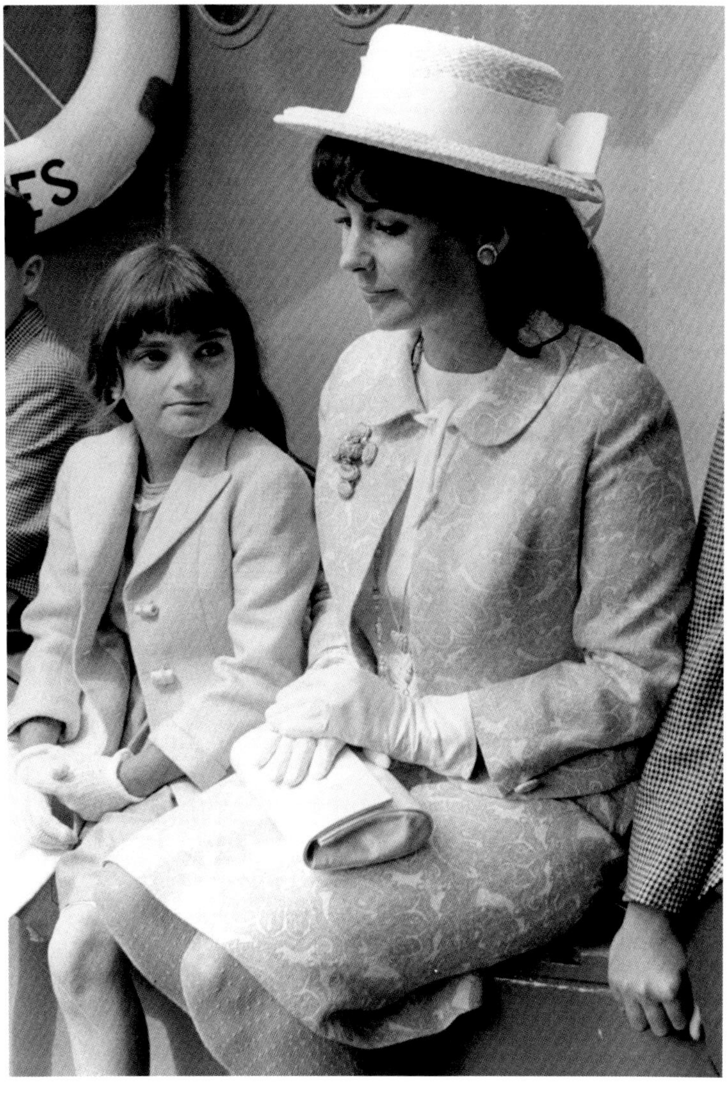

Elizabeth with her granddaughter, Naomi, 2001.

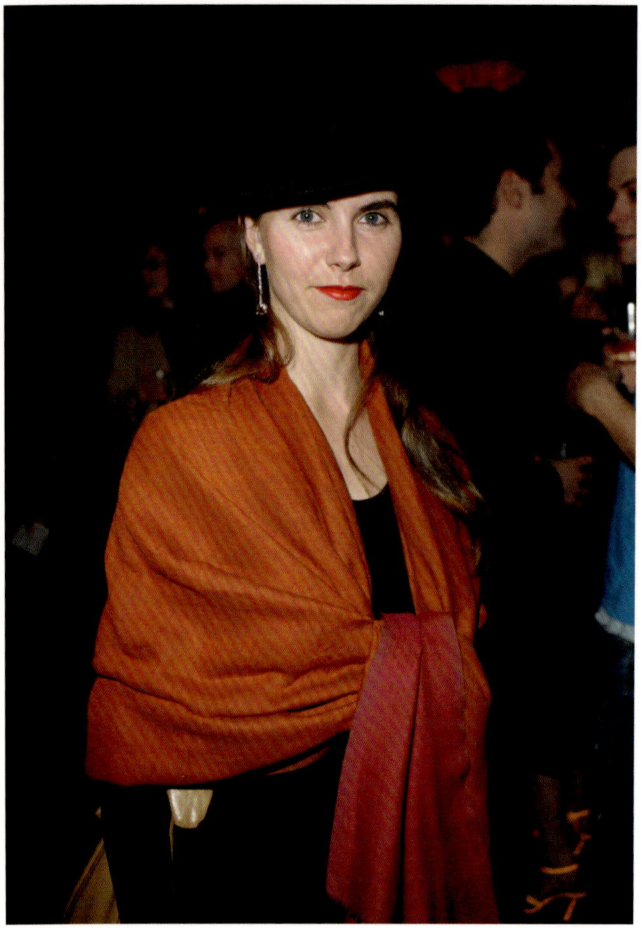

"My Granny [Elizabeth Taylor] loved colour and texture, sparkly stuff. I found it exciting when I was a kid – she sparkled for me. She always wore jewellery, sometimes playful, though – not always the big diamonds. She loved the cheap and tacky as well as the million-dollar stuff she was known for. She'd wear a ring from an arcade machine if you gave it to her."

Naomi deLuce Wilding,
2025

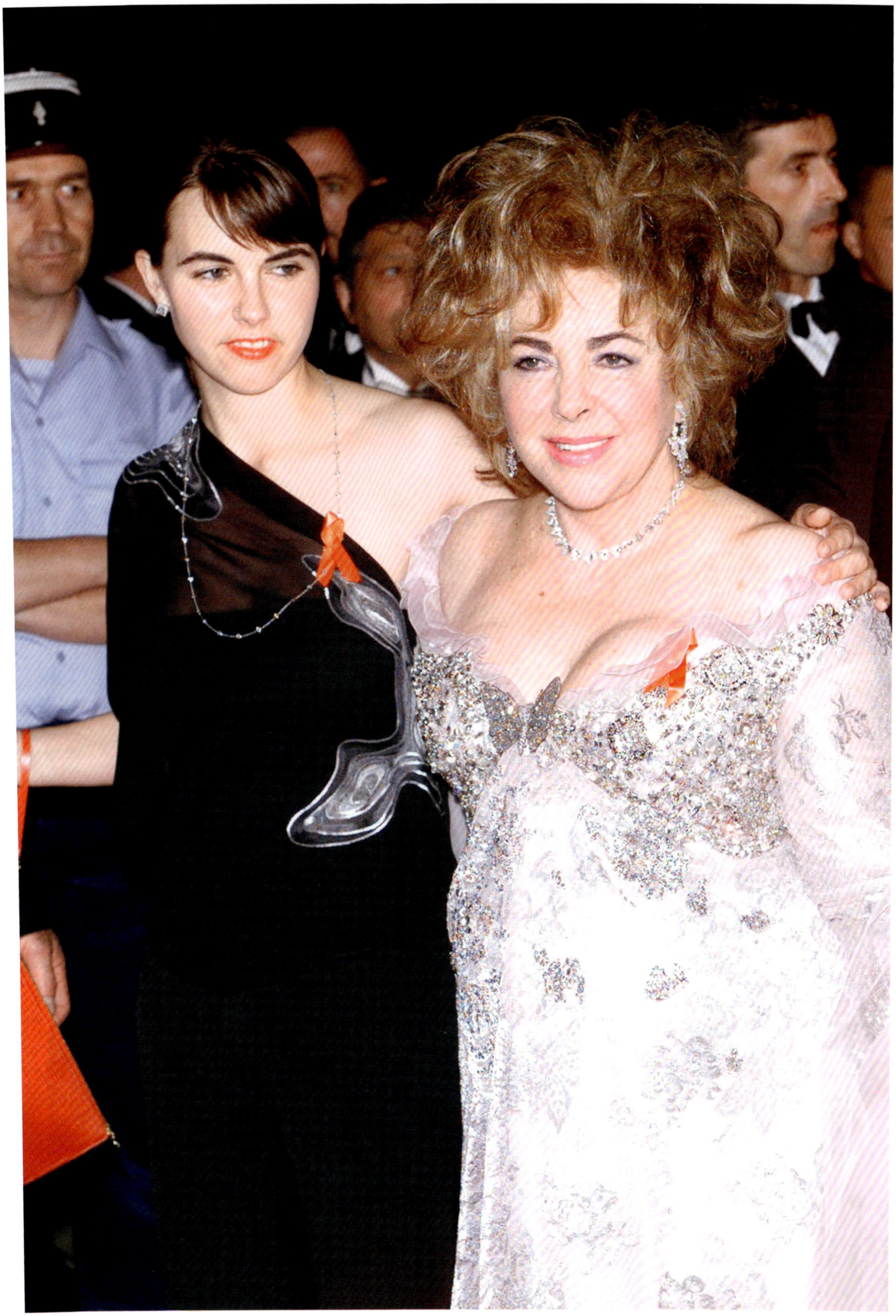

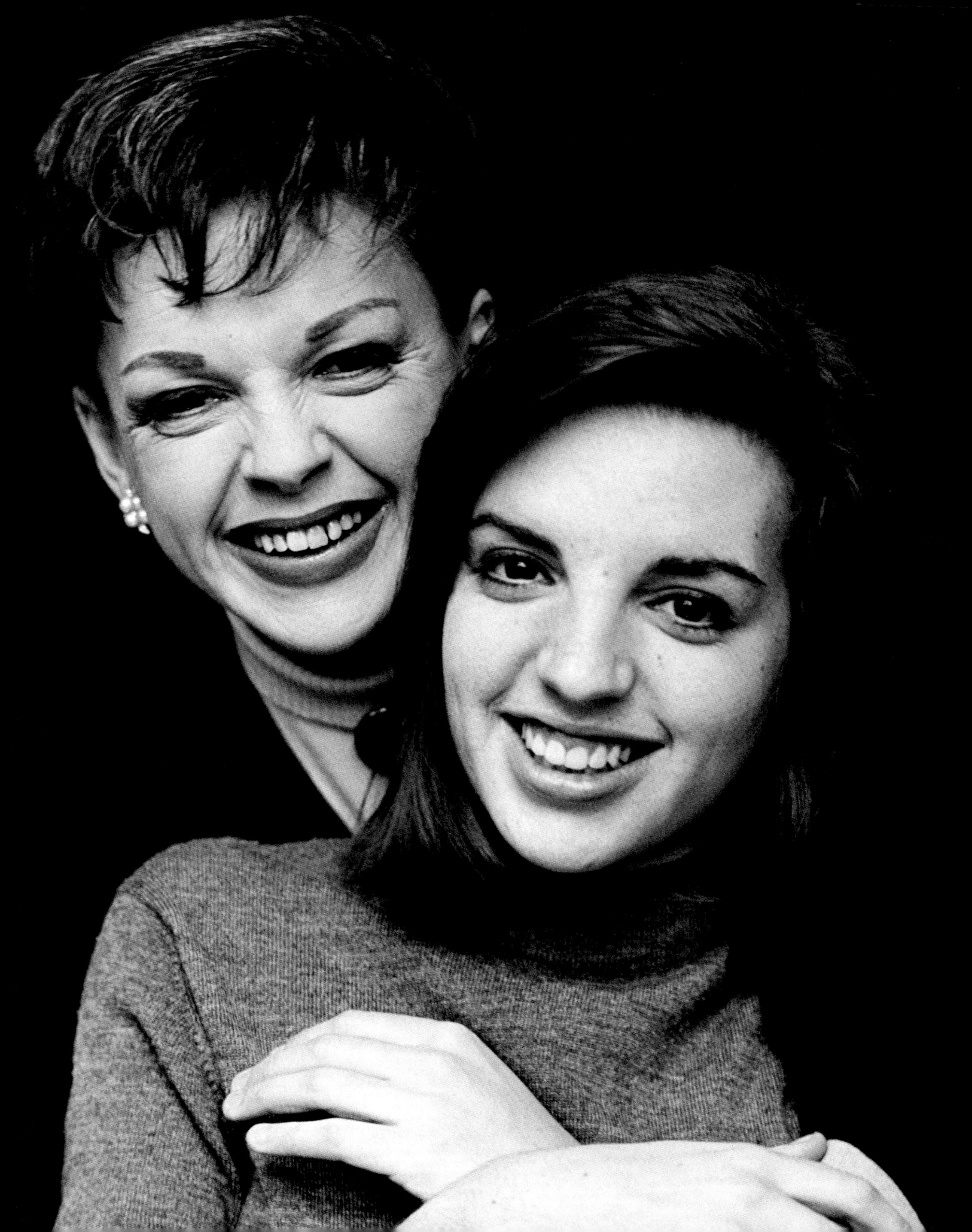

Judy **Garland,** Liza **Minnelli,** Lorna **and** Joey **Luft**

★

There are many perks to having a legendary star as a parent. Lorna Luft depicts a childhood full of ups and downs in her 1998 memoir *Me and My Shadows*, but one of the benefits of being the daughter of Judy Garland were her fabulous clothes:

> "Mama had the best closet in the world for a kid to play in, a big movie-star closet stuffed full of wonderful clothes and dozens and dozens of shoes. I spent hours in there looking around and trying things on. I loved putting on Mama's glamorous dresses and hats, and I especially liked trying on the shoes. My mom always wore those high spiked heels when she went out. I'd put my small feet into what seemed like big shoes to me and try and walk around in them. I thought they were the coolest thing there was" (Luft, 1998).

Judy Garland earned her wardrobe. She fell in love with performing, and being camera ready at all times – onscreen and off – was part of her fashion persona. At the age of two and a half, she stood on stage for the first time and sang 'Jingle Bells'. She was known as 'Baby Gumm' and would soon dominate the singing troupe The Gumm Sisters that she had formed with her siblings. Garland adored people paying her attention, and the spotlight and the approval it gave her.

However, it wasn't until 20 years later, when she appeared in her 1944 film *Meet Me in St. Louis*, that she found her grown-up signature look: red lips and long lashes. After the movie had finished, Garland proclaimed that it was the first time she had ever felt beautiful. Dottie Ponedel, who would go on to become a life-long friend, was the make-up artist on set who had bestowed the cosmetic armour. Costumes were by five-time Oscar winning, designer Irene Sharaff, who clad Garland in a now iconic pale-blue, striped cotton dress with white-lace bow tie and a red-velvet ballgown with a sweetheart neckline. Sharaff outfitted the best of Hollywood, and witnessed glamour up close. She said: "You can acquire chic and elegance, but style itself is a rare thing" (Nemy, 1967).

Referred to as "my little hunchback" by her first studio boss, Louis B. Mayer at MGM, Garland was constantly berated for her looks, size and height (Wayne, 2003). This constant battle meant she quickly learnt the chic fashion tricks of the trade and worked out how to look as elegant as possible – how a boat neckline made her neck look longer and maxi dresses made her look thinner. More critically, she discovered not just what made her look good, but what made her feel good, too: her own style consciousness. She was an entertainer who always searched for sparkle and her wardrobe was one way of always looking great on the outside. Her outfits never let her or her audience down. Onscreen and off she wore Capri pants, tights and over-sized shirts, sequins, feathers and fur, headscarves, pumps, a men's fedora and a satin-lapelled tuxedo. Dresses, heels and trouser suits by designers like Bob Mackie, Balmain and Salvatore Ferragamo, topped off with bugle beads – Garland's confident way with clothes was a conduit for her people-pleasing vivacity. Dressing, for her, was dressing for success.

Garland's style was an inspiration both while she was alive and in the present day. The gingham dress she wore in *The Wizard of Oz* (1939), designed by

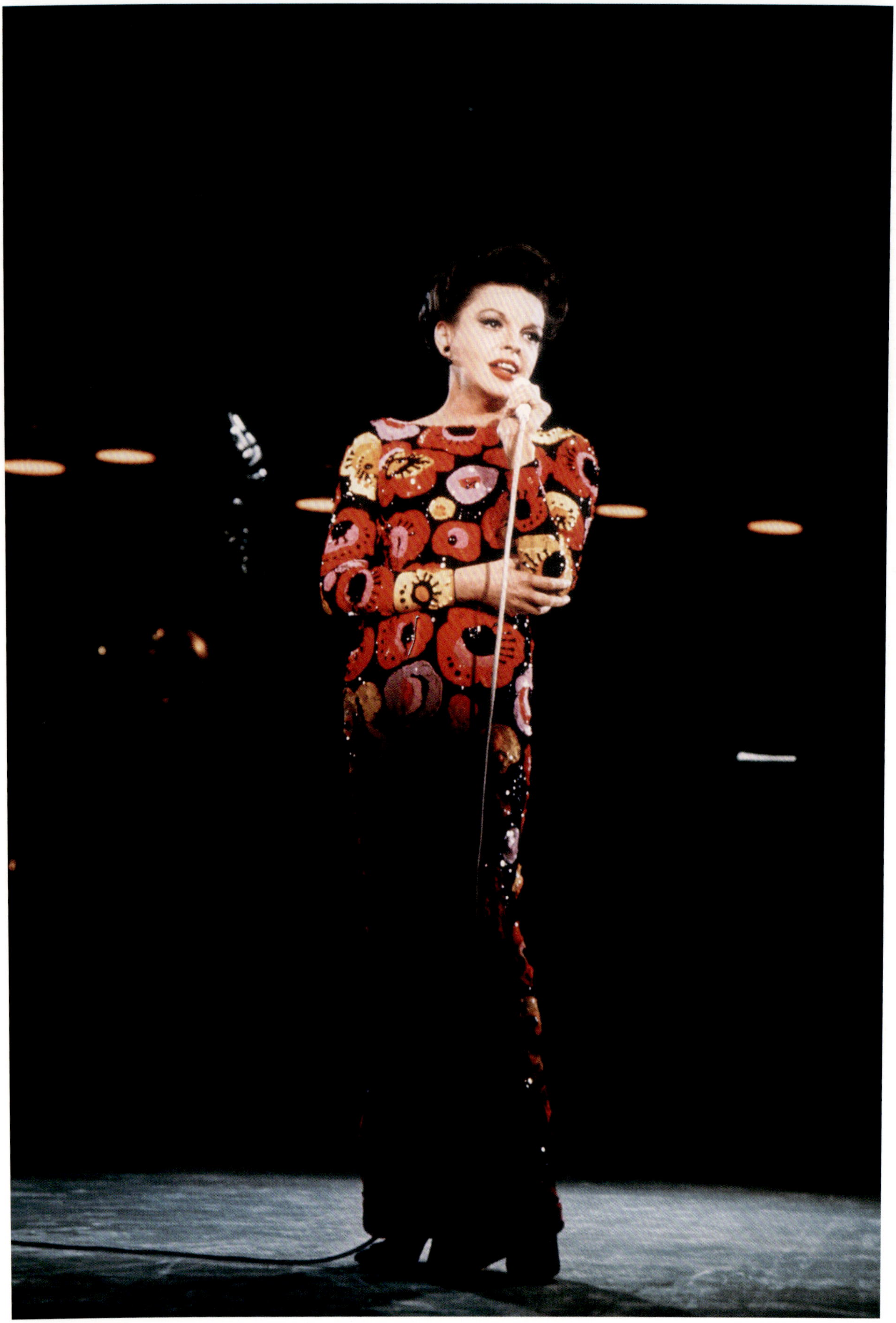

American costume designer Adrian, sold for $1.56 million in 2015 in New York. Following the release of the film, replicas were sold in stores throughout America, as well as a dress pattern that girls at home could send off for. Fashion brands, including Louis Vuitton, Rodarte, Marc Jacobs and Prada, have all been influenced by WOZ styling, creating collections that nod to 'Dorothy' detailing.

Garland loved fashion. She selected a young Bob Mackie to produce outfits for her '60s television show, and she stepped onto stage at the Glasgow Empire Theatre in couture Balmain. Five marriages meant five dresses to make an entrance in; the last she designed herself – a pale-blue chiffon and feather-boa-trimmed trapeze frock with a matching jewelled pill-box hat. They were all a stunning success, unlike the marriages themselves.

Garland's fans adored her clothes as much as she did. As early as 1940, she teamed up with knitwear brand Tish-U-Knit to create a Judy sweater collaboration, as advertised in American *Vogue* on 15 September 1940. The same year, a *Judy Garland Fashion Paint Book* (1940) allowed her fans to dress movie-star paper dolls and make-believe the star's life at home. In 1963, Garland wore a dress by Ray Aghayan to sing 'The Battle Hymn of the Republic' in tribute to John F. Kennedy, who had just been assassinated. It was a red-sequinned shift embellished with a paisley pattern that was created with bugle beads and sequins. Its three-quarter-length sleeves, scooped neck and maxi length is classic Garland. Polished, shimmering and flawless, she looked divine and sang her heart out. Reportedly the gown "fell out of her possession after trouble with the bill at The St Moritz Hotel in NYC" and was later sold to super-fan Charles Triplett (The Judy Garland Experience, 2012). Everything Judy wore is gold dust to Garland aficionados.

Lorna Luft bittersweetly described what it's like to have a legend as a mother: "Most people haven't attended a convention where most of the crowd, male and female alike, is dressed as your mother who died 30 years ago" (Luft, 1998). The craving to be near Garland through her clothes and possessions is something her equally iconic daughter, Liza Minnelli understood. In 2018, she sold a vast array of ephemera at the Profiles in History auction house in LA – including a pair of ruby-red slippers identical to the ones Garland wore as Dorothy in *The Wizard of Oz*. Commissioned by Minnelli as part of her trousseau, she wore them as a tribute to her mother when she married Jack Hayley Jr in 1974.

Minnelli inherited her mother's sense of style, dressing in pieces by designers such as Bob Mackie, Gianni Versace, Gucci, Isaac Mizrahi and Donna Karan. Halston, however, was her favourite. She told *Vogue* in 1990:

> "I had been wearing Halston since I was 20 years old. That's when we met. I didn't really have enough money to get everything I wanted, but the only clothes I ever wore were his. I wore all his clothes at one point, I think it was 1971, and became one of the best-dressed women in the world" (Allen Mellen, 1990).

The thrill of belonging to Garland's dazzling family is something that her children have each experienced uniquely. At times, their mother invited them on stage, such as in a 1963 Christmas show when Lorna, Liza and their little brother, Joey, all performed with their mother. It was presented as an 'at home with' special and ends with Judy snuggled up with her children, who are by then in their dressing gowns, singing 'Somewhere Over the Rainbow'. This is the way Joey likes to think of her. When asked how he wants the world to remember her, he said:

> "I've always thought it was an honour to have a mom like that. She was a very good mother to me. But I also knew that she was an incredible entertainer and that she was an incredible hard-working lady with a great sense of timing. Her songs and her movies are her gifts to the world. And that she was a great giving human being. And (also) that she was a great mother" (Nye, 2002).

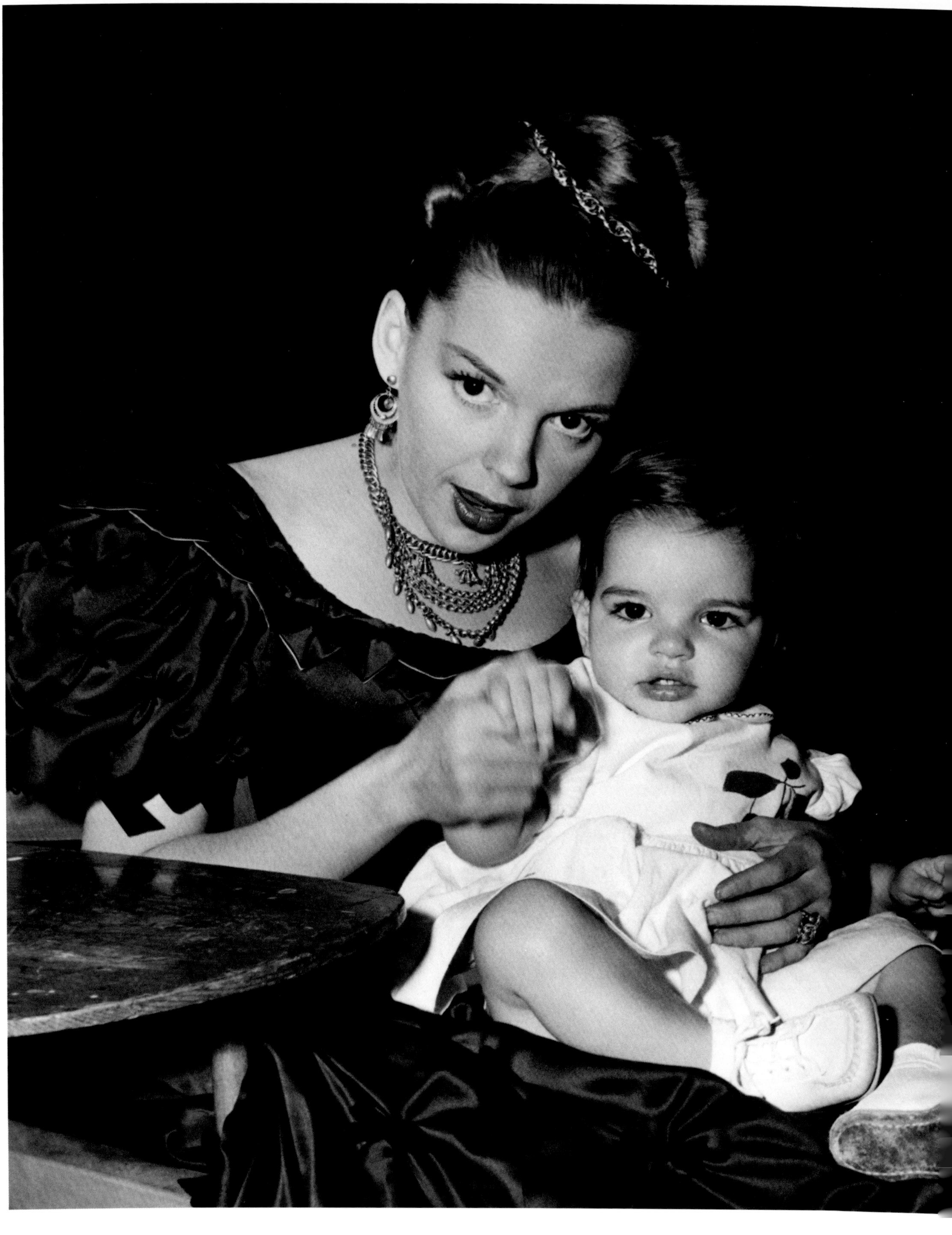

Left: Judy Garland with a baby Liza Minnelli, 1947. Right top: Judy and Liza performing together in 1963. Right bottom: Judy with her three children, Liza, Lorna and Joey, 1962.

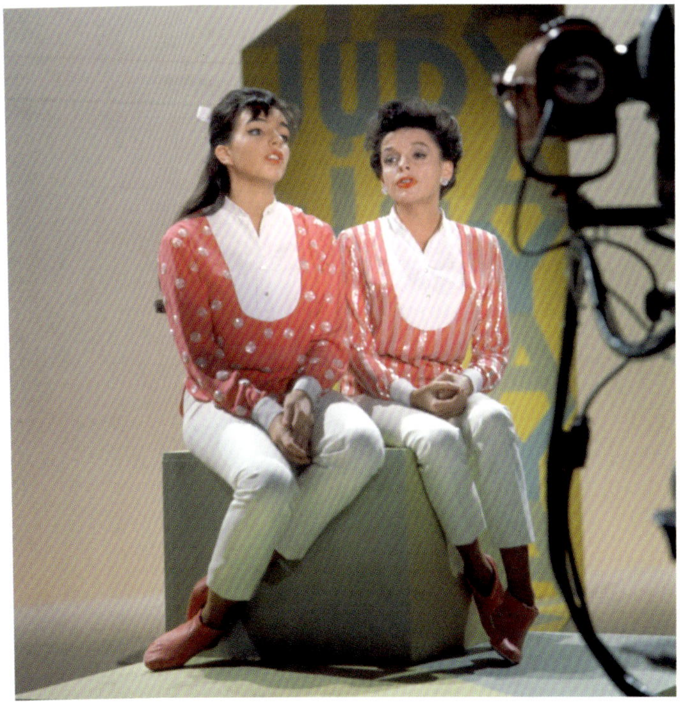

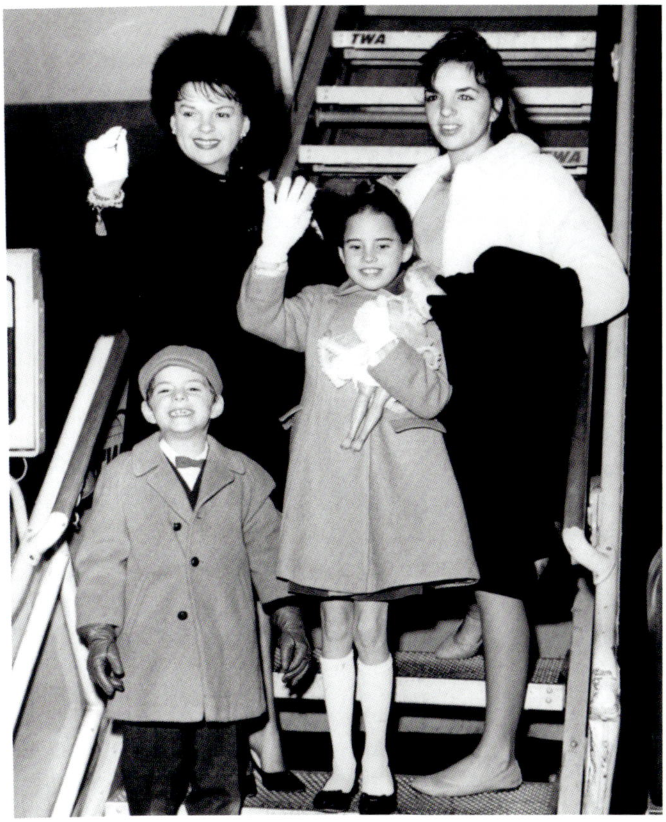

"I thought my mother was perfect, perfect. Every little thing she did."

Liza Minnelli,
CBS News, 2022

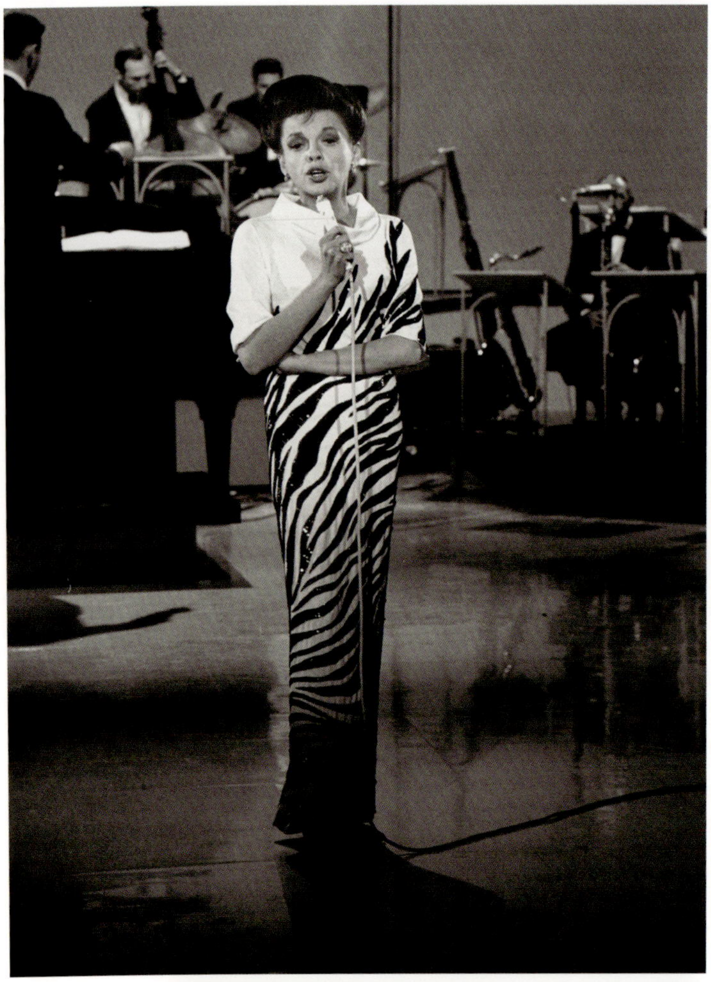

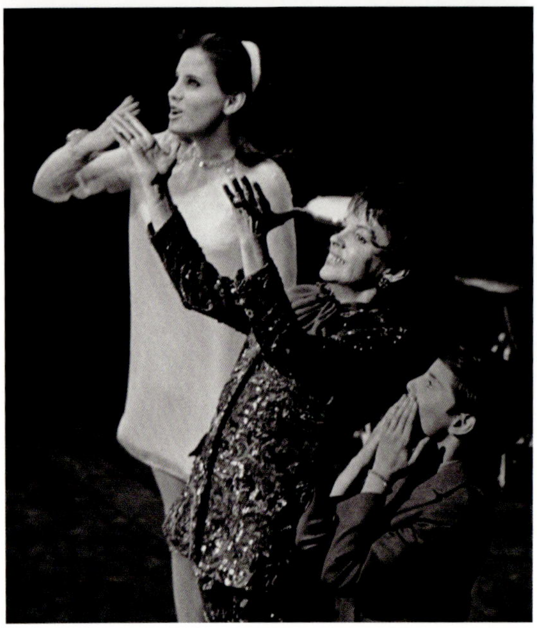

"Most people haven't attended a convention where most of the crowd, male and female alike, is dressed as your mother who died 30 years ago."

Lorna Luft,
Me and My Shadows: A Family Memoir, 1998

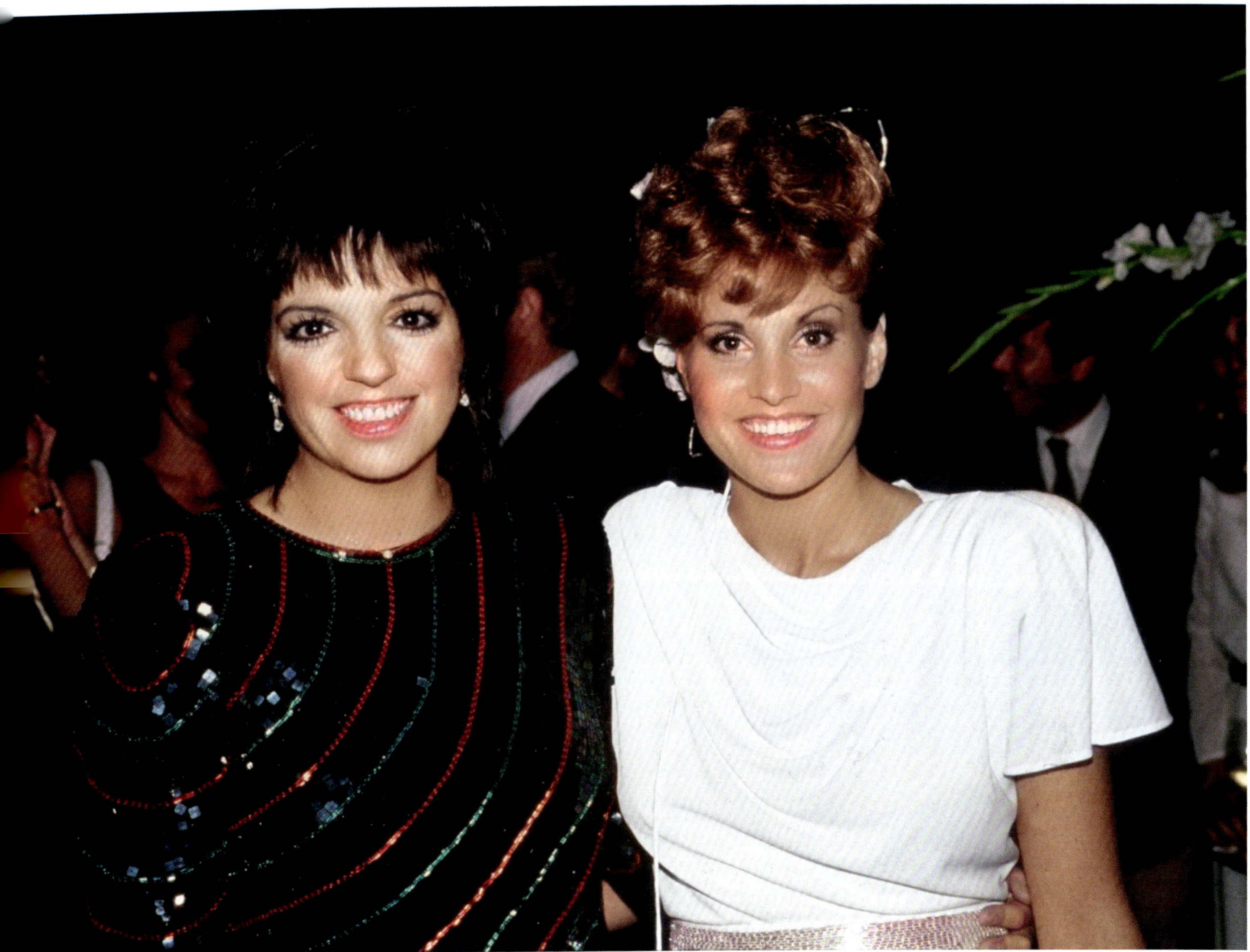

Liza Minnelli and Lorna Luft, 1983.

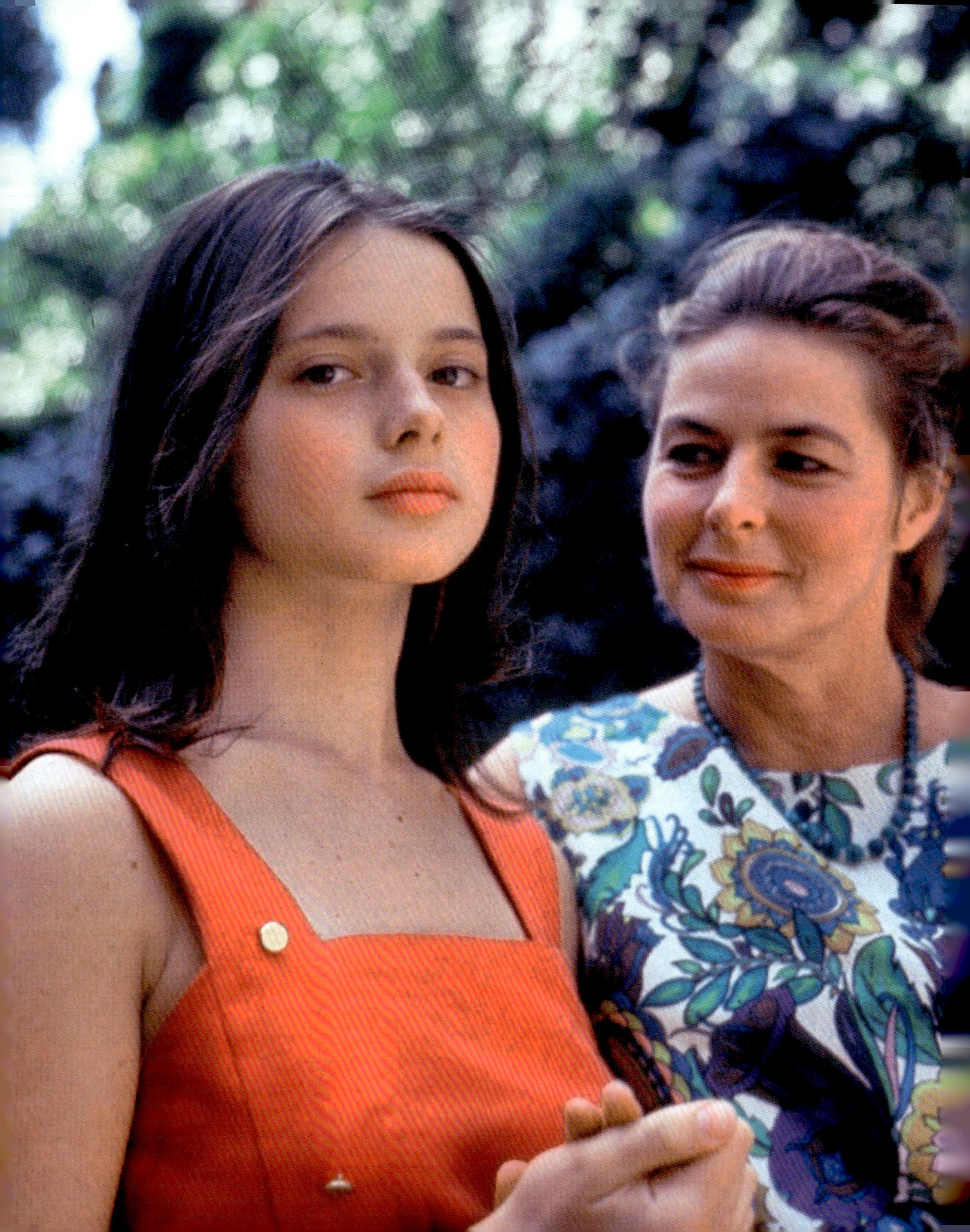

Ingrid Bergman and Isabella Rossellini

★

In February 1950, just shy of two weeks before *Stromboli* was released, the film's main actress, Ingrid Bergman, gave birth to her second child, Renato. Her son's father was the film's director, Roberto Rossellini, though she was still married to her first husband Petter Lindström, with whom she'd had a daughter, Friedel Pia Lindström. It was a moment of scandal for the Swedish actress, who lived her life in Hollywood in a way that many men of the town took for granted. Her sexual emancipation and uninhibited lifestyle were criticised to such an extent that she was ostracised from America. Divorcing Lindström and marrying Rossellini three months after her son was born, Bergman would go on to have twin daughters Isabella and Isotta with Rossellini before their marriage ended in 1957.

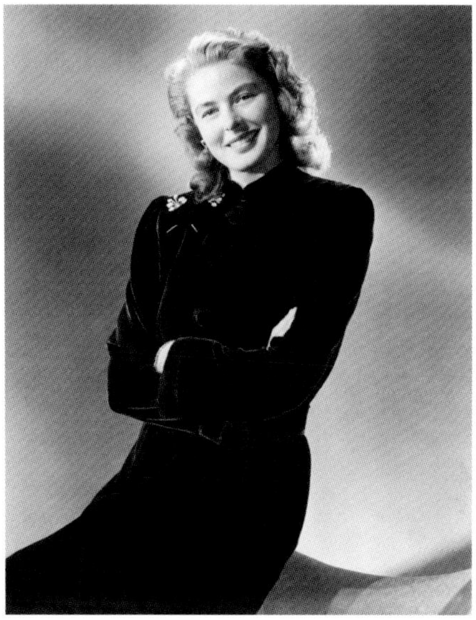

Bergman's work, including *Casablanca* (1942) and *Spellbound* (1945), continues to be considered as some of the most enduring and iconic films ever made. The clothes in *Casablanca* were designed by Orry-Kelly, the legendary Australian costumer, and although created for her character, Ilsa Lund, Bergman might have chosen the outfits in real life, they suited her so well. A short, white evening dress, a lace, puffed-sleeve gown and a chic plaid suit paired with a French beret were worn by Bergman with consummate elegance. But of all the stage clothes she wore, her black outfits in the 1948 production *Joan of Arc* were the distinctive fashion moment that inspired Maria Grazia Chiuri in her Spring/Summer 2024 Dior collection, with her emphasis on feminism and strong women.

Bergman largely avoided toeing the line when it came to behaving in the way starlets of her time were expected to, let alone a mother of four. From her gamine, boyish haircut to her easy androgynous sensuality, she didn't conform to the stereotypical prototype that prevailed. "This is how I look, take it or leave it", she famously told film producer David Selznick, who suggested she have a Hollywood makeover when she first arrived in LA (Sayej, 2015). But there were some concessions that had to be made. Her daughter Isabella revealed in a *Harper's Bazaar* interview that "actresses in Hollywood had

Isabella Rossellini's daughter, Elettra, wearing Ingrid Bergman's dress, remodelled by Fernanda Gattinoni, 2011.

a tremendous pressure to maintain a certain weight, just as they still do today. When you see her clothes, they are so small—poor Mama! She would write longingly in her correspondence about eating ice cream, which she only did about once a year, and she would dream about it" (Cowles, 2015).

Bergman was elegantly pragmatic when it came to designer outfits and when she needed to dress to impress, her closet ranged from Balmain, Balenciaga and Christian Dior, which she wore for premieres and red-carpet events. However, as a general rule, she would instruct her children not to "spend too much money" when it came to buying their own clothes; a 'buy less, buy better' philosophy that feels in tune with today's sustainable values (*WWD*, 2004).

In 2011 at the Met Gala, Bergman's granddaughter Elettra Wiedemann wore one of her grandmother's dresses – a piece by the Italian couturiere Fernanda Gattinoni – thoughtfully remodelled by the Nepalese-American designer Prabal Gurung. Following Bergman's death in 1982, the gown was found in a trunk at the home of her third husband, Lars Schmidt.

Inheriting her grandmother's classy matter-of-factness, Elettra told *New York* magazine in a 2011 interview that she rarely takes inspiration from her stylish mother, Isabella Rossellini, as they "have very different body types. So structurally that wouldn't really work...when it's just us at home, she's always very elegant. When I'm at home, I'm not dressed in a gorgeous Armani vintage men's suit. I'm in, like, an old silk slip from the Forties and ripped Seven jeans" (Baker, 2011).

Rossellini, however, is a very special fashion icon, loved by many for her originality and vision, and has appeared on a multitude of *Vogue* covers, including in 2024 at the age of 71 for *Vogue Italia*, unretouched and unrepentant. She follows closely in the footsteps of her mother, Bergman, going against the grain of expectation. It's an approach that brought her to the attention of Lancôme in 1982 when they appointed her the face of the brand, a position she held for 14 years. She returned again in 2016, testifying via her Instagram that the luxury house's "marketing research showed that I was not intimidating to women. There is a beauty that seems to attract more women than men and that is what I had" (@isabellarossellini, 2018). In 2018, Lancôme's campaign featured both Elettra and Rossellini in its Mother's Day imagery, celebrating both of their distinctive looks. Today, the mother and daughter duo are united in a conservation farm project, aptly called Mama Farm. According to their website, the farm "aims to foster the next generation of environmental stewards", raising animals, making honey and, from time-to-time, crafting fashion, such as their 2023 capsule collection which included a limited-edition 'Mama' sweater.

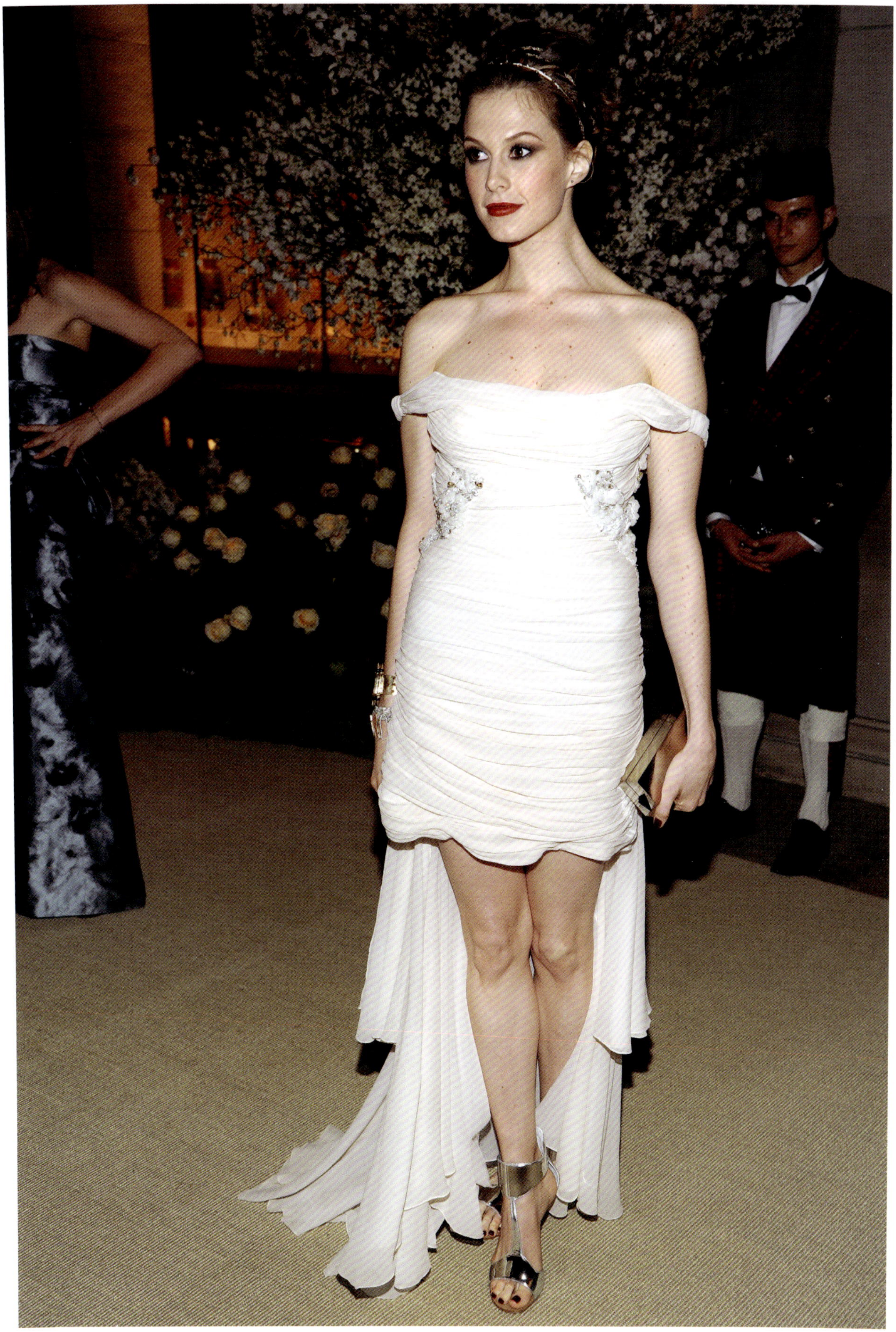

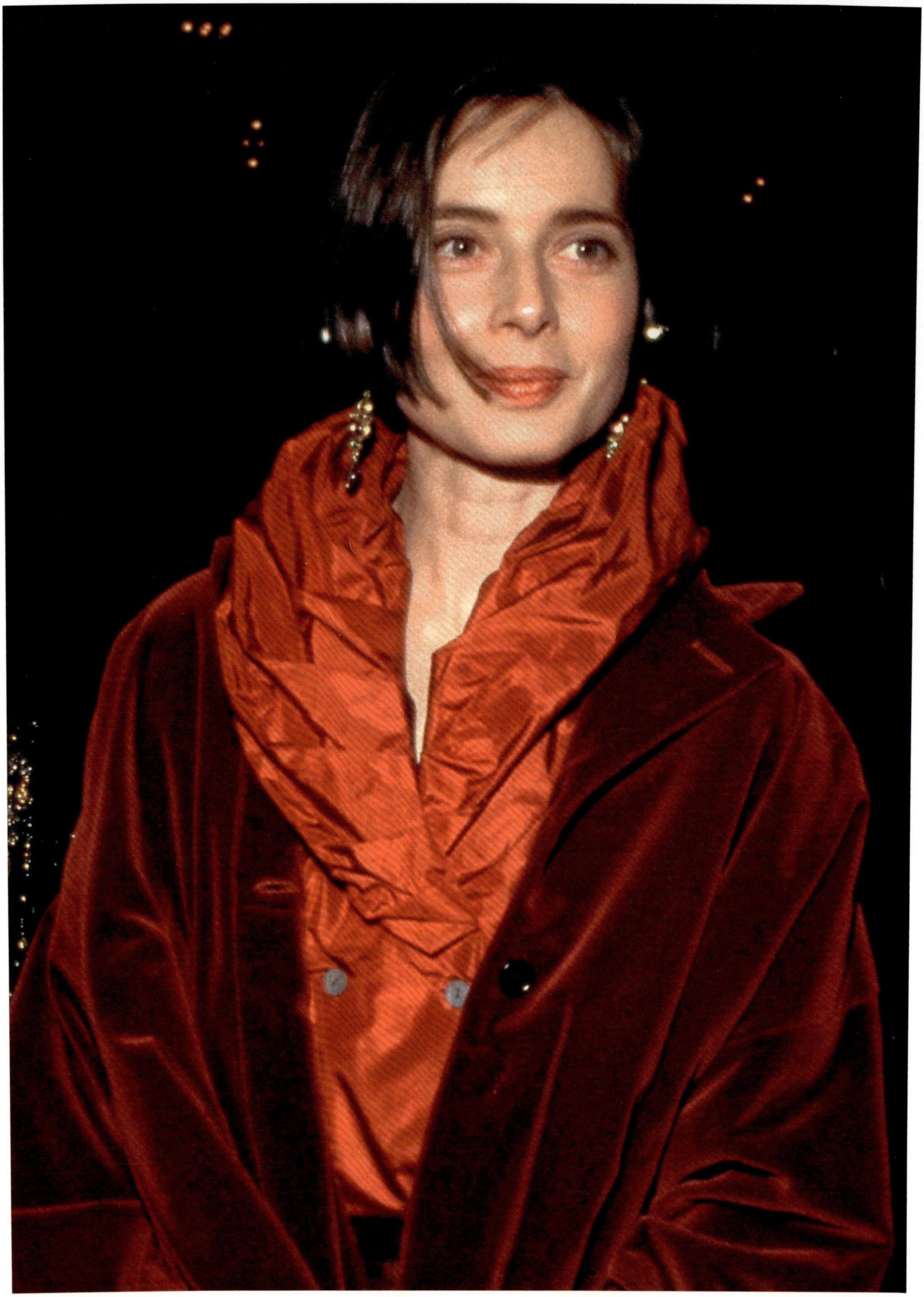

Right: Ingrid Bergman with Isabella and her twin sister, Isotta, and their brother Renato Roberto, 1953.

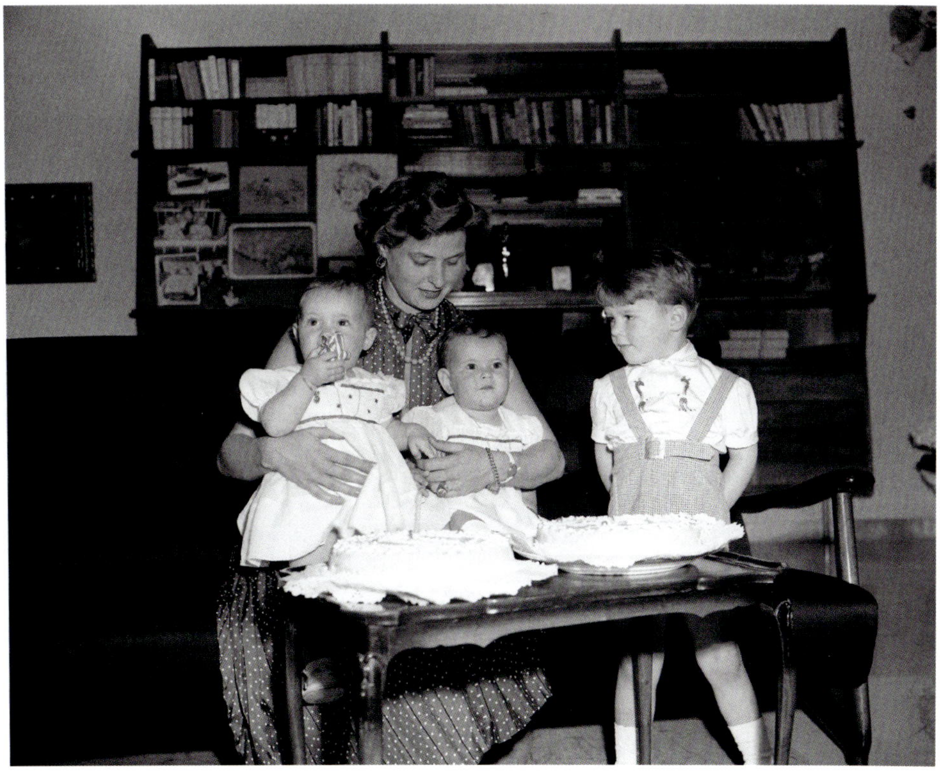

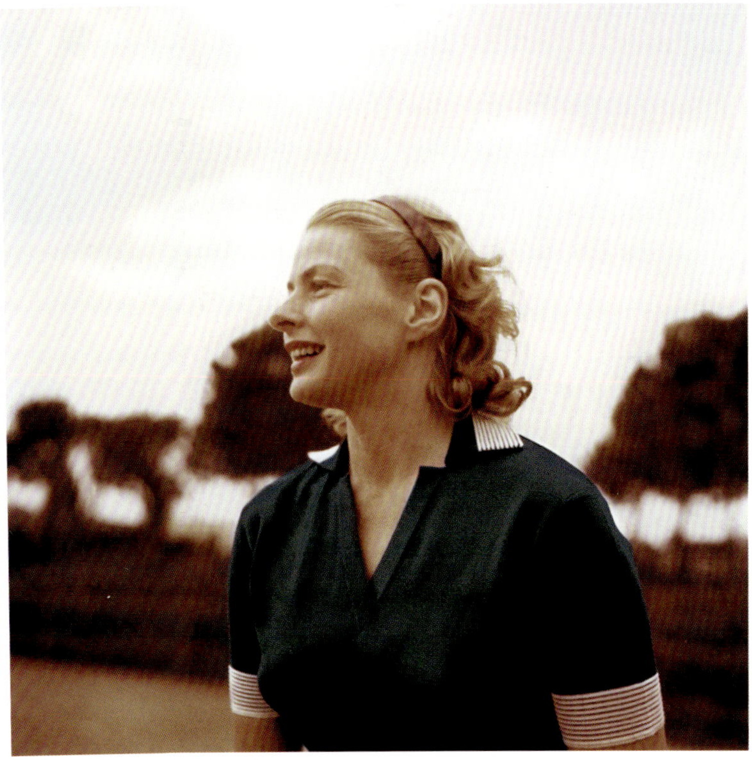

"This is how I look, take it or leave it."

Ingrid Bergman,
quoted in *The New York Times*, 2015

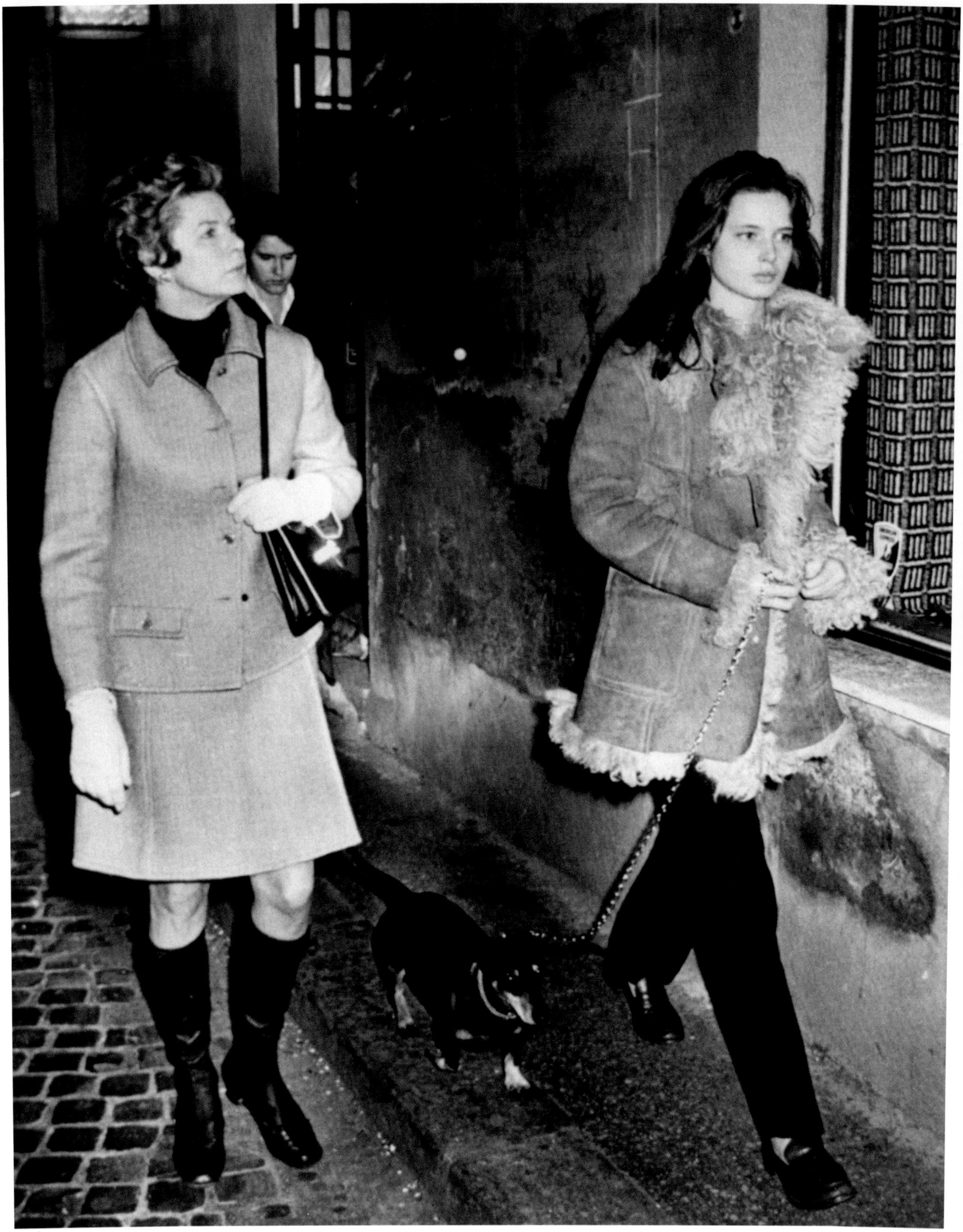

Left: Ingrid Bergman shopping with her twin daughters in the fashionable Via Borgognona in Rome, Italy, 1970.

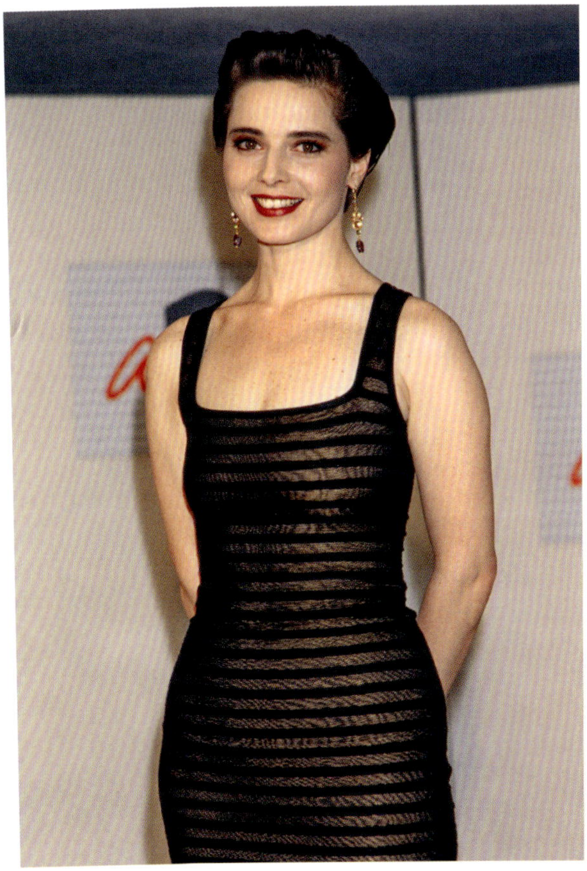

"Mother never wore much make-up and always had short hair. There was a freedom about her, and a modernity about her attitude. Being Swedish, she was very into open air, very sporty—which was unusual in Hollywood then but looks very contemporary today."

Isabella Rossellini,
Harper's Bazaar, 2015

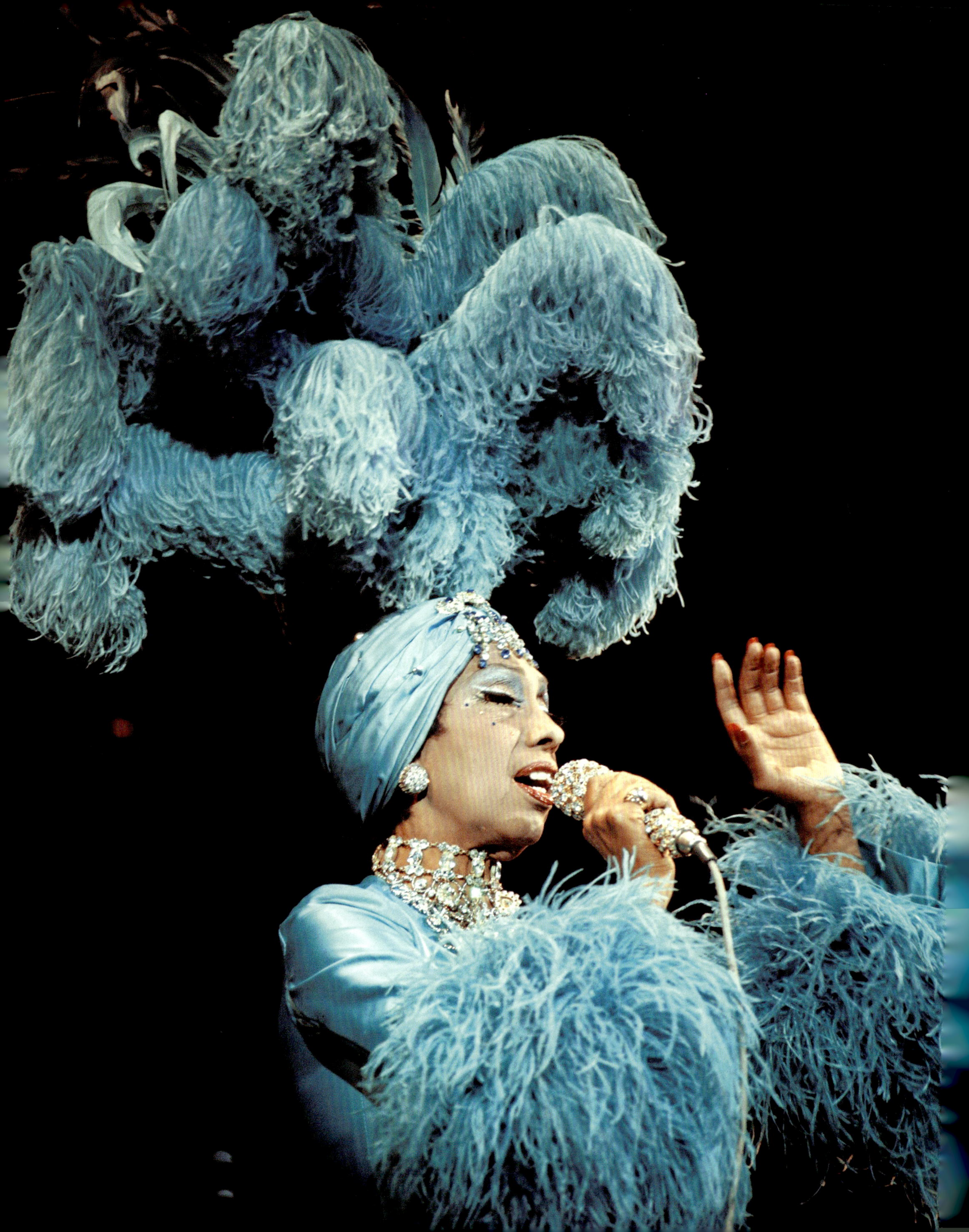

Josephine Baker and her **Rainbow Tribe**

★

The illustrious actress, singer and dancer, Josephine Baker, was almost 50 years old when she adopted the first of her 12 children and created a 'Rainbow Tribe' family. Born in St Louis, Baker moved to New York in 1922 when she was just 16, embracing and embodying the Harlem Renaissance. Three years later, in 1925, she left America for France, explaining how "one day I realized I was living in a country where I was afraid to be Black. I felt liberated in Paris. People didn't stare at me" (Holiday, 2021).

Her fabled career in Paris is part of Baker's rags-to-riches mythology. She became a Folies Bergère cabaret dancer, performing the *Danse Sauvage* wearing nothing but a banana skirt and pearls. She was a sensation, epitomising the heady world of the Jazz Age, and was courted by the finest couturiers such as Paul Poiret, Jean Patou and Madeleine Vionnet, who competed to dress her. Later, in 1951, a *Jet* magazine editorial christened her 'The World's Best-Dressed Woman' and she was shot modelling Dior and Balmain.

Baker welcomed the world of fashion and lived an intoxicating life, but when France went to war with Germany in 1939, she became a spy and worked for the French Resistance. In 1961, she was awarded the *Légion d'honneur* and the *Croix de guerre* for her bravery. In 1963, she spoke at Martin Luther King's side during his March on Washington. Activism and social justice were at the heart of all Baker's good deeds; exposure to hardship and bigotry early in life made her determined to help build wide-reaching tolerance in any way she could. A few years earlier, on a visit to Japan in 1954, she went to see the abandoned 'occupation babies' of Japanese women and American military, that had been left at the Elizabeth Saunders Home in Oiso, Kanagawa. It was a typical Baker crusade. She was there to play a series of charity concerts in aid of the orphanage, founded by her friend Miki Sawada, and returned home with two boys, Akio and Teruya (whom she later renamed Janot).

Baker returned to Château des Milandes, a castle in the Dordogne where she had lived since 1937 and shared with her husband Jo Bouillon since 1947. She had only intended to adopt one child, but the Japanese trip was indicative of Baker's life-loving spontaneity and the beginning of an adventure. The turreted palace was intended as a magical world for the children that Baker and Bouillon adopted, filling their household with foundlings from all cultures and countries to demonstrate Baker's hypothesis that people from all backgrounds can live together. She discussed her rationale in a 1964 Overseas Press Club interview, explaining, "they were adopted because of my many experiences in life...seeing that people were misunderstanding each other...separating rather than

> **"She was like a rock. For us, she seemed immortal."**
>
> **Akio Bouillon,**
> *Los Angeles Times*, 2006

"Whenever she would appear on TV, singing, half-naked, she would turn it off very quickly and tell us that 'it wasn't her'. Because she wanted us to see her as our mother... not as a dancer. There was no talk of music, dancing or singing in the house."

Jean-Claude Bouillon-Baker,
El País, 2022

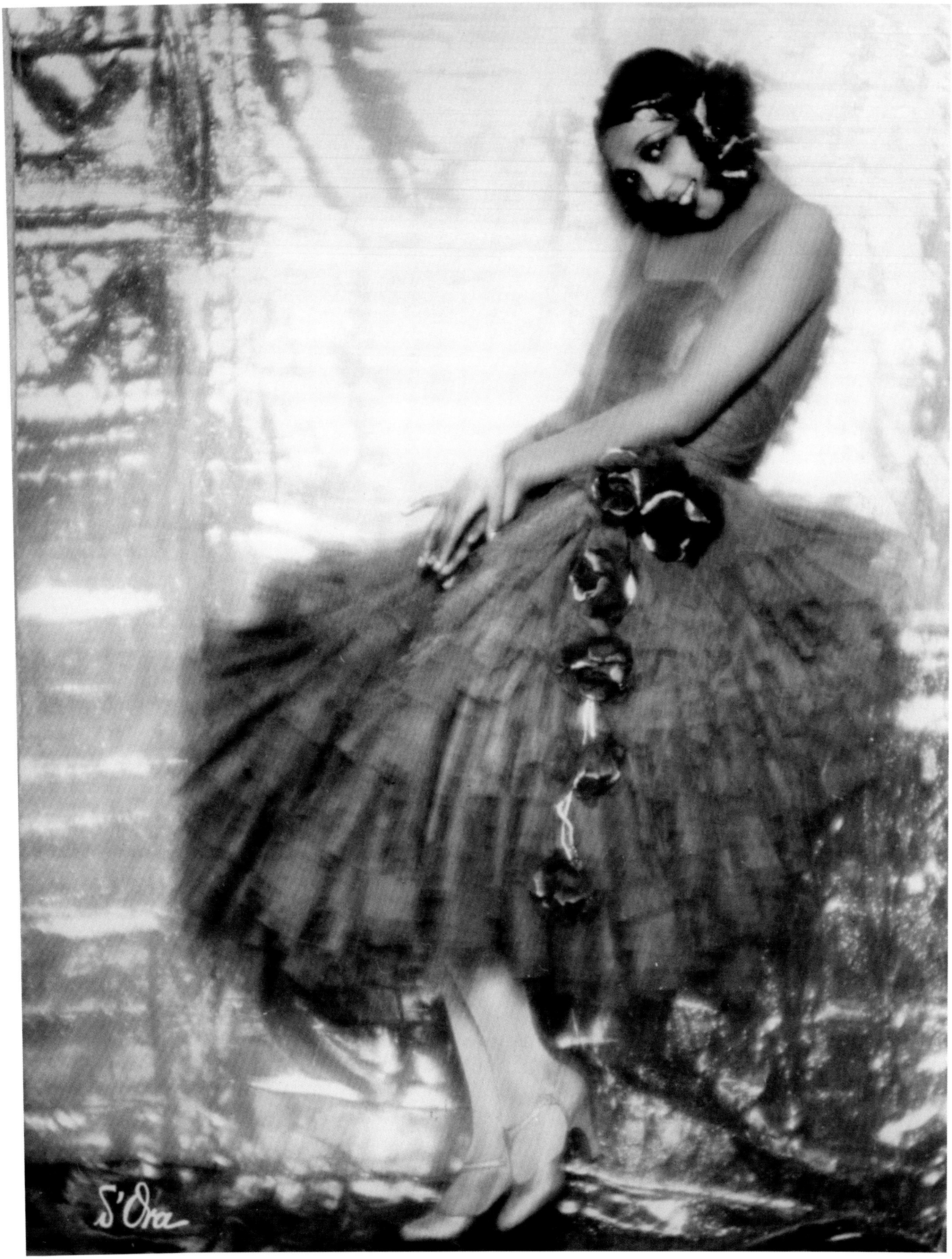
d'Ora

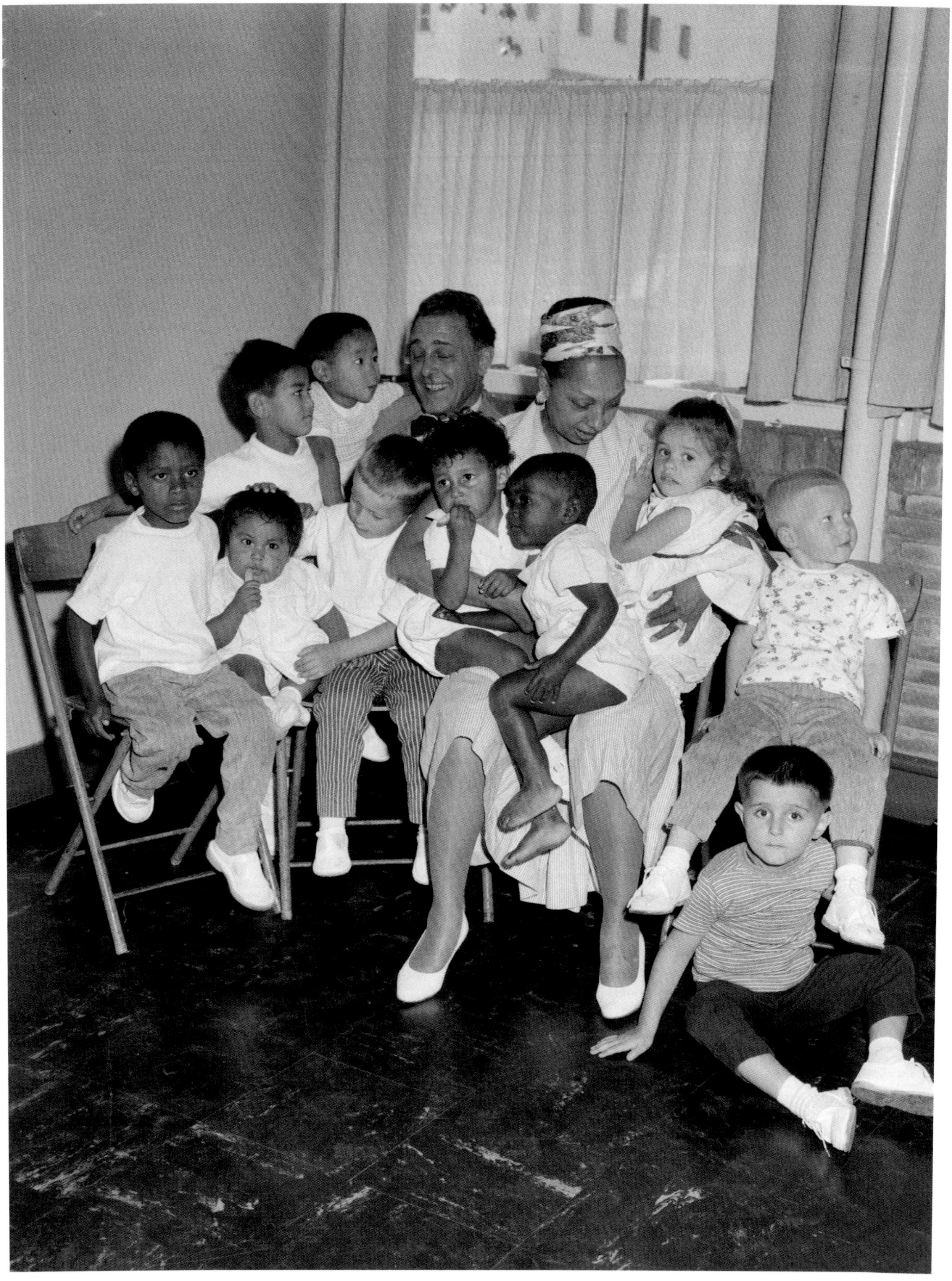

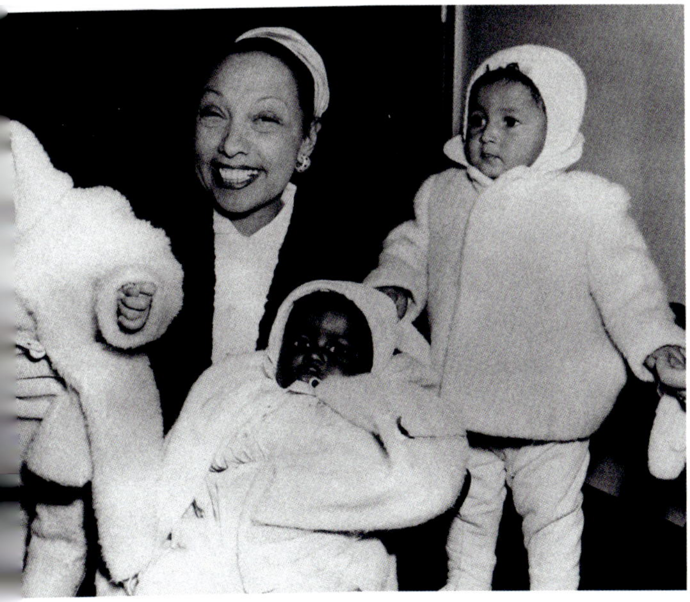

> **"My only regret is that I didn't start adopting children earlier."**
>
> **Josephine Baker,**
> Overseas Press Club, 1964

uniting" (Quarles, 2012). Her children came from all corners of the world, including Venezuela, Côte d'Ivoire, Columbia, Finland, Morocco and France. Her daughter Marianne describes: "I lived in a castle. I walked around in my mother's stage outfits. For me, life was like in fairy tales where there are princesses" (Abraham, 2019). The castle fascinated sightseers, who were charged to visit Baker's cosmopolitan domestic world and watch her children at play. In a 1974 interview she said: "My 12 children get on very well together. Too well, because they gang up on me" (Murari, 1974). However, by 1961 Baker and Bouillon had divorced, and in 1968 Josephine and her family left the Château as she could no longer afford its upkeep.

Baker would keep on dancing and performing for a living, continuing to mesmerise her audience. Following a show in 1973, a review in *The New York Times* declared that Baker "brought a full house at Carnegie Hall to its feet cheering and applauding Tuesday evening merely by stepping into a spotlight wearing a spangled body-stocking that left no doubt about the slim, trim, youthful lines of her figure, topped by an outrageously towering headdress of flamingo-coloured plumes that was as tall as she was herself" (Wilson, 1973). She had just celebrated her 67th birthday.

Her fashion legend lives on in myriad ways, including through pioneering drag artist Lynne Carter who was a happy recipient of her beautiful costumes, declaring: "Josephine Baker once gave me three taxicabs full of gowns" (Klemesrud, 1971).

> **"I have not had the honour of being a mother, in the sense that we understand, naturally. Many mothers have to take what they get. I was lucky enough to go around the world and choose."**
>
> **Josephine Baker,**
> Overseas Press Club, 1964

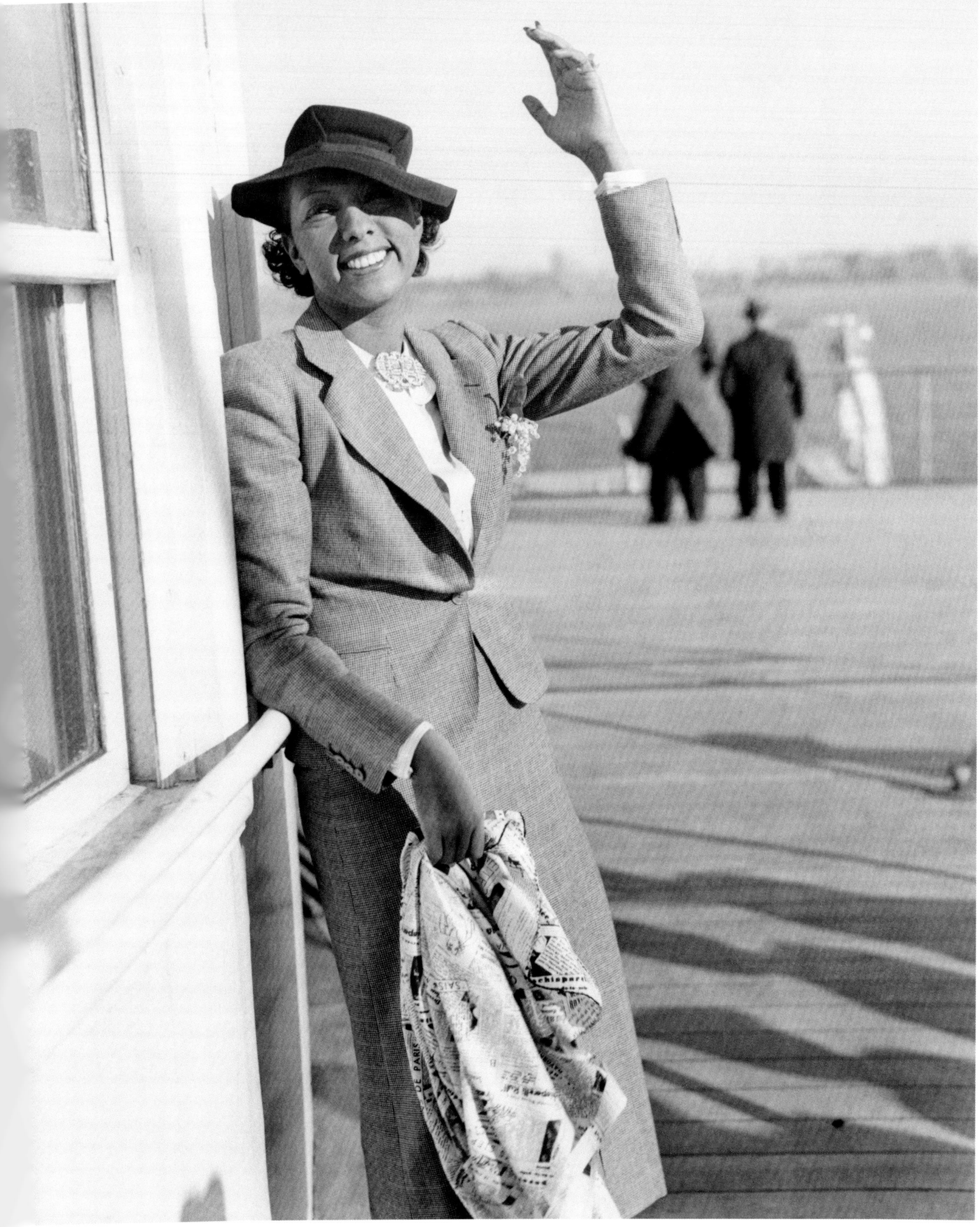
DE PARIS

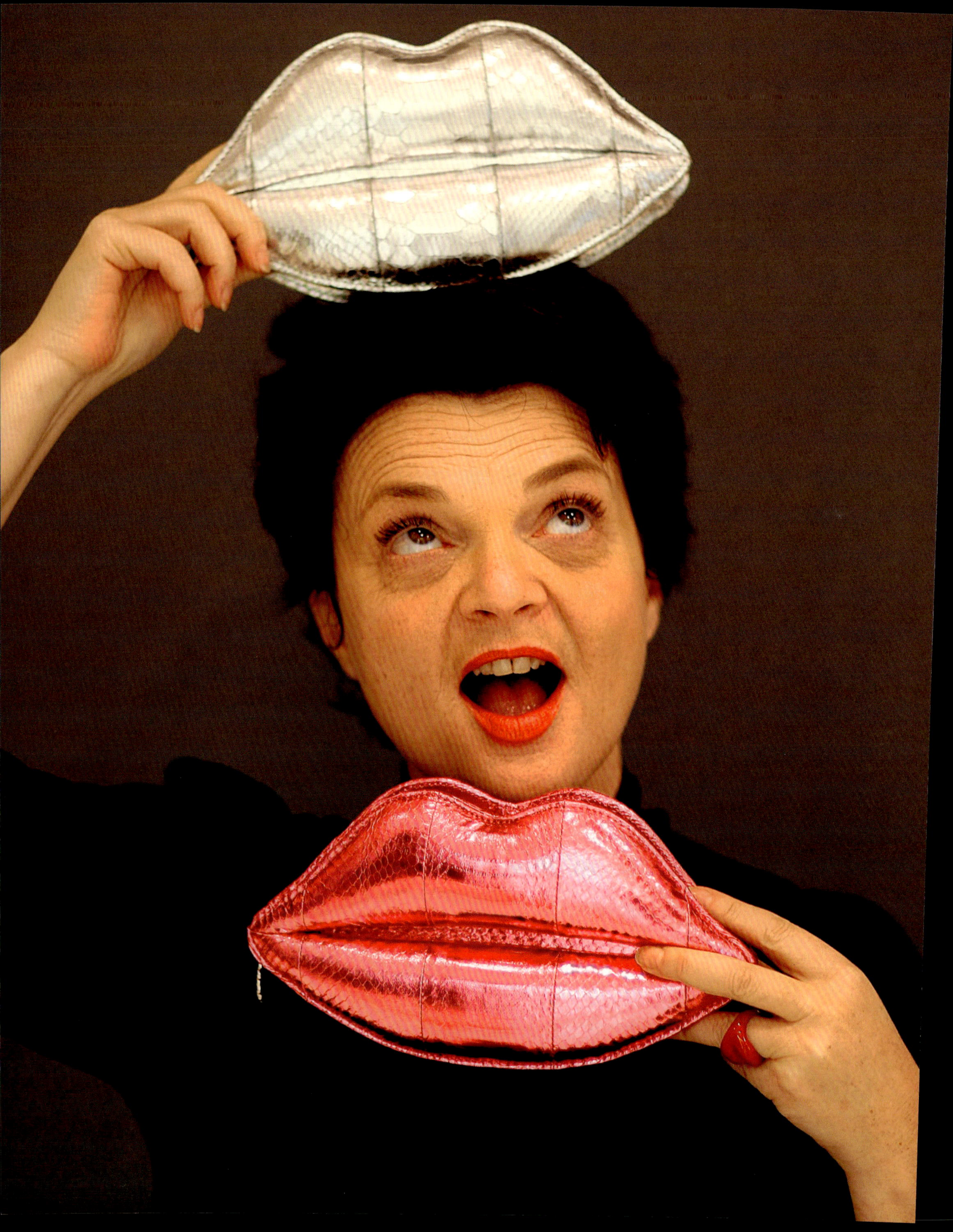

Lulu and Madeleine Guinness, **and Tara** Kelway-Bamber

★

Lulu Guinness is one of British fashion's national treasures. She cheers people up with her characterful accessories and boldly unconventional designs that are contrary to trends and instead forge an individualistic style of their own. Think about her iconic 'Rose Basket' bags, now displayed in the V&A in London, which she created because of her love of flowers; or the pillar-box 'Red Lips' clutch bags that reflect her own Betty Boop-esque mouth. A signature emerges that is all her own and has been adopted lovingly by her fans around the world who adore her special kind of wit and wisdom.

She began her company in 1989, debuting a vermillion-lined leather briefcase for working women, complete with compartments for necessaries like lipsticks and Filofaxes. She followed this with another functional item: a baby bag, made in black and created for smart power-dressing women who want something to wear with a Thierry Mugler suit. It's this kind of practicality that she is coming back to today, having just re-made her famous baby bags, again inspired by functionality, after refurbishing her latest project – a magical new house in the English countryside, which has since been featured in *T: The New York Times Style Magazine*.

She has two daughters, Madeleine and Tara, who, while growing up, always appreciated the spirit of both their mother's clothes and the interiors she created for them. Maddy remembers:

> "I 100% knew she was a very hard worker; I always thought she was a badass – an assertive person overseeing a lot of things and holding it down. I was and still am very proud she was such a highflier. Her personal style was always chicer than anything else I saw – she never wore casual and still wears red lipstick at all times and little finishing touches like leather gloves. I knew that our house was wonderful – but it was also fun. Our home has always been beautiful – mum would find a bird painting or a knick-knack that other people might overlook and use it in an interesting way that made the house feel artistic. She would always leave a lot of exciting things around the house – swatches of lovely materials and sketches of bags that I used to colour in. She once used material from a sheer effervescent bag to make me a fairy wing. I used a lot of her work materials to play with. In terms of her having the most amazing wardrobe, though, of course I dressed up and played with endless bags, floral dresses, hats and pearls. I understood she was far more into clothes than other mothers."

Today, Lulu's clothes frequently gravitate towards her daughter Tara's cupboards:

> "Mum is not very good at remembering what I've borrowed, so upstairs half of my wardrobe is hers. When I was a teenager, I thought what she wore was horrible but now I dress the same; we have the same figure, and she basically lends me things the whole time. We are so similar in our tastes now that I had my wedding dress made by Eponine, who I only knew about because of her. Mum has given me the confidence to go for it with clothes."

"Most people around the swimming pool wear flip flops but Lulu will wear heels. She has just started wearing quite cool overalls for walking the dog, but until not that long ago I had not seen her wearing trousers apart from when we went skiing. The first time she put on salopettes, we all couldn't stop laughing."

Tara Kelway-Bamber,
2025

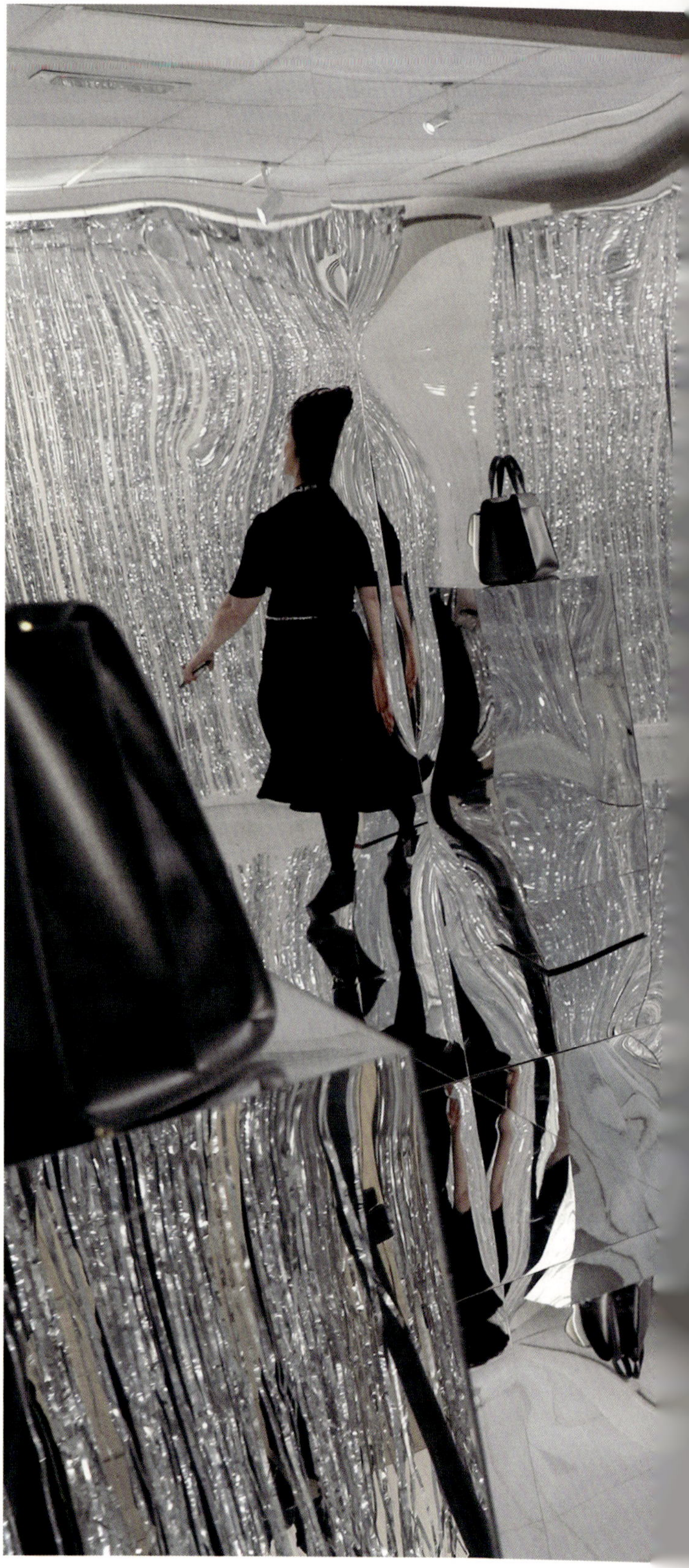

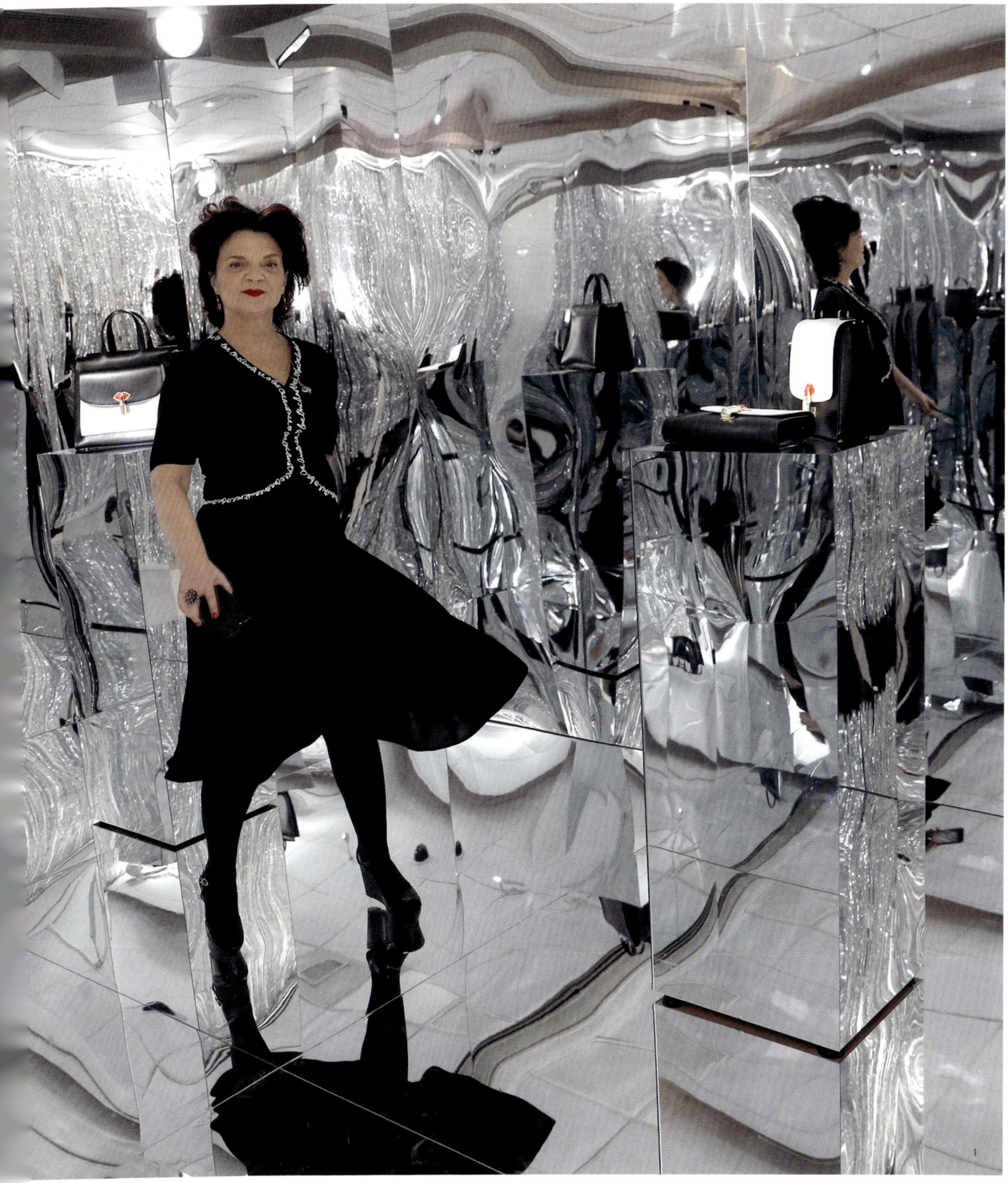

Lulu's style, like her work, has evolved. She came from a loving and firmly traditional family where creativity was a curiosity. Though born in England, she grew up in Malta and Singapore, where her naval captain father, Baronet Sir Miles Rivett Carnac, worked, before returning to England to live in Devon. Her mother, Lady April Rivett Carnac, was, Lulu describes, very much a 1950s girl living in the '60s, who knew the aristocratic rules of dress. Lady Rivett Carnac would never dream of wearing brown shoes in town and had London clothes and country clothes she wore exactingly. It was a hard sartorial act to follow, especially when Lulu gave birth to Tara and suffered from severe post-natal depression:

> "While I did try to keep up appearances, I do remember a lot of time being spent in bed wearing a nightdress. But the important ethos of keeping it together, which came from my mother and her mother, too, was still there. My maternal family were Jewish, and they chose to live deep in the country. There is nothing that brings out class etiquette more than those trying to live the hunting, shooting and fishing life. They didn't want to be caught out by doing something wrong, so their clothes were very important. My mother wore what my granny before had worn, and that included pearls; it was so firmly entrenched. My mother was on a diet all her life. If she was ever a size 12, that would have been too much for her. She was terribly rigid and so was her mother. I have always wanted to be different though. One of the things my mother would say about my choice of outfits was: 'It's all very bright, isn't it?'"

Despite her intention to dress differently from her mother, Lulu's own style growing up gravitated towards the 1950s, too, and she has always worn lots of vintage. It's something she learnt to appreciate from her great grandmother, who wore couture: "I would go and stay with her a lot and we would spend hours dressing up in her evening coats and examining her bags." From an early age Lulu understood the value of fit and proportion – something learnt from scrutinising the intricacies of her grandmother's bespoke wardrobe. But instead of Parisian fashion houses, Lulu found her treasure at Portobello Market.

> "I didn't have long legs; I just had a tiny waist, so could wear frocks with cinched middles. I always chose high heels, so I'd look taller. Body shape is so important when thinking about what to wear and the 1950s silhouettes worked for me. It's not that I didn't love '70s clothes, but when I tried them on, they looked ridiculous. Maddy has long legs and wears these massive chunky boots, as if she is standing on a brick, and very short skirts – it suits her. She can show these things off. Tara looks as if she is Spanish and always wears orange or red. We both suit gold colours, but in the days of my mother and grandmother, wearing shocking pink was an act of rebellion."

Lulu's love of clothes was something she thought carefully about when she became pregnant, admitting:

> "I don't think I enjoyed anything about how I looked when I was pregnant. At the time, it was coming up to my first-ever fashion week and I had to look smart. I had waited all my life to do fashion week and then I was eight months pregnant, so I had these blue and pink coats made with buttons up the front. I was as wide as I was tall. My legs swelled up so much that I had these shoes that I cut down the front to wear. I had always worn high heels as they were the most the important thing, but I couldn't when I was pregnant, so instead I had my hair up to make me look taller."

Garments worn as a mother often become markers of emotional states, social expectations, and the negotiation of selfhood during a time of profound transformation. They can be about resilience and freedom, as well as constraint, and Lulu reflects:

> "My creativity didn't go with post-natal depression. I thought I was hopeless, so I tried even harder. But I just loved my girls and dressing them was so much fun. I went to New York often where I had an office, and I bought unusual things for them there. If they needed casual clothes or shorts, they'd come from Lilly Pulitzer.

Above: Lulu with her mother, Lady April Rivett-Carnac, 2012. Below: Lady April Rivett-Carnac as a young woman, circa 1956.

It goes back to always wanting to be different – this has manifested in the way I decorate my house, the way I dress, and the way I design my bags. This sensibility has also gone into the way I dressed my daughters."

Maddy concedes: "I look back and me and Tara were immaculate and adorably dressed – embroidered-collar dresses and patent shoes. But I can see in the photo albums when there was a turning point – when I wanted a Hello Kitty T-shirt instead."

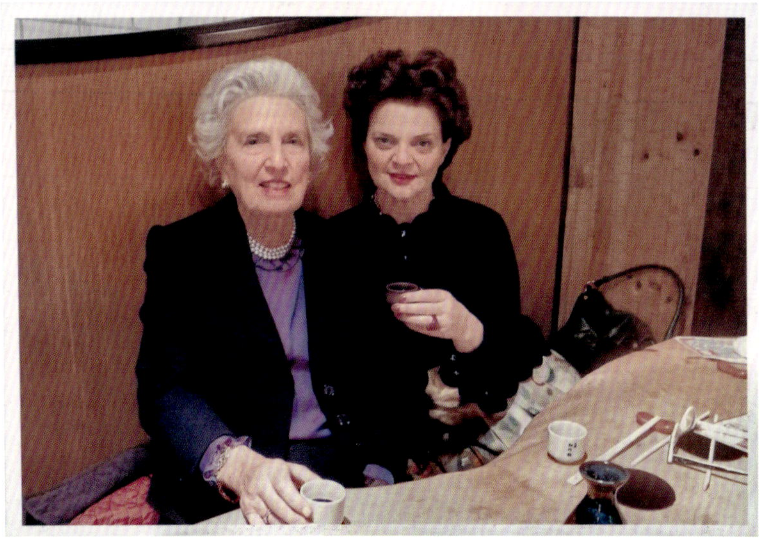

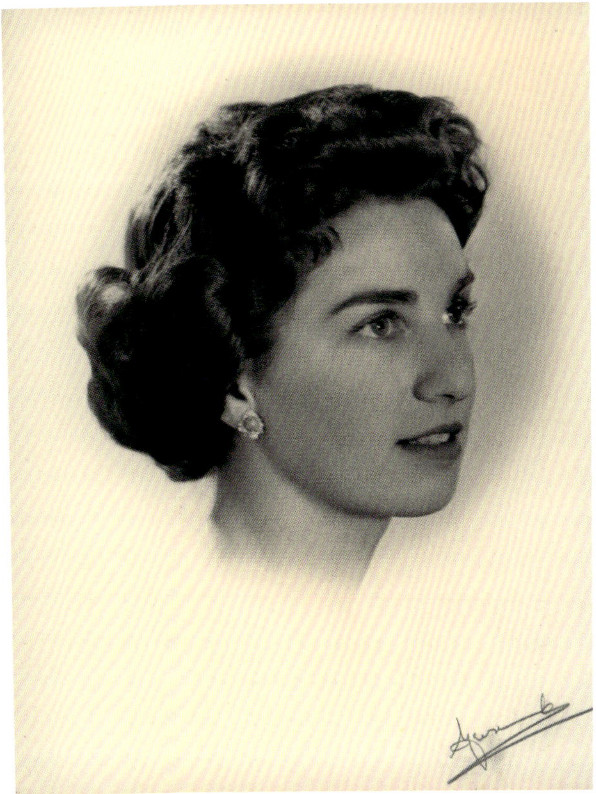

"One of the things my mother would say about my choice of outfits was: 'It's all rather bright, isn't it?'"

Lulu Guinness,
2025

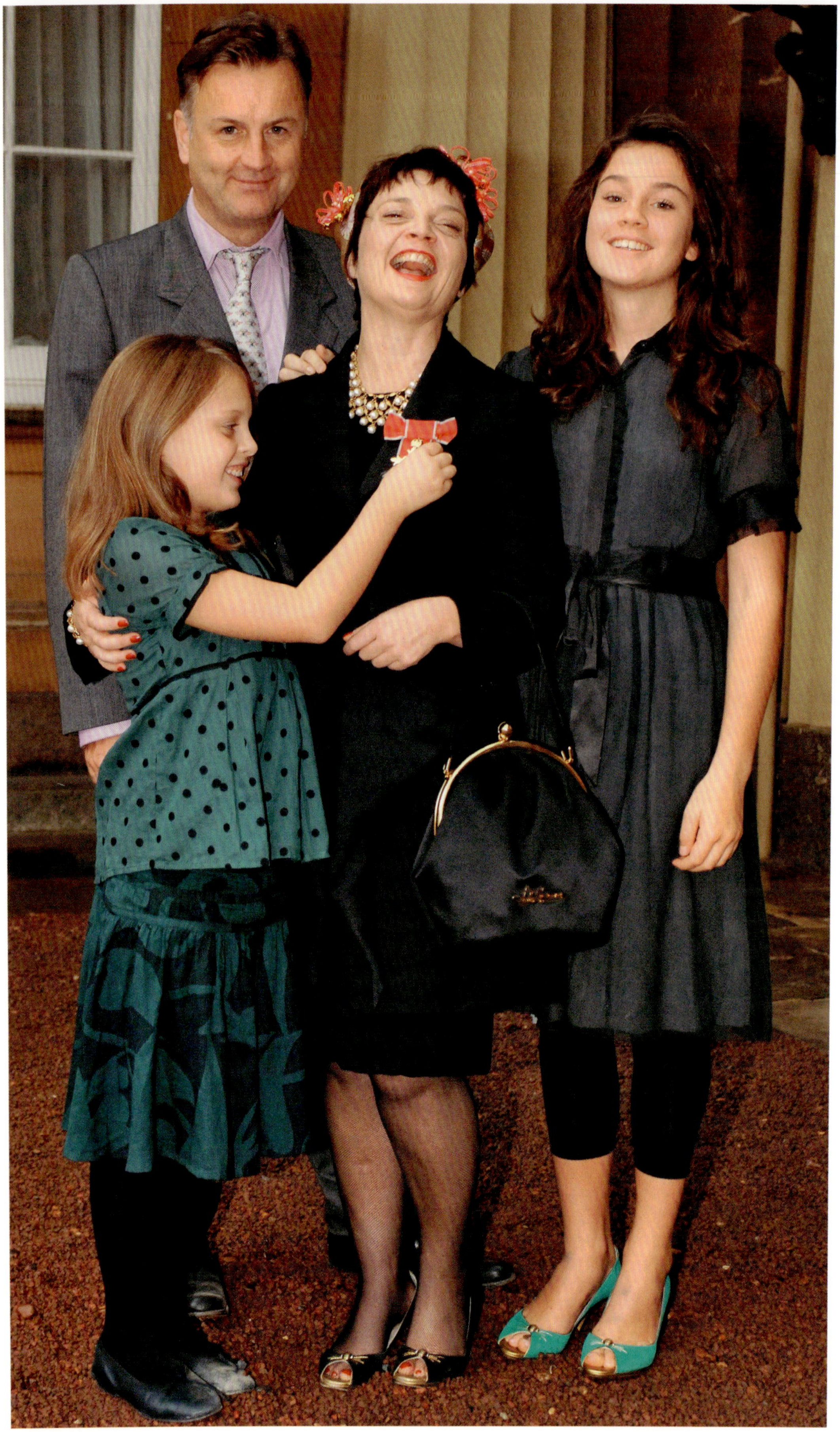

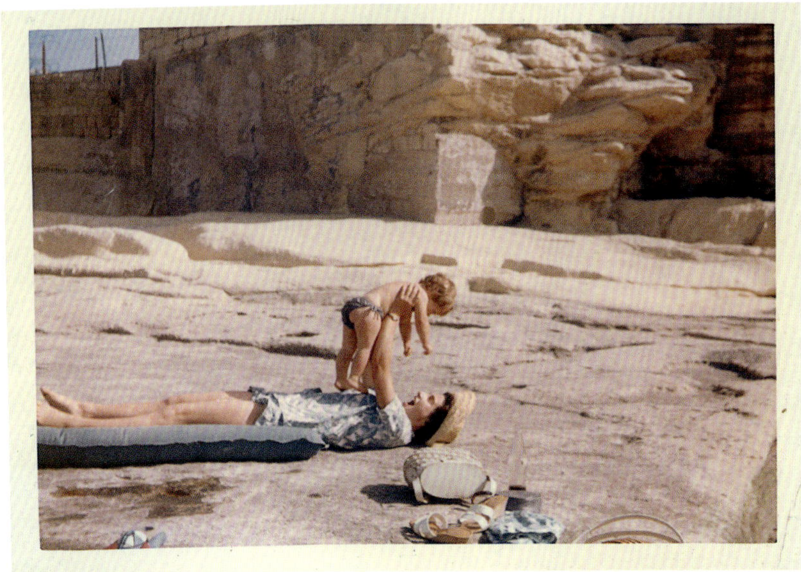

Lulu as a baby with her mother, 1961.

"None of my mum's bags were off limits. The bird-cage bag I used as a music box. I adopted a lot of her bags as pets. I used the black poodle bag in a vet game and tied lots of loo roll around it. She didn't mind!"

Madeleine Guinness
2025

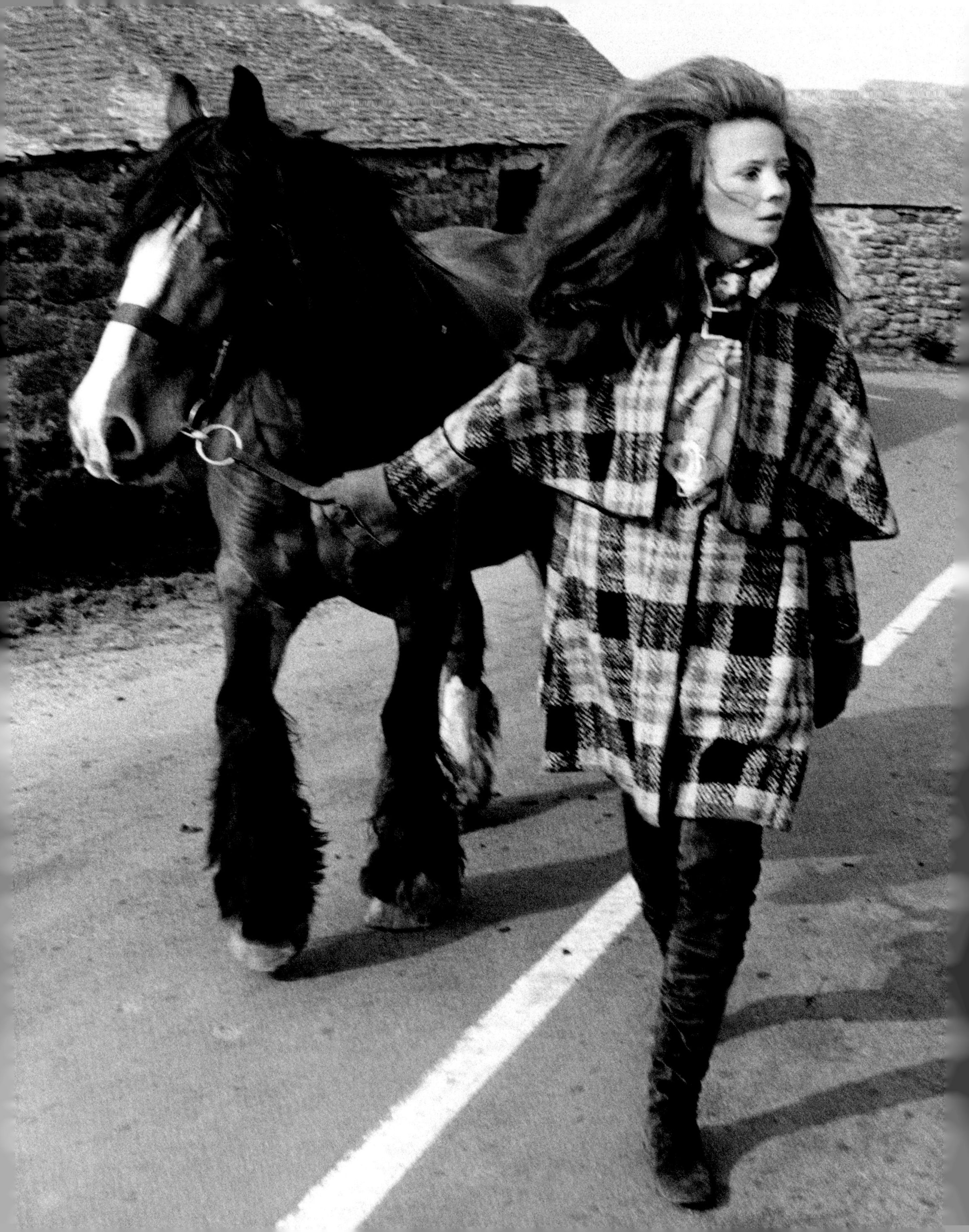

Penelope Tree as a young model in 1968, and more recently in 2024.

Marietta and **Penelope Tree**

★

In 1967, Diana Vreeland commissioned legendary photographer Richard Avedon to shoot Penelope Tree for the 1 October issue of *Vogue* magazine. Up to that point, the 17-year-old had planned to take up a place at Sarah Lawrence, a liberal arts college in New York. Instead, the pictures Avedon produced set her career alight as the face of fashion. Tree created her own look: her artistic make-up, described by *Vogue* as 'outrageous', was something she started a few years earlier at the age of 13, "to annoy my friends' parents... now I do it all the time", she admitted to the writer Polly Devlin in the accompanying interview (Devlin, 1967). Her painted, psychedelically intoxicating face defined the times. Everyone wanted her, including David Bailey who swept her off her feet and became her boyfriend. Penelope's mother, Marietta Peabody Tree, did not approve; she didn't like Bailey, who told her tersely: "Just be glad I'm not a Rolling Stone" (Seebohm, 1997).

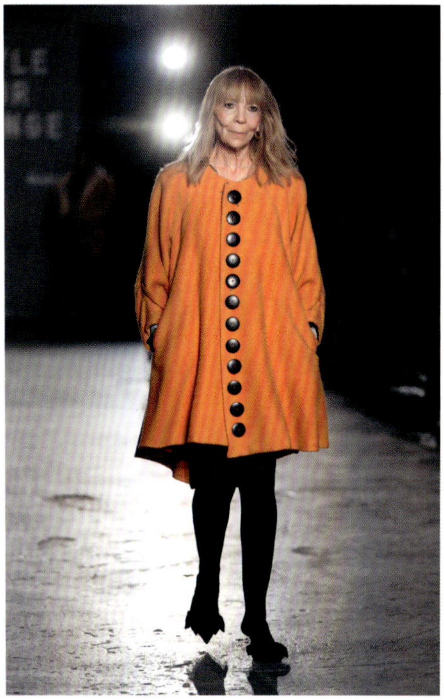

Marietta was a statuesque woman: 5 ft 10 in. by the time she was 14. In 1934, while in finishing school in Italy, she attended an audience with Pope Pius XI, wearing a black-veiled hat and red nail varnish, which was outré at the time. Later, in 1936, a debutante Marietta worked as a model for John Wanamaker's iconic department store in Philadelphia – one of the first to open in America. Like Penelope, she had also failed to take up a place at college, instead leaving home to find adventure. The parallels between them are clear in retrospect but mother and daughter were far from kindred spirits. Penelope recalls:

> "She just did not have a maternal bone in her body and as soon as I was born, I was just handed over to this, actually, wonderful nanny. Thank God I had her. My mother was very ambitious, and she was out every night, or they had people to dinner every night. You know, one thing or another. It was just very rare that I ever, ever saw my mother on her own."

The only exception was when Penelope was young, in the mid-1950s, and her nanny had Thursday afternoons off.

> "Although I would scream because I didn't want to be left, the really good thing that I remember about those afternoons is that me and mum would go down Madison Avenue to the shops and she would look at

all the 'off-the-peg fashion', as she would call it. We'd go to Saks Fifth Avenue or Bergdorf's, where she'd try on clothes and I'd sit on a chair and say what I thought looked good or if I liked a silhouette or a colour. And she'd go, 'Wow, you have a really good eye'. And I was very excited by that because it was just about the only – I guess what I knew to be – sincere compliment from her. And so, I think that that's where my love of clothes began."

The outfits worn by socialites like Marietta were impeccably refined and demure, and her wardrobe mesmerised Penelope:

> "She bought couture twice a year from Paris. She went to the shows, and she picked out what she wanted. Her favourite pieces came from Balmain, Balenciaga and Givenchy; suits and cocktail dresses but nothing insane and extravagant because she wasn't insanely extravagant. She had a lady's maid, who dressed her every night and put all her clothes out on the bed and then helped her because a lot of the couture dresses she wore had tiny little eyelets and tiny buttons on the back. And she'd take quite some time to get ready. And so, I'd sit and watch her get ready. And that was kind of exciting."

Later, Penelope would start experimenting and using clothes to craft her identity, too:

> "From about the age of 12 to around 15, I wore black only. It was sort of beatnik – I was in love with Edgar Allan Poe and the dark side. I was thinking about it today. How funny that you almost take something on as a style, but then it becomes an attitude. It's more than a style. It's a sort of inner attitude as well. It drove my parents crazy, which of course I loved."

At the age of 16, Penelope famously attended Truman Capote's Black and White Ball. It was an event for the great and the good of New York society, and she was the youngest person there. "My mother looked amazing. She wore a dress, it could have been Balmain, that was her favourite, and an amazing headdress with black cock feathers and lots of diamonds; it moved all over the place." Penelope's sense of style shone through that evening, too. She was wearing an incredible dress that she had asked newly graduated designer Betsey Johnson to make her. They'd met because Johnson worked in Paraphernalia – the Manhattan equivalent of Biba in London.

> "I was obsessed with modern ballet, and I love dancers, clothes, and the whole thing of rehearsals and sweatpants and tight jersey leotards. So, we made something that had that vibe. As soon as I put the dress on, I knew that it was going to change my life; it was very special. I just had a feeling and intuition about it."

Penelope and Marietta's gowns were in direct opposition to each other: one a symbol of old-school couture elegance; the other radically subversive, heralding a new generation of fashion that was built on youth and counterculture. Mother and daughter personified each outlook. Marietta had become famous as a well-connected jetsetter with a wardrobe to match. In 1944, as Mrs Desmond Fitzgerald in her first marriage, the New York *Daily News* would write about Marietta's wardrobe, with its elegant labels that included Hattie Carnegie and Valentina. After marrying again and becoming Mrs Ronald Tree, the wife of an English aristocrat and Penelope's father, her wardrobe became even more

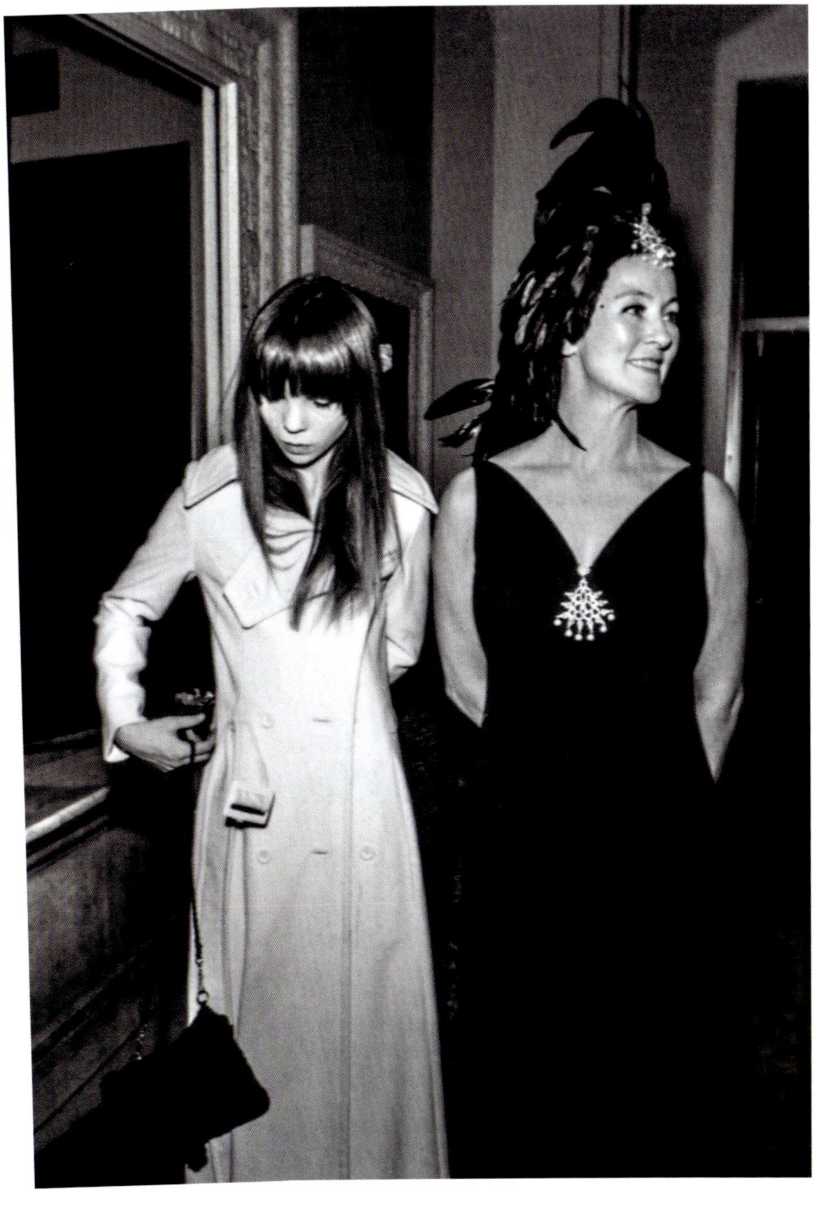

"My mother looked amazing. She wore a dress, it could have been Balmain, that was her favourite, and an amazing headdress with black cock feathers and lots of diamonds; it moved all over the place."

Penelope Tree,
2025

newsworthy. Outfits were shipped in from Paris to be worn to meet the Queen of England, attend horse racing at Ascot or entertain Babe Paley in New York. Marietta had built a life as the best hostess in town, but also a profile as a career woman. Rising to the heights of the United States representative to the United Nations Commission for Human Rights, she had the wardrobe to cover all eventualities. "Marietta wore a lot of colourful suits, and I remember a lot of nice jewellery. She wasn't flashy, but everything, even her lingerie, was beautifully made. All her bras were made for her, everything was silk and wonderful", remembers Penelope.

The Tree family spent lot of time in Heron Bay, Barbados, where in the early 1970s Marietta's deluxe wardrobe morphed as she stopped visiting Paris for couture and instead began wearing bohemian designers, such as Bill Blass, Thea Porter and Oscar de la Renta, paired with silver, black or gold slippers. Zandra Rhodes remembers her in Florence wearing "huge summer hats and floaty dresses, looking... as though she had stepped out of a Gainsborough portrait" (quoted in Seebohm, 1997).

As her opulent lifestyle continued, Penelope and Marietta drifted further apart. After Ronald Tree died in 1976, Penelope didn't speak to her mother for over a year. She built her own life, moved to LA and gave birth to a daughter, Paloma.

> "When my daughter was born, I had no idea what I was doing at all, and we really had to muddle through. I was quite determined to be a better mother than my mother had been, and even though I didn't know how to really achieve that, I certainly loved her. I was very lucky in that as soon as she was born, I absolutely adored her, so that made it easier. The thing is I was never really that great a parent, but she is a fantastic daughter, and it's all worked out. I just feel like that has been the best huge thing in my life, you know, having her."

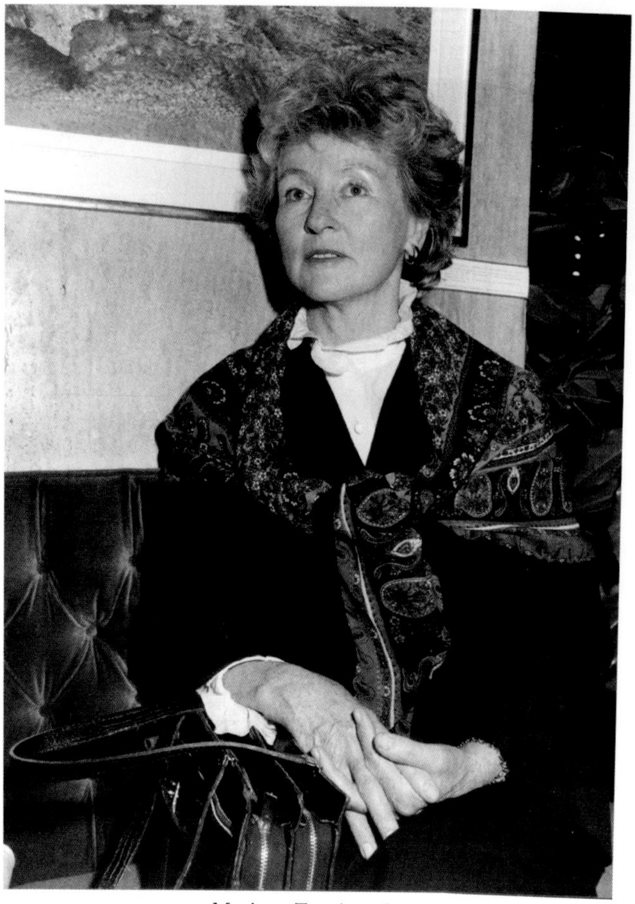

Marietta Tree in 1981.

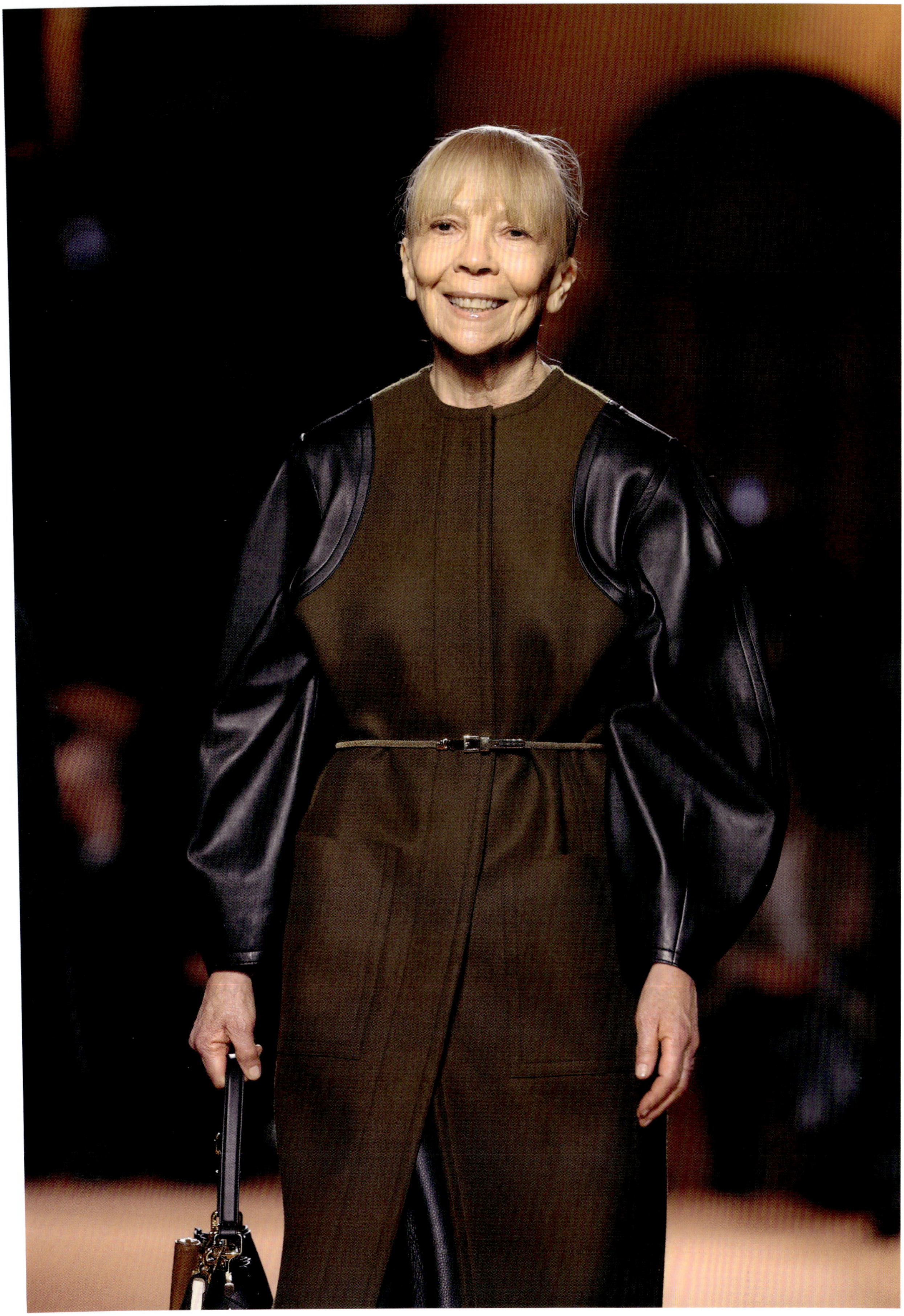

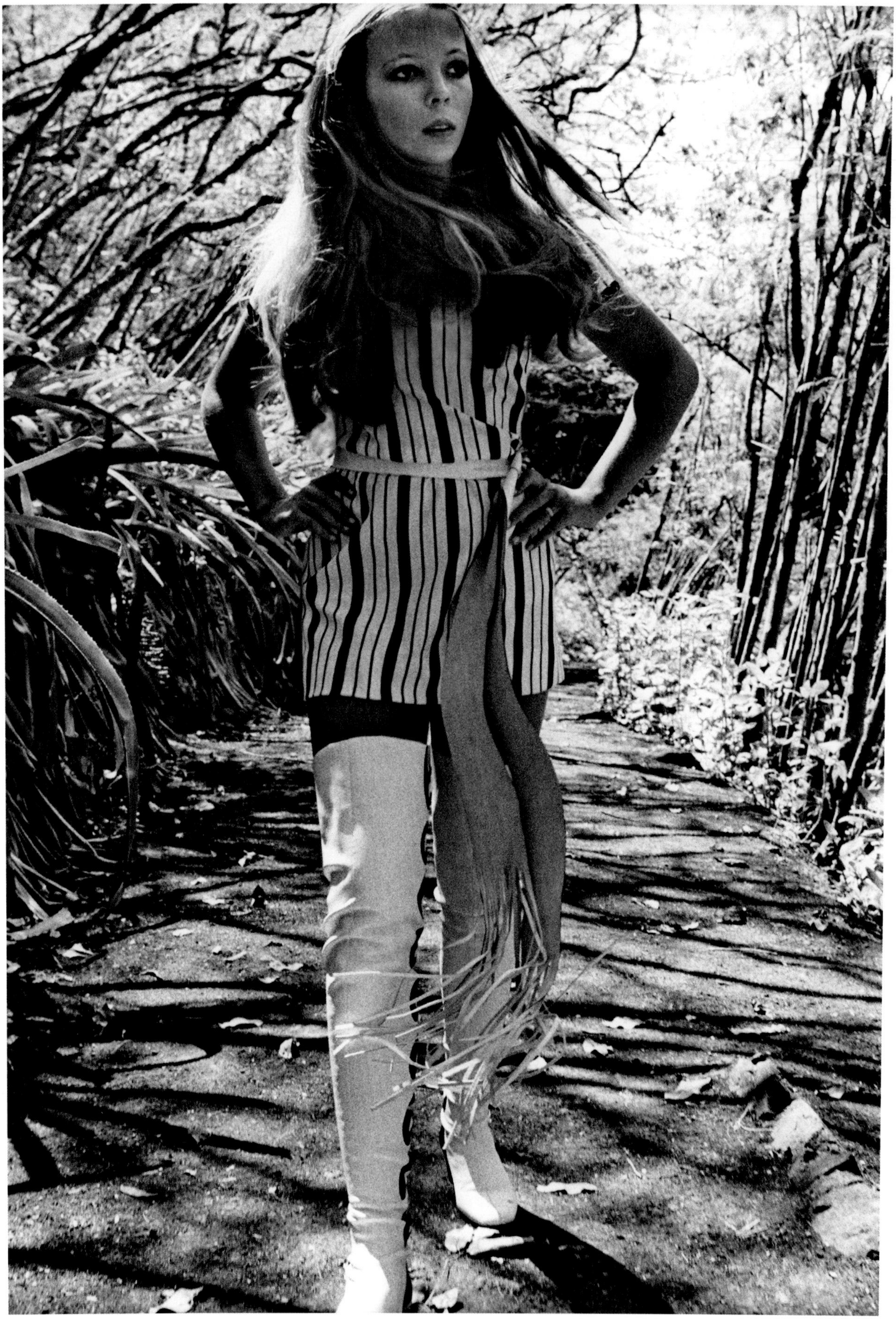

"In the 1970s
my mother's
look was made
up of these long,
floaty caftans,
with her hair up,
accessorised with
long earrings. And
she'd sort of sweep
through the room
like a galleon in
full sail."

Penelope Tree,
2025

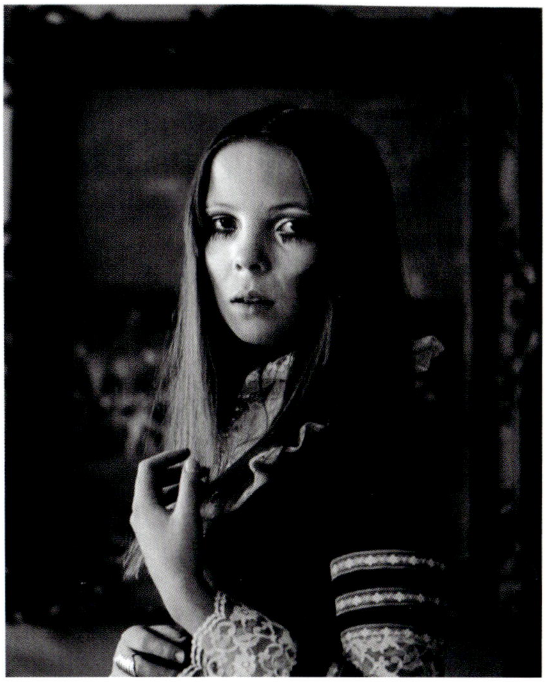

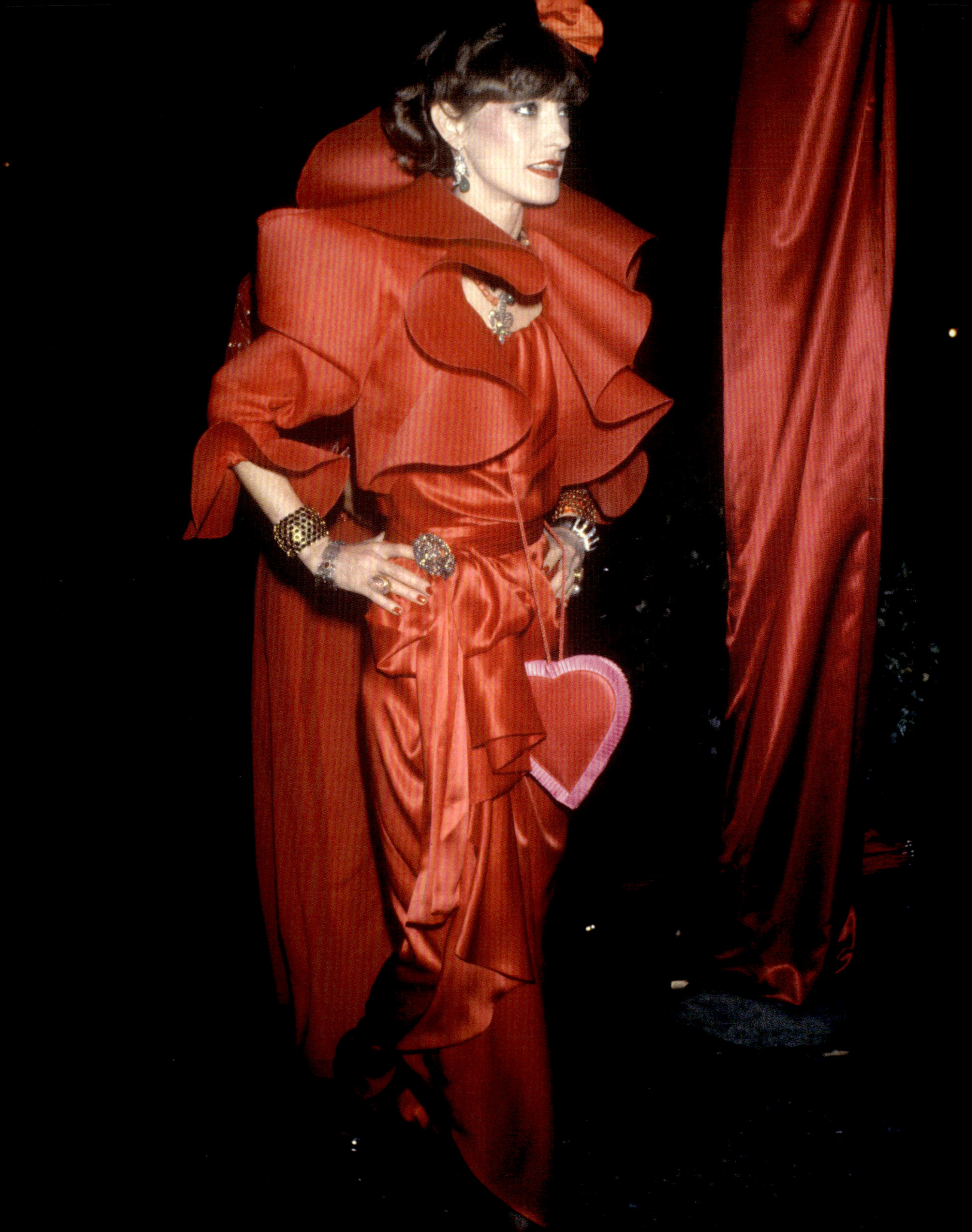

Left: Loulou de la Falaise at Nelson Seabra's Red Ball, 1980. Right: Rhoda, Lady Birley, photographed for Vogue in 1926.

Rhoda, **Lady Birley**, and Maxime **and** Loulou **de la Falaise**

★

Alongside first-wave feminism, the emancipation of women around the world unfurled slowly during the 19th and 20th centuries; yet a dichotomy continued to exist for many, despite this evolving autonomy. The feminist literary and cultural critic Jaqueline Rose points out that for the philosopher and activist Simone de Beauvoir, "becoming a mother is for a woman the most fundamental alienation of her freedom, certainly in the unequal world as it then was in the middle of the last century, and is still in so many ways today" (Rose, 2018). Two years before Beauvoir's seminal text *The Second Sex* (1949) was published, Maxime de la Falaise, muse of the avant-garde Italian designer Elsa Schiaparelli, became a mother to Loulou, who would herself go on to become the muse of French fashion legend Yves Saint Laurent. Maxime side-stepped convention and, to some criticism, forged her own unique method of motherhood – abandoning it to gain her freedom. A privileged, bohemian heritage encased her and inoculated her perspective; she wasn't born to be compliant.

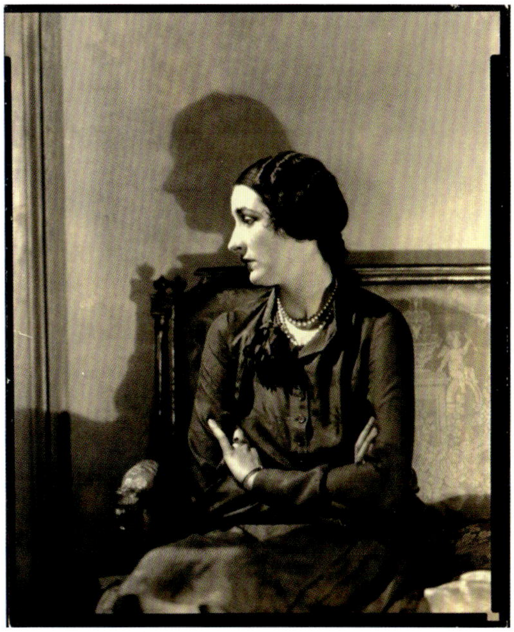

She was christened Maxine and came into the world in 1922 to live a life of free-spiritedness. Her own mother, Rhoda, Lady Birley, was an avid gardener and artist, and was often photographed. Though looking chic, wearing a black day dress in a frontispiece portrait taken for *Vogue* in August 1926, Hubert de Givenchy paints a picture of a woman that is far more unconventional: "I saw Rhoda every year in Palm Beach...Our group was artistic... Lady Birley made belts and jewellery with shells that she sold from a friend's boutique on Worth Avenue, standing in front with her wild gypsy hair and baroque pearls, waiting for customers, looking like she was about to read your palm" (Petkanas, 2018). She was often to be found in the grounds of her English country home, Charleston Manor. In the 1970s, she was photographed among her prize shrubs by Valerie Finnis for the Royal Horticultural Society, looking eccentric and dashing with a straw hat askew, beige trousers, green oversized sweater and a clashing purple scarf.

Rhoda had learnt her style codes from her mother, Vavarina (Catherine) Pike, born around 1858 in County Wicklow, Ireland. In a 1992 *Vogue* interview, Maxime describes her grandmother as wearing "only cream and natural colours; an ivory fedora, heavy silk shirts with pearl buttons, beige tweeds and a gold pince-nez on a fine chain. I remember her in those manilla-coloured cashmere cardigans

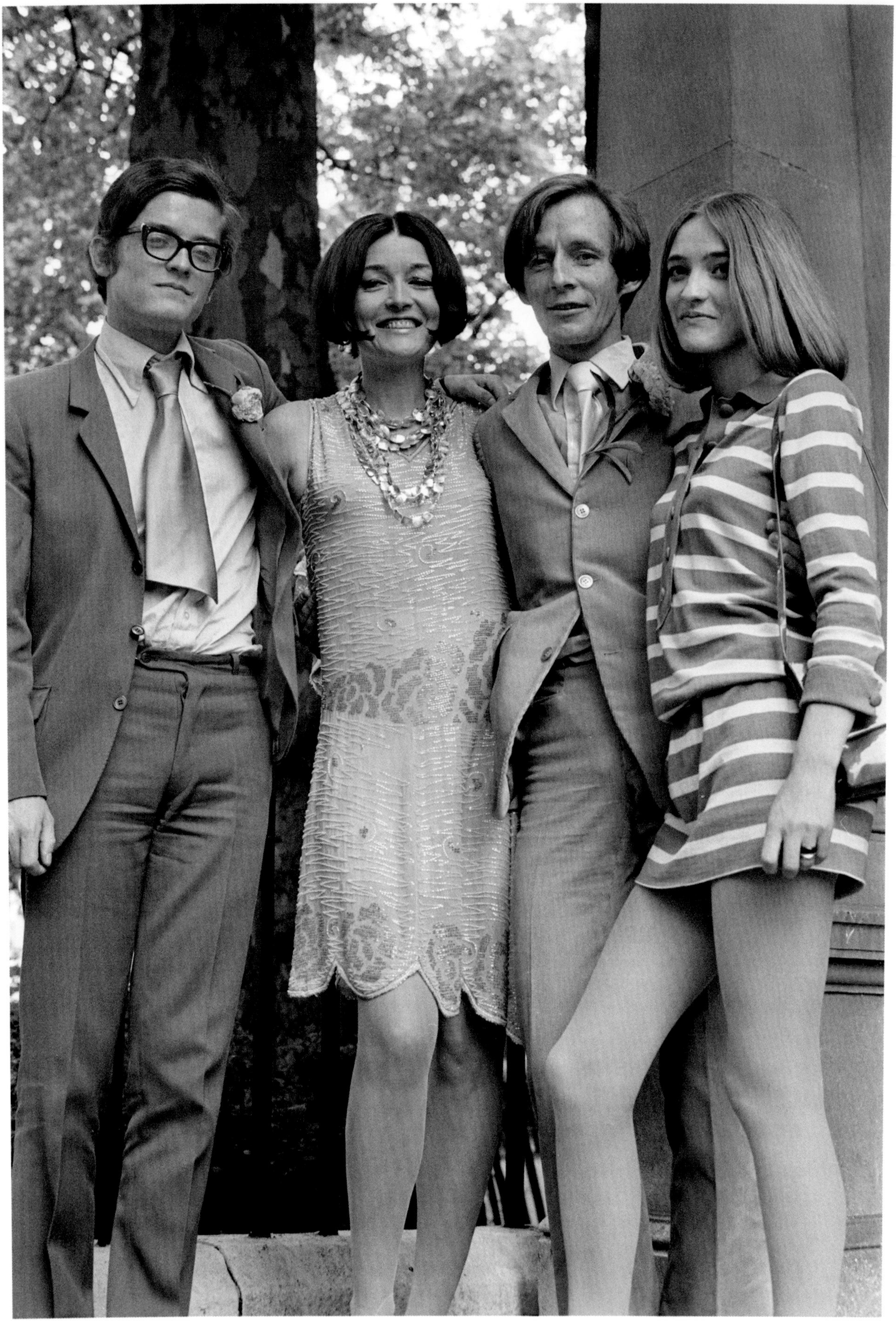

Maxime de la Falaise weds John McKendry in London, 1967. Loulou (far right) attends the wedding with her husband Desmond Fitzgerald (far left).

from men's department stores in London". Maxime inherited her mother and grandmother's characterful style, which she in turn passed on to Loulou, who completely understood the family codes and made them all her own, declaring: "We're self-invented creatures. You start by creating yourself. You have to be quite brave about it. You've got no choice unless you bind yourself to rules you don't like" (Howell, 1992).

The Birley–de la Falaise women were not just style originals, they worked for a living. Despite being bred among the higher echelons of society, money was relatively scarce for Maxime once she was wed. In 1946, post-war and after a spell on assignment at Bletchley Park as a codebreaker, Maxime married Comte Alain Le Bailly de la Falais, who had a grand name but little income. They lived in Paris, where the new Comtesse de la Falaise, aged 24, found employment at the house of Schiaparelli as a muse to bring in rich English customers. She became fast friends with Hubert de Givenchy, who described her thus: "Before I met Audrey Hepburn, Maxime was my feminine ideal...She was my idol, a Gruau drawing come to life" (Petkanas, 2018).

Loulou described her mother and grandmother as coming "from a family of artists; beautiful women who were stylish but penniless, so they had a lot more imagination in their dress" (*Crash*, 2015). Maxime divorced her first husband in 1950, by which time she had begun modelling, appearing on *Vogue*'s Best Dressed list together with the likes of Babe Paley and the Duchess of Windsor. She was contracted as a designer at Paquin as well as Schiaparelli, for whom she designed 'Schiap Bebe'. The surrealist childrenswear line was avant-garde, humorous and experimental, and included dresses in 'toadstooly' colours, embroidered with poisonous mushrooms. The pièce de la résistance, reportedly inspired by Loulou, was a straitjacket adorned with pink ribbons for "children who played with matches" (Petkanas, 2018).

It was only natural that Maxime would find employment in and around the world of fashion, but her take was always ingenious. She always looked radically chic, as confirmed by fashion journalist André Leon Talley: "Her day uniform was a Schiaparelli herringbone tweed coat lined with purple satin. But at night she would turn the coat inside out, roll it up into a gigantic muff – adding dash to a little black dress – and head out for a cocktail party" (Talley, 2009). Later, Maxime would design together with Gaby Aghion for Chloé and in 1960 created the legendary 'Embrun' dress. It was one of Aghion's favourite pieces. She recounts:

> "Maxime suggested a supple jersey, like a man's pullover. Then I realized I couldn't add a lining to the sleeves and the collar with the jersey; it was too thick. Maxime went to Max on the Champs-Elysées and returned with twill fabric for ties. We lined the collar and cuffs with it. It was adorable. Ravishing. Embrun was born. It was very avant-garde to make a shirt dress like that, like you would design a tee shirt. Women were fighting over it. It had plenty of charm with its tie twill facings—a masculine detail on feminine clothes. I have always mixed everything together; I do this because I'm nonchalant. And this dress was tremendously successful because it says, 'I'm nonchalant'" (Petkanas, 2018).

Insouciance was at the heart of Maxime and Loulou's fashionable appeal and, at times, this extended to some extent to their mother–daughter relationship. After Maxime's divorce and having been designated *une mère indigne* (an unfit mother), she left Loulou and her brother, Alexis, who were ordered to stay with their father, saying: "I should have been stronger...but I was streaking off with a boyfriend. I know the kids suffered terribly badly...a lot of Loulou's strength lies in the fact that she protected her brother and made herself strong" (Petkanas, 2018). Later, Loulou and Maxime reconciled: "Finally, I was sent to live with my mother in New York in 1964. We were both rather neurotic at the time. It was a rather wild time for both of us" (Petkanas, 2018).

In the 1970s Maxime became part of Andy Warhol's Factory set, mentoring Robert Mapplethorpe and his girlfriend Patti Smith, and writing cookery columns for *Vogue* – a feast of fun for the young Loulou, who was just 17. In 1976 Maxime reflected on their newly established bond, saying: "If she weren't my daughter, she would probably still be my closest friend" (Lau, 2010).

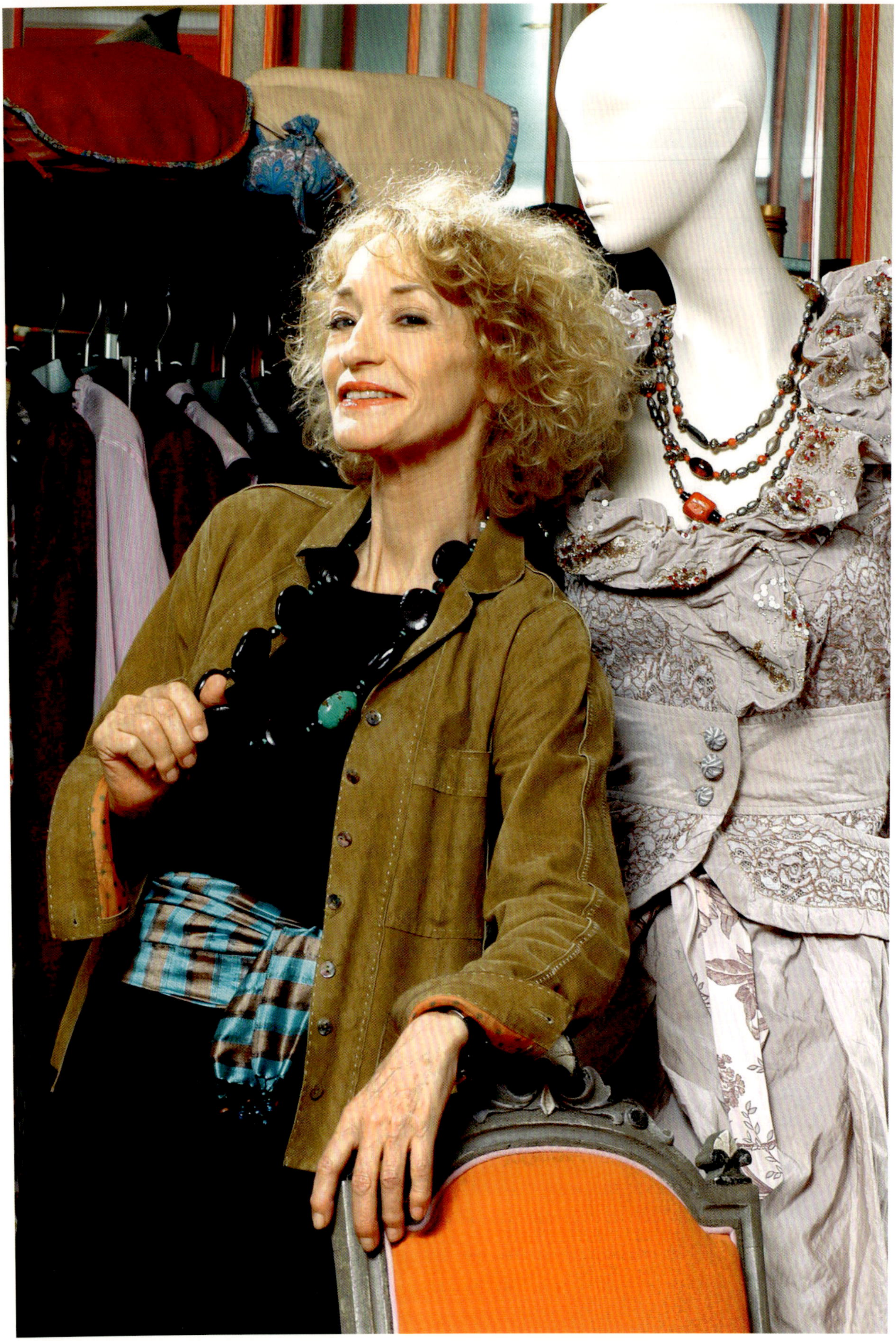

Loulou grew up to become just as dazzling as her mother; according to former fashion director of *Vogue* Grace Coddington, "You took one look at Loulou and gasped" (Ravenel and Fraser-Cavassoni, 2014). In 1966 she married Desmond Fitzgerald, 29th Knight of Glin, who owned an Irish castle, with Maxime co-ordinating an eccentric wedding wardrobe. She was typically creative, writing in a letter to Veronica Villiers, Desmond's mother, "I think I've gone a bit overboard on the trousseau. Also – the 1900 wedding dress fell apart at the cleaners, so it now has to be recopied in new material" (Petkanas, 2018). Maxime also gifted the couple a Habitat kitchen for their Knightsbridge flat. The marriage, however, was brief and by 1970 was over.

By this time, Loulou already knew Yves Saint Laurent and in 1972 she went to work officially for the designer in Paris, creating jewellery and overseeing knitwear, among other less tangible duties. She explained how Saint Laurent "mostly wanted my spirit, rather than saying: 'she'll do this or that'. He wanted me to be nearby. He needed to feel my presence. And he wanted to see how I combined different things. It was my personality that interested him, my way of interpreting things...everything was a lot less structured than now. Studio work was less 'who's doing style, who's doing this?'; it was more Bohemian" (*Crash*, 2015).

Former European editor of *Women's Wear Daily*, Marian McEvoy knew Loulou when she was in Paris at this time:

> "When she arrived at about 9am every day to the YSL couture studios on Paris's Right Bank, it was an event. The pants, jackets, skirts, blouses, dresses, stockings, shoes, shawls, bags and jewellery that she assembled and donned each morning in her 14th arrondissement apartment were unlike anything anyone else in Paris wore, or had ever seen. Heiresses, countesses, models, movie stars and scores of fashion editors wanted to look like Loulou" (McEvoy, 2014).

Loulou's second marriage to Thadée Klossowski, son of the painter Balthus, was the fashion event of the year. Yves's partner, Pierre Berge, organised their wedding ball, which was held in the Bois de Boulogne public park with 300 of the great and the good, from Karl Lagerfeld and Kenzo Takada to Princess Marina of Greece and Denmark, Nico, and Mick and Bianca Jagger. Loulou remarked: "It was the first time in Paris there was such a mix of age, class, activities, a jumble of characters...there were some French punks, everyone was frightfully interested by one another" (Petkanas, 2018). That night, the world reflected Loulou's signature view of fashion: a collage of theatre, the unexpected and fun. Just like her mother, who had innate charm and elegance, Loulou found beauty in unexpected combinations and counterintuitive ways of doing things and, according to good friend Betty Catroux, "saw life in pink" (Cowles, 2014). Both mother and daughter were kaleidoscopically stylish, and their legacy lives on, not least in Anthony Vaccarello's YSL Spring 2025 collection, which was inspired by Loulou with glimpses of Maxime, featuring boxy, brocade jackets in gemstone shades, multi-textured, pleated-and-laced mini skirts and oversized statement necklaces.

> **"Some families are born to money, some to politics or music. The blood of this family confers style. A dynasty carried through the female line."**
>
> **Georgina Howell,**
> *Vogue*, 1992

Left: Rhoda, Lady Birley poses in the studio of her husband, painter Sir Oswald Birley, for Vogue, *1935. Right: Maxime de la Falaise in Paris, 1976.*

"This is how my family are: the women have always played a hugely significant role. I am thinking of my mother, who now lives in New York, and of my grandmother, a ravishing woman of exceptional elegance: both have always treated life as an odyssey, always living freely, as if by magic...with a superb taste for enjoying themselves and for light-heartedness, and all without ever losing their sensibility for the truly important values in life."

Loulou de la Falaise,
Vogue, 1986

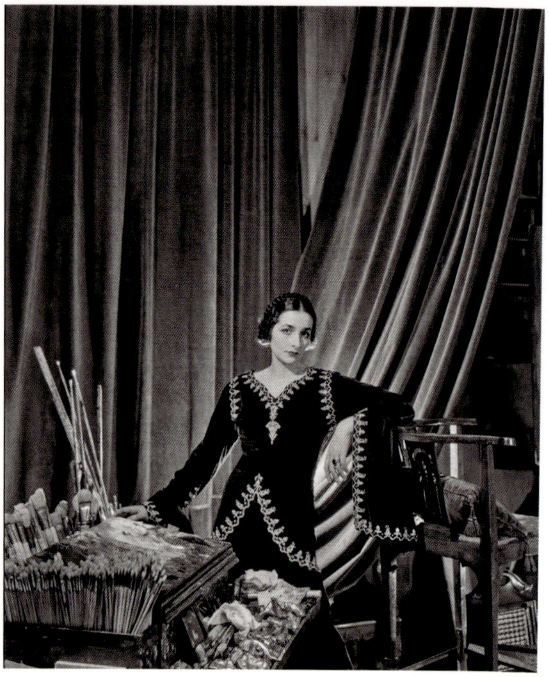

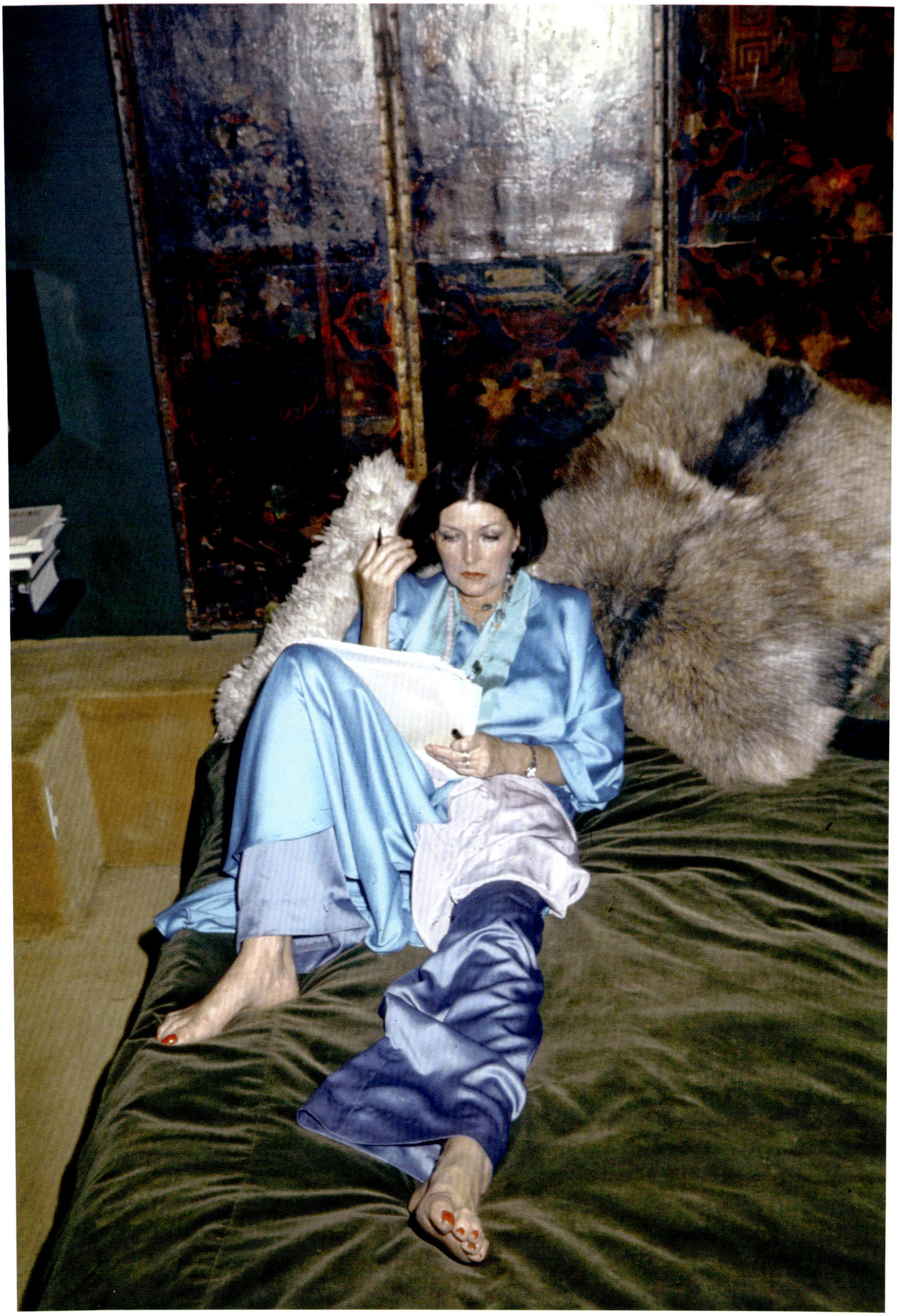

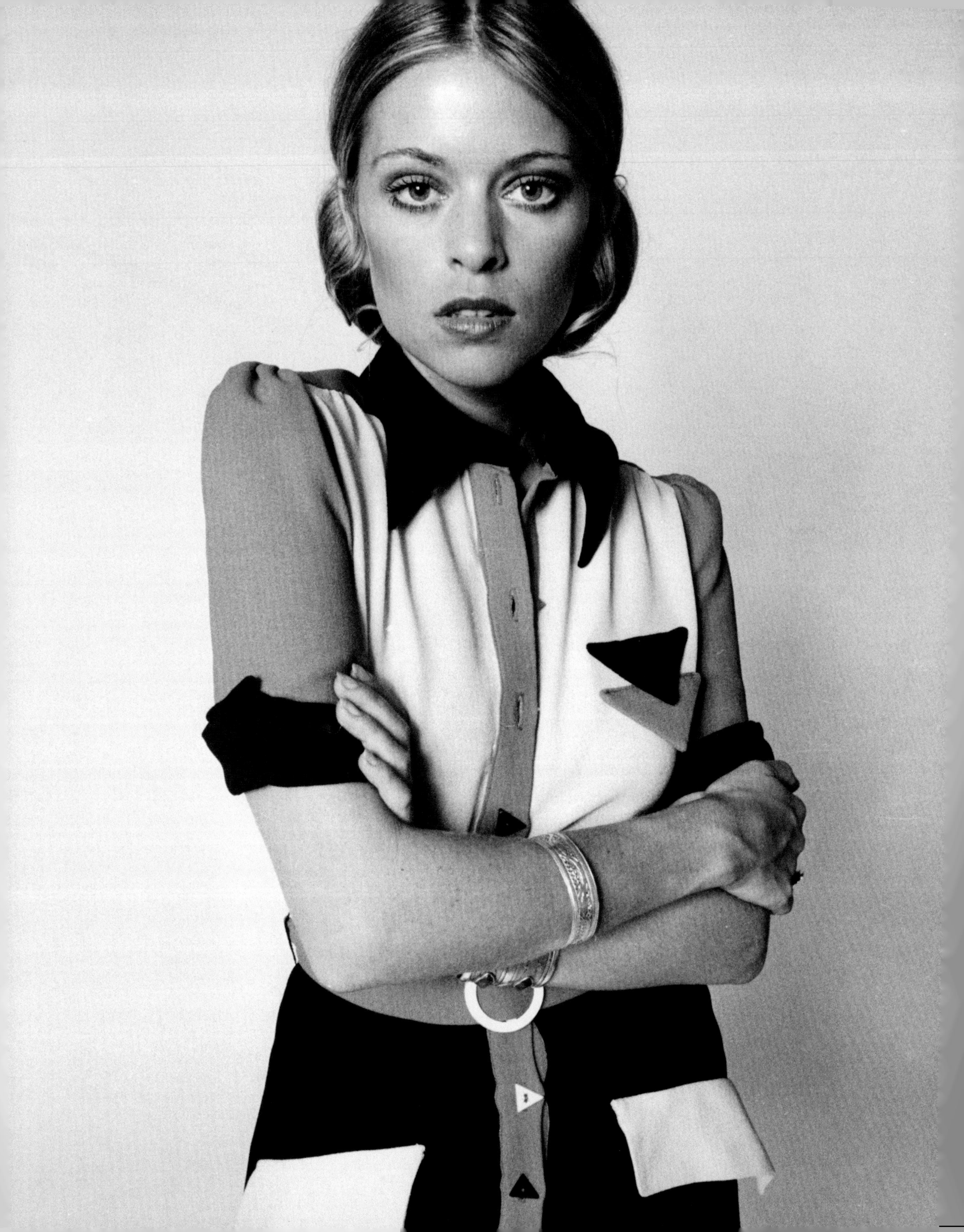

Edith and **Edina Ronay**

★

Edith Ronay was born in Budapest around 1918, though her daughter, the designer and actress Edina Ronay, admits that "My mother always lied about her age. We fled Hungary before the Iron Curtain came down. My mother came to England in 1946 and my sister and I a year later. I was just four". Despite the economic hardship following World War II, the world they left behind was one of privilege and money, though also, under Soviet occupation, unpredictability. Edina's father was the legendary restauranteur, food writer and critic Egon Ronay, whose family ran the best eating establishments in Hungary. Good food and wine were in the family DNA.

> "My father was Jewish and exceptionally wealthy. My mother, a Catholic, came from a very well-heeled but not super-rich family and had always dressed smartly. When married, things became super-charged and from then on she always wore couture. Edith was tiny and favoured elegant, tailored suits and high heels."

Their sumptuous clothes came in suitcases following their escape to London. Edina remembers how her mother "had everything sent out along with her silver and crystal. All the amazing stuff – hand-embroidered silk satin sheets. My father Egon was also a great dresser. And there was this pig-skin leather coat that arrived too".

As the Ronays adjusted to a new country, they never failed to put their best foot forward. Like their mother, Edina and her older sister Esther, a documentary filmmaker who passed away in March 2025, went to the dressmaker. "We always had clothes made for us when we were younger. I was a bit annoyed that I had to wear the same things as my sister, but I remember I was very excited by my first communion organza dress that had a matching veil." Growing up surrounded by beautiful things to wear turned Edina into a fashion connoisseur, who was in tune with what London and Europe in the late 1950s had to offer, including revolutionary designs recently created by Cristóbal Balenciaga: "When I was 15 and sack dresses were all the rage, I made my own; it was a very simple T-shape."

A year later Edina enrolled at Saint Martin's School of Art, but left after being cast by a film producer in *The Pure Hell of St Trinian's* (1960), a British comedy about a boarding school for girls. This opportunity led to a place at RADA, which served as a springboard to a successful acting career. However, all the while Edina was in love with clothes:

> "In the early days as an actress, I bought things from the Chelsea Antiques Market and that's how I started in fashion really. I'd buy vintage things and customise them, and then I had a stall in Antiquarius and later found a shop on the corner of Flood Street and King's Road to sell it all. I loved retro silhouettes, and my style was all about the fabulous old pieces I came across. My favourite period was the 1940s; the dresses were similar to the ones my mother would have worn as a young girl. I also wore lots of velvet and satin shirts in bright colours with great patterns and mixed and matched them with Hungarian blouses. Individuality was everything."

Edina Ronay with her daughter, Shebah, London 1999.

Marrying the photographer Dick Polack in 1971, Edina's gown was designed by Ossie Clark, and very much echoed her personal styling. "It was a cross-over dress with a fully pleated, pink-tulip print on black by Celia Birtwell. Dick wore white jeans and a denim jacket", she remembers. Going on to launch a fully-fledged label was a natural step, and after designing a range of Fair-Isle knitwear from old 1930s patterns, a whole range ensued. In 1971, Edina's daughter Sheba was born, and she was similarly kitted out:

> "I found a tiny Afghani coat she used to wear and knitted her a bright-coloured jacket and crocheted a hat. I bought some fabric in Morocco and made her a dress with smocking – it was all very roughly done. I wasn't a great craftsperson – I had my collections made up by experts."

Out of these bohemian foundations, the Edina Ronay label became a mainstay of chic wardrobes in the mid-1980s, and high-profile customers included Princess Diana and the model Jerry Hall. All the while, her heritage and mother's wardrobe served as key inspirations: "I used to design lots of pleated skirts and jackets that were modelled on our national costume but also the beautifully made-to-measure clothes my mother always wore." Edith was a huge fan of her daughter's work and from the time the brand took off, she wore little else. Edina recollects her much loved memories of those times: "She made them look so chic and wore these black lurex knits. I noticed, after she died, that her wardrobe contained huge amounts of my crêpe-de-Chine pieces."

"My mother personified a kind of old-world glamour that no longer exists. I remember when I was growing up, she always looked amazing."

Edina Ronay,
2025

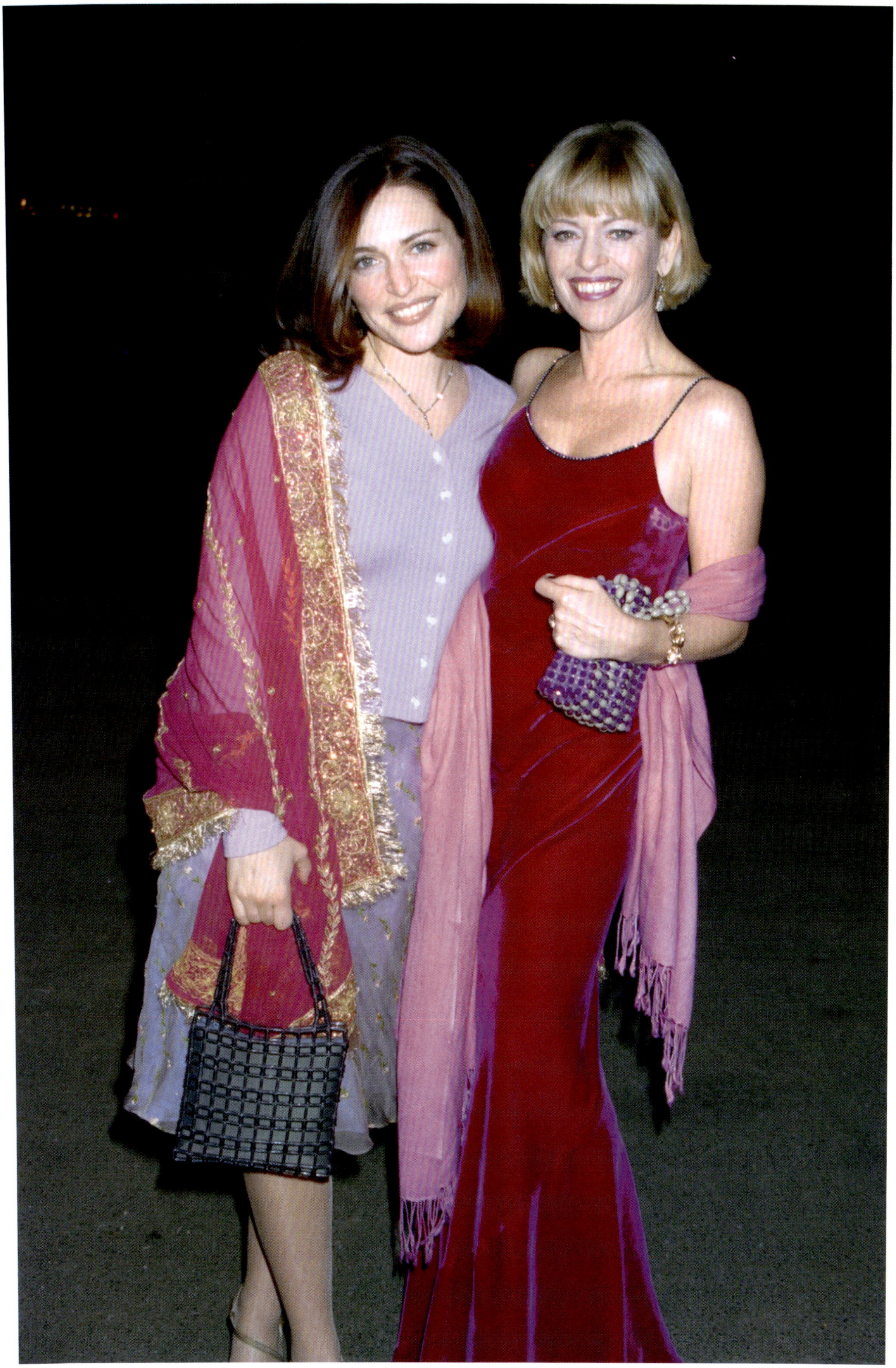

Edith and Egon Ronay, 1946.

> **"Edith was tiny and favoured elegant, tailored suits and high heels."**
>
> **Edina Ronay,**
> 2025

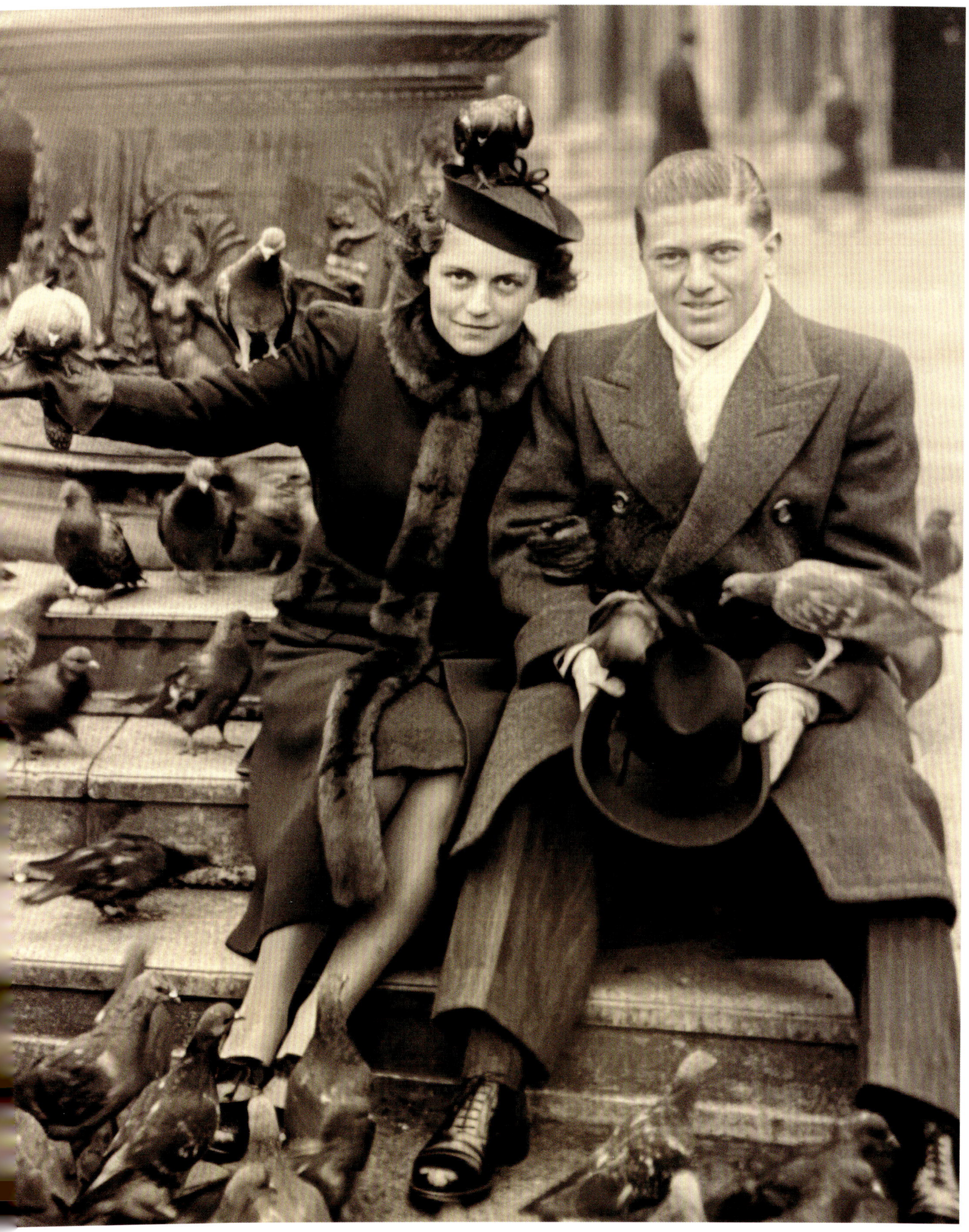

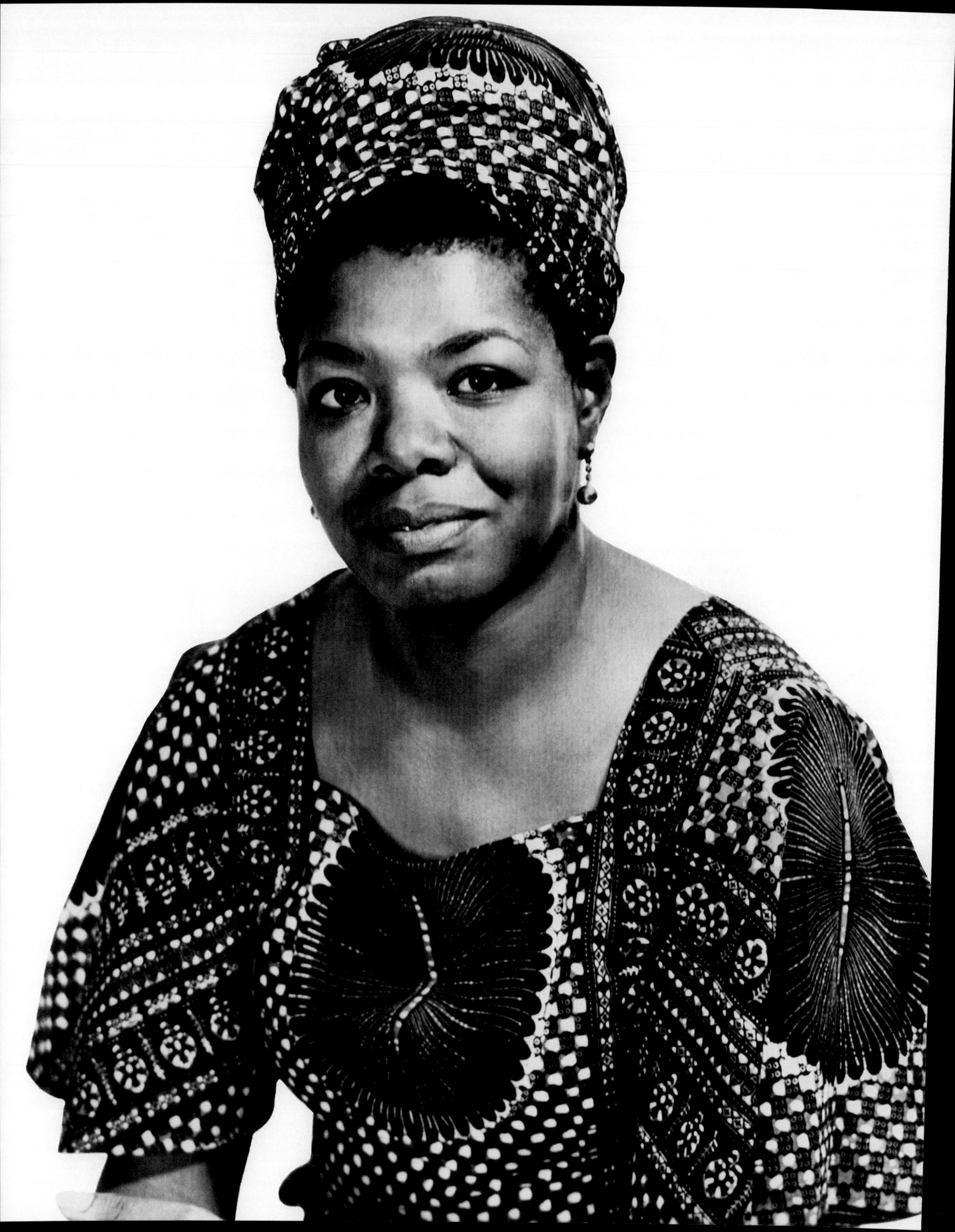

Vivian Baxter, **Maya Angelou**, and **Guy** Johnson

★

A young girl in the 1950s, the legendary author Maya Angelou was a working actress and singer, wearing cocktail dresses and kitten heels, beatnik leotards and capri pants. She was also the mother of a young son, Guy, having fallen pregnant at just 16 years old. At the age of 24, she toured between 1954 and 1955 for the European production of *Porgy and Bess*; a few years later, in 1960, she put on *Cabaret for Freedom* with the stand-up comedian Godfrey Cambridge, a show in aid of Martin Luther King's civil rights organisation, the SCLC, where she would go on to work. A year later, she performed in Jean Genet's play *The Blacks* at the St Mark's Playhouse off Broadway.

She lived with her son in the Crown Heights district of Brooklyn, where life could be tough. Guy described it thus:

> "The hours were long and there were many times [Angelou] worked weeks without taking a day off. Money was always tight during her tenure with the SCLC. Sometimes she would not even take her full salary. She would often ask me, 'What's more important to you, the struggle for freedom, or your creature comforts?' I always responded, 'The struggle for freedom.' I really couldn't answer anything else" (Johnson, 2017).

Shortly after, she moved to Cairo and lived there for a year with fellow activist Vusumzi Make, becoming associate editor of the *Arab Observer* before leaving for Ghana to study. It was here that brightly printed, patterned sarongs and scarves became her signature style in the African heat. This look evolved into loose-fitting batik sundresses accessorised with statement beaded necklaces when she moved back to the States in 1964 to help Malcom X and Martin Luther King with their campaigning. Her proud cultural dress conveyed a dignified and significant unity with tradition. However, as a child, Guy saw things differently. In an interview in 2014, he revealed:

> "What I mostly remember about my mother is that she would come to school wearing her African clothes and her hair natural, and some idiot kid in the class would say, 'Your Mama from lost Africa,' and I'd have to pop him. And generally, he was bigger than I was so I would take most of the beating, even though I would start it. And when I would come home, I would ask my mother, 'Don't you have a sweater skirt outfit? Or one of those Penney's things?' And she would say to me, 'This is your history, you come from Kings and Queens'" (Johnson, 2014).

Conversely, Angelou was in awe of the clothes her own mothe, Vivian Baxter, wore. In the last book in her series of autobiographies, *Mom & Me & Mom*, published in 2013, she describes Baxter wearing "perfect makeup and diamond earrings, and a silver fox scarf", going on to reflect candidly on how "she was admired by most people in San Francisco's Black community and even some whites" (Angelous, 2013). Baxter had been absent for a large part of Angelou's childhood, and living with her grandmother in Stamps, Arkansas, Maya saw her so infrequently that even calling her 'mother' was difficult. In her biography, Angelou recounts a conversation she had with her mother when Vivian asked why. "Because you are beautiful, and you don't look like a mother",

Angelou responded (Angelous, 2013). Despite this, when Maya became unexpectedly pregnant her mother was fully supportive of her. Angelou describes how:

> "[She] never made me feel as if I brought scandal to the family. The baby had not been planned, and I would have to rethink plans about education, but to Vivian Baxter that was life being life. Having a baby while I was unmarried had not been wrong. It was simply slightly inconvenient. By the time I was 22 I was living in San Francisco. I had a five-year-old son, Guy, two jobs and two rented rooms, with cooking privileges down the hall" (Angelou, 2013).

Though Angelou would never give birth to another child, she published a book of essays in 2008 titled *Letter to my Daughter*, where she talks to women the world over:

> "I have lots of daughters. Black ones, white ones, Asian ones and Jewish ones and the Spanish-speaking ones... Sometimes I'll get a thousand pieces of mail a week from young women who think I'm wise. So they use me as a mother and I think of them as my daughters" (Younge, 2009).

She had learnt life's lessons carefully and, in the book, talks about her relationship with her son: 'The birth of my son caused me to develop enough courage to invent my life. I learned to love my son without wanting to possess him and I learned how to teach him to teach himself." (Angelou, 2008).

Angelou's 1978 poem 'Phenomenal Woman' was first published in *Cosmopolitan* magazine, introducing the world to her style of feminism. As a public speaker in later life, she dressed to impress as the very epitome of a phenomenal woman: little black dresses and elegant polo-neck sweaters accessorised with pearls and earrings were her favourite outfits. Looking smart and feeling good about yourself was an Angelou signature that she had worked hard to cultivate, and one she carried all her life. The year before her death she was photographed for the Cole Haan 1928 campaign, laying down the gauntlet for looking great at 85 years old.

"My greatest blessing has been the birth of my son. My next greatest blessing has been my ability to turn people into children of mine."

Maya Angelou,
Huffpost, 2013

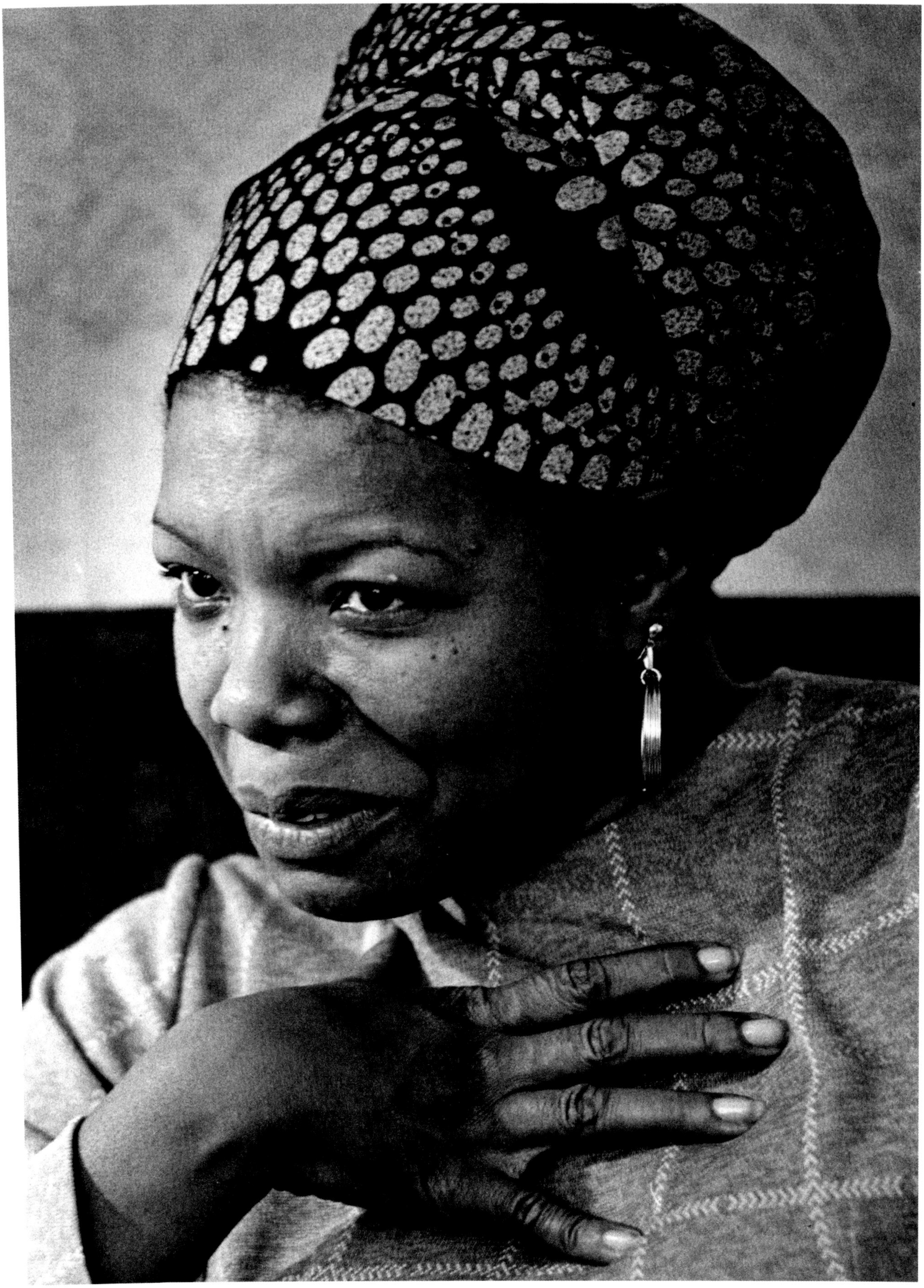

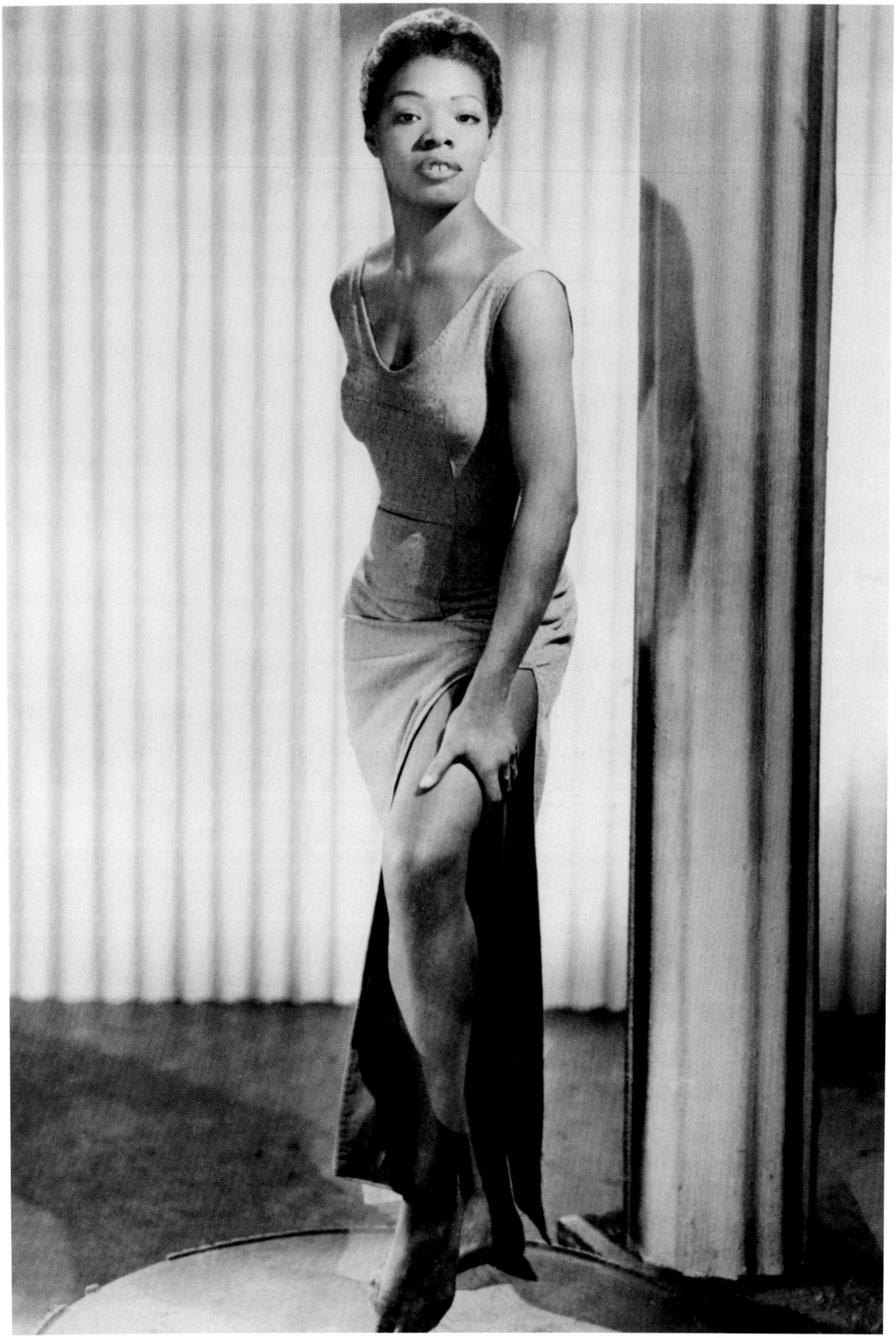
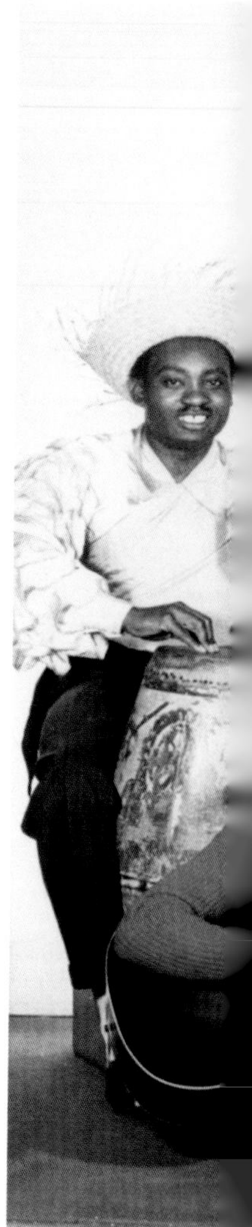

Maya Angelou in 1957. Bottom: Guy Johnson in 2005.

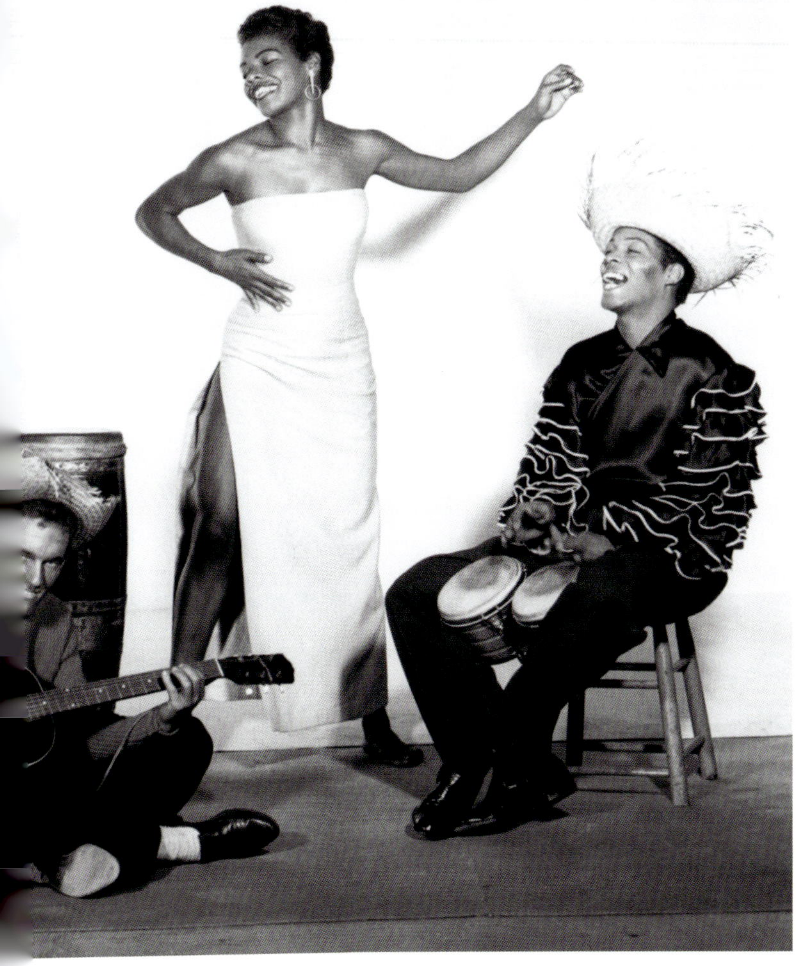

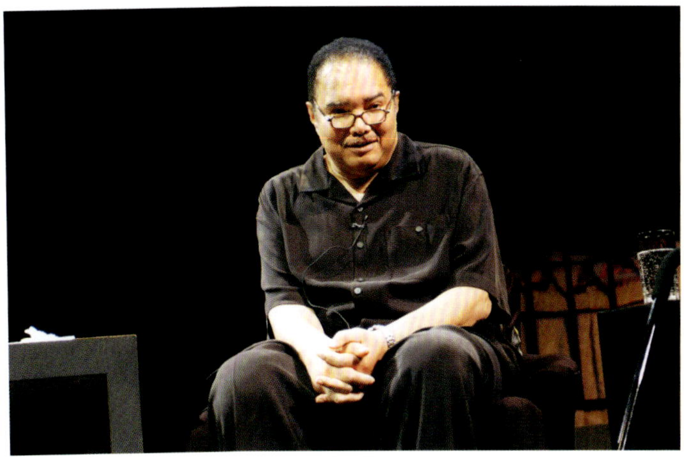

"My mother really is remarkable."

Maya Angelou,
Vogue, 1982

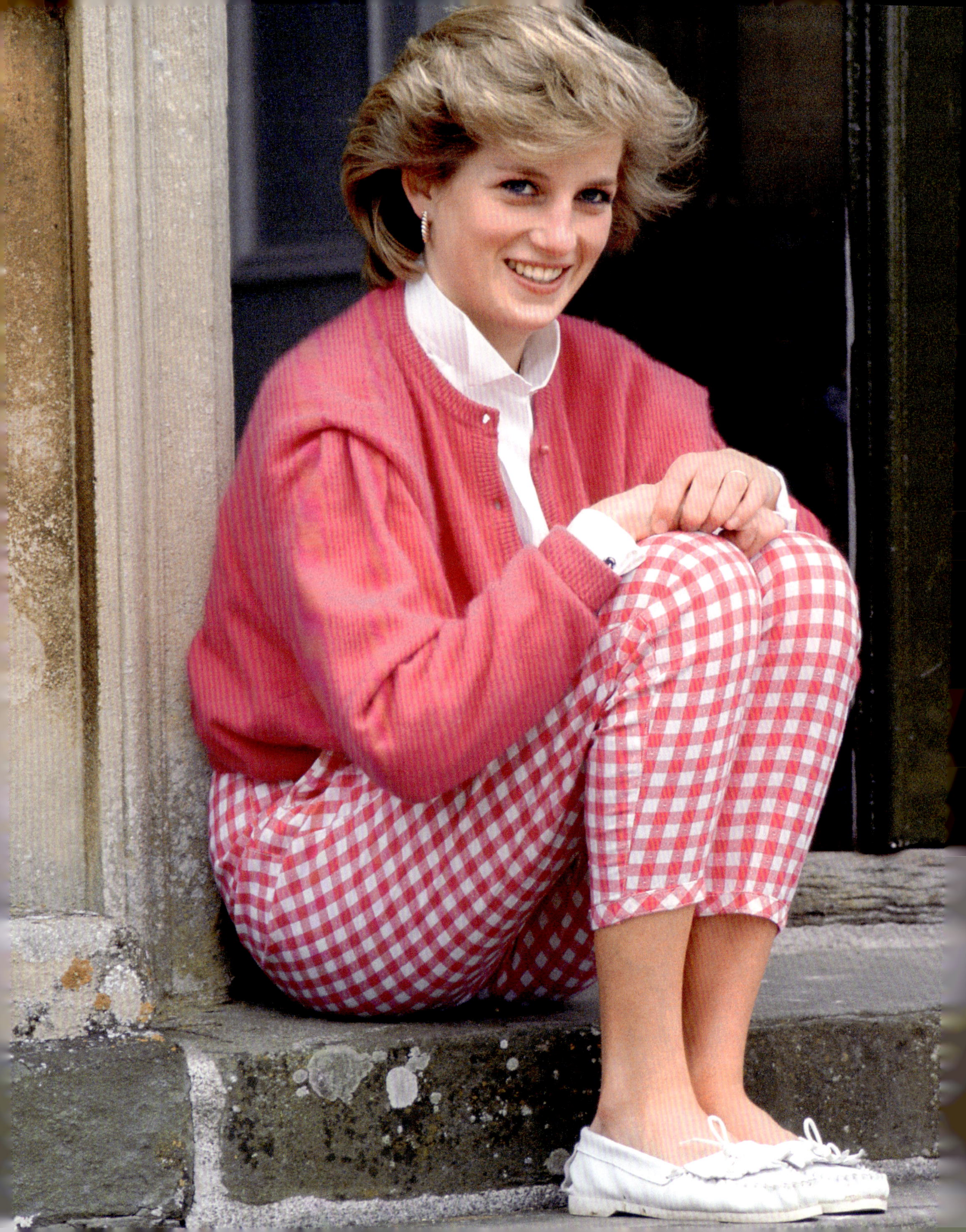

Diana, **Princess of Wales**, Prince **William** and Prince **Harry**

★

A mother's effect on a child is rooted in their own changing stories of innocence and experience. Lady Diana Spencer's life in the global media spotlight was tracked from 'Shy Di' to the 'People's Princess', and along with it a wardrobe that metamorphosed as she did. It is fascinating to see how this transformation also affected the clothes she chose to dress her children in and how an empowering relationship with fashion – something that strengthened her character – also infused and reorientated the world of her children in a way the British royal family could never have anticipated.

Diana's wardrobe when she was a young mother reflected the environment and social boundaries she lived within. As the 11th great-granddaughter of Mary, Queen of Scots, and daughter of an earl, Diana had the lineage of the landed gentry. In July 1981, when she married then Prince Charles, the heir to the British throne, it was natural that she would continue to adorn herself in the traditional raiment of girls of her class – clothes that held codes of power. However, it was at this time that this style of clothing was roundly satirised by Peter York in his legendary book, *The Official Sloane Ranger Handbook* (1982). 'Sloane' is a term used to describe an upper-middle- and upper-class person, characterised by *The New York Times* as someone who "emigrated to spend the weekend in the country houses of friends and relatives" (Brown, 1984). It flew off the shelves, not just because of York's laser-sharp reading of class but also because, in a canny move, Diana was its cover girl. She was, however, a 'Super-Sloane' – no ordinary posh miss. "She wasn't a nice upper-middle-class girl. She was an absolute, oak-tall aristocrat. When the first Earl [of Spencer] got married, the diamonds on his shoes were worth – in contemporary money – £3m", York told *The Guardian* newspaper in 2020 (Cochrane, 2020).

After attending the Institut Alpin Videmanette, a finishing school in Switzerland, Diana bought a flat with an inheritance from her great-grandmother and shared it with friends she'd met on the ski slopes or been to school with. They all wore a similar 'sloany' uniform of pie-crust-collared blouses and cardigans or lambswool tank tops, accessorised with velvet headbands and pearls, changing their loafers for Hunter wellington boots and Barbour jackets when in the country. It was a classic upper-class look that in many respects was a generational hand-me-down. Wearing conservative, slightly frumpy fashion was not an unfamiliar habit for monied families. A 2016 *Harper's Bazaar* feature points out that "it was not until 1946, the year before she became engaged to Philip Mountbatten, that Princess Elizabeth was allowed to select her own clothes. Marion Crawford, her governess, observed that her taste followed her mother closely: silk or thin-wool frocks with matching coats, in pastel shades" (Eastoe, 2016). Some years later in 2024, *British Vogue* reported that it was in fact Diana's mother, Frances Shand Kydd, who often bought her daughter's clothes: "She frequently wore dowdy garden-party hats from milliner John Boyd and blousy, floral dresses courtesy of Donald Campbell" (Maitland, 2024).

The unconscious cultural and symbolic habitus of the aristocracy and royal family was one that Diana had been surrounded by from birth; it was her heritage. When she was first married, her clothes were created by haute-couture designers such as Catherine Walker, Bruce Oldfield and Victor Edelstein, signalling her status as future queen. At first, she dressed sons Harry and William in outfits that rigidly replicated not just her rank, but their own. In January 1988, Diana dressed her boys, aged just three and five at the time, in matching pale-blue tweed coats. As they played on a vintage fire engine

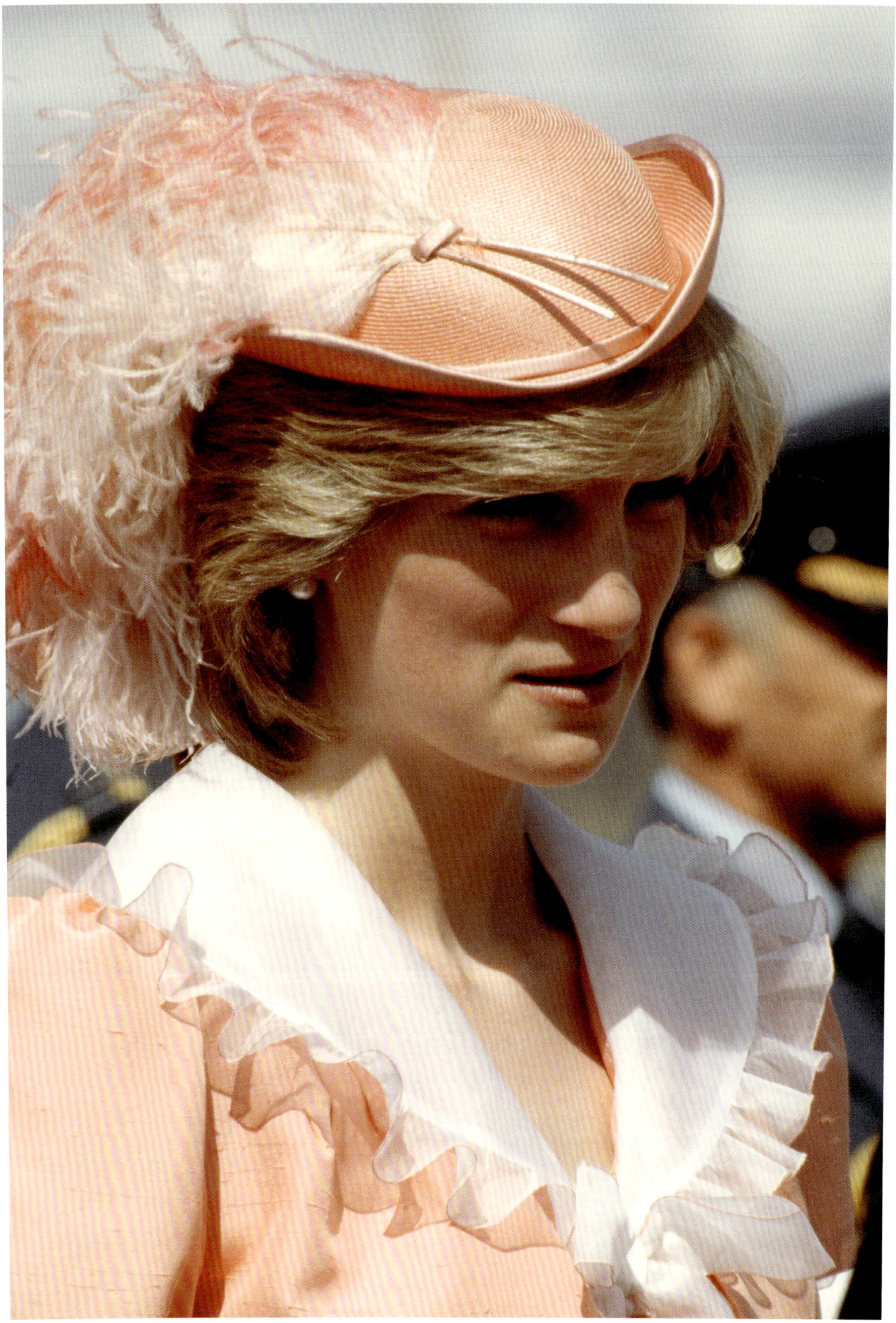

with their cousins Zara and Peter, their typically starched attire represents the stately prescription of prim formal wear for children of the family. A 1965 photo of Diana shows her sporting a similar Peter Pan-collared wool coat to the one her sons wore.

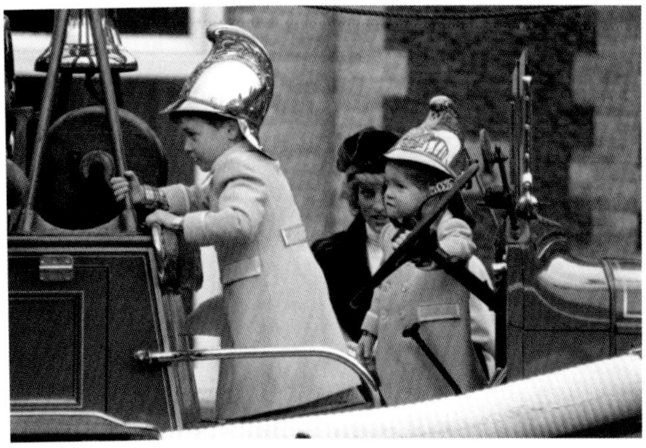

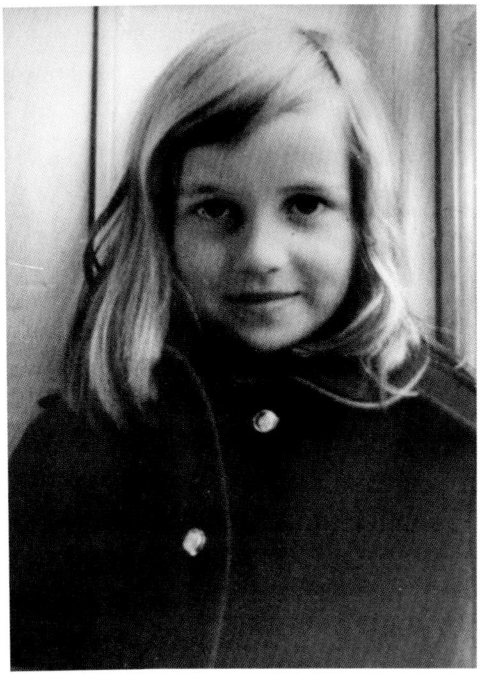

The fashion bubble that the royal family lived in was rarely punctured, but that didn't mean this very particular look wouldn't find its way outside of the royal gates. The little coats the princes wore mirrored silhouettes found that season in Vivienne Westwood's 'Harris Tweed' collection, which was based largely on the wardrobe Queen Elizabeth II and her sister Princess Margaret wore in the 1930s. Westwood's heritage Red Label wear that year was designed to subvert and reappropriate upper-class silhouettes and spin traditional British culture in an avant-garde direction – deflating but also celebrating it. Westwood's work was often about undermining the status quo of class, but high-profile nobility at the time did not see the sedition and, regardless, continued to wear their customary attire.

In the 2017 documentary, *Diana, Our Mother: Her Life and Legacy*, Prince Harry reflects:

> "I genuinely think she got satisfaction out of dressing myself and William up in the most bizarre outfits – normally matching. It was weird shorts and little shiny shoes with the old clip-on. Looking back at the photos it just makes me laugh and I think, 'How could you do that to us!' And funnily enough, we got to the age when William would turn around and go, 'This is ridiculous, I'm the older brother. Why do I have to be dressed the same as him?' And I'm sort of thinking, 'Hang on a second, if you're going to dress differently, I'm not going to be the only person dressed like this. This is ridiculous!'"

As Diana evolved and gained confidence with her own wardrobe, she similarly began to relax the clothes her sons wore and made a point of choosing them when she could. In 1991, the royals visited Canada and Harry and William were photographed wearing double denim, accessorised with a baseball hat. Later, in 1993, two years after Charles and Diana had officially separated, she took them to Thorpe Park, famously making a point of queuing with the rest of the public for the water rides and rollercoasters. The princes wore jeans once again, while Diana wore a leather jacket and black trousers. She wanted her boys to experience normality and freedom both in what they wore and what they did.

Anna Harvey, who worked as a stylist for Diana, revealed that the princess "did go down to Kensington High Street and do the odd bit of shopping, but I think it was mainly for the boys". She continued:

> "It was much freer after the divorce. You will notice that necklines dropped, and skirts rose. Much more leg was shown. I don't blame her – she had amazing legs. And she was building a new life for herself. She wanted to be positive, and I admire the way she picked herself up and got on with life and didn't sink into a sort of oblivion" (Holt, 2017).

Top: Prince William and Prince Harry in 1988. Bottom: Diana as a girl, 1965.

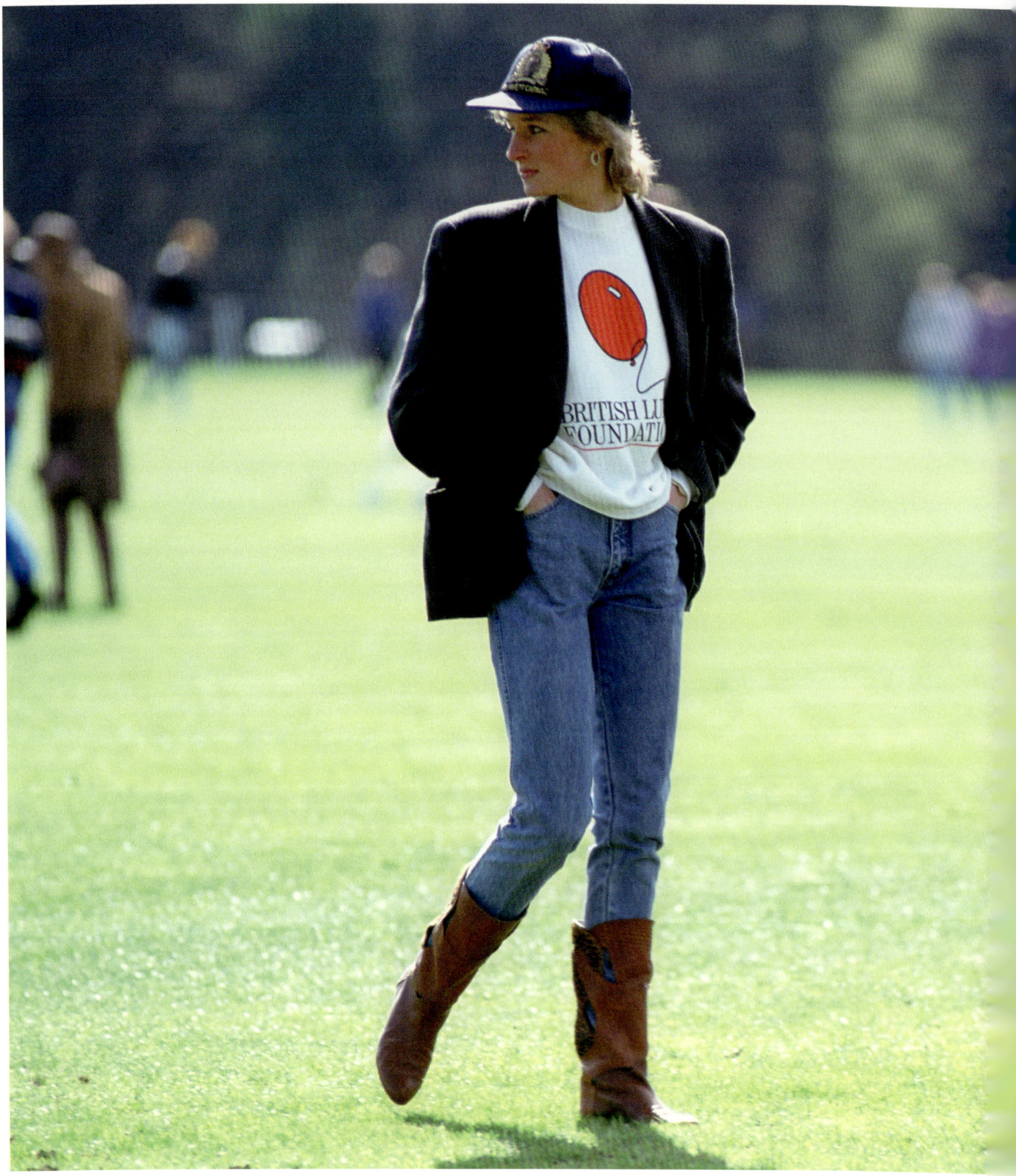
BRITISH LU
FOUNDATIO

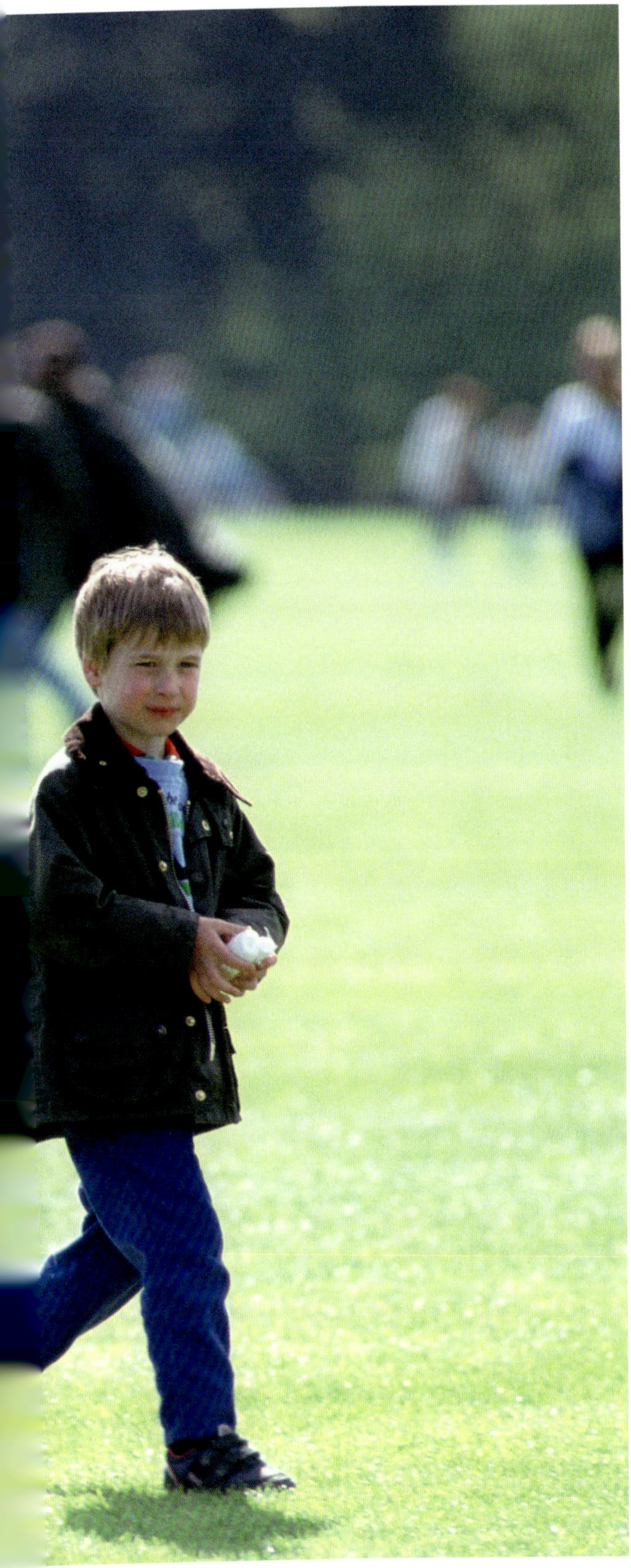

She certainly changed. By 1996 she was poised enough to wear a satin slip dress by John Galliano for Dior; the designer had fitted it with a corset but the princess asked for it to be removed so she could feel more relaxed. In 1997, the year of Diana's death, legendary fashion editor Carrie Donovan reflected: "We all admired her so much as a woman. At the beginning she didn't look too hot, but who would? She was dressed in the royal way. I remember, her first trip to the U.S. she had some terrible hats" (*WWD*, 1997). Karl Lagerfeld agreed: "She had never looked so good, so fashionable as in the last six months. I don't know why for sure, but I think she probably felt more free without all the people from the court to worry about. She was finally free from all that stiff English fashion" (*WWD*, 1997).

"The Princess of Wales delivers her sons to school wearing jeans, cowboy boots and baseball caps, and sends sales of boots and caps soaring."

Liz Smith,
The Times, 1991

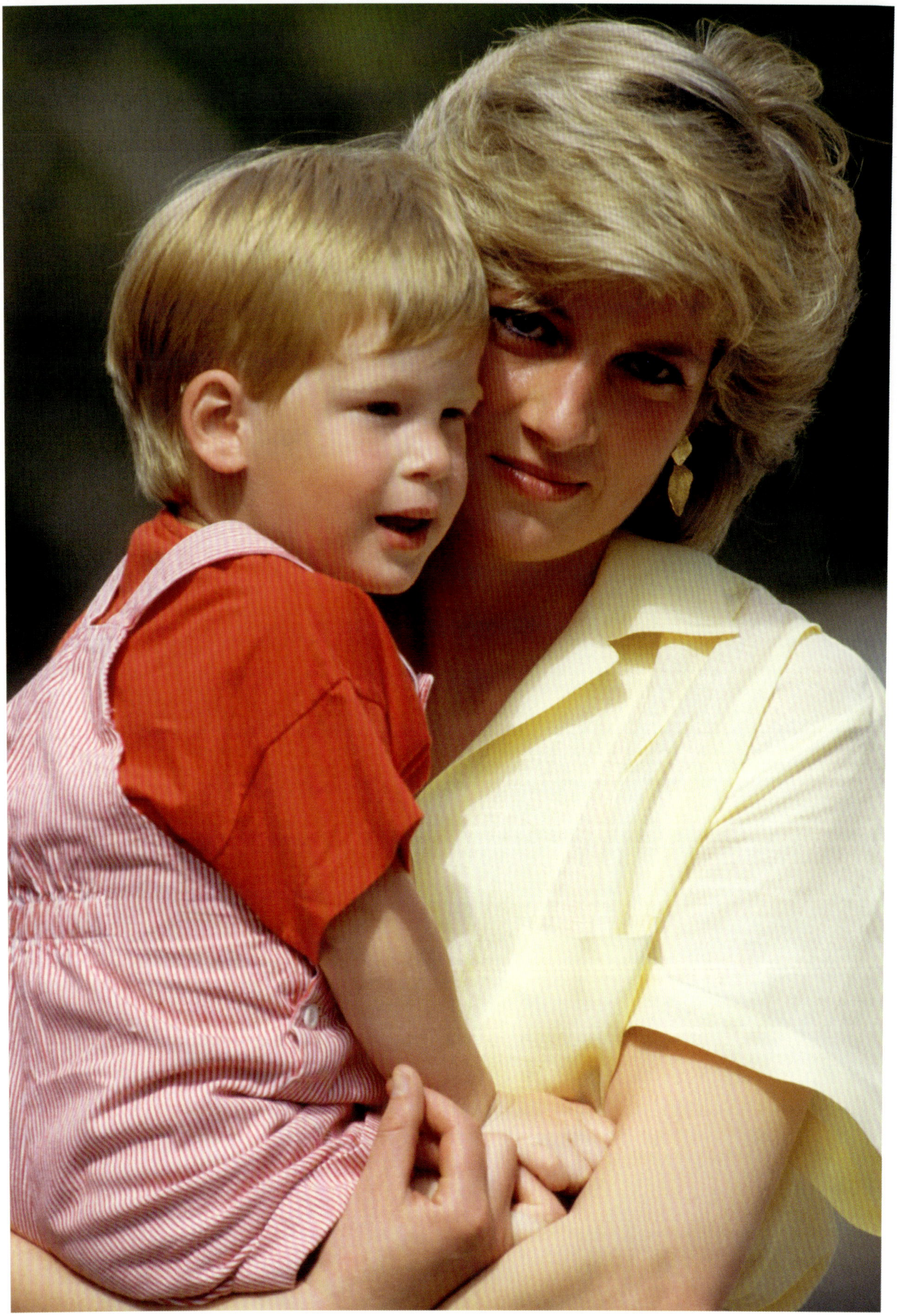

"She was an inspiration. She was a saint. As for fashion, like a designer, her knowledge was gained over years of experience."

Alexander McQueen,
WWD, 1997

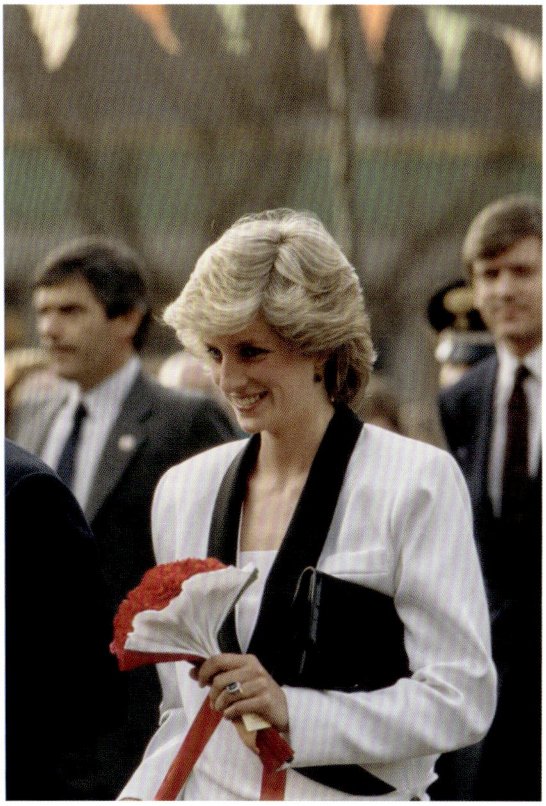

Bibliography

Abraham, Anne-Laure (2019) 'Villiers: Joséphine Baker et sa "tribu arc-en-ciel" racontées par sa fille', *Le Parisien*, 17 February.
Allen Mellen, Polly (1990) 'Fashion: Halston: 1932–1990, Liza Minelli', *Vogue*, Vol.180, issue 7, 1 July.
Andy Warhol Museum, The (n.d.) 'Time Capsule 21: Julia Warhola'. Available at: https://www.warhol.org/timecapsule/andy-warhols-time-capsule-21/time-capsule-21-julia-warhola/. Accessed: May 2025.
Angelou, Maya (2008) *Letter to My Daughter*, Random House.
Angelou, Maya (2013) *Mom & Me & Mom*, Random House.
Baker, Rachel (2011) 'The Inheritance', *New York* magazine, 12 August.
BBC (2024) 'How Elizabeth Taylor's mother shaped her career: Elizabeth Taylor – Rebel Superstar – BBC', YouTube, 30 September. Available at: https://www.youtube.com/watch?v=Kg1isLWk7e4. Accessed: May 2025.
BBC Studios (2009) 'Vivienne Westwood on corsets and Sadie Frost – British Style Genius – BBC', YouTube, 31 May. Available at: https://www.youtube.com/watch?v=kSV-poYEE30. Accessed: May 2025.
Bender, Abbey (2024) 'Elizabeth Taylor's Assistant of 20 Years Shares Her Beauty Secrets: "She Was the Real Deal"', *Woman's World*, 24 December.
Bennett Kinnon, Joy (2003) 'Serena and Venus on the fabulous Oracene, mother of the Williams Dynasty (Mother Power)', *Ebony*, Vol.58, Issue 7, May.
@blackfashionarchive (2025) 'Josephine Baker celebrated as world's best dressed woman in 1951 issue of Jet Magazine', Instagram, 7 March. Available at: https://www.instagram.com/p/DG5onstMfVO/?img_index=2. Accessed: May 2025.
Bobb, Brooke (2019) 'Timothée Chalamet Took His Mom to the Golden Globes—and She Wore Fashion's Buzziest Label', *Vogue*, 6 January.
Bossi, Andrea (2023) 'How I Shop: Venus Williams', *Fashionista*, 14 November.
British Vogue (2023) 'Rebel Rebel', Vol. 213, Issue 9, November.
Brown, Erica (1984) 'On the Trail of London's Sloane Rangers', *The New York Times*, 25 March.
Caligor, Livia (2025) 'Lady Gaga: "My Mental Health Always Played a Really Powerful Role in Making Music"', *Teen Vogue*, 26 March.
Carlson, Devon Lee (2024) 'Lila Moss Loves Matcha, Movies, and Devon Lee Carlson', *Interview*, 18 April.
CBS News (2021) 'Philadelphia Music Legend Kathy Sledge Talks About Her Deep Roots In Music, How The Pandemic Has Helped Her Evolve', 9 February. Available at: https://www.cbsnews.com/philadelphia/news/philadelphia-music-legend-kathy-sledge-talks-about-her-deep-roots-in-music-how-the-pandemic-has-helped-her-evolve/. Accessed: December 2024.
Chloé (n.d.) 'Chapter 6: A dress which says "I'm nonchalant"', LinkedIn. Available at: https://www.linkedin.com/posts/chloe_chlo%C3%A9-activity-7265771068051664900-74EC/. Accessed: May 2025.
Cochrane, Greg (2010) 'Lady Gaga defends VMA "meat dress"', *BBC News*, 14 September. Available at: https://www.bbc.co.uk/news/newsbeat-11295879. Accessed: March 2026.
Cochrane, Lauren (2020) 'Pie crusts and pearls: the unexpected return of the Sloane Ranger', *The Guardian*, 26 November.

Comenas, Gary (n.d.) 'Andy Warhol: From Nowhere to Up There: an oral history of Andy Warhol's early years', warholstars.org. Available at: https://www.warholstars.org/nowhere/andy_warhol_p4.html. Accessed: May 2025.
Cooke, Rachel (2007) 'My art is a form of restoration', *The Guardian*, 14 October.
Coon, Caroline (1974) 'Yoko Ono: The Whole World Is My Mother-In-Law', unpublished, *Rock's Back Pages*. Available at: https://www.rocksbackpages.com/Library/Article/yoko-ono-the-whole-world-is-my-mother-in-law. Accessed: May 2025.
Cowles, Charlotte (2014) 'Loulou de la Falaise: An Icon Remembered', *Harper's Bazaar*, 21 August.
Cowles, Charlotte (2015) 'My Mother, Ingrid Bergman', *Harper's Bazaar*, 27 July.
CR (2024) 'Angelina Jolie: "To Create is to Live"', 20 September.
Crash (2015) 'Loulou de la Falaise on Continuity'. May issue. Available at: https://www.crash.fr/loulou-de-la-falaise-interview/. Accessed: May 2024.
Dailey, Hannah (2023) 'Taylor Swift recalls surprising her mom with secret "Fearless" track during Mother's Day concert', *Billboard*, 15 May.
Daily Mail, *The* (2014) '"My daughter is my style critic": Kate Moss on how Lila tells her what NOT to wear as she launches new Topshop collection', 9 April.
Dazed (n.d.) 'Charlotte Gainsbourg on style and fronting Saint Laurent'. Available at: https://www.dazeddigital.com/fashion/article/37484/1/charlotte-gainsbourg-on-style-and-fronting-saint-laurent. Accessed: May 2025.
Devlin, Polly (1967) 'The Penelope Tree', *Vogue*, 1 October.
***Diana*, Our Mother: Her Life and Legacy** (2017) directed by Ashley Gething, Oxford Film and Television.
Dowd, Nancy E. (1994) 'Review: A Feminist Analysis of Adoption', *Harvard Law Review*, Vol. 107, No. 4, February, pp. 913–36.
Drenon, Brandon (2023) 'Tennis great Serena Williams named "fashion icon"', *BBC News*, 7 November.
Eastoe, Jane (2016) 'A regal look', *Harper's Bazaar*, No. 3644, June–July.
Elkann, Alain (2014) 'Loulou de la Falaise', *Alain Elkann Interviews*, 10 December. Available at: https://www.alainelkanninterviews.com/loulou-de-la-falaise/. Accessed: May 2025.
Ellis, Sydni (2024) 'Taylor Swift's Mom Reportedly Disapproved of One of Taylor's Signature Styles', *She Knows*, 3 April.
ExtraTV (2025) 'Timothée Chalamet Shares How Mom Kept Him HUMBLE After SAG Awards Win (Exclusive)', YouTube, 24 February. Available at: https://www.youtube.com/watch?v=ffiG3yO6ZYo. Accessed: June 2025.
Ford, Ashley C. (2019) 'Serena Williams: The Power of Unapologetic Greatness', *Allure*, 10 January.
Foreman, Katya (2009) 'Singing About Jane', *WWD*, Vol. 197, Issue 1, 5 January.
Fornés, Nora G. (2022) 'Joséphone Baker's son: "For us, her most obvious legacy is tolerance"', *El País* 50, 17 November.
Fraser, Emma (2021) 'There are No Costume Repeats for Lady Gaga in *House of Gucci*', *Elle*, 26 November.
Friedman, Vanessa (2022) 'Serena Williams' Best Looks', *The New York Times*, 29 August.
Gangewere, R. Jay (1997) 'Ten Years Later – What Would Andy Say?', Carnegie Museum, May/June. Available at: https://carnegiemuseums.org/magazine-archive/1997/mayjun/feat4.htm. Accessed: May 2025.
Germanotta (2018) 'Lady Gaga's Mum: What My Daughters Taught Me About Anxiety & Depression', *Refinery29*, 8 May.

Giuliano, Charles (2015) 'Gerard Malanga on Andy Warhol's Mother Julia', *Berkshire Fine Arts*, 4 June. Available at: https://berkshirefinearts.com/06-04-2015_gerard-malanga-on-andy-warhol-s-mother-julia.htm. Accessed: May 2025.
Greenstreet, Rosanna (2014) 'Q&A: Yoko Ono', *The Guardian*, 20 December.
Haynes, Kevin (1999) 'Anna Wintour; Excerpts from a 1989 interview in which Vogue's editor in chief talks about her first year at the helm', *WWD*, 13 September.
Higgins, Andrew and Miroslava Germanova (2018) 'Andy Warhol Said He Came From "Nowhere". This is It', *The New York Times*, 7 October.
Hirschberg, Lynn (1992) 'Strange Love: The Story of Kurt Cobain and Courtney Love', *Vanity Fair*, 1 September.
Hirschberg, Lynn (2025) 'Angelina Jolie's Major—and Misunderstood—Diva Moment', *W* magazine, 3 January.
Holiday, Harmony (2021) 'A Dinner in France, 1973: Josephine Baker, James Baldwin, and a Very Young Henry Louis Gates, Jr', *Literary Hub*, 11 March.
Holt, Bethan (2017) 'Remembering Princess Diana's style by Anna Harvey, the woman behind her wardrobe', *The Telegraph*, 23 June.
Howell, Georgina (1992) 'Features: A Line of Style', *Vogue*, Vol.182, Issue 3.
@isabellarossellini (2018) 'I was on the cover of Vogue 23 times.', Instagram, 26 April. Available at: https://www.instagram.com/p/BiCHpvDj6um/. Accessed: December 2024.
Isaiah, Texas (2021) 'Betye Saar, Her Daughters, and the House That Never Stopped Making Art', *Harper's Bazaar*, 13 May.
Jacques, Rajni Lucienne (2011) 'Our Q&A With Jane Birkin & Lou Doillon (Including The Story Of How The Hermes Bag Came To Be!)', *Glamour*, 4 November.
Jeff Zest (2022) 'Diahann Carroll: Biography', YouTube, 9 July. Available at: https://www.youtube.com/watch?v=snxcfK1ofjg. Accessed: May 2025.
Johnson, Guy (2014) 'Guy Johnson, Maya Angelou: And Still I Rise', directed by Rita Coburn and Bob Hercules, American Masters Digital Archive (WNET), 22 April. Available at: https://www.pbs.org/wnet/americanmasters/archive/interview/guy-johnson/. Accessed: May 2025.
Johnson, Guy (2017) 'Guy Johnson, Maya Angelou's Son, on his Mother's Love of Art', *KQED*, 23 February.
Jonathan, V.M. (2000) 'Fashion: Stella McCartney's Cheeky Chic', *Vogue*, Vol. 190, Issue 7.
Judy Garland Experience, The (2012) 'Journal Entry #3: The Battle Hymn Gown', 13 March. Available at: https://thejudygarlandexperience.blogspot.com/2012/03/relics-3-battle-hymn-gown.html. Accessed: May 2025.
Julien's Auctions (n.d.) 'Sara Sothern Taylor Evening Dress'. Available at: https://www.juliensauctions.com/en/items/52364/sara-sothern-taylor-evening-dress. Accessed: July 2025.
Julien's Auctions (n.d.) 'Sara Sothern Taylor Evening Gown'. Available at: https://www.juliensauctions.com/en/items/52248/sara-sothern-taylor-evening-gown. Accessed: July 2025.
Kaufman, Michael T. (1973) 'Josephine Baker Speaks As Artist and as Person', *The New York Times*, 4 June.
Klemesrud, Judy (1971) 'A Female Impersonator Who Likes Being a Man', *The New York Times*, 16 January.
Kors, Michael (2011) 'Michael Kors Talks to Dame Elizabeth Taylor', *Harper's Bazaar*, 23 March.
Krentcil, Faran (2024) 'A New Anita Pallenberg Documentary Sheds Light on the Style Icon's Private Life', *Elle*, 24 May.

La Ferla, Ruth (2013) 'From Isabella Rossellini, Creature Moms', *The New York Times*, 12 May.
Landy, Ann (1997) 'A Biennial Perennial, Still Changing Styles', *The New York Times*, 9 March.
Lang, Helmut and Nancy Spero (2007) 'Dear Louise Bourgeois', *Tate etc.*, Issue 11, 1 September.
Larocca, Amy (2015) 'In Conversation: Anna Wintour', *The Cut*, 4 May.
Lau, Susanna (2016) 'Simon Porte Jacquemus On His Mother', *AnOther*, 1 March.
Lau, Vanessa (2010) 'July 22, 1976: Maxime Impact', *WWD*, 26 October.
Lesavage, Halie (2024) 'Serena Williams Started a Tennis Fashion Movement "Without Even Trying"', *Marie Claire*, 18 April.
Luft, Lorna (1998) *Me and My Shadows: A Family Memoir*, Simon & Schuster.
Maitland, Hayley (2024) '"Prince Charles Was Completely Overshadowed" The Forgotten Story Of Princess Diana's First Revenge Dress', *British Vogue*, 25 November.
Marie Claire (2017) 'Angelina Jolie Takes Us Inside Her First International Beauty Campaign in a Decade', 17 April.
Marshall, Richard D. (2007) 'Interview with Louise Bourgeois', *Mary Ellen Mark*. Available at: https://www.maryellenmark.com/bibliography/magazines/article/whitewall/interview-with-louise-bourgeois-637531442193851489/W. Accessed: May 2025.
McEvoy, Marian (2014) 'Lou Lou de la Falaise, The Real Deal', *The New York Times Magazine*, 22 August.
McNeil, Liz (2022) 'Dionne Warwick on the Legacy of Cousin Whitney Houston and Aunt Cissy: It Was Just Preordained', *People*, 11 February.
Meter, Jonathan van (2000) 'Stella McCartney's Cheeky Chic', *Vogue*, July.
MoMA (n.d.) 'Louise Bourgeois: Motherhood & Family'. Available at: https://lb.moma.org/themes/motherhood-family. Accessed: May 2025.
Mooallem, Stephen (2017) 'The Ballad of Sean & Yoko', *Harper's Bazaar*, 31 July.
Mower, Sarah (2009) 'Fashion & Features: Skinny Genes', *Vogue*, 1 April.
Murari, Tim (1974) 'Josephine Baker', *The Guardian*, 26 August.
Nemy, Enid (1967) 'Mata Hari Lives Again in 30 Designs by Irene Sharaff', *The New York Times*, 9 November.
Nnadi, Chioma (2023) 'Angelina Jolie, Rebel Rebel', *Vogue*, Vol. 213, Issue 9, 1 November.
Nolfi, Joey (2021) 'Lady Gaga's House of Gucci costumes are an ode to her mother's Italian elegance', *Entertainment Weekly*, 1 October.
Norment, Lynn (1995) 'Whitney and Cissy Houston on the joys and worries of motherhood', *Ebony*, May, Vol. 50.
Nye, D. (2002) 'Judy Garland, subject of PBS special, was a great mother', Knight Ridder/Tribune News Service, 11 March.
O'Brien, Glenn (2019) 'Andy Warhol on Junk Food, Coca-Cola, Drugs, Painting, God and His Morning Routine', *Interview* magazine, 4 February.
Okura, Lynn (2013) 'Guy Johnson On Being Maya Angelou's Son: "I Grew Up In Her Light"', *Huffpost*, 16 October.
Otriová, Jana (2023) 'The incredible story of the mother of the pop art king', *The Slovak Spectator*, 13 November.
Paterson, Judith (1982) 'Maya Angelou—a Passionate Writer Living with Brains, Guts, and Joy', *Vogue*, 1 September.
Petkanas, Christopher (2018) *Loulou & Yves: The Untold Story of Loulou de la Falaise and the House of Saint Laurent*, New York: St Martin's Press.
Petrarca, Emilia (2019) 'Anna Wintour Reveals What You Should Actually Wear to a Job Interview', *The Cut*, 4 March.
Pratt, Alan (1997) *The Critical Response to Andy Warhol*, Greenwood.

Project, The (2023) 'Cynthia Germanotta On When Lady Gaga Needs her Mum', YouTube, 31 August. Available at: https://www.youtube.com/watch?v=sLW8J5Fhj3w. Accessed: June 2025.

Quarles, Philip (2012) 'The Evolving Motherhood of Josephine Baker', *Annotations: The NEH Preservation Project*, WNYC, 1 August. Available at: https://www.wnyc.org/story/192729-josephine-baker/. Accessed: May 2025.

Ravenel, Ariel de, and Natasha Fraser-Cavassoni (2014) *Loulou de la Falaise*, Rizzoli International Publications.

Restless Rick (2017) 'Cissy Houston Interview 1 Year After Whitney Houston Death', YouTube, 19 July. Available at: https://www.youtube.com/watch?v=SyaWR4CzaC8&t=312s. Accessed: May 2025.

Robert, Melvin (2025) Interview with Timothée Chalamet, *Extra*, Telepictures Productions, 24 February.

Rogers, Sam (2017) 'Angelina Jolie On Her Mother and Ageing', *British Vogue*, 28 March.

Rose, Jacqueline (2018) *Mothers: An Essay on Love and Cruelty*, London: Faber & Faber.

Runtagh, Jordan (2021) 'Janis Joplin's Scrapbook "Days & Summers" is an Intimate Self Portrait of a Rock Icon', *People*, 16 August.

Runtagh, Jordan (2025) 'Kidnapping, Tears and Reconciliation: Inside Yoko Ono's Decades-Long Saga to Find Her Missing Daughter', *People*, 1 February.

Rusinko, Elaine (2022) 'Andy and Julia in Rusyn: Warhol's translation of his mother in film and video', *Journal of Art Historiography*, No. 26, June.

Sanchez, Rosa (2025) 'Rihanna Gushes About Her Sons' Wildly Different Personalities', *Harper's Bazaar*, 22 Feb.

Sayej, Nadja (2015) 'Isabella Rossellini on Her Mother Ingrid Bergman's Enduring Style', *The New York Times*, 6 August.

Seebohm, Caroline (1997) *The Life of Marietta Tree*, Simon & Schuster.

Shome, Raka (2014) *Diana and Beyond: White Feminity, National Identity, and Contemporary Media Culture*, University of Illinois Press.

Sims, Gail Ronan (2007) 'Florez Kathy Sledge, 79; her daughters were Sister Sledge', *The Philadelphia Enquirer*, 25 May.

Spano, Susan (2006) 'Castle that housed Josephine Baker's fairy-tale dreams now honors her', *Los Angeles Times*, 3 August.

Sykes, Pandora (2014) 'What's It Really Like To Grow Up With Anna Wintour As Your Mum?', *Grazia*, 8 May.

Talley, André Leon (2009) 'Maxime de la Falaise, 1922–2009', *Vogue*, 15 May.

Teen Vogue (2014) 'Bee Shaffer on What Life is Like As Anna Wintour's Daughter' YouTube, 6 May. Available at: https://www.youtube.com/watch?v=ogMonEWxhf4. Accessed: May 2025.

Tennis Australia (2010) 'Meet Serena and Venus Williams' Mum', YouTube, 11 January. Available at: https://www.youtube.com/watch?v=uG_TA-1giSY. Accessed: June 2025.

@thewarholmuseum (2023) 'Warhol's interpretation of what's in style', Instagram, 2 June. Available at: https://www.instagram.com/thewarholmuseum/reel/Cs_8q-Ugvzx/?hl=en-gb. Accessed: May 2025.

Today (2017) 'Diahann Carroll interviewed by Al Roker on the *Today Show* (Today Living Legends)', *NBC*, 6 October.

Today (2019) 'Serena & Venus Williams' Mom Shares Secret to Raising Strong Women, Through Moms Eyes', YouTube, 21 August. Available at: https://www.youtube.com/watch?v=ZQGKi5GT-YM. Accessed: May 2025.

Van Meter, Jonathan (2002) 'Vogue Point of View: Body Beautiful', *Vogue*, Vol. 192, Issue 4, April.
@vegasetc2739 (2024) 'Taylor Swift Fashion decision with mom', Instagram, 17 March. Available at: https://www.youtube.com/shorts/o-7EdQvoaDs. Accessed: March 2026.
@venuswilliams (2021) 'When @serenawilliams and I wore our iconic beads…', Instagram, 16 November. Available at: https://www.instagram.com/p/CWWRCIBjoPq/?utm_medium=copy_link%2F%3Futm_medium%3Dwebsite&utm_source=website_internal&utm_campaign=web_link_1. Accessed: May 2025.
Vesilind, Emili (2014) 'As a fashion icon, Elizabeth Taylor could turn simple into sexy, elegance into excess', *Los Angeles Times*, 14 March.
Vogue (2023) '"Lila's The One Setting Rules For Me": Kate Moss On Her Model Daughter – And Lila On Her Super Mum', 16 November.
Walker, Tim (2023) '"Lila's The One Setting Rules For Me": Kate Moss On Her Model Daughter – And Lila On Her Super Mum', *British Vogue*, 16 November.
Ward, David (2004) 'Liverpool becomes a huge gallery for its biennial', *The Guardian*, 17 September.
Wayne, Jane Ellen (2003) *The Golden Girls of MGM*, Carroll & Graf Publishers.
Whitney Houston Platinum Club, The (2024) 'Rare! Cissy Houston Talks About Whitney on Motherlode', YouTube, 29 January. Available at: https://www.youtube.com/watch?v=NvCg3Zz7MTU. Accessed: May 2025.
Williams, Gilda (2007) 'Warhol stumbled across "The Real America" in the pantry of a woman who never adapted to the American way of life', *Tate etc*, 1 May.
Willman, Chris (2020) 'Taylor Swift: No Longer "Polite at All Costs"', *Variety*, 21 January.
Wilson, John S. (1973) 'Josephine Baker Sings, Talks, Dances and Captivates', *The New York Times*, 7 June.
WWD (1997) 'A Symbol of Style', Vol. 174, No. 44, 2 September. Available at: https://wwd.com/fashion-news/fashion-features/article-1119235/. Accessed: Dec 2024.
WWD (2004) 'Fashion Scoops: Beauty is Dirt Cheap…Green Grass', 30 April. Available at: https://wwd.com/fashion-news/fashion-features/feature/fashion-scoops-beauty-is-dirt-cheap-green-grass-597075-1942042/. Accessed: May 2025.
Younge, Gary (2009) 'Interview: Maya Angelou: "I'm fine as wine in the summertime"', *The Guardian*, 14 November.
Zany (2020) 'Johnny Carson Interview Diahann Carroll Jul 26 1979', YouTube, 4 May. Available at: https://www.youtube.com/watch?v=q7zBYfYzOHk. Accessed: May 2025.

★

Picture Credits

p.2 (left and right) Courtesy of Terry Newman
p.8 Express Newspapers / Hulton Archive via Getty Images
p.11 NTB / Alamy Stock Photo
p.12 Gijsbert Hanekroot / Redferns via Getty Images
p.14 Footwear News / Penske Media via Getty Images
p.15 Courtesy of the Serena Rees Archive
p.17 Dave Benett / Dave Benett Collection via Getty Images
p.18 Fiona Hanson / AFP via Getty Images
p.19 (left) Courtesy of the Serena Rees Archive
p.19 (right) Dave Benett / Dave Benett Collection via Getty Images
p.20 (left) Dave M. Benett / Dave Benett Collection via Getty Images
p.20 (right) Vittorio Zunino Celotto / Getty Images Entertainment via Getty Images Europe
p.21 Julien de Rosa / AFP via Getty Images
p.22 Evan Agostini / Getty Images Entertainment via Getty Images North America
p.23 Sipa US / Alamy Stock Photo
p.24 Victor Virgile / Gamma Rapho via Getty Images
p.25 Vittorio Zunino Celotto / Getty Images Entertainment via Getty Images Europe
p.27 Stefania M. D'Alessandro / Stringer / Getty Images Entertainment via Getty Images Europe
p.28 Courtesy of Angela Missoni
p.29 Courtesy of Angela Missoni
p.30 Eamonn M. McCormack / Getty Images Entertainment via Getty Images Europe
p.32 Abaca Press / Alamy Stock Photo
p.33 (left) Rich Gold / Alamy Stock Photo
p.33 (right) Trinity Mirror / Mirrorpix / Alamy Stock Photo
p.34 Associated Press / DPRF/STAR MAX/Ipx / Alamy Stock Photo
p.35 Abaca Press / Alamy Stock Photo
p.36 Jason Lloyd Evans
p.38 John Phillips/BFC / Getty Images Entertainment via Getty Images Europe
p.40 WWD via Getty Images
p.41 Jason Lloyd Evans
p.42 © Rankin
p.43 Rune Hellestad - Corbis / Corbis Entertainment via Getty Images
p.44 Dave Benett / Dave Benett Collection via Getty Images
p.45 Ian Gavan / Getty Images Entertainment via Getty Images Europe
p.46 Marc Piasecki / WireImage via Getty Images
p.47 Dave Benett / Dave Benett Collection via Getty Images
p.49 Ron Galella Collection, Ltd. / Ron Galella Collection via Getty Images
p.50 Arnold Jerocki / GC Images via Getty Images
p.51 Mike Marsland / WireImage via Getty Images
p.52 Michael Loccisano / Getty Images Entertainment via Getty Images North America
p.55 Ron Galella Collection, Ltd. / Ron Galella Collection via Getty Images
p.56 John Shearer / WireImage via Getty Images
p.57 (top) Images Press / Archive Photos via Getty Images
p.57 (bottom) Rose Hartman / Archive Photos via Getty Images
p.58 Dimitrios Kambouris / Getty Images Entertainment via Getty Images North America
pp.60–61 Sipa US / Alamy Stock Photo
p.62 Erik Pendzich / Alamy Stock Photo
p.63 (top) Associated Press / Jae C. Hong / Alamy Stock Photo
p.63 (bottom) Abaca Press / ABACAPRESS / Alamy Stock Photo
p.64 WWD / Penske Media via Getty Images
p.66 Dave Hogan / Hulton Archive via Getty Images
p.67 Dave Hogan / Hulton Archive via Getty Images
pp.68–69 Courtesy of Herbie Mensah
p.70 Associated Press / Kevork Djansezian / Alamy Stock Photo
p.73 (top) Kevin Cummins / Premium Archive via Getty Images
p.73 (bottom) Vinnie Zuffante / Archive Photos via Getty Images
p.74 AFF / JPA / Alamy Stock Photo
p.76 Gijsbert Hanekroot / Redferns via Getty Images
p.78 (top) Sipa US / Alamy Stock Photo
p.78 (bottom) Terry Wyatt / Getty Images Entertainment via Getty Images North America
pp.80–81 Patrick McMullan via Getty Images
p.82 Kevin Mazur/AMA2010 / WireImage via Getty Images
p.84 Denise Truscello / WireImage via Getty Images
p.85 Doug Peters / Alamy Stock Photo
pp.86–87 Kevin Winter/ACM2015 / Getty Images Entertainment via Getty Images North America
p.88 Glasshouse Images / JT Vintage / Alamy Stock Photo
p.90 Al Pereira / Michael Ochs Archives via Getty Images
p.92 Ron Galella Collection, Ltd. / Ron Galella Collection via Getty Images
p.93 Michael Ochs Archives via Getty Images
p.94 PA Images / Yui Mok / Alamy Stock Photo
p.96 Dimitrios Kambouris / Getty Images Entertainment via Getty Images North America
p.97 (left) Abaca Press / ABACAPRESS / Alamy Stock Photo
p.97 (right) Associated Press / Greg Allen / Alamy Stock Photo
p.98 UPI / Jim Ruymen / Alamy Stock Photo
p.99 Associated Press / Blair Raughley / Alamy Stock Photo
p.100 C Brandon / Redferns via Getty Images
p.103 (top) Courtesy of the Pauline Black Archive
p. 103 (bottom) Courtesy of the Pauline Black Archive
p.104 PA Images / Tony Harris / Alamy Stock Photo
p.105 Associated Press / Alamy Stock Photo
p.106 Associated Press / David Bookstaver / Alamy Stock Photo
p.107 (top) MediaPunch Inc / Media Punch / Alamy Stock Photo
p.107 (bottom) Chris Walter / WireImage via Getty Images
p.109 Everett Collection Inc / Courtesy Everett Collection / Alamy Stock Photo
p.110 Jack Mitchell / Archive Photos via Getty Images
p.113 Jack Mitchell / Archive Photos via Getty Images
p.114–15 Jack Mitchell / Archive Photos via Getty Images
p.116 PAGES Francois / Paris Match Archive via Getty Images
p.117 Courtesy of the Corbett family
p.118 Courtesy of Sarah Rossigneux
p.120 (top) Courtesy of Sarah Rossigneux
p.120 (bottom) © Fiona Hanson
pp.120–21 Courtesy of Sammy Adams
p.122 Popperfoto via Getty Images
p.124 Jack Mitchell / Archive Photos via Getty Images
p.125 Malcolm Park / Alamy Stock Photo
p.127 Archivio GBB / Bridgeman Images
p.128 Marc Piasecki / WireImage via Getty Images
p.129 Associated Press / Michel Euler / Alamy Stock Photo
p.131 Abaca Press / ABACAPRESS / Alamy Stock Photo
p.132 Pierre Suu / Getty Images Entertainment via Getty Images Europe
p.133 Marc Piasecki / WireImage via Getty Images
p.134 (top) Jeff Spicer / Getty Images Entertainment via Getty Images Europe
p.134 (bottom) Laurent Maous / Gamma-Rapho via Getty Images

p.135 STILLS / Gamma-Rapho via Getty Images
p.136 Dia Dipasupil / WireImage via Getty Images
p.139 Frazer Harrison / Getty Images Entertainment via Getty Images North America
p.140 PA Images / Anthony Harvey / Alamy Stock Photo
p.141 ZUMA Press Inc. / ZUMA Press / Alamy Stock Photo
p.142 Associated Press / Kevork Djansezian / Alamy Stock Photo
p.143 Abaca Press / ABACAPRESS / Alamy Stock Photo
p.144 (top) Bob Riha Jr / WireImage via Getty Images
p.144 (bottom) Dave Hogan / Getty Images Entertainment via Getty Images Europe
p.145 Frank Edwards / Archive Photos via Getty Images
pp.146–47 Doug Peters / Alamy Stock Photo
p.148 Everett Collection Inc / Courtesy Everett Collection / Alamy Stock Photo
p.149 Michael Ochs Archives via Getty Images
p.151 (top) Reg Innell / Toronto Star via Getty Images
p.151 (bottom) PictureLux / The Hollywood Archive / Alamy Stock Photo
p.153 Anthony Barboza / Archive Photos bia Getty Images
p.154 Associated Press / Mark Avery / Alamy Stock Photo
p.156 Keystone / Hulton Archive via Getty Images
p.159 Everett Colleciton Inc / Courtesy Everett Collection / Alamy Stock Photo
p.161 (left) Keystone / Hulton Archive via Getty Images
p.161 (right) Keystone-France / Gamma-Keystone via Getty Images
p.162 J. Vespa / WireImage via Getty Images
p.163 Dave Hogan / Getty Images Entertainment via Getty Images Europe
p.164 © Terry O›Neill / Iconic Images
p.166 Hulton Deutsch / Corbis Historical via Getty Images
p.168 George Rinhart / Corbis Historical via Getty Images
p.169 (top) CBS Photo Archive / CBS via Getty Images
p.169 (bottom) Everett Collection Inc / Courtesy Everett Collection / Alamy Stock Photo
p.170 (top) PictureLux / The Hollywood Archive / Alamy Stock Photo
p.170 (bottom) Ron Galella / Ron Galella Collection via Getty Images
p.171 Images Press / Archive Photos via Getty Images
p.172 ZUMA Press Inc. / ZUMA Press / Alamy Stock Photo
p.173 Bettmann via Getty Images
p.175 WWD / Penske Media via Getty Images
p.176 MediaPunch Inc / Media Punch / Alamy Stock Photo
p.177 (top) Associated Press / James Pringle / Alamy Stock Photo
p.177 (bottom) Bettmann via Getty Images
p.178 Bettmann via Getty Images
p.179 Pool Arnal/Garcia / Gamma-Rapho via Getty Images
p.180 David Redfern / Redferns via Getty Images
p.183 ullstein bild Dtl. / ullstein bild via Getty Images
p.184 BNA Photographic / Alamy Stock Photo
p.185 Associated Press / Alamy Stock Photo
p.187 Bettmann via Getty Images
p.188 PA Images / Julien Behal / Alamy Stock Photo
p.190–91 Dave Benett / Dave Benett Collection via Getty Images
p.193 (top) Courtesy of Lulu Guinness
p.193 (bottom) Courtesy of Lulu Guinness
p.194 PA Images / Fiona Hanson / Alamy Stock Photo
p.195 Courtesy of Lulu Guinness
p.196 David Bailey / Condé Nast Collection / Condé Nast Collection Editorial via Getty Images
p.197 Dave Benett / Dave Benett Collection via Getty Images
p.199 Santi Visalli / Archive Photos via Getty Images
p.200 Fairfax Media Archives via Getty Images
p.201 Daniele Venturelli / WireImage via Getty Images
p.202 David Bailey / Condé Nast Collection / Condé Nast Collection Editorial via Getty Images
p.203 Pictorial Parade / Archive Photos via Getty Images
p.204 WWD / Penske Media via Getty Images
p.205 Charles Sheeler / Condé Nast Collection / Condé Nast Collection Editorial via Getty Images
p.206 Mirrorpix via Getty Images
p.208 Abaca Press / ABACAPRESS / Alamy Stock Photo
p.210 Cecil Beaton / Condé Nast Collection / Condé Nast Collection Editorial via Getty Images
p.211 Penske Media via Getty Images
p.212 Evening Standard / Hulton Archive via Getty Images
p.215 Dave Benett / Dave Benett Collection via Getty Images
p.217 Courtesy of Edina Ronay
p.218 Everett Collection Inc / Courtesy Everett Collection / Alamy Stock Photo
p.221 The Washington Post via Getty Images
p.222 Everett Collection Historical / Everett Collection / Alamy Stock Photo
p.223 (top) Everett Collection Inc / Courtesy Everett Collection / Alamy Stock Photo
p.223 (bottom) Moses Robinson / WireImage via Getty Images
p.224 Tim Graham / Tim Graham Photo Library via Getty Images
p.226 Princess Diana Archive / Hulton Royals Collection via Getty Images
p.227 (top) Brian Purdy / Alamy Stock Photo
p.227 (bottom) Central Press / Hulton Royals Collection via Getty Images
pp.228–29 Tim Graham / Tim Graham Photo Library via Getty Images
p.230 George De Keerle / Hulton Archibe via Getty Images
p.231 Tim Graham / Tim Graham Photo Library via Getty Images

Cover images: Front cover: Etienne George / Sygma Premium via Getty Images
Back cover: (top) © Terry O'Neill / Iconic Images; (bottom) Associated Press / Kevork Djansezian / Alamy Stock Photo

ISBN: 978 1 78884 373 7

A CIP catalogue record for this book is available from the British Library

The author and publisher gratefully acknowledge the permission granted to reproduce the copyright material in this book. Every effort has been made to trace copyright holders and to obtain their permission for the use of copyright material. The publisher apologises for any errors or omissions in the text and would be grateful if notified of any corrections that should be incorporated in future reprints or editions of this book.

Publisher: James Smith
Senior Editor: Alice Bowden
Designer: Mariona Vilarós Capella
Design Tech: Craig Holden
Production Manager: Simon Walsh
Reprographics Manager: Corban Wilkin

EU GPSR Authorised Representative:
Easy Access System Europe Oü, 16879218
Address: Mustamäe tee 50, 10621 Tallinn, Estonia
Email: gpsr@easproject.com Tel: +358 40 500 3575

MIX
Paper | Supporting responsible forestry
FSC® C008047
www.fsc.org

Printed in China by C&C Offset Printing Co. Ltd
for ACC Art Books Ltd, Woodbridge, Suffolk, UK

www.accartbooks.com

ACC ART BOOKS